THE
TORCH
OF
FREEDOM

TWENTY EXILES
OF HISTORY

Illustrated by
ESTA COSGRAVE

KENNIKAT PRESS
Port Washington, N. Y./London

THE TORCH

OF

FREEDOM

Edited by

EMIL LUDWIG *and* HENRY B. KRANZ

THE TORCH OF FREEDOM

Copyright 1943 by Holt, Rinehart and Winston, Inc.
Reissued in 1972 by Kennikat Press by arrangement
Library of Congress Catalog Card No: 71-153251
ISBN 0-8046-1504-7

Manufactured by Taylor Publishing Company   Dallas, Texas

ESSAY AND GENERAL LITERATURE INDEX REPRINT SERIES

CONTENTS

PREFACE

Exile is not an invention of our times. Even in democracies like ancient Athens, men who fought for progress were ostracized. But never before today have there been so many thousands of exiles wandering over the face of the globe. The tragedy of exile is on a vast scale.

The exile of today can enter into the experience of the exiles of yesterday, can understand their motives, their suffering, their hopes, their destinies. Our purpose has been to look into the lives of the great exiles of history through the eyes of men who now are exiled from their native lands. How did these famous exiles live? What did they dream about? What did they contribute to the history of their times?

The choice of the exiles portrayed was not based on any political considerations. The men selected were important in their day or became important many years afterward. They were poets, kings, scientists, statesmen, peasants, and soldiers. But they were all fighters. Men who did not fight in exile for freedom and human progress were not included. Napoleon I, Napoleon III, Richard Wagner have no place in this book. Other prominent exiles of history had to be omitted because their era or their cause was represented by someone else—in a sense Trotsky is represented by Lenin, for example. Limits had to be set or this book would have become a veritable encyclopedia of exile.

The men chosen were influenced by exile in different degrees and in different ways. The personalities of Garibaldi and Karl Schurz unfolded after they were exiled, and, probably, because they were exiled. Other men, such as Sun Yat-sen and Lenin, had to suffer many years of banishment before they came to power in their native countries. Voltaire and Victor Hugo matured in exile to become the greatest humanitarian thinkers of their time.

Some, like Bolivar, died in desperation. Some, like Kosciuszko, died resigned to their lot. And still others, like Heinrich Heine and Byron, on their deathbeds, romanticized their fatherlands and looked wistfully back to them. Stefan Zweig broke down in exile. Ovid grumbled and wrote his most beautiful verse.

It was originally intended to have each of these lives of famous exiles written by one of his own countrymen. But this proved to be impossible. Some exiles of history, such as Sun Yat-sen and Bolivar, have no countrymen in exile at this moment. Their lives have been written by present-day exiles of another country. On the other hand, some famous writers now in exile live in places with which it is difficult to communicate in time of war. Our original plan has been followed as closely as was feasible.

All the men portrayed found exile a great experience. All of them learned through exile. All of them were torchbearers of freedom, politically or spiritually, like their countrymen in exile today. The editors of this book hope to suggest that the role of the exiles in the years after this war, while it cannot now be foreseen, should not be underestimated.

The Editors

September, 1943.

OVID

by

LION FEUCHTWANGER

LION FEUCHTWANGER

was born in 1884 in Munich. He is proud of the fact that he wrote a "pronouncedly revolutionary poem" the first one published during the First World War. It appeared in October, 1914. Its refrain was "We are waiting." In 1925 he wrote a novel warning against Hitler, but people ridiculed his prophecy. *Jud Suess* (*Power*) was his first international success. *The Ugly Duchess,* his second historical novel, was no less successful. In 1930 he wrote *Success,* a modern and anti-Nazi novel which made him highly unpopular with Hitler. Lion Feuchtwanger was in Washington at a banquet given in his honor by the German ambassador when Hitler usurped power in Germany. His money was confiscated and he was expatriated. In 1937 he went to Moscow and wrote a book about the strength of the Red Army, but did not attract much attention. His next novel, about Nazi Germany, was written in 1938 while he was in France. In 1939 he was interned by the French. His experiences and his flight from a concentration camp are described in his book *The Devil in France.* American friends brought him to this country. His *Josephus* trilogy portrays Roman and Jewish characters at the time of Jesus in Palestine, Rome, and Alexandria.

OVID
by Lion Feuchtwanger

I N ENUMERATING the names of great exiled men of all times and countries, that of Ovid—as I know from experience—is one of the first to come to one's mind. If we study the man more closely we quickly recognize that he never felt himself as representative of any established political or religious group; nobody stood by him, and he stood by nobody. He never felt that he was in exile as a martyr for his convictions. On the contrary, he never really understood the deeper meaning of his exile. To him it seemed nothing but a piece of colossally bad luck.

Nevertheless, Ovid may not be omitted from any list of famous exiles, for nobody has found more beautiful, enduring words to describe the sorrow of banishment than he.

Publius Ovidius Naso was, and still is, renowned as the greatest poet of his generation.

His world was Rome at the time of Christ's birth, the Rome of Augustus. The empire had become consolidated after wild tempests; there was peace, permanent peace. Enormous wealth had been amassed. The owners of these riches did not care a rap for politics, but wanted to enjoy themselves to the full. Customs became polished and lax. The absolute ruler took care of the state. Olympus had been stripped of its gods a long time ago; nobody was enthroned there to dispense reward and punishment. Thus one devoted day and night to the social whirl, to intricate pastimes, to subtle eroticism.

The poet who expressed the views of this society in the sweetest, most impudent, elegant, and convincing way was Ovid.

The aging Emperor Augustus saw with displeasure how the stern, patriarchal customs of the former Rome were crumbling away. He wished to found his state on a body of powerful patricians, wished to entrust the affairs of the empire and the army to his nobles. But these, interested in nothing but a life of wild and untrammeled pleasure, slunk off in the most ignominious and unscrupulous manner when it came to business. They let their families die out. Seeing in marriage only a vexatious duty, they were careful to produce no legitimate offspring. They did not wish to burden themselves with tiresome responsibilities, or give up more of their amassed wealth than was strictly necessary.

The emperor, aided by a small group of puritanical senators, proclaimed stern marriage decrees, published ever harsher laws against the dissolute customs. But he could not defeat the spirit of the age. As a matter of fact, the gilded, imperialistic youth considered the severe customs of that heroic epoch, during which Rome had worked its way up from a provincial town to the capital of the world, as superfluous or even slightly ludicrous. And the spokesman of these young men, the "Neoteroi," the moderns, was Ovid.

The poets of the past decades, Horace and Vergil, had praised the state, empire, and army, the emperor, his organization and his campaigns. Ovid sang of no campaigns other than the maneuvers necessary to win a beautiful woman, taught nothing but the methods of light, fashionable eroticism. "May others long for the old days," he confessed; "I am happy to be this century's son." And, "Let us praise our ancestors, but let us live our own life." He wrote a subtle, daring handbook of love-making in graceful verses and represented in a pleasing collection of rhymed novelettes—*Metamorphoses*—the gods and goddesses of the Roman pantheon as fashionable men and ladies about town.

The puritans fought him tooth and nail. But what did he care? He was not a politician; he scrupulously avoided attacking existing laws and flattered the emperor with exaggerated adulation. However, he did not conceal his individualistic-libertine world view: he lived as he liked and wrote what he liked.

The emperor, who had showered Horace and Vergil with

honors, bestowed no favors on this frivolous poet of modern life; but neither did he proceed against him. Much to the anger of Ovid's enemies, the latter remained unmolested. The poet recorded, not without bitterness, how a "certain nobody," a "quidam," a literary competitor, had wanted to use one of the great puritanical campaigns of the Senate for the purpose of getting rid of his rival, Ovid, by instigating a violent attack on his immoral behavior. But the quidam was unsuccessful. Despite the severe laws against the growing moral laxity, Ovid lived and poetized in Rome.

Ovid had already arrived at the threshold of old age—he was over fifty—when, abruptly and unexpectedly, disaster crashed down on him.

It is the year eight after Christ. Rome witnesses a sensational scandal revolving around Julia, the emperor's granddaughter; and Augustus, not for the first time, is forced to execute his laws at the expense of his own family. Full of grief and shame, grim and bitter, he must send his granddaughter into exile, as punishment for her emancipated way of life.

The luckless Ovid is involved in the affair; not deeply, only superficially. But he knows about it, has been "witness of the crime," and had concealed his knowledge. Of course, the whole affair is dragged into the limelight; and the emperor, growing increasingly sour and bitter with the years, spares the poet no longer.

Without trial, he sentences Ovid to exile—the milder form of banishment called "relegation." Ovid's fortune is not confiscated, nor the sale of his works—except *The Art of Love*—prohibited; but they are removed from the shelves of the public libraries.

The emperor's harshness is indicated by his choice of the place destined to be the poet's future residence. He sends him to the farthest frontier of the realm, a forsaken spot on the inhospitable shore of the Black Sea. Perhaps he wishes to put as much space as possible between himself and the troublesome poet.

We cannot be quite sure of the immediate causes leading to Ovid's banishment. However, his verses give us sufficient hints for guessing his so-called "crime."

"Why," he laments, "did I let my eyes partake in a crime? Was not my only guilt that I have eyes?" He wails that he is being punished for an error, a "stupidity." After becoming witness of the crime he should have exposed it on the spot. The whole thing had been caused by an unfortunate chain of events. If the emperor only knew in what calamitous fashion he, Ovid, had been dragged into this affair he would surely forgive him.

It is almost proved that the "crime" in question was an act of adultery committed by Julia in company with a certain Silan, a young man of noble family. Evidently a merry group of moderns, of Neoteroi, had been caught at an orgy whose participants included not only the imperial granddaughter and her young lover, but also Ovid. It seems the latter was foolish enough to testify that he knew nothing of the whole business—or something to that effect.

It is certain that this petty misdemeanor furnished only the pretext for inflicting such severe punishment. The deeper reason lay in Ovid's whole life work, his verses. The deeper reason lay in his libertine and individualistic world view, standing in opposition to the state morality protected by Augustus.

In spite of this, any attempt to make Ovid out to be a political martyr is futile. He wished to be nothing of the kind. On the contrary, he steadily bewails his unhappy lot, raves against the verses which have hurled him into misery, and flatters the emperor with all the means at his disposal. He cannot and will not understand the political and sociological considerations which have led the emperor to his resolve. For him his exile is nothing but the bewildering consequence of a chain of silly, fateful circumstances.

Nevertheless, the accidental, unheroic nature of the incidents resulting in his exile does not lessen his sorrow. It only increases his torment. He had lived in an ivory tower, and now he sees himself suddenly thrust out of it. Why? he asks, as disconsolate and helpless as a child subjected to an immeasurable injustice. He has done no wrong, lived and let live, honored the emperor— the official highest god—by burning incense before his altar. Why does this emperor fling him, of all people, into banishment?

He suffers as deeply under his sorrow as man is capable of

suffering. Exile signifies to him a specially abrupt change, a specially deep fall.

For the first fifty years of his life Ovid was one of the happiest men in Rome. Born into a wealthy, esteemed family and provided with a good education, he soon exchanged, against his father's wishes, jurisprudence for literature. Something urged him to write verses whether he wanted to or not: "Whatever my mouth desires to utter in shape of a verse is forthcoming." An amusing anecdote of his childhood has been preserved. When his father whipped him, because he wrote verses instead of studying his lessons, the boy begged him in a hexameter to spare him: "Spare me, O father, and no more, I promise, will I make verses."

His poems soon became known. After the death of Horace and Vergil he was universally acclaimed as the realm's foremost poet. He was spoiled by society, loved life and savored it to the full, lived with one woman in happy marriage and another in happy friendship. He was on unbelievably good terms with the world into which he had been born. Everything about it seemed congenial to this boundlessly happy man. He loved many, and everybody loved him.

But this happiness was tied up with Rome. Impossible to imagine a life—let alone a happy one—away from this city. He was part of Rome, and Rome was a part of him. He claims deservedly to have formed the customs and views of his age.

Now, at the summit of his life, he found himself thrust out of Rome, thrust out for a silly, heedless mistake, thrust out into a life emptier than death. The whole thing seemed completely senseless and ridiculous.

We are thoroughly familiar with Ovid's life in exile. He has presented it in his poems *Tristia* and *Epistolae Ex Ponto* in such a way that we can visualize his last years in all their devastating monotony.

It is his last night in Rome. All the time he has hoped that he might see his daughter, his grandchildren, once more. He has sent a message to Libya where she lives. But Libya is far away, and she cannot arrive in time. His friends have not dared to visit a man in disgrace; only two have come. His wife is at his side, hardly able to bear up under this ordeal. She wants to accompany him, but it is better that she stay in town and try to procure his pardon. Three times, trying to leave, he tears himself away; three times he turns back under some pretense. The friends know not what to say to him; they can only repeat the same words again and again. The servants are weeping, just as if a funeral were taking place.

There follows the endless journey across the ocean. It is December, the sea bristling with dangers. A tempest arises and throws his ship back to the Italian coast; it is as if Italy were holding him fast. At last he reaches Greece. He passes the Greek isles, the coast of Asia Minor—places to which he once traveled under happier circumstances.

And now he reaches his goal: the town of Tomis, a small settlement on the Black Sea, near the estuary of the Danube. His anticipations, bad enough, are surpassed by reality. The place is inhabited almost exclusively by barbarians: Sarmatians, Scythians, wild people.

And how terrifying is the country itself! Nothing but naked earth, no shade, no foliage. Not a tree in sight, not a single house on the steppe. Plain and ocean seem one. Whether one turns one's glance toward the land or toward the sea, it meets nothing but an endless, naked, rolling desert. What a sad sight for eyes accustomed to Italy's flowering, varied landscape!

The country has only recently been conquered and is not domesticated as yet. The customs are wild; differences of opinion are decided by the sword; conversations quickly ripen into fight. The women are lacking in grace and seem like animals—fit only for work. Rough, fearsome men roam the streets and squares; their harsh voices are loathsome; their faces, framed by long hair and immense beards, repellent. They are never seen without weapons, invariably carrying powerful bows and long knives.

The climate is intolerable. There is no spring, no autumn, no harvest, no vintage. Ceaselessly an icy wind howls—sometimes so violently that it makes the houses topple over. Winter is endless and severe. Through many months the earth is covered with snow. Ocean and rivers are solidly frozen and can be crossed by wagons. The wine freezes in the barrels and must be cut with an ax if one wishes to entertain guests. Icicles cling to the beards of the natives who, like wild animals, are covered with fur from head to toe.

The poet sees nothing around him except ruffians of this kind. But the barbarians living on the opposite shores of the Danube are still worse. The people in Rome were under the delusion that the whole earth had been conquered and all the nations were trembling before their legions. But these barbarians across the Danube have not the remotest intention of trembling. They care not a damn for the governor, his proclamations, his legal decisions. The Danube is the only protection against them. But when the stream is frozen they come over to pillage, carrying off men and animals. Their horses are as fast as birds, their arrows poisoned. The poet shivers when he thinks of these arrows—which he does very often. Thus there is nothing to do but stay at home, locked into one's house, all winter long.

Sometimes the barbarians cross the stream in great masses and beleaguer the town. Then even poor Ovid must do his part. He, who shirked military service in his youth, must play at soldiering in old age. Those damned poisoned arrows fly right into the street. Ovid picks one up and sends it to a friend, accompanied by a poem. It is the only present he can send; the country produces nothing else.

Such is the environment in which the world's most fashionable author, the poet of sweetest, tenderest love songs, has to live. What can a man do under these circumstances? He can only lament.

And that is what he does. He does it persistently and—as he is a poet—by way of verses.

> So then 'twas fated for me to visit even Scythia, the land that lies beneath the Lycaonion pole; neither you, ye learned throng of Pierians, nor you, O son of Leto, have aided your own priest. It avails me not that without real guilt I wrote playful verse, that my Muse was merrier than my life, but many are the perils by land and sea that I have undergone, and now the Pontus shriveled with constant frost possesses me.

I, who once shunned affairs, who was born for a care-
free life of ease, who was soft and uncapable of toil,
am now suffering extremes; no harborless sea, no far
journeys by land have been able to destroy me. And my
spirit has proved equal to misfortune; for my body, borrowing strength from that spirit, has endured things
scarcely endurable.
Yet while I was being driven through the perils of land
and wave, there was beguilement for my cares. And my
sick heart in the hardship; now that the way has ended,
the toil of journeying is over, and I have reached the land
of my punishment, I care for naught but weeping; from
my eyes comes as generous a flood as that which pours
from the snow in springtime. Rome steals into my thought,
my home, and the places I long for, and all that part of
me that is left.

Ah me, that I have knocked so often upon the door of
my own tomb but it has never opened to me! Why have
I escaped so many swords? Why has not one of those
gales that threatened so often overwhelmed an ill-starred
head? Ye Gods, whom I have found too steadily cruel,
sharers in a wrath on my laggard fate, I beseech you;
forbid the door of my destruction to be closed!

But oh! he feels—and this is his deepest sorrow—how his
talent is being destroyed by these unfavorable conditions. The
Romans call any man not understanding the Latin and Greek
languages a barbarian. But here *he* is the barbarian, for nobody
can understand him. He must live among wild men who cannot
understand his language, must continuously listen to their raucous
gibberish. He fears that the juices nourishing his art may dry up.
These are feelings likely to overcome every genuine writer
forced to live outside his element, separated from his living
mother tongue. And the verses into which Ovid clothes his sorrow
ring as true today as then.
"No books have I here," he laments, "to nourish and spur
me. There is no one in this land for whom my verse can have
meaning; no one fit to lend me his ear and advise me. Into the
open country I may not wander. Ramparts are guarded, gates

are closed against the hostile barbarians. Sometimes I try to remember the name of a place, the name of a person. 'Tis in vain—and no one can I find to help me. Nay—I am deeply ashamed to confess it—often a word I am hunting for seems to elude me. My own language I am forgetting. Thracian, Scythian tongues are croaking around me, and before long I shall have become a writer of Getic verses. I am even afraid that Pontian phrases and turns are creeping slowly into my Latin."

His only happiness consists in writing verses, sending verses to Rome. In spirit he accompanies his manuscript on the whole trip: visualizes it arriving in Rome, crossing the town, reaching his own house. He vividly pictures—and we with him—how the new manuscript is joined to his former works, how it is being placed on the shelves of his fine library.

He believes that his verses will please his friends and addresses them to the residences of former companions. But a grievous disappointment is in store for him. The friends do not wish to be compromised, they chide him for not keeping quiet. They had kept away from him when he left for his exile. Now they are much concerned about him and his dignity. In their opinion, the only thing to do in Ovid's position is to keep his mouth shut.

Ovid has always conformed to the judgment of the world, but he deeply resents this demand, touching the very core of his life. Anyone who suffers must have at least the right to lament. "The captive man, condemned to the chain gang, reduces through songs the burden of his toil. The galley slave sings while plying his oar, the slave girl while at the loom she is weaving." No, he will not stop lamenting.

He knows his Rome, where life is speedy and things are quickly forgotten. He has no wish to be forgotten. He is famous, deservedly famous, and wants to hang on to his fame. With bitterness he speaks of his cowardly, faithless friends. In an elegy addressed to one of the few who have remained loyal he grimly complains that his friends have disappeared along with success. Eternal truths are uttered in this beautiful poem, such as anyone in exile has experienced. They are variations on the theme: As long as you are happy you have numerous friends, but when under a cloud you stand alone.

Again and again—and what émigré has not done the same?—
he tries to bask in his radiant past. He thinks of his recitals and
his successes. From the coast of the inhospitable sea he envisions
Rome's temples, the marble theaters, the porticoes, the lawn of the
Campus Martius, the parks filled with a throng of merry, well-
groomed people. On each holiday he is back in Rome in his
dreams. "Now they are mounting their horses, now attending the
sports events. Now, on the stage, the curtain is rising. Ah! to
be there once more, to see Rome again in my lifetime." And
when he returns from such a dream excursion to his wretched
Tomis the place seems doubly bare and miserable.

Eight long years he spends in exile. Finally he learns the
language of the country and, after a few attempts, succeeds in
writing Getic verses. The natives, the "barbarians," are flattered. As a token of their gratitude they exempt him from every
tax and offer a wreath to him. Somewhat tactlessly he mentions
the mixed feelings aroused in him by these honors. Of course, he
is reminded of Rome and all the victories he attained there.
Ceaselessly he stares at the city "looking down from her seven
hills on the conquered earth at her feet." We may well believe
that only the hope of return can uphold him.

At one time this hope is almost realized. Pardon and return
are dangled before his eyes. One of his friends writes that he
has succeeded in winning over Augustus.

But already the next mail reports that the helpful friend himself has fallen into disgrace.

Soon after this, Augustus dies and with him the last hope of
pardon, for the Caesar succeeding him is Tiberius. And Tiberius
is a harsh adversary but little inclined to grant pardon.

Now a note of resignation creeps into Ovid's verses. "Pardon
me, friends, that I counted too much on your favor. Never again
shall such a mistake be committed by me. Fate has doomed me,
'tis clear, to die in the land of barbarians. Others may cling to
hope who have not been fooled by its trickery. Wounds exist
that are poisonous only when tied with a bandage. Better to let
oneself sink into sorrow once and forever, than to resist with arms
that are weakened and helpless."

Despite all these arguments he keeps on hoping. For three

more years he bears up; always trying to convince himself that there is no hope, and yet eternally hoping. Senseless as it is, he swamps the Emperor Tiberius with pleas and flatteries. Death comes to the poet of fifty-nine while he is occupied in revising an old manuscript and interlarding it with cajoleries for the emperor.

Ovid had no interest in politics. He was no rebel. For him it was a matter of course to worship the men in power. Thus his adulation of both emperors is more than exaggerated. Interminably he kisses the hand chastising him, endlessly he praises the generosity of the tyrant who has banished him. "Nothing in all the world can equal the mildness of Caesar. High above Jupiter stands he; for the Olympian is but a god created through the fancy of mankind. But a visible god is Caesar, of flesh and of blood his form is created." Statuettes of the emperor and the imperial family are sent to Ovid. Immediately he erects an altar to them in his house and rants with the most effusive enthusiasm: "Never shall you, O sacred image, be snatched from this altar. Rather shall this head of mine fall from my shoulders, my eyes from their sockets. Consolation you bring and comfort amidst all my sorrow. Should the barbarian slay me, this image shall I press to my heart as it breaketh—I swear it."

When his friends rebuke him for his unmanly attitude, his eternal plaints, his abject pleas for mercy, he answers with irresistible candor: "Well may you compare me to women who are sentimental and silly. Why not admit that my heart is too weak to endure this disaster? Born I was for the joys of this world, and always I shuddered when confronted by serious affairs. Never before this have I ever been touched by sorrow or toiling."

At all times there have been people who chided Ovid for his weakness. Some of them have been so warped by their moral indignation that they have even condemned Ovid as poet. They do not wish to concede that such a lax, weak man could have written good, let alone eternal, verses. But they wrong him. Ovid's flabby attitude has made his verses not weaker, but more sincere. It is no accident that they have survived two thousand years. It is no accident that Dante read and used Ovid, that several passages of Shakespeare are reminiscent of the Roman poet.

Ovid is a writer with every fiber of his being. Without inhibitions, he expresses whatever he thinks and feels. In shamelessly sincere verses he sings of his happiness in love; in shamelessly sincere verses, of his suffering in exile. Everything he sees and hears is brought into relation to himself. He is sentimental and ironical, frivolous and reveling in sorrow. He speaks about anything that comes into his head; and it does not matter to him in the least if the thing he says today contradicts his assertion of yesterday. Now he seems unbelievably vain, then again possessed of sniveling humility. He proclaims with pride that every syllable written by him shall endure through eternity, but execrates his verses a moment later and considers them miserable failures. His praises and his vituperations are equally boundless. He pursues his own advantage with supreme, naïve, and candid egotism.

It is just this naïvely egocentric trait which makes his verses so charming and invests them with so much directness and sincerity. His poetical works tell more of him and his age than the most objective description could do.

He often reminds us of Oscar Wilde's fashionable elegance, and often of Heine's ironical sentimentality. However, he lacks Heine's mental acuteness and strength of convictions; he lacks the hysterical intensity with which the aging Oscar Wilde throws himself into religion. But he commands an immense ability. Verses come to him at will; he is sensitive to the slightest discord. His character is one of extraordinary elegance and brilliance, concerned with trifling feelings but full of inner music.

It is strange that people should frown on him because he was not changed in his exile. It seems to me that it is this very fact that speaks for him. It speaks for his artistic integrity that he expresses himself and his suffering only with his own means and avoids bombastic words.

The ancients demanded no self-control of a man in distress. Nothing was further from their mind than Kipling's ideal of a gentleman. The ancient heroes roared if somebody hurt them;

they roared in unison and excessively loud. Homer's heroes bellow most lustily; and Philoctetes fills a great part of Sophocles's play with melodically unmelodic wailings caused by his bodily pains. Thus Ovid did not have the slightest desire to appear as a steadfast and forceful man.

He remains in miserable, barbaric Tomis what he had been in Rome: a fashionable gentleman.

He does not even suppress a good joke or quip for the sake of poetic atmosphere. In the midst of bitter complaints about the deathly climate the thought comes to him that now, when sea and river are frozen, Leander might walk to his Hero instead of swimming. Continuously he makes macabre jokes. It occurs to him that he might just as well augment his *Metamorphoses*—his "transformations"—with an account of his own case. Another time he jests that one should excuse the limping verses of his elegies because they had come a long way.

His fear that unfavorable alien conditions had robbed his verses of their melody is unfounded. Ovid did not lose his lilting voice in Pontian exile. Though some of his verses may be trifling and frothy, the best are of Mozartian sweetness and airiness.

Many objections have been raised against the books *Tristia* and *Ex Ponto*. These nine books of elegies have been charged with monotony. It has been said that the endless complaints are boring, in many parts full of triviality and mannerisms; and that the coquettish, affected tone as well as the numerous fashionable allusions to mythology make the work at times almost unendurable.

These objections are not unfounded. There are about six thousand verses; and though Ovid may have considered six thousand verses as only a moderate amount of complaining at the great suffering of nine years, these eternal lamentations do become decidedly monotonous after a while. But only if we read the elegies at one sitting. Reading each one by itself we find in every one touching verses. Studying them closer, we must admire the poet who found ever new forms and turns for his unchanged sorrow.

It is not easy to do justice to Ovid. A hard, factual age like ours is particularly unable to do so. The poems also lose a great deal of their beauty in translation; and though Ovid was deservedly proud of having smoothed the harsh, marblelike Latin, we are not much impressed by this historical merit.

But even the most bitter critic will have to admit that innumerable verses of his deserve to be universally quoted. Despite all his sentimental flourishes, the art of this poet is great and genuine: genuine in its sorrow over his banishment. Beneath all his artificiality lies genuine longing for his fatherland.

And again and again there breaks out of these verses the genuine suffering of the great, the born writer prevented by a harsh, a senseless fate from shaping what no one could have shaped as he: the light, depraved, marvelous, tasteful, scintillating life of Rome, his own city. And again and again there breaks out the fear lest he lose his gifts, his language—the language he had made so pliant that it could emulate Greek.

There are the elegies reflecting his meditations on the faithlessness of friends who slink away when misfortune appears. In their bitterness, their artistry, and their artificiality these verses remind us occasionally of Shakespeare's sonnets. There is the epitaph on the unfinished works left behind at home. And there, too, are his laments about winter and the great emptiness. These and many other things have hardly ever been expressed in a more melodious and stirring way.

> O that my soul would perish with my body and that so no part of me might escape the greedy pyre! For if my spirit flits aloft deathless in the empty air, and the words of the Samian age are true, a Roman shade will wander among Sarmatian ghosts, a stranger forever among barbarians. But my bones—see that they are carried home in a little urn: so I shall not be an exile even in death.

Ovid was a lackey, a lackey who had been suddenly chased away, he knew not why. But this discharged lackey was a great poet who suffered deeply and genuinely in his banishment. Therefore his verses will express the sorrows of exiles until the end of time.

No, the name of Ovid may not be omitted from the great names of exiles of all countries.

KING OLAV
by
SIGRID UNDSET

SIGRID UNDSET

was born in 1882. Her Lillehammer house, built ca. 1650 A.D., was furnished with genuine Norse antiques. She won the Nobel Prize for literature in 1928. Her first successful novel, *Jenny*, was her third to be published. It appeared in 1920. Her greatest works are novels of thirteenth and fourteenth century Norway: *Kristin Lavransdatter* and *The Master of Hestviken*.

When the Germans invaded Norway in April, 1940, Mrs. Undset reported for service with the Norwegian military authorities in Lillehammer, while her sons joined the army. During the stand of the Norwegian army in the valley of Gudbrandsdal, her elder son was killed in action. When the Germans were about to enter Lillehammer, the Norwegian commander ordered Sigrid Undset to leave for the north of Norway, where the Norwegian forces were still fighting. In *Return to the Future* Mrs. Undset has told the story of her journey through a bombed and burning countryside into Sweden. Before she could reach the northern front, however, the Norwegian army had to surrender, and in the autumn of 1940 Mrs. Undset and her younger son came to America. Her son later went to Scotland, where the remnant of the Norwegian army was reorganized, but Mrs. Undset is still in this country.

KING OLAV
by Sigrid Undset

N ORWAY's transition from paganism to Christianity began in the second half of the tenth century. At that time Håkon, one of the sons of the Norwegian king Harald Fairhair, was educated in England and brought a number of English priests home with him. But the people killed the missionaries and burnt the churches King Håkon built. They were convinced that departing from the pagan ways of their forefathers would bring disaster.

One man in particular, Earl Haakon, conscientiously opposed Christianity and seems to have sponsored a pagan revival. But when it was rumored that during a crucial battle Earl Haakon sacrificed his little son as an offering for victory, the people disapproved. They were no longer able to understand such a belief in the old gods.

Fifty years later King Olav Tryggvesson renewed the attempts of King Håkon. But he lived only five years.

After King Olav's death the Norsemen along the coast, who were in constant touch with the countries across the sea, remained Christians of a sort. But the land about the Trondheim fiord and farther north, the core of Norway, with its broad arable fields and mighty lords who owned big ships and herds of cattle and slaves, returned defiantly to the gods of their fathers and the old, gorgeous sacrificial celebrations of Midwinter, Spring, and Harvesttime. The interior of Norway, away from the sea lanes, had scarcely been touched by the new faith, or by any new ideas or ways of life.

So it may, or it may not, be true that King Olav Tryggvesson had visited Asta, widow of his kinsman Harald Grenske, up in one of the valleys inland, and had persuaded her to be baptized and to let him be the godfather of her baby boy. When the child was lifted out of the baptismal fount and noticed the burning candle that his godfather, King Olav, carried, the little boy called out, "Light, light, light."

The name of Olav does not occur anywhere else in the line of Harald Grenske, so it is just possible that King Olav actually was the godfather of Olav Haraldsson. Asta's husband, Harald Grenske, had been a petty king on the south coast of Norway and according to the sagas a good-for-nothing. Some years after his death Asta married Sigurd Syr, king of Ringerike, like King Olav, of the Harald Fairhair line.

King Sigurd ruled his small kingdom wisely and was famed for his management of his estates. His young stepson, Olav Haraldsson, however, did not approve of King Sigurd's peaceful ways. Once, when the king told Olav to go and saddle a horse for him, the boy returned leading a big ram decked out with the royal riding gear—this, Olav said, seemed to him as fitting a mount for a farmer king as a horse for a knight. So when he was twelve years old his parents sent Olav out to be a viking—as parents in other ages send their boys to a university or military academy to get the education proper to their station in life. His foster father, Rane, was the real master of the ships, but the boy Olav was given the name of sea king.

Olav Haraldsson was with the vikings who harried the shores of the Baltic Sea and of Holland and England in the early years of the eleventh century. Eventually he joined a fleet of viking ships, bound for the Mediterranean, but when he lay with his ships off Gibraltar he dreamed that a giant appeared to him and said, "Return to the land of your inheritance, for you must become king of Norway eternally." Olav took this to mean that he was to win the kingdom of Norway for himself and his descendants.

First he went to Rouen and was baptized. When he left he took with him priests and a bishop, Rudolf, a cousin of the Duke of Normandy. But instead of proceeding directly to Norway, Olav

decided to help the two young sons of the English King Ethelred
fight to hold England against the Danes under their king, Canute.
The English princes were defeated, but in England Olav learned
that Canute had made his brother-in-law, Earl Eirik of Lade,
come to help him conquer England. Earl Eirik was the virtual
ruler of Norway, and his presence in England meant a chance of
a sort to the young Norwegian prince.

That Olav should grasp his chance the way he did shows a
recklessness that can be explained only in one of two ways:
either Olav Haraldsson was a perfect daredevil, ready to stake
everything on a desperate gamble, win or lose; or he was convinced that to take Norway back from the usurping Dane,
Canute, and the Earl of Lade was his duty as well as his right,
and in doing his duty he ought to rely on divine justice to help
his daring attempt.

Olav left his warships in England, and late in the fall of
1015 set out with two small vessels and two hundred and twenty
hand-picked men, sailing for Norway in a violent storm. He
landed on Selja, a small island on the west coast. As he stepped
ashore he slid and dropped down on one knee. Rane, his foster
father, said, "You did not fall, king—you took foothold in your
country." Olav laughed. "Maybe, God willing!" He was at the
time twenty-two years old.

The oldest sources for the story of Olav Haraldsson are the
verses of his skalds, a long poem *Glaelogn* (the word means ocean
stillness, the radiance of the sea at rest on a windless day), the
readings in Breviaries, and the Missals of the Church, some of
them composed less than fifteen years after Olav's death. And in
these oldest sources Olav is above all the saint, who by his zeal
for the conversion of his people, as well as by his life of prayer
and mortification, has won the crown of everlasting glory.

It is worth while to remember that the Icelandic sagas about
Olav were written a century to two and a half centuries later.
They are reconstructions—probably drawing their subject matter
from oral tradition among men, whose forefathers remembered
the king as a puzzle, not always easily understood, and not always

an admirable or likable character, but always a man fascinating to those who followed his banner.

This development of the Olav tradition culminated with Snorri Sturluson's full-length portrait in his great saga of the royal house of Fairhair. With consummate psychological insight Snorri tells of the development that made a saint out of a self-willed and proud viking king—a man who during his lifetime was a symbol of contradiction, beloved as few men were ever loved by his few intimate friends, hated by his enemies, and an enigma to the mass of his people. So vivid is the picture that Norwegian historians still take sides for or against this Olav that Snorri has given to us.

Young authors of the Marxian school refuse to see in his achievements anything but an ambitious and stubborn young man's greed for power. Some die-hard romantics denounce Olav because he curtailed a time-honored freedom. When he wanted to make Norway a united kingdom and the local barons refused to co-operate, he took away their traditional right to oppose their king. But the fact remains that the shape of the Norwegian nation that has prevailed up to our time was fundamentally the work of Olav Haraldsson.

Certainly he was ambitious. He loved the power he needed to achieve his aims. Contrary to the run of kings of his race, he had a sense of economy. He might lavish gifts and favors on men he wanted to win over to his side, he endowed what churches he permitted to be built, he was generous toward the poor and needy. But he never spent money the way the old kings had done, indiscriminately, just to be praised for their lavishness and to show off their wealth. Olav was seasoned enough in warfare abroad and trained enough in political thinking to know what use money may be put to, and his goal was larger than personal prestige.

He had nothing of the radiant charm, the fascinating virility of the handsome Olav Tryggvesson. None of the historians try to pretend that he was even particularly good-looking—he was of medium height and stocky, with fair hair and a red beard. His features were "well shaped," nothing more. But his eyes, the saga says, were strangely compelling, beautiful when he was glad and friendly; but when he was angry most men shrank from meeting his glance—and the old Norsemen were not usually afraid to look an angry king full in the face.

To be able to improvise a short poem in the artificial style of the times, when occasion called for it, was part of the education of well-bred young Norsemen of that day. But if the poems the sagas quote as Olav's really are by him he was no mean poet. Through the severely conventional patterns of the old verse break deep emotions of love and hate and caustic wit. When he landed in Norway in the fall of 1015 he was still very young—merry with his merry men, when they took their chances together, easily impressed by the beauty of women. But as a convert to Christianity, Olav wistfully resigned the easy way of his fathers with fair women and found in that sacrifice a source of poems, half sad, half humorous.

During those first years it looked as though Olav would succeed in everything he undertook. Luck and Olav's reckless daring made the young son of Earl Eirik of Lade fall in his hands. Olav granted the lad life and liberty but made him swear never again to fight the king of Norway. Then he let the young earl go straight to England to his father and King Canute, his uncle.

Olav sailed on along the coast, and when he arrived in the south, where his father had had his small kingdom, he found plenty of followers willing to hail him as the new king.

In the summer of 1016 Olav could take time off to ride inland to Ringerike and visit his mother and stepfather. Snorri's picture of life on a small old-fashioned royal manor has always been dear to the Norwegians. It was harvesttime, and King Sigurd Syr was in the fields, supervising his shearers, when his wife sent messengers with his finest robes and his best steed. They were to tell him that her son, King Olav, was coming. Among the sheaves of grain King Sigurd changed into royal splendor and rode home to receive his stepson and preside at the feast the Lady Asta was preparing.

From Ringerike Olav marched overland to Trondheim. Part of the Trondheim men acknowledged him as the heir of King Harald Fairhair. Then the younger Earl of Lade, Swein, sur-

prised him with vastly superior man power. Olav had to take
to his ships and flee, and the earl burned his buildings.

The following spring, however, Earl Swein let himself be
enticed into offering King Olav a battle at sea. Olav had not been
a sea king since the age of twelve for nothing. The earl suffered
defeat and fled to Denmark. Olav returned to Trondheim and consolidated his power over the northern parts of Norway.

But on the coastal plains to the south, Jaedern, Erling
Skjalgsson of Sole, ruled as king in everything but name. A
sort of agreement between Erling and Olav was achieved, but
several times they came very near to breaking it. No love was
lost between the young king and the old chieftain. Erling has
been remembered by history mainly as the man who staked out
for his slaves a fair day's labor and let them work for themselves
in their off time, to raise the sum that would buy their freedom.
Many of his slaves managed to earn freedom for themselves
and their children in three to five years.

While Olav was busy with Erling, the kinglets whom Sigurd
Syr had persuaded to bow to his stepson's rule staged an insurrection. The new king meant to rule over them in more than
name, and they disliked it. Olav took the lot of them prisoners
by a surprise attack. Some he outlawed, some he maimed, but his
contemporaries regarded Olav's treatment of the conspirators as
Christian clemency.

The King of Sweden, who had moved his frontiers into
Norway, regularly sent his tax collectors across the border. As a
result, the border warfare and unsettled state of affairs between
Sweden and Norway was a curse to the common people on both
sides. According to the sagas, the Swedes compelled their king
to make peace with the Norwegian king. The frontier line was
fixed, and it was agreed that Olav should marry Ingegjerd,
daughter of the Swedish king.

The historical facts are that this marriage was agreed upon,
that the King of Sweden broke his word and married his daughter
to a Russian prince, that Olav married Ingegjerd's half-sister
Astrid without the consent of her father, and that he entered
upon an alliance with his brother-in-law, Anund Jakob, who succeeded his father as king. The sagas say that, although they had

never met, Olav and Ingegjerd were lovers. She loved him for what she had heard about his prowess and Christian zeal, he loved her beauty and high-mindedness, praised by the skalds. Irked by his daughter's praise of Olav, the jealous and dull old King of Sweden sent her to Russia.

But before she left, Ingegjerd entrusted her half sister Astrid—baseborn on her mother's side—with her love token to Olav, the silken shirt she had sewed for her bridegroom, and with a message that she would always do all she could to further his happiness and his honor. Secretly Astrid escaped from home and made her way to the frontier town where Olav had prepared his wedding and now smarted under the insult offered him and the loss of his bride. Even after Astrid had seen him and delivered her message Olav remained silent and glum. Then the girl made an offer on her own account. "Here I am in your power. If you married me, without the consent of my father, would you not get even with him?" And when she saw that Olav was tempted by her advice she went on: "True, my sister Ingegjerd is peerless among women. Though the priests say," said Astrid, piously and cunningly, "that she who serves is the greatest." And so Olav celebrated his wedding, with Astrid for bride.

The old history of Norway scarcely mentions the queens— many of the kings were never married at all, but did very well with the daughters of the land. Of Astrid the sagas tell a good deal: she was her husband's loyal friend, a canny counselor, a tactful lady.

Now Olav was king of all Norway—he had ousted the vassals of foreign kings and the native kinglets. To keep in check the old aristocracy of the countryside Olav created a new class of locally powerful men who were to lead the defense in time of war, manage the royal estates, and maintain the laws of the land and the rights of the common people. Olav chose them from the old yeomanry.

Since time immemorial the free peasants of Norway had assembled at the Thing to rule their own affairs. Summons to a local Thing might be issued whenever a man wanted to complain of an injustice or a crime against his honor or safety—his neighbors would then hear his case and sit in judgment. At the annual Thing of a larger area new laws, proposed by the king, were accepted or refused by the free men, and matters of interest to the whole community were settled. The natural leaders of the men at a Thing had been the heads of the greater landowning families, men who stood for an ordered society and peace in the land. This aristocracy was not willing to surrender any of its power to a king.

The old laws also had maintained the rights of the little man. They were not identical with the rights of the mighty, but they were rights. Society, however, had developed a system of legislation without developing a system of law enforcement. When a man had won his case at the Thing it was up to him personally to have the verdict carried out. The common men could do so only with the help of their hereditary leaders, so it was no more than natural that these leaders should administer justice in a somewhat arbitrary manner and think they should interpret the laws or decide to what extent they would obey them.

Olav's new body of men in authority—the nucleus of a civil service and a police force in Norway—was bound to enforce the laws impartially. And there is plenty of contemporary evidence, in the verses of the poets, that nothing alienated the old lords of the land from Olav more than this. "In vain did the rich robbers offer red gold to the king, to buy exemption from punishment. Thus the peace in the land of the prince was furthered."

The new laws aimed to end the whole business of viking raids as unseemly for Christian men. To the old-fashioned lords it must have seemed intolerable that this upstart king, with his outlandish ideas of effective government, should threaten to punish them as robbers when they did only what they had come to consider their time-honored right. And if they disregarded his new laws they were to be punished in the same way that they themselves had always punished the common people.

But to Olav the important side of his kingship was his vocation to make Norway a Christian country. The Norwegians declared that this was true less than a year after the king had been killed, and our nation has maintained it ever since. It is of course impossible to decide in detail how much of our body of

medieval laws really is identical with the laws which Olav Haraldsson and Grimkjell, his bishop, formulated and which the king
made the Norsemen accept. They were not written down until
about one century later. But they were always called the laws of
St. Olav. The opening paragraphs of one of the oldest run:

> This is the beginning of our law, that we shall bow
> toward the east and pray to Holy Christ, for a good har-
> vest and for peace, and that we may keep our country
> settled and our king happy. May he be our friend, and
> we his friends, and may God be the friend of all of us.
> A land should be built with law, and not destroyed by
> lawlessness. And he who will not let his neighbor enjoy
> the protection of the law, let not the law protect him.

The times of King Olav Haraldsson afterward came to be
called "Sidaskiptid"—the changing of our way of life. The king's
efforts to create a central government, to strengthen the position
of the Church, and to establish co-operation between the Church
and secular government, were all measures aimed at making the
Christian faith rule Norwegian morals and manners. Men and
women were to understand their duty toward their Creator, and
in the light of the new faith to accept new duties toward their
fellow men.

In Trondheim and farther north Olav went about his missionary work in much the same highhanded way as the first Olav.
But he lacked Olav Tryggvesson's gift for winning either a
grudging admiration from his enemies or the exuberant devotion
of men whose pride it was that they followed the strongest and
handsomest man in the land.

In spite of this, Olav went stubbornly and recklessly on with
his work to unite and Christianize his kingdom. He even reached
out for the Norwegian settlements in the North Atlantic. The
islands north of Scotland nominally owed allegiance to the crown
of Norway, but the attempts of the Norse kings to enforce their
sovereignty usually brought them a great deal of trouble and not
much else. Olav meddled in the fratricidal strife of the Orkney
earls and kept as a hostage a son of the earl he supported.

Iceland had always been independent, an aristocratic republic.

And however eager the Icelanders were to serve the kings of
Norway as bodyguards, skalds, and later as scholars, they
jealously prevented the kings from gaining influence in their
homeland. The Icelanders accepted Olav's help in revising their
ecclesiastical laws and his gifts of bells and building material for
a church on the Althing, their place of parliament. But further
advances they politely staved off.

About the year of 1020 Olav undertook to bring Christianity
to the valleys in the interior of Norway. In the northern part of
the Gudbrandsdal the people accepted Olav's missionary efforts
more or less willingly. But at Hundorp, in the middle of the
valley, the pagan chiefs prepared to fight the king. Olav defeated
their vanguard and sent the young leader, the son of Dale-Gud-
brand of Hundorp, home to his father with the message that the
king was coming to parley with the peasants. The dramatic story
of the Thing of Hundorp came to be regarded as the final
victory of Christianity in Norway.

An armistice was agreed upon, and for several days the king
and the pagan peasants met to talk things over. But to Dale-
Gudbrand and his friends, Olav's talk about a God who had
never been seen by him or anybody else did not make sense: they
had a god they could see whenever they wanted, the big idol of
Thor in the local temple. Every day he was fed offerings of bread
and meat, and since the food always disappeared during the
night it was evident that Thor ate it. They threatened to take
Thor to the Thing "if Olav could make his god send sunshine
tomorrow," as Thor did not like to go out doors on a rainy day.

Olav spent the night fasting and praying, and after Mass
he went to the Thing. The bright sky at dawn promised a fine
summer's day. The Hundorp men arrived, carrying their idol—
a huge figure of a man, all decked out in gold and silver.

"Where is your god now, king? I suppose he bows his
beard low on his breast; fearful to meet the fierce eyes of our
god." Olav rose and spoke, until the first spark of sunlight
started burning the tops of the spruce on the mountain ridge
east of the Thing plain.

"And now," Olav commanded, "look up and look toward the

east—see how our God comes riding in a great light." While
the Dale men looked on the rising sun a man of Olav's bodyguard crashed the idol with his mace. It broke in pieces, discharg-
ing rats and mice and grubs. "See what you have fed with your
meat and bread. Now pick up all these ornaments of silver and
gold from the grass, and take them home to hang on your
womenfolk."

So the men of Gudbrandsdal accepted baptism; the temple was
torn down and a church built on the site. Soon churches rose up
and down the valley, and Gudbrandsdal became for centuries the
center of exquisite religious architecture and sculpture.

Like many other people, the old Norsemen had combined
barbarian morals with highly refined artistic tastes—their arms,
their tools, their wood carving, and their ships had a streamlined
and perfect loveliness. The blending of the old style with the
Romanesque and Gothic styles introduced by the Church brought
about a blossoming of the arts and crafts, nowhere more beautiful than in Gudbrandsdal.

By the year of 1025 King Canute had consolidated his powers
in England. Now he meant to enforce his claim of conquest upon
Norway. His messengers arrived before King Olav and offered
him the right to hold Norway as a fief under Denmark, which
had conquered the country in the year 1000. Olav must pay
homage to Canute and send him yearly tribute. Olav replied
that he would defend his country to the utmost.

In the summer of 1026 Olav assembled a fleet and sailed
for Denmark. But several of the mighty men of Norway had disregarded the king's call. When Canute arrived from England
with a vastly superior fleet, Olav had to retire into Swedish
waters, where he was joined by his brother-in-law, King Anund
Jakob. Sometime afterward Anund Jakob made a separate peace
with King Canute, and Olav had to make his escape by a dash
through the Danish sounds back to Norway.

The smoldering resentment of the old aristocracy up to now
had mostly found expression in petty attempts to frustrate the
king's plans, unwillingness to support his measures, underhand
intriguing. Now the chieftains openly defied Olav. In vain Sighvat
the Skald tried to rally the Norse lords. "Those who sell their

liege lord for gold must be yearning for black hell. There they
will be punished. . . . Above all sins, God hates treason."

All over Norway the great lords received the emissaries of
King Canute, with their gifts of gold and their fair promises,
and pledged support to the Dane. And in the summer of 1028
King Canute himself came to Norway with a fleet of Danish and
English ships. At a Thing in Trondheim he was proclaimed King
of Norway and started on a tour of the country, to receive the
homage of the Norwegians.

In the meantime, Olav with his few ships had hidden in a
fiord in his native south district. But as soon as King Canute
had returned to Denmark, Olav took off and sailed along the coast
westward. Rounding the southernmost tip of Norway, he sailed
past the domains of Erling Skjalgsson and stood north. This was
reported to Erling, who hurriedly manned his ships and started
in pursuit.

Erling's own ship outsailed the others, and when he overtook
the king and attacked, the king had the upper hand. Every man on
Erling's ship was dead or wounded when Olav with some men of
his bodyguard boarded it and went along the bloody deck to where
Erling himself stood alone on the high poop, waiting to face the
victor. Sighvat the Skald has preserved their words, when they
met :

"So you are turning your face toward me today, Erling?"

Erling answered, "Eagles should fight eye to eye."

Olav could not master his resentment toward his opponent.
And he did a mean thing—with the edge of his battleax he
grazed the chin of the old man : "A traitor to his king ought to
carry a mark."

One of Olav's men rushed forward and cut down Erling.
"Woe to you for that stroke—now you have struck Norway out
of my hands," the king cried. And so Olav Haraldsson had to die,
before he again could become the king of all Norwegians.

Now the whole of the west of Norway was up in arms
against him. He had to run into one of the fiords that crisscross
the Norwegian coast line, desert his ships, and in the middle
midwinter make his way on foot over the wild mountain ridges

that separate the coastlands from Gudbrandsdal. Even the chiefs who had sided with him up to now gave up his cause as lost.

King Olav fled overland into Sweden, where he left his queen and their only child, a girl, with King Anund Jakob. In the spring Olav went on into exile. He took with him his four-year-old son Magnus. The mother of the boy had been a bondwoman of Queen Astrid's.

Of all places, Olav found refuge in Gardar, the Russian principality which belonged to Jarisleiv and his lady, Ingegjerd. According to the sagas, he had never met her. But a lovely short poem ascribed to Olav during his stay in Gardar is heavy with emotion : He is standing on the castle wall and looks down where Ingegjerd is riding past. "Back in her home in Upsal she was like the fair young tree abundant with green leaves. She has faded since she came to Gardar. Yet to me her white forehead, circled with gold, is still very lovely."

How far the sagas' tale of the tremendous spiritual growth in Olav's mind during his exile in Gardar is historically true cannot be decided with certainty. But it is not the way of the legends to invent freely—rather, they underline salient traits and create a kind of conventionalized portrait, while using the impressions their object made on his environment. St. Olav of the legends and sagas is an elaboration of the thumbnail sketches surviving in the improvisations and short poems of his skalds. And the skalds speak of Olav with a deep and sincere devotion that is different from the conventional praise and official admiration that the court poets of other Norwegian kings offered to their lords.

To Sighvat Thordarsson, the greatest poet of his age, even "the high mountains of Norway seemed to laugh, when Olav was alive. Now the hills seem saddened." And when after Olav's death he saw the Dane's courtiers at their games in the meadow, where Olav used to play with his men, he felt the pang of grief make his face turn white. All his skalds loved Olav. After all, he was a poet himself, and the poets were the ones who really understood the man beneath the robes of royalty.

Disrobed, in his exile, a king without a country is just his own reticent, somewhat shy self. In some way the rumor got abroad in Gardar that if you could get the exiled Norwegian king to touch sick people and pray over them they would get well. Reluctantly Olav gave in to their importunate requests, miraculous cures happened, and more sick people came to see Olav.

Meanwhile he yearned to leave Gardar—to lead a crusade against the pagan Bulgars or travel to Jerusalem and enter a monastery. Both lives may have appealed to an exiled Christian king—either as a crusader or as a monk in the turbulent Orient he would find ample opportunity to use his ruling and organizing talents to the greater glory of God.

But one night Olav Tryggvesson appeared to him in a dream. He ordered Olav Haraldsson to return to Norway and fight for his kingdom. In Norway lay his vocation, and there he would meet the fate that God had designed for him.

Friends of the king arrived from Norway. Some of them had let themselves be bought by Canute, but remorse troubled them and they had to go to their lawful lord, begging his pardon. Others had kept their faith but had to lie low; now they could tell their king important news. The young Earl Swein of Lade had broken the promises he made when Olav pardoned him, and had returned to Norway as the earl of King Canute— only to be stricken down by a mysterious illness. Norway was without a ruler—for the present.

One Sunday evening, sunk in thought, Olav had taken up a piece of wood and begun carving (he was, say the sagas, a fine artist in wood carving). A page, shocked that the king should do manual work on the Sabbath, whispered to him, "My lord, tomorrow is Monday." The king looked up and asked the boy for the lighted torch he carried. He swept the shavings off the table, set fire to them, and let them burn in the hollow of his hand. Once more Olav proved that the commandments he had imposed on others would be kept by himself at all costs.

And now he felt it was time for action. His little son, Magnus, he entrusted to the care of the lady Ingegjerd and her husband. With his followers, some two hundred men, Olav returned to Sweden. King Anund Jakob dared not support him openly, but secretly he let Olav recruit Swedish warriors from the out-of-the-way parts of the country. Frontiersmen, settlers from the mountains, flocked to the banner of the foreign king. Olav accepted their oath of loyalty and tried to convert them.

Of Arnljot Gelline, the strong and handsome head of a band of desperate outlaws, Olav asked, "What do you and your men believe in?"

"In nothing much," said Arnljot. "We do not believe in the gods. As for me, I used to believe in my own strength and courage. But I would fain trade that belief for a belief in you, king!"

"If you want to believe in me," Olav answered, "believe in the faith I will teach you. You must believe that Jesus Christ has created heaven and earth and all men."

Adam of Bremen, the German, who wrote less than five years after the battle of Stiklestad, says of the war between King Canute and King Olav, "The Dane fought for power, the Norwegian for liberty." The men of the eleventh century did not think about nationality the way we do, and their love of the soil of their homeland was different from and more realistic than our idea of patriotism. But the feeling that an ethnic group has a right to choose its own ruler, from its own stock, was just being born in many different parts of Europe. In Norway the defeat and the death of Olav was the event which brought it home to the whole nation, and made impossible ever after for Norwegians voluntarily to submit to a foreign conqueror or obey an alien Fuehrer.

Olav himself probably did not dream of this development, as he crossed the border mountains with his small army. It was toward the end of the month of July, when the Norwegian summer is fairest, meadows and cornfields ripening during long days and short, twilight nights. The first place where his army camped, on a lonely farm on a hillside, they trampled down the fields. The king said this ought not to have happened. During the night he walked over the fields, praying. In the morning every stalk of corn and every blade of grass had been righted, and the crops looked more promising than before.

One day the king had been riding for a long while without

talking. It was where the valley opened up, and from the high ridge the plains down by the fiord and the sea came into view. The bishop asked the king why he was so sad. "A great vision came to me," the king replied, "as I looked westward from the mountain into Norway. I remembered that in this country I have been glad many a day. Then I was granted this vision: it seemed to me that I looked out over all Trondheim, and next over the whole of the land. And the longer I looked, the wider did the view unfold, until I looked on the whole of the earth, both land and oceans. I recognized the places where once I had been, but just as plainly did I see all the places where I have never been—some that I have heard about, but also all the places I never knew were there, countries where men live as well as wildernesses—all of the wide world." The bishop dismounted, and embracing the king's foot he bowed low—he said this vision was holy and beautiful.

Olav seems to have thought that the vision foreboded his death. He tried to persuade every man who joined his forces to be baptized and his old friends to confess and receive the Body of Our Lord, as he himself had done. To the priest of Stiklestad church he gave a sum of money, to have masses said for the souls of all men who were to die in the coming battle—especially for his enemies, they would need it even more than his own men dying in a righteous cause.

All Norway had mustered against Olav—or so it seemed. The army of the peasants was the largest ever seen in the country. The bulk was made up of men from Trondheim under their hereditary chiefs, but also from the north and the west country a number of lords with their troops had joined. But then it happened that these leaders of warriors could not agree who was to be commander in chief. None of them was willing to take the responsibility. The great army was really an army of men fighting each for his separate interests or private ambitions, personal aspirations or prejudices—the multitude of minor liberties for which men at all times have been willing to compromise even with foreign domination.

Against them stood Olav's small army—the king's bodyguard, the Swedes, and some troops from Ringerike and the valleys.

At break of day on July 30th the armies took up their positions. Olav was resting, his head on the lap of Finn Arnesson, when the bugles of the peasants' army sounded. The king sighed: "I dreamed a fair dream. I dreamed I did mount a ladder that led up into heaven. And just as I was grasping the uppermost rung I was awakened." Angrily Finn answered that he could not think the dream boded any good.

Thormod the Skald rallied the king's men by singing an old battle lay in his strong and beautiful voice. The king said he must reward Thormod for his singing. Thormod answered, that he wanted one thing only: "To be in your bosom and before your face, and I wish I may not survive you." One thing made him fearful. He was afraid, if both were killed in the battle, that he and the king might not be summoned to the same feast tonight. Olav promised he would pray that they might both go to the same place after death.

In Olav's army every will was welded into one. Three times his army swept through the vastly superior masses of the enemy, cutting wide swaths in the ranks of the peasants. But each time the peasants closed in on the king's firm formation of bodyguards and Dale men. When the end came, Olav's standard-bearer was cut down, thrusting with his last strength his banner stake into the ground, and under the banner the bodyguard was massacred. King Olav was wounded three times, the last wound a mortal one. Leaning against a boulder, he threw away his sword, commended his soul to God, and expired. . . .

The remnant of his army, Swedes and men from Ringerike, rallied for a last stand to avenge their king, but they were defeated and routed. The few survivors had to make their way across the mountains back to Sweden.

Late in the evening Thormod the Skald came to a farm, where a wisewoman tended the wounded. In the yard he met a peasant who told him how pleased he was to have been "on the side that got the best of it." The dying poet smiled: "I was on the side that *is* the best."

At night the farmer of Stiklestad and his son went over the battlefield, searching for the body of the king. They carried it into the woodshed, washed and shrouded it, and hid it behind the woodpiles. Toward dawn a blind beggar, who had followed the peasants' army, groped his way into the woodshed, slipped on the floor, and passed his hand, wet from the bloody water, across his eyes. When he came out into the open he could see. . . .

Less than a year passed after the death of King Olav before the men of the great compromise had their eyes opened.

From Stiklestad they had scattered in a way that was singularly unlike the homecoming of victorious warriors. Soon enough they learned that men who are banded together by private interests are liable to fall apart like dry sand, and the price of the preservation of outdated little liberties is always freedom itself. That holds good for individuals as well as for peoples and nations. The Norse lords who had hoped to have all their old privileges under a king who lived in another country were severely disappointed.

To rule Norway, King Canute sent over his own son Swein, and, since the prince was very young, Canute let the boy's mother, an English lady who had been Canute's mistress, accompany their son. With the lady arrived a train of Danes and Englishmen, and the Norwegians learned for the first time in their history what foreign rule really is like.

New laws, molded upon the laws of countries where the king had unlimited power—a situation utterly unknown in Norway— were enforced without asking the sanction of the people. Even the old aristocracy altered its opinion of Olav as a lawgiver. A drought was regarded by the people as the punishment of God upon the regicides. And rumors were rife: men and women in distress had prayed to Olav for his intercession with the God he had proclaimed, and they had been wonderfully helped. So it seemed that their own king, whom they had killed, was one of those saints the priests of the new faith told about.

One of the Trondheim chiefs, who had rebelled against the king but happened to have been abroad when the battle of Stiklestad was fought, expressed the new view on Olav: "We made a bad bargain when we traded our gallant king for a mare and her filly."

That chief sent for Grimkjell, the bishop, who had lived in retirement in Olav's old home in Ringerike since the battle. Now the farmer of Stiklestad revealed where he had hidden the body of the king. He had secretly buried it in a sand bank by the river that flows through the town of Trondheim. It was exhumed, and King Olav looked as if he had just gone to sleep, except that he was handsomer than he had ever been when living.

The bishop, the priests, and the chieftains of the people unanimously proclaimed Olav Haraldsson a saint. The body was placed in a proper coffin and enshrined above the high altar of St. Clemens' Church in Trondheim.

Pilgrims flocked to the new shrine—"an army of lame and blind and mute," says Thorarin, court poet of King Swein, "and they return to their homes, giving praise to God, because he has restored the kingdom of Norway to Olav."

A number of posthumous stories about Olav cropped up. It is impossible to decide exactly how much of the subject matter goes back to the people who remembered the man as he really was. A common characteristic is the picture of a man with exalted ideas about his dignity and his duties as a king, but with great modesty about himself as a human being. Kind and helpful in his own shy and unobtrusive way, Olav does not like anybody to fuss about the services he willingly renders.

When some drunken peasants have insulted him on a road outside Trondheim town, because they did not recognize the modestly dressed, quiet stranger, he afterward summons them into his presence and greets them with a friendly, "Hello, mates." Frightened out of their wits, they do not understand what the king means. "Why, so you hailed me the other day on the Gauldal road. I only called you here to give you a piece of sound advice. Always be polite to strangers, even if they seem to you to be people of no importance."

On another occasion, some peasants from the country have walked all the way to town to go to the solemn Mass on Whitsunday, only to discover, when they come to the river, that the ferry is not there. A man walking in the meadow on the town side sees their plight, loosens a rowboat, and comes over to take them across. A busybody of an old wife recognizes the volunteer ferryman, and starts exclaiming about royal condescension, but Olav hurriedly hushes her. He promises to give her a cow if she will not tell anybody about his slight service to some fellow Christians. So, in the story, she did not tell, until after he was dead and declared a saint.

St. Olav of the miracle stories is similar. The stranger who offers to guide a cripple to St. Olav's Church near London Bridge and disappears at the lich gate with a friendly nod; and the healer who comes to help the maimed English priest left to die in a hut on a Norwegian mountain side—in each case, the character seems to dislike any fuss being made about his good deeds. Asked who he is, he always murmurs, "Oh, it's Olav from Trondheim," —and vanishes.

The *Passio & Miracula Beati Olavi,* written about 1180 by a Norwegian archbishop exiled in England by the then ruling king of Norway, is the most vivid and intimate picture we possess of everyday life in Norway in the Middle Ages. It tells of a people, hard-working, winning a modest living as farmers and fishermen and sailors, as hunters and woodsmen. They love their babies and their wives, and their old people, are helpful or mean, forgiving or revengeful, merry or sad—and for all their great and little woes, their hopes and disappointments, a people's king, who has the ear of Almighty God and is eternally concerned about everybody's well-being in this life and the hereafter, sits enthroned in Trondheim, ready to listen to all complaints and petitions and to help his people.

To make Christianity a living force, a beloved thing, and a source of activity as well as of art and poetry, the Norwegians had to find the new faith embodied in a man who was of the very bones and blood of the people, a man belonging to the life of everyday reality in Norway and exalted above it in high heaven. Like the old Norse wooden churches, built of the same timber as the homes and barns and byres, but sculptured and towering above them, St. Olav is of the same stuff as all Norwegians.

He became the ideal of his nation for five centuries. Even today the social conscience that built up the Norway which now is temporarily destroyed by usurpers and unlaw, is rooted in our humane and wise medieval laws, which the people agreed should be called St. Olav's. The beautiful words in one of them, about the responsibility of a man who by neglect causes the death of a

pauper—"but may God save us all from ever becoming guilty
of a crime so heinous"—has ever since, in spite of backslidings
and human frailty and callousness, expressed a fundamental feeling in our nation.

But besides the saint of the people there is the king who
became the symbol of a united Norway. Ever since Olav's time
it has been the unpardonable sin to Norwegians to call in foreigners as umpire in quarrels among ourselves or to bow to alien rule.
(The union with Denmark came into being when a young king
of Norway, with a Danish princess for mother, was chosen by
the Danes to succeed his maternal grandfather.) And since the
battle of Stiklestad, rebellion against lawfully established government and treason toward king and country have been abhorred by
Norwegians as the sins of Judas.

Then there is a third Olav—the mythical champion of mankind and human homes against the forces of destruction and
anarchy, against the trolls of the mountains who hurl avalanches
and floods into the valleys, who wreck the boats of the fishing
fleet and drive the lonely hunter crazy. The old gods had lost so
much of their hold on the minds of the people that they were
easily superseded by the Blessed Trinity and the White Christ.
Odin, the Wotan of dark Teutonic forests and stormy nights,
returned to his old status of a demon—in medieval Norwegian
ballads he is the devil himself, or the leader of lost souls. Thor,
the red-bearded god of the hammer, who had defended the tilled
countryside and the sanctity of pledges and promises, merged into
the figure of St. Olav of the red beard.

Recently, at a banquet given to celebrate Swedish aid to our
Norwegian air force, which is now fighting the Nazis above the
Channel, the consul general of Iceland wound up his toast to
Norway with the wish that soon St. Olav might again hear the
voice which summoned him back to his kingdom.

It was not so irrelevant as it may seem to Americans to in-
voke a medieval saint, dead in the year of 1030 in a battle between
men armed with axes and spears and swords.

Olav Haraldsson of Norway was and is the everlasting king
of a nation that for more than a thousand years has managed to
live an honorable, free, and civilized life in a harsh and infertile

country, which we never took by conquest from any other people
—and which never was coveted by anybody except as booty. We
like our hard way of life, and nobody else has ever tried to
follow it.

TYCHO BRAHE

by

KARIN MICHAELIS

KARIN MICHAELIS

was born in Denmark and educated for a musical career, but she discovered that writing was her real vocation. In 1903 she wrote two books, both successes, which in less than a year were published in about twenty languages. *Dangerous Age,* in 1911, sold like wildfire and, like her Bibi series of children's books, has appeared all over the world. Many of her books have been made into motion pictures. The last one America saw was *Star For a Night* in 1936. As a lecturer, Miss Michaelis has traveled widely and has spoken against Hitlerism in America and in most of the countries of Europe. She is now working on her autobiography.

TYCHO BRAHE
by Karin Michaelis

MOST people who hear that someone has gone into exile think that political or religious persecution must have been the cause. There have indeed been many martyrs for their faith as well as for their political convictions, but apart from these two reasons for exile there is a third which is just as unbearable.

We would never use the word "exile" to describe a common criminal or a man who sought new pastures because he could not pay his wife's bonnet bills. But the lack of freedom to work as a scientist, the interference of foolish or malicious people, the constant presence of spiteful or envious enemies who try to tear off the spiritual wings which carry the scientist or inventor high over everyday life—this lack of freedom sucks the life out of the most healthy and strong-willed man and leaves him a wreck or forces him to go into exile.

About such a man this story will be told; about the Danish astronomer, Tycho Brahe.

Denmark was until recently one of the places where culture and education had reached a high peak, a country where life was easy and the soil well-cared-for, where there was prosperity everywhere and little real poverty.

Now, of course, the Danes have been drained of their blood, have been robbed and gagged into silence by gangsters from a neighboring country, and no one is left his inborn right to be a free man, to say what he thinks and act as he sees fit. The

43

Denmark of today is a closed prison with high walls, so that we do not even hear the victim's moan.

After the last war, in which the Danes—through the Germans—were involved, hard times swept the country and work became scarce. Many whole families, as well as young boys, emigrated in order to try their luck in places with still unbroken soil, where possibilities were said to be bountiful.

And so the Danes made their way to the United States, not in thousands but in hundreds of thousands. These people were not exiled, they were settlers. They kept as their holy secret—like a little day-and-night-burning candle on the altar of their hearts—the wish to return to Denmark and enjoy their last sleep in their beloved homeland.

The Danish people believe in freedom. They need freedom.

Had Tycho Brahe lived in Denmark under Germany, either he would have been slowly tortured to death or, if lucky, he would have found refuge in America.

In the Teyn Church of Prague, in the country of Bohemia, a silver coffin contains the dust that was Tycho Brahe. If the coffin were opened one would doubtless find in it a strangely shaped lump, a mixture of gold and silver—the artificial tip which he glued to his nose daily but which he could never make grow on to his face, in spite of his great chemical knowledge and his famous elixirs.

Tycho Brahe was born in 1546, a Danish nobleman. He was to have become a warrior or a statesman. But when once his eyes had been opened to the marvels and the greatness of the sky he followed and depicted the silent, unceasing wanderings of the stars until the day he died—in exile.

He was despised by his contemporaries because he dared to study something so unimportant as the senseless wanderings of the stars. And also because he dared to marry a simple peasant girl.

In Denmark, in Tycho Brahe's time, there were, of course, some people who had a peasant mother and a nobleman for a father. But these noblemen usually turned their backs on the peasant girls and their "brats," whereas Tycho Brahe until his death treated his Christina as it behooves any nobleman to treat his highborn wife. How great a part of his exile was due to his marriage will probably never be known, as the statements contradict each other. I, as a woman, am strongly inclined to believe that the hatred of the chancellor, Christoffer Walkendorf, was due mainly to Tycho's choice of the woman who was to become the wife who presided at his table and the mother of his children.

Tycho's father, the "austere knight" Otto Brahe, was of a good old family. He must have been a little queer. At least to us it seems queer that a young husband, with only one child, a girl, should promise his second child to his brother, if that child should be a son. Evidently he forgot to ask his wife's permission. For when the boy arrived she said an emphatic No.

But Tycho's uncle, Joergen (George) Brahe, insisted that a promise is a promise. He let the mother keep her boy until he was weaned; and when, shortly afterward, boy number two arrived Joergen kidnaped the older one, Tycho, and the matter was settled.

Joergen was a wealthy and respected man, and the child was in good hands under his care. The mother acquiesced, and fate rewarded her by giving her half a score of children in all.

Tyge, as his name is in the good old Danish, was thus almost a changeling. But his life would hardly have developed differently if he had remained with his parents and had grown up with his brothers and sisters, instead of being his uncle's only heir.

It is told about Nijinski, the Russian dancer by God's grace, that he once had his legs X-rayed and they appeared to be partly human and partly birdlike. If anyone had been able to examine Tycho's eyes in the same way, they would probably have been found to be partly human and partly the eyes of an eagle.

So far as we know, no one before or after his time has been equipped with eyes as sharp, as piercing, or as enduring as the stargazer Tycho Brahe's. Only one thing in the whole world could have prevented him from following his vocation: the calamity of having been born blind.

Probably the intelligent boy was rather spoiled by his uncle;

yet he was not allowed to loaf, but was sent to school at an early age and began his Latin when only five.

He was enrolled at the university at the age of eleven—which shows that the requirements of a university at that time were nothing compared to what they are now. Tyge was neither very diligent nor very lazy, but probably like most boys of his age.

In his twelfth year something happened that would have stirred the imagination of any schoolboy as greatly as a murder or a large fire. But for him it decided the entire course of his life.

A total eclipse of the sun took place on the day and at the hour predicted; while observing it Tyge's mind was thrown into as great a turmoil as if he had been shaken by an earthquake.

How could people foresee what was going to happen at that unmeasurable distance? The boy had a religious bringing-up, and during his whole life he kept his child's faith with all its contradictions and misunderstandings. To calm himself, he tried to explain the eclipse as something divine, but it was of no use. He stood as before a wall: they had known the day and hour . . .

While the black disk slowly advanced and finally covered the entire sun, killing its rays, Tyge Brahe was conceived and born anew. When again the golden light reached the earth with its reviving glow it was the astronomer Tycho Brahe who wiped the perspiration off his brow, his eyes trying in vain to penetrate the infinite space.

He probably did not realize that from now on nothing would matter to him except the exploration of the firmament with all its mysteries. He was only a boy, with all the helpless limitations of a child. But he had become another; his orbit was marked out. He had only one aim: to be able to predict the strange ways of the sun. If he did not succeed in doing that he would never find peace.

He spent his pocket money on books about the stars and their influence on the destiny of man. He was convinced that the earth was the center of the universe and that we small human beings were the most important part of the whole creation. He never realized that we move around in space with almost unthinkable, but exactly calculated speed.

His most precious possession now seemed to be the little celestial globe which he bought secretly. It was no larger than an apple, but to him it seemed to contain the wisdom of the whole world.

No game, no reading, no excessive eating could make him sleep enough to forget his wandering stars. They were his friends; he began to distinguish them as one tells one face from another. He conceived their many different hues as a painter conceives the colors that he mixes on his palette. He seemed to hear the earth tremble with beautiful sounds, produced by the soaring, wandering, floating bodies. He never tired of gazing into the enigmatic world of the cosmos.

In those childhood nights he laid the foundation of his later calculations, so unbelievably exact, written down daily through many years. Tycho Brahe was the first of all astronomers to realize that any certain knowledge about the stars demands uninterrupted, patient, and systematic study of their courses, singly and relatively.

Joergen Brahe began to worry about the eagerness with which Tyge threw himself into the new studies. To deter him from this obsession, his uncle sent him abroad to Leipzig to study law for three years. He studied hard, but not law.

Joergen Brahe died and Tyge took possession of his inheritance. While abroad he had been homesick for Denmark; but when he came back and was received with jeers and contempt because of his enthusiasm for something so improper as stars and planets he lost heart and went abroad again. His mother's brother, Steen Bille, was the only one of his kin who defended him.

For a time he stayed in Rostock, where the beer was good and not so strong as in Denmark. Here the "famous" duel took place between him and the Danish nobleman, Mandrup Parsbjerg. The two madcaps had disagreed about something and had to fight it out. Instead of doing this in the normal way, they decided to have their duel in absolute darkness. As a result, Tyge lost the tip of his nose and perhaps also a piece of the bone. He might possibly have got a nice little wax nose, but that did not appeal to him. So he made an alloy of gold and silver, from which he formed a nose that suited him. During all his later days he went around with wax and glue in his pocket, in case his fine nose threatened to come off.

On this journey he met the feared and honored Cyprianus, who influenced him a good deal. For some time he had been occupied with alchemistic experiments which, if they proved successful, might bring him much money. He who found out how to "make gold" would be rich all his days. With his practical mind he knew that astronomy is a science that demands riches, if one is to acquire the necessary instruments.

Tycho returned to Denmark and met Christina. Without awaiting the blessing of the Church they established their lifelong "conscience marriage."

In his biography of Tycho Brahe, Gassendi expresses the opinion that Tycho chose a peasant girl because it suited him better to have a useful woman in the house than a doll who would make all kinds of demands. Others maintain maliciously that he had to content himself with Christina because no highborn girl would take a man with a maimed nose. What foolishness!

Tycho could doubtless have had a dozen girls if he had wanted them. He was good-looking, interesting, the owner of one estate and part heir of another, and was already famous abroad.

His biographers ventured many guesses. No one seems to have suspected the obvious reason, that he was in love with the girl and felt that she was the one with whom he could find happiness for life. Which turned out to be true.

Among his foreign friends was the Landgrave of Hesse, a man as fanatically engrossed in astronomy as himself. The story goes that the landgrave was one evening absorbed in the contemplation of a very beautiful star. Suddenly he was called— "The castle is burning!" The landgrave did not turn. What did it concern him that the castle was burning—once, twenty times? His star was certainly of greater value than a castle!

At the request of the king, but without great enthusiasm,

Tycho gave lectures for one semester at the University of Copenhagen. After that he again went abroad, leaving wife and child in Denmark. The Landgrave of Hesse, fully convinced of his genius, invited him as a guest, enticing him with a completely equipped observatory. Tycho, however, found the instruments imperfect, and the landgrave's measurements, therefore, inexact.

Meanwhile the landgrave had dinned the ears of the Danish king with praises of the crown jewel which the king possessed in Tycho, telling him in plain words that he would make himself immortal by calling Tycho home and giving him the place that was rightly his due.

Tycho went home to see Christina and his little daughter, but prepared to leave and settle down where no one would jeer at him for what was to him the holiest of holies.

But then Frederick II sent a messenger, asking Tycho to come to court at once. He was most cordially received, and immediately the island of Hveen was deeded to him for life. The king had chosen Hveen as a suitable place for a scientist who had to live in a quiet place, and yet be able to get in touch with the rest of the world easily and quickly. His Majesty declared himself willing to bear all expenses of building an observatory, a residence, and workshops. The deed to Hveen was signed and provided with the royal seal.

The island of Hveen is situated between Denmark and Sweden. The cliffs rise steeply from the coast and end in a plateau. The view is beautiful, the soil fertile. There is plenty of grass which yields fine hay, and therefore the cattle are good. There are small deer and hares, many birds, and an abundance of fish. The farmers are wealthy. There are thirty-two farms and a church.

The cornerstone of the castle, the later world-renowned Uranienborg, was laid at sunrise. Many noblemen were present, and the ill will against Tycho seemed to be forgotten. Luxurious meals were served while congratulations poured in.

The castle was built according to Tycho's plans, and the still existing pictures of the finished building show that Tycho was not to be despised as an architect. But unless the building material was grossly deficient, it seems unbelievable that this

stately castle deteriorated so completely after Tycho's death that
soon no stone was left.

Uranienborg was sixty feet long, sixty feet wide, and consisted of two stories rising to a sort of pyramid in the middle,
and two seventy-five-foot towers at the sides. Large ponds provided the kitchen with fish at all times of the year. All sorts
of fruits and vegetables were raised for the large household.

A luxuriant flower garden was laid out, since Christina loved
beautiful and strange flowers. There were deep vaulted cellars,
one under the other. In them were wines and provisions and,
doubtless, material for the costly instruments which Tycho already
was planning.

The construction went slowly and, as the castle neared its
final stage, the owner furnished and decorated all according to
his personal, refined taste. He put in so perfect a water system
that there was fresh drinking water to be had in every room in
the castle. His restless brain seems even to have worked with
problems that in those times were considered only in the home
of a Leonardo. Thus he established a quite modern "telephone
system" with which he enjoyed surprising his guests. Casually
he would touch a small button, unnoticed by others, while whispering softly, "Christina," or perhaps, "Peter." After a short
while the door opened and the desired person stood on the
threshold. "Did you want me?"

Tycho's observatory was the most nearly perfect of all then
in existence. Besides, as the years passed, he continued con-
structing larger and more complicated instruments which by far
surpassed all heretofore seen. He had his own printing press, his
own glassworks, where artistic glass objects were made as
souvenirs for distinguished guests. Each of his many disciples,
who flocked to him from all countries, had his own small apartment, which made it possible for Tycho to watch the work of
each one and see that none plagiarized another. On the walls of
the disciples' rooms hung cords of different lengths. When one
of these cords began to move the pupil knew at a glance that his
presence was desired, and where he was to appear.

Tycho spent what he calls "a barrelful of gold" of his own

means, partly to beautify Uranienborg, partly to construct his extremely costly instruments.

A few duties were required of him, and it does seem that he might have performed them in return for all that was done for him. He was to keep up the lighthouse of Hveen; in case a ship was in distress he was to summon help. He was to keep the cathedral in Roskilde in good condition. All this he neglected with complete indifference. Even serious admonitions from the authorities had no effect.

During the following twenty years Tycho let no night or day pass without taking careful, patient observations which he wrote down minutely and exactly. At all times his house was full of disciples glowing with enthusiasm, besides the many foreign transients, prominent men who honored Denmark by their eagerness to visit the legendary figure, Tycho Brahe. His brain seems to have been indefatigable in its endurance and intensity, and for some years he could still tax his vigorous body with the excess of food and drink that was typical of his time.

Having unlimited strength himself, he often demanded super-human efforts from others. Thus he constantly ordered his peasants to do whatever work there was to be done, instead of keeping within the number of days due him. This created ill feeling. He, who in his innermost soul did not acknowledge any difference between highborn and bondsman, treated his bonds-men like thralls. As he thought of his own work he thought of theirs: the work must be done, must be done *now!*

Also his pupils had to work hard. They had instruction in mathematics, philosophy, alchemy, medicine, some astrology, and, of course, astronomy. Tycho Brahe was a passionate dabbler in medicine, perhaps because of his friendship with Mistress Liva, a servant in the family who reached the ripe age of a hundred and twenty-four years. Her plasters were said to have been miraculous. This was also said about some of Tycho's concoctions, especially his "elixir," which protected against all contagion. The elixir was cheap and sold like wildfire. Later he gave it freely to all who wanted it.

At the death of Frederick II in 1588, his son, Christian IV, was only eleven years old, and was naturally put under a regency. Among his guardians, Christoffer Walkendorf was the most important. This highly intelligent man was filled with such a burning hatred of Tycho Brahe that he poisoned the mind of the young king against the man whom his father had favored so generously. The reason for this hatred has never been fully discovered. Something has been said about a dog which belonged to Tycho and snapped at Walkendorf. When the latter kicked him, Tycho, a great friend of animals, flared up. But there were doubtless other reasons; Tycho was a scientist who demanded full freedom for his work—and there was also his marriage with "the peasant girl." Aside from this, Walkendorf was what is called "a good man." He was thoroughly patriotic. He was virtuous and did not countenance loose morals.

While in our time anybody will acknowledge that Tycho Brahe's conduct toward Christina does him credit, we have to admit that it was a grievous sin according to the moral code of his contemporaries and equals. It was not considered sinful for noblemen to beget children with the daughters of peasants. But one thing was strictly forbidden: to place the peasant's daughter at the head of one's table, to treat her as one's wedded wife. That was a blow in the face of the high Danish nobility of which Tycho was a member, although he was neither a count nor a baron. These titles were not introduced into Denmark until the following century.

Like everyone else who has gained great honor and fame, Tycho made enemies. Shortly after the death of Frederick II these enemies began to conspire against him, knowing full well that Walkendorf would back them. Tycho heard the rumor that something was brewing, but he smiled and shook his head. Why should anyone want to harm him?

Then the first blow fell. He was accused of spending too much money on Hveen. It was said that Roskilde cathedral had not been kept up. There were spiders in every corner; the whitewash was falling off the ceilings; some chapels were threatening to collapse. Tycho had been warned and had not heeded the warnings. His brother, Steen Brahe, understood that this time it was serious. Persecution was being started and he did what he could to prevent the worst. But since Christoffer Walkendorf, the mightiest man in the kingdom, was behind it, all was in vain.

Finally it was more than Tycho could bear. One by one his sources of income were taken from him. His personal fortune was not large enough to cover the expenses of maintaining his home and the observatory on Hveen. He owned a house in Copenhagen; it would cost far less to live there. With a heavy heart he left his beloved island.

For a short time it seemed that the tables were going to turn. The whole city talked of the petty persecution of the great man. But Walkendorf played a final trump. He sent two "well-informed" men to Hveen to look into the matter. When they saw Uranienborg partly broken up, the furniture removed, instruments packed, they gave a verdict unfavorable to Tycho. They declared that the entire establishment was not only superfluous, but—even "harmful." Incredible as it sounds, Tycho was bidden not to undertake "such" in the future.

The town bailiff delivered this order in the name of the king, while the king was abroad and in total ignorance of the matter. Compared with this outrage, it was only a trifle that Tycho was attacked in the street.

He realized that all hope was gone. He chartered a ship and sailed for Germany with his family, servants, and furniture. Rostock was his first stop. His exile had begun.

As soon as Emperor Rudolf heard the rumor that Tycho Brahe was in disgrace he wrote and begged the Danish scientist to come to Prague, where everything would be arranged according to his wish. But for the present Tycho stayed in Rostock, hoping, expecting, to be called back.

The king's grandfather, who lived in Rostock and was a passionate admirer of Tycho, wrote to his grandson and impressed upon him the fact that Tycho had been grievously wronged. He received no answer, but Tycho Brahe was honored with a letter from the twenty-two-year-old king. This letter was unworthy of a king's conduct toward one of his subjects, of a man toward a fellow man, of a youth toward an older person. It was filled with freezing contempt and gross insults, and failed to recognize a king's duties toward the man who had gained imperishable honor for his country.

We know from Tycho himself what he suffered before burning his bridges behind him and accepting Rudolf's generous offer. There still exists a letter written to a friend, Anders Sorensen Vedel. In this letter, plainly written with posterity in view, Tycho renders an account of the happenings in a dignified, manly, and candid way which does not allow any doubt about the truth of his words.

He relates how he had been deprived of all his sources of income but did not become aware of the conspiracy until he was told that the Roskilde chapter had been transferred to Walkendorf. He moved to his house in Copenhagen with the intention of taking observations from the tower, the use of which had been granted him in writing, with the signature of all the king's councilors attached. Now even this was forbidden him.

He went to Rostock, and there received the king's letter. One might expect him to feel justly indignant about this letter. Instead, Tycho utters only a few words about his deep chagrin. His letter to Vedel shows a meekness which suggests that his vitality and courage had been broken for life.

He spent a year in Holstein as the guest of a friend, constantly hoping for the impossible, the request to return to Denmark. Finally he accepted the emperor's invitation and went to Prague, leaving his family in Holstein. Prague was at the moment afflicted with pestilence, the "Black Death," and the emperor advised him to stop in Dresden and remain there until the epidemic passed and the court could return.

Here follows the account of his first meeting with the art-loving Rudolf, who was exceedingly kind and gracious to him. Tycho presented the emperor with three books from his own printing press, and seems to have been happy to learn later that the emperor read day and night until he had mastered their contents.

The meeting with the emperor must have seemed a fairy tale or a dream. Tycho was offered three thousand gold ducats a year, besides several thousand for expenses. Rudolf added that several of his councilors looked askance at such generosity, since no one in the emperor's service, were he count or baron, had anywhere near this salary.

Before Tycho had recovered from the shock of this brilliant offer the emperor promised him an inheritable fief as soon as one was vacant. In addition to this, he was offered any one of the imperial palaces within a convenient distance of Prague. Tycho was taken from castle to castle in the vicinity. He pointed out, as the one that appealed most to him, the castle of Benach, and there he finally settled down.

In his joy at having secured for his country and his people the greatest living authority on the stars, Rudolf crowned his work by offering to erect a new Uranienborg as magnificent as the former one, a picture of which he had seen in one of the books. To make Tycho feel completely secure and at ease, the emperor sent Barvicio to him with the following message: "If the means placed at your disposal should not be sufficient you must bear in mind that the emperor's arm still reaches far, and that your own mouth is not muzzled."

We learn all this, and still more, from the letter to Anders Sorensen Vedel. Tycho tells him where the new observatory is to be erected, how it will be arranged in order to house properly all the costly and unique instruments. The emperor was even willing to defray the cost of a new laboratory for chemical research.

"And now I have reported all, exactly as it happened. I wish that all history writing were as reliable as this."

He suggests that Vedel "make a summary, or whatever you wish, to be entered into your annals or chronicles for the sake of posterity."

Tycho Brahe was happy about Benach. He was bursting with anxiety to take up his work again, perhaps sensing that he had not much time left.

But Muhlstein, the treasurer of Benach, could not produce the necessary money; it simply wasn't there. Tycho took his troubles to the emperor, who was altogether on his side. Of

course, he was to have whatever he wanted, every single thing!
He got it—on paper. But behind the emperor's back his secretary
whispered to Tycho that he would do much better to move to the
city. He did. For a short time he lived at an inn in Hradsjin,
where the noise nearly drove him mad. In February, 1601, he
moved into the Curtius palace, where he remained until his death.

The house was soon again filled with eager disciples whom
he initiated in the mapping of the stars. It had long been his
purpose to leave to posterity the exact courses of one thousand
stars. It seems, however, that he kept certain discoveries or
observations to himself, or at least confided them to no one
except his closest associates. Thus Kepler writes to a friend:
"With my best intentions I cannot tell you all that I learned
from Tycho Brahe. There are certain things which I had to
promise on my honor not to reveal without his permission."

Kepler was, without the slightest doubt, the man closest to
Tycho. The two men corresponded for years, mutually admiring
each other's wisdom and enthusiasm for the same work. They
were very different. Kepler was a quiet, sickly man who struggled
all his life to keep the direst poverty from his door. Tycho Brahe
was enchanted with young Kepler's brilliant genius, and his delight was not impaired by the fact that Kepler did not always
agree with him. He looked forward to the visit of his friend
as to one of the red-letter days of his life. When the latter was
on the way Tycho sent his son-in-law, Tengnagel, to welcome him
and accompany him on the last day's journey.

We do not know what Kepler expected, but it is certain that
he was disappointed in several ways. He found a wild turmoil
of people coming and going. Never was there any quiet, never
any silence. Too many guests. Too little room. The meals were
grossly extravagant. Even the host himself ate and drank im-
moderately, and became riotous when in his cups.

Kepler's nerves were on edge and he could not understand
the situation. Although far from suspicious, he had the feeling
that Tycho did not wish his presence personally, but only wanted
to exploit his work.

They agreed to work together. But Kepler was methodical,

careful in business affairs. He wished a contract to be made out, wished to know exactly where he stood. Tycho thought this completely senseless between friends.

At last the whole thing became too much for Kepler. He made a scene and left. Some days later he wrote a violent and offensive letter. But instead of showing indignation, Tycho Brahe took this outburst of nervousness quietly and meekly. Finally Kepler realized how wrong he had been and wrote a letter which in its sincere regret and withdrawal of all accusations is as pathetically beautiful as the insolent scrawl of Christian IV is odious.

One can imagine Tycho Brahe smiling happily while reading letter number two, and then shaking his head. Angry? He had not been angry one single moment. He had nothing to forgive. Kepler was his friend, his precious, beloved friend. How can friend insult friend? Impossible! Friendship is eternal!

They met again and no discord separated them.

But Tycho's strength was already broken when he came to Prague. Fate did not long allow him to enjoy a peaceful and secure existence in the country which felt honored by his presence. Death overtook him on October 24, 1601.

When the news of his death reached Denmark the rumor naturally arose that he had been poisoned by his enemies. Poisoned? Not literally. His enemies had simply broken his heart, robbing the proud and strong man of all resistance. That is the inexorable truth. During his long, hard agony he mumbled time after time, "I think I have not lived all in vain . . ."

Until the last he was engrossed in his work and the results of the everlasting, painfully scrupulous observations. Kepler gave him his solemn promise to see to the publication of the so-called "Rudolphine tables," the courses of the thousand stars. It is certain that Kepler could never have attained his success had he not had these observations of Tycho's to guide him in his work, and even to Copernicus they were a great help.

For several years after his death Tycho's instruments were crowded together in a room in the Zcernine palace in Prague, where no one was permitted to see them, not even Kepler.

For the large sum of twenty thousand ducats the emperor

bought all the instruments with the intention of keeping them together. But the treasury was empty; the money was not to be raised. Little by little, part of the sum was paid to Tycho's widow and children. Christina died soon after her husband. Although the children married into the Bohemian nobility, in the course of the years every trace of Tycho's direct descendants disappeared.

The instruments were sold at a public auction, and thus scattered. By strange chance Prince Frederick, the son of Christian IV, got hold of the costly globe, which he sent back to Denmark. It was received with great enthusiasm. It is no longer in existence. With many other treasures, it was demolished by the great fire in Copenhagen in 1728. If we did not possess Tycho's own detailed descriptions of his instruments no one would know that they had ever existed.

Tycho Brahe had his faults and shortcomings, but all in all he was an unusually forthright and honorable man. And his faults were insignificant compared with the crimes committed against him by fools as well as by people who knew better.

He was said to have been obstinate, insisting on his opinion —until convinced that he was wrong. He was also said to have had "a grudge against the high and mighty." The latter was perhaps true, for two reasons! Partly because of his natural feeling for the "little man," partly because he was often insulted by the Danish nobility—for his studies and for his marriage. Naturally now and then he felt satisfaction in striking back.

His funeral oration, delivered in Latin, says among other things:

> He was lively and gay, generous to the poor, trustworthy, truthful, modest. Hypocrisy and dishonesty were repulsive to him. He was candid, straightforward. To him research was the goal of existence. Contemplation was his diversion. His riches consisted in science. He despised haughtiness, resented any bragging about noble descent. He did not brood over insults, but forgave willingly and completely. He was always ready to do himself what he demanded of others. He wished to be of use to all, wished to harm none.

It is a shame for Denmark that Tycho Brahe had to go into exile, but, well—even the sun has its spots.

I am proud to state that in the centuries from about 1590 to 1940 Tycho was the only outstanding Dane who had to leave his native land and seek refuge in exile.

VOLTAIRE
by
YVAN GOLL

YVAN GOLL

was born in 1891 in Saint Dié, France, near the Alsace-Lorraine border. He studied philosophy and law in Strasbourg.

From 1919 to 1939 he lived in Paris, which became the battlefield of Europe's poets and thinkers. Yvan Goll took part in the peaceful fights between the factions of different "isms," which finally led to—exile. "Twenty years largely wasted, the years of *l'entre deux guerres,*" regrets T. S. Eliot. Is he right?

Yvan Goll wrote several books of poetry. *Jean Sans Terre* is the best known and is partially translated into English, and a poetical essay *The Eurococcus,* in which he pointed out, in 1930, that Europe had been infected by a bacillus which destroyed all ethical measurements.

Since 1939, Goll has lived with his wife Claire, also a noted author, in New York. He is the editor of *Hemispheres,* a French-American quarterly of poetry.

VOLTAIRE
by Yvan Goll

THE eighteenth century was called by Hegel "The Age of Intelligence," by others "The Age of Voltaire." The terms are synonymous. Voltaire had the most lucid and incendiary mind of his time.

Yet all his life Voltaire stood alone. The king had his armies; the Jesuits had the devil and the hangman: Voltaire had only his pen, which he handled like a rapier, a rapier tempered in logic, adorned with poetry, a rapier with which the thinker, on the steps of the thrones, challenged the men of evil and the dragons of superstition.

Voltaire was admired by kings and emperors, beloved by many a princess and duchess, recognized by his fellow philosophers all over the world—and yet he was cast into prison, compelled to live about sixty of his eighty years in exile and to see his books banned, and burned by the public hangman.

Wherever he was, guest in a palace or prisoner in the Bastille, he worked every day of his life. He wrote over two hundred volumes and ten thousand letters. He thought and fought by day and night, often awaking his secretary at two in the morning to dictate a new story. He wrote poetry, tragedies, novels, short stories, works of history and philosophy, pamphlets, and articles. By that incessant labor he forged the weapons and tools which the French Revolution used in overthrowing the palaces and monasteries of his oppressors.

Young François Marie Arouet was not born to be a martyr. He had in him something of the Paris gamin, but his education

63

destined him for success in the fashionable world. When he was
ten his father, a wealthy notary, sent him to the Louis-le-Grand
College, where the Jesuit fathers, like sculptors, loved to mold
man. They soon discovered the boy's extraordinary gifts. They
stirred his ambitions, and set him up as an example for his fellow
pupils, who were sons of the upper classes, princes and marquis.
At school young Arouet got the habit of placing himself on an
equal footing with the nobility.

His godfather, the Abbé de Châteauneuf, was enormously
proud of him. When François Marie was twelve, the abbé introduced him to the celebrated Ninon de Lenclos, who left him in
her will a sum of two thousand francs "to buy books." Later,
when François Marie left college, the same prelate introduced him
to the dissolute society of the Temple, which had nothing religious about it. Love and poetry flourished there, along with
dissipation.

A critical and decadent nobility is the first to attack, from
within, the monster of tyranny. It does this almost unconsciously,
through moral dissolution. Vice and debauchery putrefy the
nobility. The virus of satire gets busy. The epigram becomes
more important than the drama. The pamphlet is a secret weapon.
The stiletto supplants the goose quill.

Young Arouet became the man of the hour, the champion
archer with poisoned arrows. His epigrams were handed about.
His witty remarks were the delight of the salons. The following
story is told about him: The regent boasted that for reasons of
economy he had sold half the horses left by Louis XIV, whose
funeral was just over. Arouet remarked that it would have been
better to get rid of half the donkeys that filled the palace.

Then a frankly nasty verse about the Duchess de Berri brought
down on the poet's head the order to leave town. He was allowed
to go to the château of Sully-sur-Loire, whose owner was a friend
of the elder Arouet. There, as in all other castles, the year was
a round of festivals, balls, fireworks, and "white nights" in the
parks.

In the dissolute Parisian society, where the regent had a love
affair with his own daughter and where every priest had a mis-

tress, exile, far from being shameful, had become a sort of halo. Upon his return from Sully the young poet's vogue only grew greater. Any witty remark that went the rounds was credited to Arouet.

The regent, feigning clemency, set a spy on his heels, an officer named Beauregard, who soon denounced Arouet as the author of two satires. In the first, the things which he claimed to have seen were among the main causes of the Revolution to come:

> I have seen the Bastille filled with brave citizens . . .
> I have seen Port Royal torn down . . .
> I have seen the altar, polluted . . .
> I have seen all this, and I'm not twenty . . .

The other satire, called "Puero regnante," was a still more violent attack: "Under the reign of a child, under the government of a poisoner, the councils are ignorant and unstable, religion still more unsteady, the treasury cleaned out, sedition approaching . . ."

At dawn on May 16, 1717, the day of Pentecost, a Monsieur Bazin brought guards to arouse Arouet in his room at the Green Basket, near Notre-Dame, where he was peacefully sleeping. He politely invited him to get into his carriage and took him straight to the Bastille.

Shut up for eleven months in the "King's House," Arouet did not waste his time. They refused him paper and ink, but he wrote with a pencil between the lines of a Homer several cantos of the *Henriade,* and finished his tragedy *Oedipus.*

When Arouet was released from prison the regent, on the recommendation of one of his roués, received him and awarded him a pension. This act brought forth the remark: "I thank his Royal Highness for being so kind as to see that I have my board, but I beg him not to worry any more about my lodgings."

All differences between him and the regent seemed forgotten. The Comédie-Française staged *Oedipus* under the author's new name, Voltaire. The play was a striking success and the Parisian upper classes crowded the theater to see it. The scandalmongers attempted to discover in the choice of the subject an allusion to the private life of the regent. But the poet had taken the precaution to dedicate his play to the regent's wife.

Voltaire at twenty-four was at the height of fame. His name was on all lips. He was hailed and hated on all sides. He became the lover of the great ladies of the period. The Marquise de Rupelmonde took him in her carriage to Holland. He went from château to château, from triumph to triumph. But there were still aristocrats who looked with a supercilious eye on the rise of the young commoner. One evening in a box at the Comédie-Française the Chevalier de Rohan-Cabot demanded:

"Monsieur de Voltaire, Monsieur Arouet, what *is* your name?"

"I do not trail a great name about; but I honor the one I bear," answered the poet.

Several days later, when Voltaire was dining with the Duke de Sully, someone inquired for him at the door. Trustingly he walked toward a cab waiting in the street; immediately de Rohan's men rushed at him, beating him with cudgels. The chevalier in the cab shouted to them, "Not on the head; something good may still come out of it!"

Bruised and outraged, Voltaire returned to the Sully mansion and begged his friends to go with him to the police. They refused. One does not swear out a warrant against a Rohan. Voltaire then undertook to defend his honor himself. He vainly sought the chevalier all over town, trying to force an apology. The all-powerful Rohan family obtained a lettre de cachet against him. For the second time he was shut up in the Bastille. He was released after several days, however, on condition that he sail immediately for England.

Across the Channel, Voltaire stepped into a real bath of freedom. He found codified into laws the feeling for social justice and human dignity which he had sensed developing in Paris. Coming from French dungeons he was blinded by this unsuspected light. Freedom of thought suffered no restrictions. Poets and philosophers openly published and discussed the most advanced and startling ideas, capable of revolutionizing the whole philosophical system and moral structure of the still medieval continent.

It astonished Voltaire to find that in England each man had

the right to believe in a God of his own choosing. There were twenty different sects, none of which claimed to speak the One Truth or wished to exterminate the others. But after analyzing them closely, Voltaire mocked them all. His very special smile, at once sharp and fatherly, first appears in his *English Letters*. In his description of the Quakers there is a foretaste of his beneficent irony, from which later was to come *Candide*.

The English spirit formed the counterpart of the Jesuit spirit which had first nourished him. Voltaire arrived too late in England to meet Isaac Newton, the "legislator of the heavens," but just in time to attend his funeral in Westminster Abbey. Watching the English people honoring and weeping over a great philosopher with the respect due to a king, Voltaire thought with bitterness that this same philosopher would, in France, be deprived of a decent grave, as was Molière.

Voltaire studied the work of Locke, the founder of the philosophical school of sensationalism, which armed him for his attack on the Cartesian system. He met the poets Young and Pope. Gay read him scenes from his famous *Beggar's Opera* and Jonathan Swift was to have a great influence on his satiric style. Such are the benefits of exile.

Upon his return to France, Voltaire so clearly understood the explosive value of his *Letters* that he hesitated to publish them until 1734. But copies of the manuscript, circulated under cover, had already caused sensational damage. Before risking another lettre de cachet or another banishment, Voltaire put on several plays which he had written in the meantime. *Brutus* caused a scandal: *Zaïre* was a tremendous success. If he had wished, merely by living quietly and smiling, the author might have quintupled his worldly success and become a well-paid courtier at Versailles, a rare bird in a gilded cage.

Voltaire's egotism has often been mentioned. The end of his life was to prove his magnanimity and generosity. But long before that he revealed the quality of his friendship.

Adrienne Lecouvreur was the greatest tragic actress of her time. Because she was extremely sensitive and had an exceptional capacity for love, she suffered greatly all her life. She died almost alone, abandoned by everybody except Voltaire and another friend.

The Church refused her Christian burial because she was an actress and had not renounced her profession, as the laws of the Church demanded. The night she died, without a word to anyone, the police carried off her corpse and threw it in a potter's field known as La Grenouillère.

To avenge the death of Adrienne, Voltaire wrote one of his finest poems, into which he wove memories of the England that knew how to honor her great:

> They have refused a resting place
> To one for whom of old her altars Greece had dressed
>
> .   .   .   .
>
> Is it upon the English strand
> Alone that thought can dare be free?
> O Athens' rival, though, O London, happy land!
>
> .   .   .   .
>
> Immortal gods! Why has my country ceased to be
> The home of worth and fame?

This outrageous treatment of a dead body haunted Voltaire for the rest of his life. The anger it roused in him never died. Again and again he repeated his battlecry, "Écrasez l'infâme!" In the meantime, his wrathful elegy was regarded as an indication of dangerous publications to come. The forces of fanaticism were aroused against him.

Voltaire prudently sought refuge in Normandy for a few months. In Rouen he watched the printing of his important *History of Charles XII,* which was instantly suppressed. Now he knew what would happen to his *English Letters,* in which he showed clearly the contrast between the liberty and religious tolerance in England, and the despotism in France.

As he was setting to work on the publication of these *Letters,* an unscrupulous editor, Jore, who had obtained the manuscript somewhere, brought out a clandestine edition, and was immediately cast into prison. The book, condemned as "scandalous, contrary to religion, to good morals, to the respect due the authorities,"³ was burned by order of Parliament, and a lettre de cachet issued against the author.

Luckily the author happened to be at Monjeu, celebrating the marriage of his friend, the Duke de Richelieu. One of the guests present, the Marquise du Châtelet, invited him to take refuge at her castle which had the advantage of being situated on the border of Lorraine. In case of danger Voltaire would only have to place this border between himself and the emissaries of the king.

The author accepted and remained in Cirey for fifteen years. The marquise was one of the most brilliant women of the century. She had studied Newton's *Principia,* which she later translated into French. She also knew by heart whole passages from *Henriade* by Voltaire. She was, moreover, the kind of woman necessary for Voltaire's feminine and febrile nature, one who would hold him both by maternal affection and intellectual qualities.

Madame du Deffand, Voltaire's old and witty friend, said of the marquise, "Picture a tall, gaunt, hipless, waistless, flat-breasted woman, with long arms, long legs, and enormous feet . . ."

But Voltaire began his famous ode "On Newton's Philosophy" with these lines:

> You called me to you, genius, bright and mighty,
> Minerva of France, immortal Émilie!

The Cirey romance is one of the most touching episodes in French literature. The morals of the period permitted Voltaire to settle in one of the wings of the castle, in spite of the marquis, who was absent on military duty a great part of the year, and of two children, whose education Voltaire supervised. At his own expense, Voltaire built a chemistry laboratory, where the two lovers indulged in the enthralling study of the natural phenomena first discovered by the English philosophers.

It was a period of work and peace. Voltaire wrote several plays and began his *Essay on the Morals and Spirit of the People.* This essay inaugurated a new method of writing history, by giving a picture of civilization rather than a collection of anecdotes on wars and kings.

The evenings were pleasant in Cirey. At supper Voltaire was gay and witty. Private theatricals were a favorite pastime. Voltaire's tragedies, old or just finished, were staged in the little theater, and the geometrically shaped Émilie became through love a great actress.

Work was from time to time interrupted by journeys to Lorraine, Belgium, and Holland, where Voltaire had kept up his international friendships. Together the couple were invited to the tiny court of King Stanislas at Lunéville. It was there that a young officer named Saint-Lambert brought tragedy into their lives. The masculine temperament of the marquise, so long given over to study, sometimes played tricks on her: toward the end of her forties she indulged herself in a passing affair with Saint-Lambert and became pregnant. Several days after she had given birth she died of fever. Émilie's death was the greatest sorrow in Voltaire's life.

After that, Paris forgave him and pledged forgetfulness. Madame de Pompadour, who had been a mistress and admirer of the young poet, at that moment governed Louis XV and, through him, France. She obtained for Voltaire the title of royal Historiographer, which carried with it a pension.

Again Voltaire reconquered the capital. His *Catilina* was staged and praised, although it castigated a period in Roman history which strangely resembled his own, and in the play he paraphrased Juvenal's Sixth Satire: "The spirit of pleasure, more than that of war, threatens Rome and will avenge the world."

But Voltaire could never really be a good courtier: with each bow his clothing split at the seams. Each phrase, each chiseled epigram, was impregnated with the acid of his wit. A single verse about La Pompadourette lost him the favor of the king's mistress. Vexations, threats, legal actions began all over again.

Voltaire decided to accept King Frederick's invitation to the Prussian court, although he did not at all want to go. A smile from Louis XV was all he needed to change his mind. But when during a hunting party at Compiègne he asked the king's authorization to leave France, he was infuriated by the stinging reply: "You may leave whenever you wish!" To his courtiers Loúis XV added, "That will be one more jester at the Prussian court and one less at mine!"

The die was cast. Frederick II appointed Voltaire chamberlain at his court and gave him a pension of twenty thousand francs. During his first weeks in Potsdam the festivals, concerts, parades, and operas enchanted Voltaire. He had his suite of rooms in the palace of Sans-Souci. Each evening at supper the king assembled the select company of poets and philosophers who gave his court its famous luster. There Voltaire met Maupertuis, who was president of the Berlin Academy of Science and whose ambitions were boundless.

But little by little Voltaire's pleasure in the court deteriorated. The German mind and the French mind can never become close. In each German there lurks both Faust and Mephistopheles.

At Potsdam, Frederick II was a two-faced king; he would weep over a sonata and the moment after declare a war. At dawn he would review his troops in a lather of sweat, and in the afternoon hammer out Alexandrines.

Voltaire, infatuated by the compliments and kindnesses bestowed upon him, forgot that he was the guest of a tyrant, a liberal tyrant, a freethinker and poet, but still a tyrant. He set his spiritual royalty against the autocrat's royalty. Was not Frederick his pupil?

One evening, after having corrected a royal manuscript, the author of the *Henriade* stated with his usual sarcasm that he had just washed his Majesty's dirty linen. This was repeated to the king. Another day Voltaire heard that the king, in speaking of him, had said, "One sucks the orange and casts away the peel." Voltaire was so offended that he complained of this threat in several of his letters. But he did not for a moment think that his royal host might also be offended.

Moreover, whenever Frenchmen foregather they quarrel. The Potsdam philosophers did not lead a very philosophical life. Maupertuis, vain to the point of folly, could not abide the presence of such a satirist as Voltaire. A dispute soon estranged the two men, who became so embittered that Voltaire wrote a pamphlet against his rival, *The Diatribe of Doctor Akakia*. This pamphlet was considered irreverent to the king, and was seized and burned, just as it might have been in Paris. Was it really necessary to go so far away into exile?

Voltaire became guilty of other blunders which caused the smiling royal face to become a steely-eyed, impassive mask. He could never get over it. He could never understand this "Northern Solomon," who was in league with hell.

The other Frenchmen, for their part, poured oil upon the flames. After three years of rancor, reconciliations, sudden ecstasies, and cruel silences, the vanquished Voltaire decided to leave. On the parade grounds at Potsdam, at dawn on March 26, 1753, the French poet came to the king, who was about to review his troops. "Sire," he said, "urgent business, and more especially the the state of my health, makes it necessary for me to leave." "Well, sir, I wish you a pleasant journey" was Frederick's only answer.

At nine o'clock the coach carried Voltaire off into a new exile. "Go toward the west!" was the only direction he could give the driver.

Voltaire drove back over the highways of Germany, a man without a country, an outcast. He reminded himself that he had never had a home. He had moved from castle to castle, from city to city, from country to country. He had thousands of friends but none on whom he could call for help in his distress.

To gain time he let Fate have its way. He was going to play truant. By roundabout ways he would eventually reach a home.

He stopped off at Leipzig, the capital of printing. He accepted an invitation from the Duchess of Saxe-Gotha to stay with her. He spent a few days at Cassel with the Landgrave of Hesse, before going, on May 31, 1753, to Frankfort, where he took rooms at the Golden Lion Inn.

There occurred an adventure which made all Europe laugh and which revealed a strange side of Frederick's character. At dawn of the day following Voltaire's arrival the Resident of Frankfort burst into the traveler's room and demanded, in the name of the King of Prussia, that he return his chamberlain's key of office, his cross of the Order of Merit, and a volume of the sovereign's "boetry" which the fugitive had carried off with him.

With a light heart Voltaire handed over the insignia and the medal, but the precious volume, alas, was in a trunk which had already gone on to Strasbourg with other luggage. This seemed very grave in the eyes of the municipal authorities, who decided to hold the foreigner until he returned what he had taken from their monarch.

One can easily imagine Voltaire's state of excitement. He tried to leave town surreptitiously, accompanied by his secretary, Collini, but they were caught at the city gates, brought back under guard, and kept in a house before which sentinels were stationed. Madame Denis, the poet's niece, who rushed from Paris to help him, was locked up and rudely manhandled by the soldiers. It was only after thirty-five days, when the book and a very tardy order for clemency from the king had arrived, that Voltaire was allowed to continue on his way.

The enforced stay in Frankfort had been painful, but once more freedom was his. Where could he go now? There is no worse fate than to feel as free as a bird but not be awaited anywhere, to have not a square foot of land to call one's own. From Mainz, Voltaire wrote his friends to try and get him permission to return to Paris. After all, he was a "gentleman-in-ordinary to the king." But the reply to his request was negative. D'Argenson, a Cabinet member, noted in his daybook: "Permission to return to France was refused Voltaire . . . to please the King of Prussia." Kings have long arms and a strange psychology.

"I'm like a wandering Jew," Voltaire said, and continued blindly on his way to spend a few more days at Strasbourg. Then he went on to Colmar, seeking a resting place all along the Alsatian border, while he waited for his recall to Paris. He became the ancestor of all the men without a country who, in the centuries to follow, wandered between France and Germany, belonging neither to the one nor to the other, tossed about from left to right.

The author of *Zadig* fell ill at Colmar and stayed several weeks with the Goll family, before going to the Abbey of Senones, where the Benedictine fathers nursed him and placed at his disposal their well-known library. He borrowed innumerable documents, which he later used against those who had harbored him. After six months he left the abbey, with the ingratitude of a spoiled child, and called Senones, "a town of Hottentots governed by German Jesuits."

"They said that I was a Prussian," he wrote. "It would be most unjust not to regard me as a Frenchman, since I have always kept my house in Paris and paid the head tax there. Can it be seriously said that the author of the *Siècle de Louis XIV* is not French?"

Finally, when hope of returning to France had completely evaporated, Voltaire slowly continued his journey toward Switzerland, later to become the classic land of exiles from Byron to Lenin. He settled down in Geneva, near the French border, so that in case the call ever came he would be able to go with ease from one country to the other. Although he was a Catholic, he was allowed by the Calvinist authorities to buy a nice little house, which he christened "Les Délices." It was built on a hill, on the bank of the Rhone—"the stream I sent into France." But it was only a summer house; he soon bought a more sturdy one for winter use at Lausanne. As always in the beginning, he was thrilled with the reception he received from the people of Geneva. But the same old story occurred in Calvin's city. Voltaire's subversive mind soon frightened the authorities.

A new scandal burst on Paris. An unscrupulous publisher, without the author's permission, brought out the satiric epic, *La Pucelle,* in which Voltaire had treated Joan of Arc after the manner of Italian farces, and with a Rabelaisian touch.

That this book was burned in Paris by the public hangman was not at all surprising. But when the High Council of Geneva followed the same course and forbade its citizens to attend the performances of Voltaire's tragedies in the little theater he had built at Les Délices, the eternal outcast complained of having to live in "the narrowest of republics." For his personal security he decided to settle on the other side of the border, in the territory of Gex, in France.

He first bought the Château of Tourney, with which went the title of count; then he bought the Domain of Ferney. He could thus write: "I have four feet instead of two: the front two are in Lausanne and Les Délices, the two hind feet in Ferney and Tourney. To my left in Mount Jura, to my right are the Alps, and I have the Lake of Geneva in my front yard. Crawling thus from one lair to another, I escape kings and their servants . . . A philosopher should always have two or three holes to shelter him from the dogs."

Now like Anteus, touching earth, Voltaire renewed all his creative and fighting forces. In his sixties he began a new life with all the ardor of youth. He transformed his property to suit his taste, planting orchards, gardens, raising horses, building a church with the inscription *Deo Erexit Voltaire*. He also started, in the village of Ferney, such industries as watchmaking and lacemaking, which brought the peasants both comfort and happiness.

"After having lived with kings," he wrote, "I have become a king of my own."

Ferney became the intellectual capital of Europe. Voltaire kept up an intimate correspondence with six reigning sovereigns, and with cardinals, military leaders, and philosophers everywhere. He received more than fifty letters a day and answered them by return mail. From all corners of Europe people made pilgrimage to the modern Mecca of Ferney.

Voltaire could be as courteous as he was malicious. His famous smile hid all the recesses of the human soul. He had the courage to incur the hatred of the mighty by denouncing them, but through his own intellectual power he was greater than they. He wanted to crush religious intolerance, political despotism. He became the conqueror, shining and smiling, at the dawn of a new Europe.

The Encyclopedists, a group of French philosophers and writers struggling against the Church for the emancipation of man, were the subjects of constant legal action. Voltaire was one of their most ardent supporters: he wrote and edited articles for them, and obtained funds and supporters from all over Europe.

Catherine II, Empress of Russia, admired Voltaire and sent him highly flattering letters; she adopted his liberal ideas and tried to apply them to her still barbaric empire. Failing to persuade

Voltaire to visit her—at his age he was no longer able to make long journeys—she invited Diderot and the other Encyclopedists to her court.

At the end of his letters Voltaire still wrote "Écrasez l'infâme," which had become his war-cry against oppression. From his place of retirement he took up the cause of innocent victims of superstition. He redressed the wrongs which the Church had done to Calas and the Chevalier de la Barre, and fought the law courts to obtain their rehabilitation. But to do so he sacrificed years of labor and much money. The whole of Europe watched the struggle and cheered the victory of the just.

Voltaire's authority was uncontested. There were two kings in France then: the temporal at Versailles, the spiritual at Ferney. It was the latter who held the real power. Few human lives have been so complete as that of Voltaire. Even in exile he was Luck's child.

Gradually Voltaire became a legendary personage. And what nicknames they gave him! The Patriarch of Ferney. The Geneva Prometheus. The malicious old man. And a hundred others.

"Philosophers have bowed before kings too long," Frederick II, with whom he had become reconciled, wrote to him; "it is now for kings to bow before philosophers."

He was truly a force against which other forces spent themselves. When the Bishop of Annecy asked the French queen to rid his diocese of the presence of the philosopher, Louis XV answered: "What can I do? Were Voltaire in Paris, I would exile him to Ferney."

Suddenly, at the age oi eighty-two, Voltaire became homesick and returned to Paris without permission. His return was transformed into a triumph, an apotheosis. The people of Paris recognized him as their liberator and cheered him in the streets. At the opening night of a new play of his at the Comédie-Française he was presented with a wreath of laurel. When he fell ill the greatest personalities visited him. The Académie Française sent a delegation. The English ambassador came to his bedside. Benjamin Franklin brought his grandson and asked Voltaire to bless him. With his hand outstretched over the kneeling youth's head, Voltaire said, "God and Liberty."

These words were to be the heritage of the United States of America. The French Revolution was to adopt them later as a motto.

Shortly after this Voltaire died. But freedom had been born into the world.

All his life Voltaire had only to burst out laughing to overcome extravagant pomp, grotesque prejudices, and barbaric traditions. The task of clearing away the residue, the rust and muck of centuries, made him a Hercules more powerful than the mythological one. He used every kind of stratagem to overcome his enemies, who were the enemies of man.

To man himself he said, "Arise! No one has the right, none has the power to take from you the treasures of the soul which were given to you at birth."

And the people finally heard him. They attacked the Bastille and destroyed it! The Age of Voltaire ended with the French Revolution, with the triumph of the people who recognized in the philosopher their inspiration and gratefully carried his ashes to the Pantheon.

TADEUSZ KOSCIUSZKO

by

JOSEPH WITTLIN

JOSEPH WITTLIN

was born in Dmitrow, Poland, in 1896. He spent his childhood in the country in Podolia, where his family had lived for generations. He attended high school in Lwow and studied at the University of Vienna and the University of Lwow.

His first published work was a volume of poems. His translation of the *Odyssey* first appeared in 1924. It received the Polish P. E. N. Club Prize in 1935.

In prose he has published two volumes of essays and the first volume of his trilogy dealing with the Patient Infantry Soldier. This first volume, *Salt of the Earth,* begun in 1925, was not completed until ten years later. It has been translated into ten different languages.

Salt of the Earth won two literary prizes. Joseph Wittlin was awarded the Golden Laureate of the Polish Academy in 1937. Since 1939 he has been Poland's candidate for the Nobel Prize.

He is now in the United States to complete two more volumes of his war epic. In 1943 he was awarded the Arts and Letters Grant by the American Academy of Arts and Letters and the National Institute of Arts and Letters. Wittlin has been called both the Polish Barbusse and the Polish Remarque.

TADEUSZ KOSCIUSZKO
by Joseph Wittlin

I

IN THE neatly cultivated parks and squares of a
dozen or so American cities stands the bronze figure of a young
officer. Not very tall, he is clad in the colorful uniform of
Washington's day, and the day of the Directory. From under his
cockaded bicorn, a braid of powdered wig falls to the nape of
his neck, or à la Napoleon in Egypt, his hair tumbles in a long
bushy stream to his shoulders. In Chicago and Milwaukee he
straddles a horse cast like himself in bronze and flourishes a
sword aloft. In Washington, D. C., in Boston and in Cleveland
he is merely a pedestrian though no less theatrically bellicose and
domineering. Only in the park of the Military Academy at West
Point and in the little town of Yonkers, above New York, is his
attitude one of modesty: the sword is sheathed, as no doubt it
was when he stood before his superiors, the generals Horatio
Gates and Nathanael Greene.

It is evident from the prominent cheekbones and the fleshy
nose that this officer—pride of so many American lawns—did
not belong to the Anglo-Saxon race. Which is to say that he did
not comply with the popularly accepted image of an Anglo-Saxon.
His cheekbones, in fact, rather confessed a Tartar-Mongol strain,
and the snub, fleshy nostrils—but enough of the bones and noses
of heroes. It will profit more to decipher the name chiseled so
carefully on the pedestal. For the majority of the townspeople
who pass these statues daily will have little success making out
the name. Except perhaps in Chicago, which until recently held

more Poles than the whole of Warsaw. There one might ask, "What is the name of this bronze snub-nosed equestrian?" and occasionally receive the phonetically faultless reply! Kosciuszko.

The average American will twist his brain as well as his tongue trying to recall who Kosciuszko was. At school something or other had been mentioned about him, but that has long since passed out of the mind. Much more is known of that other Pole, Casimir Pulaski, who not only distinguished himself—as did Kosciuszko—in the American fight for Independence, but actually gave his life in its cause during the battle of Savannah, when he was only thirty-three. Pulaski became known as the father of American cavalry. Kosciuszko, on the other hand, was no cavalryman, he did not fall in battle; in fact, when the fighting ceased he left the United States in excellent health. He returned to Poland a brigadier general, as modest and unassuming as when he had left. In the American army he had been engaged chiefly as an engineer of defense fortifications. The opportunity for bravura never came to him, even had his disposition been so inclined. Small wonder then if he is not so noted a figure in the United States as Pulaski. In Poland, however, only one of them can claim the enthusiastic love of the people to this very day, and that is Kosciuszko.

He was a gentle warrior, a man of peaceful heart. As he expressed it, he wished rather to be loved than feared. It would help little to scrutinize his life—gay as it was with romance and adventure—for symptoms of vanity or violence. But he was not altogether the docile lamb. On the contrary, his White Ruthenian —or Lithuanian—obstinacy was capable of asserting itself before the most powerful figures of his day: the czars of Russia, Napoleon, and such shrewd statesmen as Fouché, Duke of Otranto. Nevertheless, all who knew him joined in praise of his profound modesty, disinterestedness, and singularly winning manner. Necessity made of him a soldier and warrior. But had history dealt differently with his motherland Kosciuszko might well have become a painter. A nearly feminine sensitivity and tenderness was strangely mingled in him with a stubborn resolve. He was one of the few contemporary Polish revolutionists who refused to succumb to the magic of Napoleon. For Kosciuszko understood quickly enough that the murderer of the French Revolution would never fulfill his commitments toward Poland.

All his life Kosciusko grappled with the tragic problem of realizing the ideals of two great revolutions: the American and the French. But most tragic of all for this Jacobin *sui generis*—this Jacobin without atrocity—was the very land in which he had hoped to sow the ideals of the republican revolution; this was the Polish land already plowed and torn by the bayonets of Russia, Prussia, and Austria.

It is safe to assume that the United States would not have raised so many monuments to a single engineer of the war of 1776-1783—true, a distinguished and devoted officer of the engineer corps—had he not later in Poland become a symbol of the freedom for which his own people were fighting so desperately, so hopelessly, and indeed so illogically; and had he not been one of the first to champion democracy in Europe. Kosciuszko owes both his historical and his legendary fame, not to any great victories—of which there were few—nor to any military or political genius—which, it seems, he did not possess: Kosciuszko's greatness emerged from disillusionment and defeat.

The world today is less and less sympathetic to heroism of this kind. Power and success hold our admiration. We raise monuments to victors, spoilers and virtuosos of violence. Occasionally the hero of a lost cause is graced with a day of sympathy and then buried without éclat.

But for those who still may wish to ponder the heroes of lost causes and limitless sacrifices there are the works of the English romantic poets, there are the tales of Byron. Here, perhaps, one may learn how it happened that greatness and fame could come to this modest engineer of Fort Ticonderoga, Saratoga, and West Point. And perhaps then it will be understood that the greatness of Kosciuszko was a greatness of soul.

II

Andrzej Tadeusz Bonawentura Kosciuszko Siechnowicki was blessed not only with a long and difficult name but with a long and difficult life as well. He was born on February 12, 1746, in

a village hitherto unknown and with a name probably chosen
with the deliberate purpose of preventing any foreigner from
ever uttering it. The name—with the indulgence of all Anglo-
Saxons—was Mereczowszczyzna.

Our hero passed the years of his childhood at Siechnowicze,
on his father's estate, and from here he was sent to the school
of the Piarist Fathers in Lubieszow in the province of Wolyn.
No doubt, it was at the Piarists' that young Tadeusz first discovered that ancient world of heroes unveiled in the works of
Cornelius Nepos and Plutarch. According to Kosciuszko's own
report, it was the figure of Timoleon of Corinth, that fascinated
his youthful imagination most of all. This figure became a model
which he was to follow his entire life.

This youth, who later so nearly achieved the liberation of
Poland, found in Timoleon the attributes of a true patriot and
wise legislator, and the idealism of a reformer and champion
of republican freedoms. Besides, he admired the magnificent
leadership of Timoleon who at the head of scarcely five thousand
soldiers had managed to inflict a disastrous defeat upon an army
of seventy thousand Carthaginians. Yet it would be difficult to
say that Kosciuszko felt the soldier's impulse in his youngest
years or that he betrayed any of the traits of a revolutionary.
True, at the age of nineteen he joined the recently organized
Cadet Corps in Warsaw, but it was from personal rather than
ideological motives. The last and most miserable of the kings of
Poland, Stanislaw August Poniatowski—raised to the tottering
throne with the support of Empress Catherine II of Russia—had
founded the corps as a "School for the Knights of his Majesty
the King and the Republic" during the first year of his reign.
Perhaps even then he foresaw that someday it would serve as a
living altar at which to expiate the sins he later committed against
the Polish nation. In its own way this school was important as
a reservoir of moral health. It gave certain firmness of character
to young men who were exposed from birth to the depravity of
the privileged gentry, a class that fell into corruption during the
reign of the Saxon dynasty. In those days, Poland was ruled not
by the king but by the Russian ambassador, and the king visual-

ized a section of the youth educated in the spirit of Western Europe whose enlightenment he admired so greatly.

Admission to such a school, whose students numbered not more than eighty, was a great distinction for the son of a moderately rich nobleman. Kosciuszko owed his selection as seventy-ninth among this group, to the influence of a certain high personage, with whose daughter, by a strange quirk of fate, he later fell in love.

Contemporary documents prove that Kosciuszko was a leading student in the School of Knights where, in addition to the humanities, the basic principles of tactics and military architecture were taught. "He excelled in diligence, decorum, penmanship, and draftsmanship." He also enjoyed a certain esteem, so that upon graduation he remained with the school as a paid instructor with the rank of captain. He even drew to himself the attention of the king, whose court receptions the cadets often attended. Despite the high ideals in the name of which this school was founded and by which it undoubtedly sought to abide, its first graduates more quickly achieved notoriety as the "golden youth" of Warsaw than fame as promising Catos. There is little reason to believe that Kosciuszko was any different in this respect. We can only quote one of the historians, to the effect that under the influence of the School of Knights "a consciousness of public duty awoke in him as well as a civic and patriotic honor." These were virtues not to be snubbed in the days of the moral disintegration of the social class to which he belonged and on the eve of the first partition of Poland.

The tale of every hero abounds with legends bred after the fact. And when a hero shines as the champion of an enslaved people, primitive biographers—we should call them hagiographers—generally discover somewhere in his youth the inclinations which have led him onto the chosen path. Kosciuszko was no exception. The legend is told, and repeated by even serious historians, that he went abroad to study after the tragic death of his father, who, it was said, had dealt with his serfs so harshly that they murdered him. So horrified was Kosciuszko by the reprisals taken against the peasants that he is reported to have

left his family home, swearing to dedicate his life to the liberation of the village people.

Be that as it may, what we do know is that it was the king
who sent Kosciuszko abroad to study; of course, at the king's
expense. As to what he studied, here again historians disagree.
There are those who claim that the royal protégé studied in
France for five years, first at the school of engineering and
artillery in Mazières, and then at the Paris École Militaire.
Others dispute this fact, with the argument that Kosciuszko's
name does not appear in the files of either of these schools. They
do agree on one thing, however: he did study in France, but it
was not military science, it was—painting. During the years
between 1769 and 1774 he is said to have been a student at the
well-conducted Academy of Painting and Sculpture in Paris,
then under the patronage of the court of Versailles and especially
guided by the lady who held all of Versailles at her beck and
call—Mme. de Pompadour. Among his foreign friends Kosciuszko, future champion of Polish democracy, is said to have
availed himself of the title of count, a title which did not exist in
Poland. If so, this innocent departure from the truth renders
Kosciuszko all the more human for us, and confirms the fact
that greatness is not always above vanity. Balzac too employed
the "de" arbitrarily between his Christian and his surname.

We do not know what actually was the case with that Paris
painting of "Count" Kosciuszko, for neither the Louvre nor
the Versailles Palace contains any of his canvases. This proves
nothing, of course. Some of his drawings of later years were
preserved along with a portrait of Jefferson. In any case, it is
clear that the intellectual atmosphere of prerevolutionary France
brought immeasurable gain to Kosciusko's intellectual development. His sensitive mind was drawn to the movement of the
Encyclopedists, to the works of Voltaire and Jean Jacques Rousseau. In addition, this count, captain, and artist-painter avidly
studied economics. He was especially excited by the teachings of
the so-called physiocrats, whose works dealt with the material
status of the peasants and with the reform of taxation which was
so painful a burden on this social class during the reign of
the last Louis. In Paris, Kosciuszko delved into the work of

Turgot, *Reflexions sur la formation et la distribution des richesses,* and Dupont de Nemours's *La Physiocratie.* Jules Michelet, an enthusiastic French follower of Kosciuszko and a friend of the Poles, rightly noted that "Kosciuszko's ideology and his humanitarian tolerance reached maturity in France."

Independently of these studies, in his French period Kosciuszko gathered more than a little knowledge in the field of military science. He attended private courses which prepared candidates for the great military schools; but he was excluded from these schools, first, because he was a foreigner and, second, because he was too old. He is also said to have studied the fortifications at the port of Brest, and to have studied military architecture under the master Perronet.

Kosciuszko returned to Poland after the first partition. He found himself in difficult straits. He attempted to join the army hoping to serve his country, which had been dishonored. But even for a person with the rank of captain, and a royal protégé at that, it was not easy in those days to join a regiment. For the entire Polish army had been reduced by the partitioning treaty to the absurd number of 11,000 soldiers, and if one wished a rank it was necessary to buy it from another officer, usually for the exorbitant sum of 18,000 Polish zlotys. Kosciuszko had no such sum at his disposal, in fact, he had no money at all. His share in the estate of Siechnowicze, which his older brother had been managing, was so small and his brother's management so disastrous that upon his return to his native land Kosciuszko stood face to face with imminent financial ruin.

It was not only his personal troubles, or the political tragedy of Poland, that made the young officer's stay in the country impossible. Unemployed as a captain and branded a "philosopher," Kosciuszko was compelled to tutor for a livelihood. He taught drawing and history to the lovely daughter of the patron who had once sent him to the Cadet Corps, the great magnate and military personage, Joseph Sosnowski.

Drawings may be drawings, and history history, but, as the old saying goes, blood and water are not the same. The tutor fell in love with his pupil and the pupil with her teacher. The parents, of course, had not the least intention of giving their daughter in

marriage to an insignificant officer without standing and with
not a penny to his name. Kosciuszko sought the help of the king
himself in winning the consent of the beautiful lady's father.
But the king, far from coming to the aid of his former protégé,
preferred to warn the father in advance and on the very day of
Kosciuszko's projected visit to the house the young lady was
packed off out of harm's way. Not long afterwards she was
betrothed to a duke, rich and well-known as a moron. Another
version of this romantic tale has come down to us. According
to this story, Kosciuszko had intended to elope with the girl in
the manner of the knights of old. Learning of the plan, the
enraged father sought to punish the daring romantic, who, it
happened, was under his strict military jurisdiction. Captain
Kosciuszko, faithful ever after to his first love, packed his be-
longings, borrowed some money and fled to Danzig. From there
he sailed for America. A more credible hypothesis states that
Kosciuszko left for France and from there sailed for America.
But it is a matter of indifference to us whether this future hero
of the American War of Independence experienced his first sea-
sickness on the Baltic or on the English Channel.

III

If Kosciuszko embarked for America not from Danzig, but
from Le Havre, then by all odds he was in Paris first where the
cafés resounded with the echo of events across the ocean. And
it was in Paris that he may have learned the exact circumstances
leading to the rise of the American colonists against England.
Perhaps over a glass of steaming tea in a café alongside the
Palais Royal he reflected on the resurgent mob which had spilled
340 cases of English tea into Boston Harbor. And a strong enthusiasm for the "rabble" of Lexington and the minute men
swept over him.

However, it is more probable that his desire to join on the
side of David in this modern battle with Goliath had already
ripened to a decision back in Warsaw, where sympathy for the
American rebels was high. The king himself favored these rebels,
and indeed so did the prominent family of Czartoryski; who

knows whether Kosciuszko did not carry with him letters of introduction from Prince Adam Czartoryski to Colonel Charles Lee, who not long before had been in Warsaw.

It would be more than tempting to bring together Kosciuszko and Beaumarchais, the author of *The Marriage of Figaro* and *The Barber of Seville*. It is well-known that Beaumarchais, together with a certain Dr. Debourg, actively concerned himself with recruiting volunteers for the American army. Unfortunately we cannot make the liaison for the simple reason that Kosciuszko was already in Philadelphia when Beaumarchais began his recruiting activities on a broad scale. Kosciuszko, like Lafayette, was among the first of those who came from Europe to aid the American revolutionaries; and he came at his own expense without the help of Rodrigo Hortalez et Compagnie, the Paris firm which in behalf of the French government busily supplied Washington with men and ammunition.

On September 31, 1776, Kosciuszko sent a memo to the Congress assembled in Philadelphia, offering his services to the Revolution. On October 18th he received a commission from John Hancock, President of Congress, as "an Engineer with the Rank of Colonel."

This commission Kosciuszko doubtlessly owed to the favorable opinion of the commander in chief, George Washington, though we have nothing to prove that he was ever personally introduced to Washington.

Thus began the seven-year service of a Polish volunteer in the American fight for independence. This was an extremely important period of our hero's life, not only because of what he gave America, but also because of what America gave him. He offered to these states as they wakened to freedom the whole of his generous soul, and all his talents—not least of which was his draftsmanship. And in return America brought to this admirer of Timoleon the first living example of how the ideal of a democratic republic could be realized, and this example he kept firmly before his eyes for the rest of his days.

Immediately upon his arrival from that chaos of political intrigue—feudal Europe—Kosciuszko acquainted himself with the simple and noble contents of the Declaration of Rights of

Virginia. No doubt he also read the eternally memorable Declaration of Independence, written by his friend of later years, Thomas Jefferson. On this native of Poland, where the life and death of millions of peasants were at the mercy of a small group of privileged nobility—on this idealist just come from France—where the peasant and the middle class of the Third Estate suffered inhuman oppression at the hands of the aristocracy—on this European—what must have been the impact of these words:

> . . . We hold these truths to be self evident, that all men are created equal, that they are endowed by the Creator with certain unalienable Rights, that among these are Life, Liberty and the pursuit of Happiness. . . .

But what mostly impressed Kosciuszko was the difference between the Congress which passed this act and the Polish Sejm (Parliament) where one vote was enough to veto the resolutions of the entire body. The Latin name of this venom that ran in the veins of the old Polish republic—a republic headed by a king—was Liberum Veto. In America fifty-six members of Congress approved and signed the Declaration of Independence; the fact that only one of these, Dickinson, opposed it was of course without importance. In Kosciuszko's motherland Dickinson's vote would have canceled the work of the entire Congress. . . .

And so he sketched and drew diligently. He drafted fortification plans for Billingsfort near Philadelphia. The Delaware River was to be closed by palisades three miles below the city and on the cape high ramparts were to be built. The work was still unfinished when Congress, in fear of the approaching English, left Philadelphia on December 2, 1776, and moved to Baltimore. The fortification of Philadelphia was to continue, but on the city side, for the English attack was no longer expected from the river. Fortunately the onslaught never took place. The Delaware did not freeze that winter and an attack across it would have been too dangerous. In January of 1777, after a successful battle at Trenton, Congress was able to return to Philadelphia where fortifications were again in progress. Kosciuszko's work on these fortifications was his baptism of fire, true, a christening without fire or smoke.

From here on Kosciuszko's activities in the American campaign link him closely with the person of General Horatio Gates, who quickly recognized the outstanding talents of this Polish engineer. For his part Kosciuszko retained a great respect and deep friendship for his first direct superior, even when the so-called Conway Cabal later brought Gates into unpleasant conflict with Washington. It is possible that Washington's obvious coolness toward Kosciuszko derived straight from Kosciuszko's friendship with General Gates. Although this attitude was apparent all through the war, Washington in his generous objectivity was finally compelled to recognize Kosciuszko's services. Coolness was altogether absent when, after many years, Kosciuszko came to America for the second time, having played a role in Poland similar to that of Washington in the United States, with the sole difference that Kosciuszko was not the leader of a successful uprising, but the unhappy hero of a defeat. It was then, in September, 1797, that Washington greeted him with these words:

"I welcome you to the land whose liberties you had been so instrumental in establishing. No one has a higher respect and veneration for your character than I have."

But now it is March, 1777. General Gates has taken command of the so-called Northern Army in the "land of hills." Kosciuszko came up in May recommended by General Patterson as a "capable engineer and one of the best and finest draftsmen." Gates's adjutant, Wilkinson, also has a high opinion of him and describes him as "timidly modest." Indeed, Kosciuszko was so modest that, despite his own better judgment, he carried out the plans proposed by Colonel Baldwin, chief engineer of the Northern Army, for fortifications at Ticonderoga on the Hudson, the fortress which Washington had called "key to all colonies of New England." When the worthlessness of the plan became obvious Kosciuszko wrote to Gates, who was elsewhere at the time:

General, above all I beg you not order me do anything until you arrive. The reason is this: I desire harmony and I wish to be friendly with all if possible. And if they should be stubborn and not acceed my proposals which might be better, I will leave them freedom to do as they will, the more so that I am a foreigner. I know how cautious I must be and how much courtesy I owe to the natives. I tell you frankly I am sensitive, and I like peace. I would rather leave everything and go home and plant cabbage.

Kosciuszko did not leave everything, however, and did not return to Siechnowicze to plant cabbage. He endured his thankless post and became reconciled to Baldwin. His compromising nature won him many friends but added nothing to his laurels. Out of the shadow in which his modesty kept him he emerged into the light only after the decisive battle of Saratoga on October 17, 1777. Here his engineering superiority finally made itself felt. When General Schuyler was removed and the command resumed by Gates, Kosciuszko worked out an excellent plan of fortification for Bemus Heights. This was his contribution to the victory over the English general Burgoyne. The victory at Saratoga had reverberated around the world and brought official recognition of the independence of the United States. With the name of Saratoga the difficult name of the Polish engineer will always be linked.

After this victory Washington himself spoke of Kosciuszko in a letter to the president of Congress, Henry Lawrence, on November 10, 1777, as "a gentleman of science and merit." It would seem that a promotion was due Kosciuszko after his first major success. But whatever efforts he may have made in this direction were restricted by his modesty. For how seriously could he have been thinking of his career if he was able to write these words to Colonel Troup in January, 1777:

My Dear Colonel,
If you see that my promotion will make too many jealous tell the General that I will not accept of one because I prefer peace more than the greatest rank in the world.

In our eyes, overstrained as they are by the sight of human pride and selfishness, these characteristics of Colonel—still colonel

—Kosciuszko may qualify him rather for a cloister than for the staff of a fighting army where European volunteers in general, and the French in particular, did not hesitate to sing their own praises to the sky. Kosciuszko, however, did not enter a monastery, though all his life he remained celibate. In March, 1778, we find him at West Point, where again under the command of a French engineer, Colonel du Portail, he is extraordinarily active strengthening the defenses of the Hudson River. In this work his colleague was also a Frenchman, Colonel Radière. Colonel Radière was a Parisian; Kosciuszko, as we know, was born in Mereczowszczyzna. Naturally the Paris-born engineer considered himself cleverer than the engineer who had been no more than a student and visitor in Paris. And so the two clashed and out of the contest Kosciuszko emerged the victor.

Colonel Robert Troup, who had now become chief of staff, reported to General Gates, now chief of the Board of War in Philadelphia: "The works in West Point are in a great state of forwardness. Kosciuszko is very much esteemed as an able engineer, and has made many alterations in the works, which are universally approved."

In August, Washington himself rode down to inspect the fortifications at West Point. That was the first time Kosciuszko saw the commander in chief. As to how Washington appraised the engineer's work—judging from Kosciuszko's letter to Gates on October 6, 1778, not too badly. But one could not have expected Kosciuszko's report about himself to have been other than the following:

"His Excellency was here with General du Portail to see the works. After all, conclusions was made that I am not the worst of Engineers."

"Not the worst of engineers" remained at West Point from March, 1778, to the summer of 1780. And his achievements there? Here is what George Bancroft has to say: "West Point was a solitude, nearly inaccessible, now it was covered with numerous redoubts, constructed chiefly under the direction of Kosciuszko as engineer, and so connected as to form one system of defense which was believed to be impregnable."

So far as the saintly inclinations of this man who converted a

desert into an impregnable fortification were concerned, he continued to follow where they led him. British prisoners were kept at
West Point. The food could not have been particularly appetizing
if American soldiers and twenty-five hundred civilian employees
at the defense center constantly complained of hunger. Our "not
the worst of engineers" lived so modestly that from his savings
he was able to feed the starved prisoners. This information has
come to us by way of a certain Pole (who, incidentally, did some
research on the life of Kosciuszko in America). It seems that
on a trip to Australia this Pole was stricken with the yellow fever
in Queensland. He was nursed back to health in the home of
a shopkeeper whom he had never seen before. And upon inquiry
he learned that the Queensland shopkeeper hoped in this way to
pay a debt of gratitude to another Pole who once had saved his
grandfather from starvation. That was at the time of the American Revolution in the fort at West Point, where the shopkeeper's
grandfather had been held prisoner as a soldier of his Majesty's
army. The Pole's name had been Koskesko, or something similar.

Even if this story is not true, out of all the credible documents touching on Kosciuszko's activities in America there
emerges the silhouette of a man whose actions were dominated by
his heart. Today it is difficult to understand how a man possessed
of so great a heart and such sensitivity to human suffering could
ever have reconciled his temperament to the perilous duties of
military service. It can be said of him that he detested slavery,
oppression, tyranny, but never did he hate the people who were
the instruments of these forces. It is hard to say whether Kosciuszko ever himself killed a soldier clad in the uniform of the
enemy. We do know, however, that in later years, when at the
head of the Polish insurrection against czarist Russia and Prussia
he held dictatorial powers, he was not to be compared with those
who personify the dictator type today. When the insurgent
Warsaw mob, on its own initiative, strung up a few royal
traitors in the streets of the capital, Kosciuszko—supposedly a
Jacobin who had seen the French guillotine—was enraged and
declared that he would rather lose two battles than live again
through this June day.

But we are still far from the day when Kosciuszko became

commander in chief of the Polish insurrection of 1794. For the present, it was March, 1780, and Kosciuszko was chief engineer of the American armies. For this position he owed thanks to the British, who had captured du Portail, his predecessor. Before long, however, Kosciuszko took leave of West Point. At the instigation of General Gates he was appointed chief engineer of the Southern Army by Washington. But before he was able to reach the southern front—in the so-called "Black District" named for the many Negroes there, where a "small battle" was in progress—General Gates suffered a disastrous defeat at Camden, South Carolina, on August 16, 1780. As a result Gates was court-martialed and relieved of all command for two years. The Southern Army was now placed under the leadership of General Nathanael Greene, one of the great figures of the American Revolution. Kosciuszko struck up an even friendlier relationship with Greene than he had held with Gates. Under Greene, Kosciuszko was not simply chief engineer; his duties included the selection of strategic positions in a difficult terrain, the draining of swamps, and the construction of pontoons for river crossings.

The southern front bore another significance for Kosciuszko. Here for the first time he exchanged the "quiet of the study" for the front lines. Here he had his true baptism of fire, fighting as an ordinary rifleman, or leading a band of guerrillas. He stayed in the South until the end of the war. The entire year of 1782 he spent on the battlefield at Charleston. More and more frequently the American papers of that year referred to Kosciuszko's bravery and valor; his legend had already begun to grow. On December 14, 1782, he rode into Charleston with the triumphant American army just a few hours ahead of Greene.

During his stay in the Black District, Kosciuszko's sensitive soul was touched by the fate of the colored people. And before leaving his many years of uncollected pay to the American Negro in his will, this Polish nobleman had already shown them his kindness. On September 2, 1782, he wrote to General Greene on the matter of distributing the clothes of Colonel Lawrence, who had fallen in battle:

"I recommend to you two Negroes belonging to L. C. Lawrence . . . They are naked. They want shirts, jackets, breeches and their skin can bear as well as ours good things."

Possibly, in advocating the cause of the Negro, Kosciuszko was thinking of the Polish and White Ruthenian peasants whose emancipation later became one of his primary objectives. In Polish eyes, the figure of Tadeusz Kosciuszko is visualized not in the resplendent uniform of a general, but in the white linen peasant blouse which he wore at the time of the insurrection in memory of the battle of Raclawice fought against the Russians on April 4, 1794. Here, for the first time in the history of Poland, complete peasant formations appeared in battle with scythes for weapons—and these peasants won a decisive victory over the regular Russian infantry and artillery. When Kosciuszko called the peasants to arms, he not only visualized their liberation from statutory labor and slavery, but he saw in them the true future citizens of a democratic republic in which slavery or statutory labor would have no place.

It was in the people's army of Washington that Kosciuszko acquired a practical knowledge of the power of the people and the triumph of a republican ideal. He had come from a world where dukes, lords, counts, viscounts, marquesses, and barons were wont to achieve highest ranks in the army automatically, simply because they had been born into high station. In America it was quite different. Here lords were forced to capitulate to sons of the people, to farmers, merchants, untitled, uncrested. General Nathanael Greene had been a simple blacksmith before the Revolution. Captain Lee had been a horse merchant. General Morgan, leader of one of Greene's armies, had been no more than a coachman; General Schuyler owned sawmills in Albany. And the highest symbol of the American Revolution, George Washington, had no special privileges either. He was a farmer.

Nor was money a decisive factor in the American triumph. More often than not during the long campaign Washington's army was an assortment of ragged tramps. For one who had looked upon this army for seven years, who took part in its triumphs and its defeats, even for such a one who called himself "count," as Kosciuszko sometimes did—it was impossible not to catch the germ of freedom and want to plant it on his native soil.

At the end of the war Kosciuszko decided to return to Poland. He had been promoted to brigadier general. It was not a promotion based on individual merit, however, nor was it a reward for distinguished services. Congress had elevated all officers one step in the hierarchy of the service. But it was a great honor for Kosciuszko to be admitted into the Society of Cincinnati, organized in June, 1785. He was one of the only three foreign officers admitted to this fine group of veterans. From then on the Order of Cincinnatus, a golden eagle with diamond studded eyes suspended from a white and blue ribbon, ornamented the chest of this Pole who always retained a great love for the United States and the ideals represented by it.

He left America in June, 1784, passing through France to Poland, where he was soon to play one of the most tragic, though most beautiful, roles in the history of his country.

IV

How deeply Kosciuszko had become attached to America is apparent in the moving letters he wrote to his American friends. Each letter brims over with love for the country whose independence he helped win. One might say that the ancient noble blood running in his veins was rejuvenated by the smoke of the American Revolution. Here is a letter he wrote to his friend Williams from Paris on August 26, 1784. (Despite his long sojourn among Anglo-Saxons it is full of mistakes.)

My dear Williams, I dare say you think to this day yet, that I shall forget you—you see how often we are mistaken in our conjectures. How happy I should be if you could swallow only half scrupul of my affection, your heart would be open to the conviction, no longer mistrustful, but sure as of your own you would me always ready to render your service in my power. . . . I will not entertain you with the Eligency or afluence of Paris and the other places; because it will give any real pleasure to me or to you. We require more solid food to our unbiassed sentyment, and we are sensible of the strict conexion which nature assigned to peace the innocence, the richess to industry, to tranquility the valour, and the enjoiment of Liberty—dear Word—I wish my Country feel its influence. . . . Can you believe I am very unhappy been absent from your Country it seems to me the other world her, in which every person finds great pleasure in cheating himself out of common sense. The time may have some power to preposses my mind in your countrys favour and adopt the opinion of greater number of men, but Nature more, it is in every breast, here they take great pains to subside the Charmes which constitute real happiness, but you folow with full speed the marked road and you fined by experience that domestick Life with liberty to be the best gift that nature had to bestow for the human specie. To morrow I am going to Poland and with some relictance as am informed by one of my countrymen that the affairs of the republick as well as mine are in a very horrid situation, you shall know it in my next. . . . I must prepare for the wors, perhaps you will see me again in your country, for this reason you must use your influence in Congress in my favor, and write me as soon as you can. Adieu your sincerely Thad. Kosciuszko.

Indeed he had the worst to prepare for, though it did not come until after what Kosciuszko's biographers call a "few idyllic years."

Between the first and second partitions of Poland there was a twenty-year lull, an interlude, separating the last acts of a dark tragedy. A Shakespearean light was thrown on this tragedy of both Poland and Kosciuszko by the ermine and purple of numerous royal personages.

The shock of the first partitioning had produced great changes in the country during Koscuiszko's absence. An extraordinary flowering of arts and sciences and the intellect had occurred. At the same time trade and industry had flourished, bringing relative prosperity to the land. Brilliant political writers, and statesmen— Wojciech Turski, Hugo Kollataj, Stanislaw Staszic—came to the fore with demands for radical social reforms, proclaiming that annihilation could be averted only by a nation whose people were free. The French Revolution had given wings to Polish radical thought. And of that revolution Kollataj wrote: "A people of twenty million that dares throw aside its crafts and its tools, risking burial in its own ruins, will terrify any power." The people of Poland would never terrify the powers of Russia, Austria, and Prussia so long as they were willing to remain slaves on their own land. It can be said for the Polish patriots, however, that even before the outbreak of the French Revolution they had joined in an attempt to reform the system of the country despite the powerful opposition of Russian bayonets and native reaction.

In 1788 the four-year Sejm assembled and in 1791 the famous Constitution of May 3rd was passed. Though it was no more than a compromising act which brought equality of rights to the middle class alone and gave the peasants nothing more than vague promises, nevertheless, it may be considered an important step which might well have brought further advances had Poland been able to retain her independence. The constitution had the support of all progressive elements. The reaction, however, formed an ignominious confederacy at Targowica to oppose it; this confederacy, unfortunately, was later joined by King Stanislaw August, champion of Polish culture. To this day the word "Targowica" has the same sound to Polish ears as the word "Vichy"—though, Targowica was never famed for its curative waters.

Let us look back to the first year of the four-year Sejm. This year was significant for Kosciuszko. For a bill was passed increasing the army to a hundred thousand men. As a result, after several years of public inactivity, Kosciuszko was now able to serve in the army of his own nation. In his effort to join the reorganized army he was aided by the very lady who once had been the cause of his voluntary exile. Lidwika, née Sosnowska, Princess Lubomirska was a fervent intercessor for Kosciuszko at the king's court; the princess did not attempt to conceal the unquenched emotions she still felt for her former tutor of drawing and history. In 1790 the Sejm recommended Kosciuszko's appointment to the army as a major general.

And here the truly epic tale of the quiet engineer of West Point and Saratoga has its real beginning. Events followed one another with lightning speed. Kosciuszko quickly became the nation's leader. In the war with Russia in 1792 he led a division under the command of Prince Joseph Poniatowski, nephew of the king, who was later to become a hero of the Napoleonic Wars and a marshal of France. Superior Russian forces defeated the tiny Polish army at Dubienka in the Ukraine. Prussia, with whom Poland had signed a defense pact against Russia, not only failed to come to her aid, but betrayed her. Joining with Russia, Prussia carried out the second partition of Poland in 1793. Targowica was again Poland's Vichy. The patriots and many generals, including Lieutenant General Kosciuszko, went into exile.

L'Assemblée Législative in Paris had granted Kosciuszko French citizenship back in 1792. This honor the Polish fighter for freedom shared with George Washington, Friedrich Schiller, and Johann Pestalozzi. Using the pseudonym "Baron Poverty," Kosciuszko escaped through Saxony to France. There he sought to interest the French government in the fate of his country. The French spared no pains to prove their respect and sympathy for Kosciuszko and the Polish insurrectionist movement, but they contributed neither money nor diplomatic support. It is possible that they had little confidence in a nation ruled by the aristocracy, a nation which had not the courage to deal with its king as they had dealt with theirs. A certain Citizen Parandier, an agent of the French government, who was favorably inclined toward Poland, attempted to persuade his government to lend the Polish rebels twelve million francs after the outbreak of the insurrection. He explained to his superiors that Poles deserved from the French republic the same sort of help that Americans had received from the "Versailles despots." But in vain. It was to the advantage of France at the time not to interfere with the partitioning powers. It was preferable to have these powers occupied in the east rather than in their own territory in the west. In any case, the rulers of France had more important matters to fill their heads—which at the time sat precariously enough on their shoulders.

So Kosciuszko's hope for foreign aid was crushed. It was left to the insurrection to succeed on its own strength. It burst forth prematurely and was quickly suppressed.

The victorious battle at Raclawice, in which the peasants so nobly distinguished themselves, sent a wave of enthusiasm rolling through the land. On May 7th, in his camp at Polaniec, Kosciuszko, now leader of the nation, issued a memorable manifesto which was more or less supplementary to the Constitution of 1791. To peasants he granted personal liberty and the right of each to till his own soil. The revolutionary slogans that he proclaimed took hold of the middle class as well as the peasants. The "Raclawice miracle" was contagious. The workers of Warsaw, led by a shoemaker named Jan Kilinski, expelled the Russian troops from the capital. King Stanislaw August favored the insurrection, but his rule had been taken from him. He was now completely subordinate to the man who had once been his protégé at the School of Knights. It is easy to guess that Kosciuszko was both generous and respectful toward his former patron—a fact which was later frowned upon by the guillotinists of Paris.

The rapture of victory was short-lived for the rebels. The strategic errors of Kosciuszko—who attempted to apply his American experience to this war—and the numerical superiority of the enemy hastened the collapse. On June 6th, Kosciuszko suffered a defeat at Szczekociny. A Prussian bullet shot his horse from under him. For unexpectedly in the midst of the battle with the Russians, Polish horses and Polish men found themselves under a hail of Prussian bullets. The Prussian King Frederick Wilhelm II rode at the head of his troops at Szczekociny. On June 15th his forces seized Cracow.

But in Warsaw the heart of the insurrection still beat. A Radical Club, modeled on the Jacobins, was founded in Warsaw with Kollataj at its head. Kosciuszko led a magnificent defense of the capital in which—as in September, 1939—the civilian population took full part. The Prussians were compelled to abandon the siege. Yet the insurrection was not saved from disaster. On October 10, 1794, at Maciejowice, a superior Russian army under command of Fersen delivered a mortal blow to Poland. Kosciuszko, severely wounded in the head and leg, was taken prisoner. To the end of his days he denied that at Maciejowice he cried, "Finis Poloniae."

The third complete partition of Poland was but an epilogue

to the battle at Maciejowice and the subsequent massacre of civilians in the suburb of Warsaw called Praga.

The wounded Kosciuszko was accorded great honor by his captors. Those were knightly days, and a defeated foe was held in respect for the virtues of his spirit and the greatness of his soul. After the battle of Maciejowice the victors feasted and drank the health of the broken Polish generals.

At the command of Empress Catherine, Kosciuszko was brought to Petersburg and placed in the Fortress of Sts. Peter and Paul. There he was subjected to an inquiry—with great courtesy—by Attorney General Semoilov. The records of this inquiry are a priceless testimony to Kosciuszko's nobility of character. He took upon himself full responsibility for the insurrection. Shortly thereafter the empress ordered his removal from the fortress to the palace of Count Orlov, and here the wounded prisoner lived in greater comfort than he had ever enjoyed in his life. His wounds were attended by an English physician, Dr. Rogerson; he was supplied with a personal servant, a Negro, and with a cook named Jean. He was allowed to drive in a carriage through the city. During the two years of his imprisonment his chief diversion was a latheshop.

There exists a well-known engraving which depicts the moment when the new Czar Paul, immediately after the death of his mother, pays Kosciuszko a visit at his elegant prison. Supported by an extravagant retinue and accompanied by his son Alexander, Paul pompously informs Kosciuszko—who has not so much as stirred from his sofa—that from this moment he is free to come and go as he pleases. The chronologist who relates this event states that as Paul offered freedom to Kosciuszko he professed himself an admirer of this prisoner of his mother's, assuring him that he had always opposed Poland's partition and pledging himself to restore her liberty.

Kosciuszko was now free to go to his foster motherland across the ocean, but before he left he made what was probably his greatest sacrifice. In order to free twelve thousand Polish captives who were distributed in Russian prisons or had been deported to Siberia he took an oath of allegiance to the Marshal of the czarist court, George Wielchorski. From Paul he received

a gift of sixty thousand rubles which he planned to use in behalf
of his people. He paid a farewell visit to the czar's family at the
Winter Palace, presenting himself in the uniform of an American
general. Here he was received not as an enemy prisoner but as
a cousin. The czar embraced him, again assuring him of his
friendship, and loaded him down with gifts. To the Empress
Maria Fedorova, Kosciuszko presented a snuffbox, which he had
himself made, and the peasant russet which he had worn at the
battle of Maciejowice. The empress requested that he send her
garden seeds from America. Such were the times.

Kosciuszko traveled through Finland, Sweden, and England
to the United States. On the way he was showered with honors
as if he were a king. Ovations greeted him on every side. Orches-
tras serenaded beneath his windows, regiments paraded, elegant
ladies of the highest social rank made pilgrimages to this Polish
invalid who had lost a war and a fatherland. Stirred with emotion
they wept at the sight of him, and gazed with awe upon him
as if he were Mona Lisa. It was no doubt the greatest triumph
a conquered man had ever enjoyed in modern times. The essence
of this triumph was moral and it evokes nostalgia for a world
so completely fascinated by greatness of soul and so deeply moved
by one man's unhappiness. Kosciuszko had become the prima
donna of suffering.

On August 8, 1797 an American freighter, the *Adriana,*
brought the sick and defeated Kosciuszko to the very same Philadelphia pier at which eighteen years earlier the young, healthy
and hopeful volunteer had disembarked to join the War for Independence. In Philadelphia the triumphal ovations of Europe were
repeated. Philadelphian Quakers unharnessed the horses of Kosciuszko's carriage and themselves brought him to the house at
which he was to stay. Not long afterward George Washington
sent him a letter expressing full admiration and respect and inviting him to Mount Vernon. This invitation Kosciuszko politely
declined; he remained in Philadelphia, where he struck up a lifelong friendship with Thomas Jefferson. And it was to Jefferson
that he entrusted his last testament which read:

I Thaddaus Kosciuszko being just in my departure from
America hereby declare and direct that should I make

no other testamentory disposition of my property in the
United States thereby authorise my friend Thomas Jefferson to employ the whole thereof in purchasing Negroes
from among his own as any others and giving them liberty
in my name in giving them an education in trades or
otherwise and in having them instructed for their new
condition in the duties of morality which may make them
good neyghbours, good fathers or mothers, husband or
wives and their duties as citizens teaching them to be
difenders of their liberty and country and of the good
order of society and in whatsoever may make them happy
and useful and I make the said Thomas Jefferson my
executor of this.
5th May 1798   T. Kosciuszko

Why Kosciuszko suddenly left America, where he had intended to spend the remainder of his days farming, is a question
which historians still ponder. It is possible he was discouraged
by the antirepublican government of President Adams, which
at the time passed the so-called "Alien and Sedition Bill" directed
against foreigners. The more likely assumption, however, is that
he left upon receiving news that a Polish legion was to be formed
in the French army under the command of Jan Henryk
Dabrowski.

He beat about France to the end of his days, twinkling somehow at the edges of Napoleon's star—whom, incidentally, he did
not hold in high regard. He engaged in diplomatic and political
affairs, attended meetings and banquets at which Poland was
toasted and crocodile tears were wept. Immediately after his
arrival in France, while he still hoped that another armed uprising of the Poles would take place, he attempted to repay the
czar the debt which had been burning his conscience, the money
he had received in Petersburg, and which he had deposited in an
English bank; with the money he sent a polite note renouncing his
loyalty and obedience to the czar. The note explained that he had
taken the oath of allegiance under pressure of the czar's ministers.
Enraged, the czar refused to accept the money and declared
Kosciuszko an ungrateful traitor.

In 1806 Kosciuszko was in close contact with Napoleon.

The French emperor hoped to make use of the name of the beloved Polish leader to win over the Polish people in his war against Russia. It is said that Fouché forged Kosciuszko's name to an appeal to the Poles. Kosciuszko was firm with Napoleon; he demanded clear guaranties of Poland's independence and the liberation of the peasants from statutory labor. These guaranties however, were not given; Napoleon considered Kosciuszko a naïve lunatic. In 1812 Czar Alexander I of Russia, who like his father Paul professed admiration for Kosciuszko, sought to win him over. Again Kosciuszko demanded Poland's independence and the liberation of the peasants. Alexander invited Kosciuszko to attend the Vienna Congress in the hope of strengthening his own position as king of Poland by winning Kosciuszko's support. Kosciuszko maintained an attitude of friendly reserve. He committed himself to nothing. He was grateful to Alexander, nevertheless, for having at least restored the name of Poland in the Congress kingdom.

As a matter of fact, Kosciuszko did not take active part in any independence movements in Poland after the Maciejowice battle. His final years were spent at Soleur, Switzerland, at the home of a family by the name of Zettner. On April 2, 1817, he liberated the peasants on his estate at Siechnowicze from statutory labor. On October 15th of the same year he died, adored by his neighbors, especially the poor toward whom his kindness was almost legendary. A year later his body was transferred to Austrian-occupied Cracow, where he was ceremoniously buried in the Polish National Sanctuary—in the royal catacombs beneath Wawel Cathedral.

Today Wawel Castle is occupied by the German governor general. He has had the equestrian statue of Kosciuszko removed from the bastion. But not far from Cracow there is another monument to this great leader, a monument which no governor will ever remove. It is a high mound, an artificial hill overgrown with moss and raised in Kosciuszko's honor by the hands of the Polish people. In this mound of earth there is a bit of soil gathered from the American fields where Kosciuszko once fought. As a Polish romantic poet writes: "Wawel will fall—but the grave of Kosciuszko will remain."

Not alone will Kosciuszko's grave remain, but the songs that our people sing of him and their love will remain as well. And so will the immortal lines of Byron in which he paid his respects to Kosciuszko, as for example the lines in *Don Juan* or these meters in the *Age of Bronze:*

> Ye who dwell
> Where Kosciuszko dwelt, remembering yet
> The unpaid amount of Catharine's bloody debt!
> Poland! o'er which the avenging angel passed
> But left thee as he found thee, still a waste,
> Forgetting all they still enduring claim,
> Thy lotted people and extinguish'd name,
> Thy sigh for freedom, thy long flowing tear,
> That sound that crashes in the tyrant's ear—
> Kosciuszko!

SIMON BOLIVAR

by

J. ALVAREZ del VAYO

JULIO ALVAREZ DEL VAYO

was born in Madrid in 1891. His father was a general in the army; his mother a leading aristocrat, active in Catholic organizations. He studied law, graduating from the University of Valladolid. Upon conclusion of his studies, he went to London to study at the School of Economics and Political Science, under Sidney and Beatrice Webb.

In 1918 del Vayo took part in the German legal movement against war headed by Rosa Luxemburg, about whom he later wrote his well-known novel, *The Red Road*. It was translated into many languages. In 1920 he became European correspondent for *La Nación*, leading Argentine newspaper.

In 1931 he was appointed ambassador to Berlin. When Berlin refused his credentials because of his attacks against the rising Hitler movement he was appointed ambassador to Mexico. From 1933 to 1936 he served as ambassador to Moscow. In 1936 Largo Cavallero appointed him foreign minister of Spain and a few months later he became general commissar of war. In 1938 he was again appointed foreign minister and kept the post until the end of the Spanish War. Practically all the time he was the first delegate from Spain to the League of Nations.

Julio del Vayo is the author of several books, including *The Red Road, Freedom's Battle,* and books on Russia, Germany, and Spain. Since 1940 he has been in the United States, where he is executive director of the Free World Association.

SIMON BOLIVAR
by J. Alvarez del Vayo

U<small>NTIL</small> Bolivar was driven out of his country by the turn of military events he cannot be considered as a political outcast in the strict sense of the term.

His first voyage from Venezuela (he sailed from Guaira for Europe on February 19, 1799) was occasioned solely by his rich, teeming imagination as an adolescent; he was passionately eager to see with his own eyes a world which his guardian, Simon Rodriguez, had already conjured up for him in the most glowing colors. Nor had he yet been placed in social or political conflict with the world he was born into. True, his childhood and early youth gave indications of that restlessness and rebelliousness which were to develop into the vigorous, well-rounded personality of his manhood. But, all in all, his formative years were better calculated to foster a desire for the even tenor of comfort and well-being that characterized the old Creole families. Bolivar belonged to a class of men who were firmly attached to the existent social order by virtue of positions handed down from father to son with a hereditary regularity that was almost feudal.

Juan Vicente Bolivar, his father, died while the Liberator was still a child; he had been an official in the Treasury. The Bolivar family, one of the most distinguished in Caracas, enjoyed considerable wealth. And Bolivar could count on the generosity of his uncle, the Marques de Palacios, who, convinced of the lad's exceptional promise, resolved any material doubts the family might harbor by advancing the money necessary for his nephew's journey and financing his further education in Europe.

Thus Bolivar left Venezuela for the first time not as a political outcast but an enthusiastic quest of knowledge and adventure. Still, fatherless as he was, he could not have failed to react emotionally to his tutor Rodriguez, a man in whom the culture and worship of liberty were married to the highest pedagogical gifts. Simon Rodriguez left his mark upon his pupil; his disinterested, nay generous, attitude was obvious from the beginning. More curious and infrequent still, far from parting in rancor and hostility, teacher and student remained fast allies. Later, amid the turmoil of his public career, the Liberator was to value his quondam mentor as the political counselor of his maturity.

Rodriguez was more than a friend of liberty and a devotee of progress, he was a man of action, whose participation in the Venezuelan revolutionary movement anticipated Bolivar's and constituted Rodriguez as a genuine political émigré in 1797, two years before Bolivar's jaunt to Europe. That Rodriguez roused his charge's first impulses of revolt against certain features of the colonial regime is more than likely. Indeed, a minor incident that occurred as Bolivar set out on his first journey from his native land goes to show that he must already have begun in a confused way to resent the Spanish domination.

When the ship he was on called at a port in Mexico, then New Spain, the viceroy, Don Miguel José de Azanza, granted him an audience in the course of which the young man proved himself no mean speaker and, with all the spontaneity of youth, felt free to dispense with the niceties of protocol. Bolivar was to recall later how, as conversation progressed, he found himself openly advocating the cause of American independence. His plea must have been both empassioned and convincing, for the viceroy, deeming Bolivar's sojourn in Mexico dangerous to the state, did all in his power to speed his departure.

Trusting to the distractions that lay in store for his youthful and irrepressible interlocutor, the viceroy must have breathed more freely when the attractive Venezuelan was on his way to Spain. For Bolivar had entrée to the choicest circle in Madrid. His friend and countryman, Manuel Mallo, was persona gratissima at the royal court, a general favorite and particularly of the queen's. It was an open secret in the antechambers that the royal alcove lay open day and night for the young colonial; and it was no news in the sanctum of Godoy himself, who was premier but shared the royal pleasure with Bolivar's compatriot. Doubtless a lively personal jealousy and fear of being eliminated in favor of the Creole inspired the premier to enact against the colonists more of such injustices as Bolivar had protested against in Mexico.

As friend of her "friend," Bolivar attended the queen informally and shared the princes' sports. At tennis one day a ball from Bolivar's racket chanced to hit Ferdinand—Prince of the Asturias and heir to the throne—on the head. Angry and hurt, the infante flung down his racket, refusing to continue the game, but the queen, breaking the pride of the lad who was to become the baleful Ferdinand VII, insisted he play. Years after, recalling the incident, Bolivar wrote: "Who could have divined in this incident the omen that I was later to wrest from him the most precious ornament in his crown?"

Under Charles IV and Maria Luisa, the process of Bourbon decomposition was being hastened and intensified, and the spectacle of the depravity at court was slowly but surely working to undermine Bolivar's respect for the royal power in whose name the American colonies, including his own country, were governed. For this and other reasons he would have shortened his stay in Madrid were it not for his relations with the Marques de Ustaz, his guardian during the visit. The marques, quick to discover Bolivar's talents, devoted himself to the task of rounding out the youth's education; but his affection for his ward did not blind him to the fact that Bolivar, at seventeen, was not qualified to marry his daughter Theresa, with whom he had fallen madly in love.

A short sojourn in Paris early in 1802 tided Bolivar over until he was judged old enough to marry. Napoleon, as consul for life, was then first magistrate of the Republic; Bolivar admired him as he admired no other man in his lifetime. The romance of France's mighty historical experiment thrilled him, but he had left someone behind him in Madrid who continued to disturb his slumbers. So he made one of those swift decisions so typical of him; he returned to Spain, broke down the resistance of the marques, and jettisoning his legal studies married Theresa. Almost at once the bridal couple set sail for Venezuela, Bolivar intending to retire to his estate in the Aragua valley to enjoy in his new-won happiness a compensation for his lonely childhood days. But a few days after their arrival Theresa, who had just turned seventeen, contracted yellow fever and died. Thus our predestined orphan found himself bereaved once more. The shock was terrible; the loss of Theresa altered the whole course of his life. Over her grave Bolivar vowed never to wed again, and he kept his word. Later he said: "My wife's death drove me to follow the chariot of Mars instead of the plow of Ceres."

His grief sent him a second time to Madrid, where he had a painful meeting with his father-in-law, both of them tortured by memories of Theresa. A legal difficulty in connection with his residence wounded him once again in his pride as a "colonial" and, sharpening his hostility to the domination of the metropolis, drove him to France. He reached Paris in the spring of 1804. Meanwhile his god had turned out to be just another mortal with unlimited ambition and an inextinguishable lust for power. Bolivar's admiration changed into irreconcilable hatred which he expressed in this bitter judgment: "I worshiped him as the hero of the republic, the bright star of glory, the Genius of Liberty; but one day he made himself emperor and ever since I have looked on him as a hypocritical tyrant."

His disillusion proved so genuine that he took no pains to veil his feelings; again and again he recklessly and passionately denounced the fickleness of the French character and Bonaparte's usurpation. In a Paris beset by policemen, this frequently led to serious trouble. But Bolivar would yield neither to the pressure of friends, who considered Napoleon's evolution as an inevitable fact, nor to the advice of certain persons in high station, who feared that his sojourn in Paris would become impossible. When, on Napoleon's coronation, the Spanish ambassador invited Bolivar to join his retinue, the latter declined and, as a token of protest, remained in his quarters all day long.

His origin and wealth opened the most exclusive circles of the capital to him. In the salons of Paris, where fashionable society delighted in receiving the philosophers of the eighteenth century, Bolivar learned to think—and to love also. In the latter respect at least, France won him over completely, so that subsequently in his career, in the midst of his most violent battles, he was often to seek relaxation in dancing and in amorous dalliance. Indeed, throughout his life, he mingled military with amatory conquests. One of his happiest days was undoubtedly August 6, 1813, when he entered Caracas in a triumphal coach drawn by twelve young maidens, each more beautiful than the other.

Out of this period in Paris stemmed a friendship which lasted for many years: his pseudo idyl with Madame Dervieu de Villars, who was fired by the Liberator's ideals and who pretended to be his cousin. In a letter which this lady wrote Bolivar many years later she mentioned Louis XVIII under curious circumstances. A son of hers was about to be expelled from the army for having intercepted a letter to Bolivar; Louis XVIII, intervening in the young officer's favor, himself now wrote soliciting a picture of the American hero. "Madame," the king concluded, "I shall not live to see your cousin's marvelous destiny attain its culmination, but if he is not assassinated, you can someday do him and also France a great service by co-operating in consolidating the interests of both worlds. Farewell, madame; do not worry about your son's fate."

With the attraction of high French society in these times and the fascination of the smartest salons of Paris—"a school of discussion and thought," Bolivar called them—he might well have passed his youth in mere flirtations with the ideas and the enchanting priestesses of the day; but the providential shadow of Simon Rodriguez rose to take care that his talents and aptitudes did not go to waste. Bolivar and the teacher of his childhood in Caracas re-established contact in Paris. Rodriguez advised the young man to carry on serious methodical studies and under his spiritual guidance Bolivar worked in earnest. Helvetius d'Holbach and Hume became his favorite authors; he became acquainted with Humboldt, who just had returned from America, a tried partisan of the independence of the Spanish colonies. The great German provided a new stimulant to the future Liberator who, day by day, found himself increasingly eager to help his fellow colonists shake off the Spanish yoke.

Rodriguez was more than the teacher and counselor who, meeting a former pupil in the latter's manhood, strove to retain his ascendancy over him. Rodriguez was an alert friend, who knew his former pupil intimately and could tell to what degree the latter depended upon support and encouragement, despite his apparently excessive self-confidence. In the course of his second visit to Europe, Bolivar soon sank into a profound apathy; he seemed incapable of mustering energy enough to direct his life along concrete and determined lines and was plagued by doubts as to whether he should devote himself to science or work for the liberation of peoples or simply die. While Bolivar tarried in Vienna, a prey to the torment of this intimate conflict, Rodriguez informed him that he, Bolivar, had come into a fortune of four million francs. Malicious historians pretend that this news proved to be the best psychological treatment, and that it cured him. But this interpretation scarcely holds against Bolivar's well-known generosity, which he proved later by contributing virtually the whole of his personal fortune to financing the war.

Basing their theories upon this critical juncture in Bolivar's life, some of his biographers insist upon certain characteristic traits which, illustrated by isolated incidents in his future career, have inspired voluminous psychopathical studies of the Liberator. Among its greatest personalities, history numbers men like Julius Caesar, Mahomet, Charles V, Richelieu, Molière, and Peter the Great, all of whom, without being epileptics of the general convulsive type, yet presented what the scientist terms "epileptic equivalents." In other words, such cases offer special temperamental conditions—sudden attacks of fury, hysteria, depression, local nervous convulsions, and the like—which while epilectic in nature are also expression of a superior functional condition.

Some of the physician-biographers who have examined Bolivar's personality from this angle include him in this group of "genial epileptics." On the strength of various similar psychic activities, these commentators have drawn a psychological parallel between Bolivar and Caesar. Both were, in effect, impulsive, hyperexcitable, and highly sensitive; in both, the sexual impulse was abnormally developed and the brain constantly subject to creative tension. But the direction these qualities followed and the form these impulses took were totally different. In any case, the impression abides that in such incursions into Bolivar's psychopathology, some of his symptomatic moments have been excessively dramatized. The same Peru de Lacroix who writes in the Bucaramanga diary: "Any stranger who saw and observed him at certain moments would have thought him a madman," goes on to state: "But his fury does not last."

Of all Bolivar's erratic acts, that which proved most astounding, because of his audience and the setting, must have been the famous incident at Angostura. On the occasion of a banquet tendered him by Irving, the United States commissioner, Bolivar climbed onto the table, and striding from one end of it to the other, regardless of all that was on it, shouted: "This is how I shall go from the Atlantic to the Pacific until I have crushed the last Spaniard."

In a man of Bolivar's caliber, such contrasting and contradictory reactions formed a background against which his figure stood out with vivid immediacy; instead of diminishing him, they lent something very human to his historical stature.

As his second visit to Europe drew to its close, and the hour of returning to his country approached, Bolivar's journeys grew more frequent. In 1805 he went to Italy on a walking tour with Rodriguez; they visited Florence, Venice, Naples, and Rome. In the Eternal City one morning, with Rodriguez beside him as usual, Bolivar climbed the Monte Aventino, the Sacred Mountain, that august hill where Sicinius roused the plebians who were exasperated by the abuses of the patricians. There, moved by the spell of the hour and the site, in an outburst of civic mysticism Bolivar made the vow to free South America.

He returned to Paris, crossed Holland, and reached Hamburg whence he sailed to North America, arriving in Caracas late in 1806, after an absence of three years. He found the ground prepared by nine years of complicated diplomatic and political labor. Great negotiations had developed since December 22, 1797, when Don Francisco de Miranda, Don José de Pozo y Sucre and Don Manuel José de Salsas had signed the Pact of Paris, which empowered Miranda to approach England on the subject of the emancipation of the Spanish colonies.

Miranda, who in some ways may be considered a forerunner in the movement of South American independence, was no mediocre person. Born in Bogotá, he was nevertheless considered a foreigner during his period as generalissimo, for he had soldiered at Valmy, conquered at Ambères, enjoyed the friendship of Catherine of Russia and Joseph II, and been accounted the equal of Pitt and Bentham. A highly resourceful diplomatic agent, he had promoted British aid; and his virtues as man of action were clearly confirmed by the first military expedition to Colombia which he organized. Subsequently, the inexplicable fall of San Mateo, when four thousand men surrendered to the Spaniards without firing a shot, cost Miranda the irremediable loss of Bolivar's respect; the Liberator, who could not overlook the slightest lapse on the battlefield, went to his death regretting that he had not had Miranda shot that day. But neither Miranda at his best nor any other contemporary could vie in fortitude and leadership with the brave, handsome, ardent genius of Bolivar, "the man who freed one continent and filled another with his name," as children in the Paris schools used to sing one hundred and twenty-five years ago.

His feats of military prowess have been retailed a hundred times. They range over the periods of the hardest fighting, from the creation of Colombia (when from 1819 to 1821 he scarcely left the battlefield), through the liberating campaigns of New Granada and Venezuela, to the successive campaigns of Colombia, Ecuador, and Peru (1822 to 1826). It is difficult to conceive what tremendous effort Bolivar and his soldiers were called upon to make as they fought on against the most unfavorable odds. The crossing of the Andes and the march on Bogotá at the height of the rains survives as one of the greatest accomplishments of all times.

Bolivar was able to transmit his enthusiasm to men like Páez, a brave and imaginative leader, a product of the pampas whose sole training for outstanding military exploits had consisted in taming fillies and enraging bulls by tugging at their tails. The lack of suitable armament did not faze these native lieutenants of Bolivar's. Some of the men fought with pikes of albarico, a wood so extraordinarily hard that the tips of the pikes did not break in battle. Others used rifles seized from the enemy; others, steel lances. When their mounts—wild colts tamed in the fury of the fray—fell exhausted, the men managed to find replacements and went on fighting. The passage of the Andes to Bogotá alone took seventy days, every hour of which was fraught with hardships and danger. Hunger, the rains, and physical exhaustion decimated the troops, but they reached their goal. O'Leary, with all the phlegm and realism of an Irishman, has recorded the vicissitudes of this epic. Who can forget his cold, objective account of a soldier's wife giving birth to a child during the march and rising immediately after to join the files plodding over the jagged paths above the deepest precipices of the Andes?

Those who did not die forged on, possessed contagiously, as it were, by their great leader's faith, and, on August 10, 1819, to the enemy's stupor, the Liberator entered the city. His victories at Carabobo and Ayacucho were being celebrated throughout America. One man, Bolivar, now rose to embody the will and the aspirations of an entire continent.

If Bolivar's military genius is familiar to those who have given South American history even the most cursory glance, his ideological struggle to afford the old Spanish colonies a substantial content of freedom has been somewhat neglected by commentators in the last few decades. Fear of appearing inferentially to criticize the most powerful figure of the other America has made North American authors chary of hazarding a word which might arouse resentment in their good neighbors. Yet there is but one way to appraise Bolivar's qualities as a leader and to measure his greatness as a man. It calls for a fearless judgment upon the obstacles which he had to overcome; and it calls for a scrutiny of Bolivar's soul, tortured by the disparity between a noble ambition to make the emancipated colonies so many true, free and strong nations and the stern realities that encompassed him.

Three documents, well worth reading in the original, mark the successive stages in the development of Bolivar's political thought. They are *The Jamaica Letter*, sent by Bolivar, as the title shows, to "an English gentleman interested in American affairs"; *The Cartagena Manifesto,* issued on his return from exile in Curaçao in 1814, when, at the age of thirty, the young leader already displayed the gift of statesmanship; and *The Angostura Message,* addressed to the Congress held in that city in February, 1819, which invested Bolivar with the office of president of the Republic, and brought the Venezuelan state into being.

In *The Jamaica Letter,* the will to independence prevailed over all other considerations. The essential point was that the old colonies must break the bonds, or rather chains, that bound them to the mother country. As yet Bolivar did not seem to have troubled much about what form of government the emancipated colonies should adopt. More, a really careful reading of this interesting document warrants the belief that Bolivar was virtually justifying tyranny from within in contrast to the exterior tyranny which subjugated the peoples of the American continent. Thus, for example, he wrote:

> In absolute administrations, there is no limitation in the exercise of the governmental faculties: the will of the Great Sultan, Kan Bey and other despotic sovereigns, forms the supreme Law. This law is executed in almost arbitrary fashion by pashas, khans, satraps, and other Turkish or Persian subaltern officials. But, after all, the Chiefs of Isfahan are Persians, the viziers of the Great Lord are Turks, the tyrants of Tartary are Tartars; and China did not go to seek military mandarins in the land of her conqueror Genghis Khan. In America, on the contrary, we were subjected to tyranny from Spain which in reality deprived us of the enjoyment and exercise of our own active tyranny, impeding the latter's functions in our domestic affairs and in our inner administration.

One hundred and twenty-five years later, this rather curious reaction of Bolivar's to the problem of national independence as against the problem of domestic freedom still preserves a certain immediacy. Not that the two conceptions are contradictory; indeed, they are compatible. This is precisely the case when the cause of national unity is bound up with a really progressive movement along the home front, when the fight of a people against foreign tyranny acquires all the value of a great movement of liberation. On the other hand, it is not uncommon today, especially in Europe, to find peoples who in their nationalist obsession go so far as to adopt the most reactionary attitude, actually jeopardizing the nobler anti-Fascist cause, solely to obtain satisfaction in their so-called rights as a national minority.

The Irish offer a classic example of this tendency. A quarter century ago, at the time of the controversy over Ireland, your true Irish nationalist did not care if all Europe was destroyed by the direst reaction, if only Ireland was free. Similarly today, he does not care if the whole hemisphere bows to Fascism, if only he sees Eire completely independent. The same holds for the Croat or Slovak nationalists. For them, the only important thing in this world is to become a nation, with its own government and complete bureaucratic machinery, even though it is not self-sustaining, even though it must perforce depend upon the favor of neighbors who are ideologically at the opposite pole, even though it must receive its "liberty" from the hands of a Hitler. Friedrich Engels observed many years ago in his excellent study of nationalities that this all goes to prove that in nationalism à outrance, unleavened by a deep liberalism, independence may easily become synonymous with counterrevolution and reaction.

In the *Cartagena Manifesto* Bolivar advocated the adoption of the British Constitution as a model for New Granada and Venezuela, and enthusiastically supported the idea of a hereditary senate to balance excessive radicalism. His opinion of popular elections was less than favorable. "The people," he wrote in this document, "are wrong much more often than nature perfected by education." In a hereditary senate along the lines of Britain's Parliament at the time, Bolivar saw a check to the possible excesses of an exaggerated democracy. "We must not leave everything to the hazard and chance of elections. Only a balanced government can be free. How do you expect me to balance a democracy save by the counterpoise of an aristocratic institution? We cannot suffer a monarchic form of government to interfere with the popular form of govenment which we have adopted; but we have at least to strive to provide the Republic with an immovable

organism to assure its stability. For without stability, every political principle is doomed to corruption and ultimate destruction."
And, farther on: "Nothing is more dangerous than weakness in
the executive; if a monarchy has found it neccssary to give the
executive so many powers, how much more indispensable are
these powers to a republic? In a republic, the executive must be
strong, because every one conspires against it; in a monarchy,
the legislative must be the strongest, because here every one conspires in favor of the monarch." When the hour struck to test
the capacities of the former colonies for self-government and to
launch the peoples of America in their decisive battle against
Spanish domination, Bolivar still harbored doubts as to the wisdom of the people's will. And he also feared lest certain none
too scrupulous tyrants rise to expoit the political immaturity of
the new national entities in the process of creation.

This twofold preoccupation took on clear dramatic accents
in the most important of the three documents mentioned, *The
Angostura Message,* delivered to Congress on February 15, 1819.
It begins with a solemn declaration of democratic faith: "Happy
the citizen who, protected by the forces under his command, has
called upon the national sovereignty to exercise its absolute will.
Truly, I reckon myself amongst those beings who have been most
highly favored by Divine Providence, for it has been my honor
to assemble the representatives of the Venezuelan people in this
august congress, which is the spring of legitimate authority,
the depository of the sovereign will, and the arbiter of the nation's
destiny." Doubts as to the people's capacities for establishing a
lasting government, and a free and just one, again rose to disturb
him in the course of the address.

Pointing out the ethnic differences existing between Anglo-
Americans and Spanish-Americans, he cited the mixture of
Indians, Spaniards, and African Negroes in the latter. "Our
moral constitution still lacks the consistency to admit the benefits
of wholly representative government," he observed. The American Constitution of 1811 was thus presented as inadequate, given
the real necessities of these peoples now being born to independence in the southern regions of the Western world. "Laws
must be adapted to the physical aspect of a country, to its climate

to the quality of its soil, to the nature of the life its people lead, and to their customs. Such is the code we must consult, not that of Washington."

Faced with the prospect of a long fight, certain of military victory but questioning the victory of the ideals forged in his mind during his years of romantic pilgrimage over Europe, Bolivar tossed his old Jacobin fanaticism overboard to reconcile his loyalty with more general democratic principles. He felt it was his duty to help create the strong government which he considered indispensable in this period of violent awakening and of revolutionary growth.

In the theories of Barthélemy he believed that he had found the justification of his realistic and pragmatic evolution. One of his favorite quotations at this point in his career was that which served the famous author as a springboard in developing his conception of political relativism: "The democratic principle appears only as national ideal for which the nations must strive; but, given the social realities and the practical necessities that encompass them, no precise type of popular government can be installed." Bolivar looked and argued within himself ever more urgently as he felt himself deviating from the ideals which had inspired his belief in the sound sense of the people. Could the people really administer for the common good that treasury of progress which the ascension of humanity would deposit in their hands? "Will we, the people, be able to maintain in proper equilibrium the heavy burden of a republic? Only angels, not human beings can live free, quiet and happy while exercising all their sovereign power. . . . States fall into extremes, as absolute freedom always leads to absolute power, whereas it is the happy mean between these points that spells supreme social liberty." Bolivar's language grew complicated and rhetorical; his ideas, formerly so clear, now took on a flavor of dangerous ambiguity, and the way lay open to the most different and most contradictory solutions.

In this conflict between his unquestionable democratic convictions and his skepticism about his people's ability to rise above the state of slavery they had known under the colonial regime, Bolivar was, for a moment, disposed to accept that same escape to the throne which had scandalized him in Napoleon. "Only democracy, to my way of thinking, is capable of absolute liberty; but where is the democratic government which at once enjoys united power, prosperity and permanence? On the other hand, have we not seen aristocracies and monarchies welding great and powerful empires together for century after century? Does any government exist that is older than China's? What republic has ever outlasted Sparta and Venice? Did not the Roman Empire conquer the world? Has not France known fourteen centuries of monarchic existence? What land is mightier than England? Ay, all these nations were or are aristocracies and monarchies!" It was at this moment that Bolivar appeared most confusing and self-contradictory.

It may be said that in his lack of faith in the people Bolivar was ignorant of historical dialectics: he accepted as permanent states forms which were in fact only phases, even if they sometimes filled centuries in the universal process of the struggle against tyranny. It was as if all his stay in France were completely erased from his mind, as if the times in which he lived were not still illumined by the French Revolution and the ideals of equality proclaimed in the Code Napoléon. In his admiration for British might, Bolivar forgot that the Britain of his day was not made great by her monarchy and aristocracy but rather by her Magna Charta and her Constitution. Fortunately, however, his monarchical fickleness proved only temporary; invariably in practice he finally turned to the republican solution.

Continuing his *Angostura Message,* Bolivar exposed his political formula to Congress; it embodied the republican principle of the government, with a democratically elected House of Representatives, a technical and hereditary Senate, and a centralized executive. Of the democratic essence he accepted only a limited realization through the House of Representatives. The Senate was to act as a counterpoise; he called it "the basis and soul of the Republic." Thus Simon Bolivar's republic assumed the form of a conservative republic, directed by an intellectual elite, if not by army generals. It was not an ideal solution, as he himself recognized, but in his opinion it offered the only operating formula possible in the period of transition from colony to independent state.

At this time, leaders and partisans in the movement for independence covered all the distance between the two poles of federalism, the utopia of the extreme left, and monarchy, the utopia of the right.

Bolivar was opposed to the federal system, partly, as already shown, because the masses under the Spanish yoke had had no political education, and partly from purely military considerations. Centralization, in effect, had proved useful to his war policy and had contributed to the reconquest of Venezuela, Quito, and Peru. But thereafter, on the contrary, every attempt at federalism had turned to the disadvantage of the progress of the campaign. The future was by its experience to prove Bolivar right in the political field too. After New Granada became the United States of Colombia, there were no less than forty revolutions in twenty-five years. To a people unschooled in the defense of democracy, federalism may appear theoretically a very beautiful thing; but in practice it readily leads to the caudillismo whose defective and disorderly politics mark a whole century of South American history.

Between the federalism proposed by the left and the monarchy beloved of the right, Bolivar sought for middle ground. He believed he had found the compromise when he suggested vesting a continuity in the supreme office, which would protect it against any sudden changes in the government of the country. Besides, it would assure a strong executive, capable of quelling any local uprising under the federalist banner, and at the same time it would spare the new states the commotion and agitation that all too frequently attended popular elections. Though fully realizing the inherent dangers of his formula, Bolivar proposed life tenure for the presidency in the republics he had created, and, going even further, he proposed that the president appoint his own successor. This, he believed, would safeguard the continuity of administration yet avoid hereditary rule, the archevil of the abominated Spanish monarchy.

The statesman in Bolivar was no less great than the warrior. His political intuition and wisdom rise more clearly from the pages of his private correspondence than from the official documents we have cited or from other messages and addresses in which he considered the various opinions found in the different tendencies and groups. These letters, sent to military men and to friends during a campaign which lasted fifteen years, were couched in a clear, precise style; they were utterly without literary ostentation, save when he sought to flatter his correspondent—and succeeded admirably—or when he was addressing ecclesiastical authorities. Then, exceptionally, his language grew pompous and heavily burdened with the most baroque ornamentation.

In his letter to Antonio José de Sucre, dated Guayaquil, May 26, 1823, Bolivar wrote:

> England is the country most interested in this transaction because, from among all free peoples in America and Europe, she seeks to form a league directed against the Grand Alliance, to place herself at the head of these peoples and to command the world. It cannot please England to see a European nation, as strong in character as Spain, owning possessions like Peru in America; England would much prefer Peru to be independent under the weak authority of a shaky government.

In another letter to Colonel Tómas de Heres: "England is blindly for us," he observed. "France will do nothing; nor will the rest of Europe. No man can change the face of America against the will of God, London and ourselves."

Bolivar played his nationalistic trump shrewdly, suffering no personal feeling to mar his diplomatic strategy. A movement arose against the Grand Alliance; actually it was a crusade of the Catholic Church with Bolivar as the first crusader. Why? Because Bolivar needed England, which was fighting against the Grand Alliance, which, in turn, was attempting once again to legitimitize Ferdinand VII's right to the Spanish throne. On the other hand, when it suited his policy, Bolivar did not hesitate to align himself against Ferdinand's enemies in Spain itself. Logically, the Liberator, as patron of American liberty and foe to the Bourbons and to all they stood for in Spain, might have been expected to evince some inclination or at least some concern for the liberal movement in Spain, as represented by the Cortes of Cádiz. Apparently both parties were fighting in the same cause, namely, to shake off the Bourbon yoke and the age-old tyranny which had oppressed both the mother country and the colonies. But Bolivar's cold-blooded purpose to gain sympathy for himself at Rome committed him to a policy of criticism and contempt for the Spanish liberals fighting against his own sworn enemy.

In a letter to Monsignor Lasso, dated Guayaquil, June 14, 1823, Bolivar seized upon the persecution of the Church in Spain to feather the South American nest. "Now," he wrote, "our enemies will tell us that the Pope sets us aside from the community of the faithful, when it is they who set themselves aside from the Church of Rome. I have just read the terrible decrees enacted against the Holy See." (Bolivar here referred to decrees issued in Spain.)

In another letter, this time to Monsignor Jimenez de Enciso, bishop of Popayán, a Spaniard and a realist, Bolivar pursued his policy of captivating the higher Catholic hierarchy as follows: "From people recently arrived from Spain estra Illustrissima may gather information on the antireligious turn which the revolution has taken. I believe that your Illustrious Highness will be bound to recognize our faith by merely glancing at this, our own Constitution." (Bolivar here referred to the Constitution of Cúcuta, issued in Cúcuta, Colombia.)

Here again the politician prevailed upon the thinker. In point of fact, Bolivar's philosophical creed, which he voiced over and over again in letters, in conversations, and in cultural perorations at Bucaramanga corresponded more closely to a religious skepticism, governed by admiration of the Encyclopedists and eighteenth century philosophy. At one moment it seemed as though a doctrinaire rationalism were bringing him to absolute agnosticism. In a letter addressed to Sucre from Chancai, Bolivar, borrowing Voltaire's finest pen, could write: "The surest of all sure things is to doubt."

But Bolivar needed Rome; he must at all costs bring the new nations to a direct understanding with the Vatican, over the head of Madrid. The restoration of Ferdinand VII to the throne of Spain was a severe setback for his policy; but by 1827, when Colombia's ecclesiastical orphanage came to an end and new bishops were nominated, Bolivar was rewarded for his efforts. At last he had assured himself of the support of the Catholic Church, which, to him, meant the mainstay of such governments as attracted the favor of Rome.

Perhaps this led him further than he had intended to go. To please Poe Pius VII, who in a letter dated September, 1822, held out hopes of settling ecclesiastical affairs in South America, Bolivar closed the Masonic lodges, re-established the convents, and abolished the Chair of Public and Constitutional Law in the University of Bogotá, in favor of a Chair of Fundamentals and Apologetics of the Roman Catholic Religion. No wonder Simon Rodriguez, his childhood teacher, his mentor and guide during his formative years in Europe, and the man who taught him to read *Candide* and *The Social Contract,* felt a certain disappointment. The reformer, Jean Jacques of Caracas, still clung to his earliest political idealism; but Bolivar, in language at least, was vastly different from the youth who stood on the Sacred Hill at Rome and swore to set the peoples of South America free.

To be just, he was liberating them from the yoke of Madrid; but he was tinging the epic with conservative and clerical colors which somehow made his old teacher feel melancholy. Trusting that this was but political strategy and that Bolivar was sparring for time, Simon Rodriguez kept his faith in his disciple; Bolivar, for his part, received his old teacher enthusiastically and set him to directing his energies into a program of popular education for the country. Rodriguez's pedagogical plans, a heritage of *Émile,* collapsed before the narrow attiude of the clergy in Colombia, then, as now, one of the most reactionary factions and strongest props of the Roman Catholic Church.

Left to choose between Sucre's methodical warnings against Rodriguez's anticlericalism and his own rooted devotion for his old teacher, Bolivar did not hesitate. Rodriguez could not but feel that the arm which had supported him was now beginning to flag. Disillusioned and robbed of all hope, Rodriguez left the country, somewhat forsaken by his disciple, not in a material sense, but in the moral support of those ideals which had united them so strongly years before.

In conclusion, in spite of surface contradictions in Bolivar's character, no one who has studied his personality again and again can point to the existence of a true, inner contradiction. Deep down in his heart, throughout the evolution of his phenomenal career, Bolivar continued a liberal. Opponents and slanderers have accused him of attempting in his own person to foist an imperialist dictatorship upon the vast lands of Latin America. Possibly at one time, aware of the lack of political maturity in the men about him, he toyed with such an idea. But he did not follow it through. Even after the victory of Ayacucho, which swept him to the height of fame, Bolivar was concerned more with providing a solid organization for the young nations he had carved out with his sword than with consolidating his own position or emphasizing his indispensability. In more than one speech he referred to the "horror" that supreme power inspired in him. On accepting the title of Libertador, the only title he ever consented to accept, his first thought was to found the Order of the Liberators, designed to honor those officers who had distinguished themselves in the struggle for independence.

The meeting of the Congress of Panama in 1826, which marked the first attempt ever made to create a kind of American League of Nations, was brought about by his personal initiative; it reflected anything but a desire to establish either his own dictatorship or the dictatorship of any one of the nations he had helped to create. When Bolivar determined to outline a superstate uniting Colombia, Peru, Bolivia, Argentina, and Chile in a single vast republic bearing the name of the United States of the South, he was moved by pure altruism; he dreaded seeing the young nations involved in petty frontier squabbles or internal disorders that threatened to undermine the foundations of his work of liberation.

It is not in the criticisms of leaders like Santander (who rose in rebellion against the Liberator in his last years) that we must seek a genuine appraisal of Bolivar's worth; such pages lack the generosity and serenity of judgment necessary to solve the complex case of the hero whose name brightens the noblest chapter of South American history.

If Bolivar failed at all, then, quite objectively, his failure lay in his lack of confidence in the people. A real revolutionary can summon the requisite strength to overcome all the obstacles of his times only in the hearts of his people. With less political shrewdness and less double play, and with more faith in the masses of men he had set free, Bolivar would not have died as he did in 1830, after the most agitated life imaginable, watching his gigantic edifice crumble to pieces and uttering these terrible, last words: "I have plowed in the sea."

LORD BYRON

by

ANDRÉ MAUROIS

ANDRÉ MAUROIS

was born in 1885 in Elbeuf, Seine-Inférieure. He was educated in Rouen and Caen. His first book, *The Silence of Colonel Bramble* (1918), had a great popular and critical success, and he found himself, between one day and the next, transformed from a factory official into an author. It has been said that Maurois writes "novelized biographies and autobiographical novels." He is one of the foremost practitioners of the modern biographical method originated by Lytton Strachey. His best-known books are: *Ariel: The Life of Shelley; The Life of Disraeli; Lyautey; Dickens; The Miracle of England; Byron; Tragedy in France.* After the fall of France, he came to America, which he had often visited before.

LORD BYRON
by André Maurois

Exile, when it is connected with great events and accepted with fortitude, gives a poet a strange and durable prestige. Because he is far from his home, he sings of it with a pleasant wistfulness or with a tragic sadness. Would Joachim du Bellay have written *Les Regrets,* those lovely sonnets, had he not been an exile in Rome? Because he is far from his enemies and from the enemies of his country, the exile does write about them scathing satires that, under normal conditions, might have remained unwritten. Would Dante have placed in his *Inferno* some of the men whose crimes he immortalized if he had lived with them, in his native town? Would Victor Hugo have written *Les Châtiments* had he remained in Paris? It is at least doubtful. Byron, more than any other poet, was the creature of exile. To exile he owes not all his glory, for he would have been a glorious poet anyway, but the passionate enthusiasm with which he was loved by some of the young men and by all the women of his times. Solitary, on this foreign background, he appeared much greater than he would have been on the familiar English scene. Not that he was not British to the core; on the contrary, because he was at heart a British peer and a Scottish Calvinist, his figure detached itself with picturesque majesty on the Italian and Greek surroundings in which he passed his last years. Byron was not made by exile; he was certainly magnified by it.

I

He had never been very happy in England. He was born a lame boy and his infirmity, in a country of vigorous and hard men, inspired him with the fear of being laughed at, so that early in life he became shy, aggressive, haughty, and quick to take offense. And it was not only physically, but spiritually that, according to English standards, he felt he was a misfit. He had been brought up by his mother in admiration of the French Revolution. Lady Byron was a ruined aristocrat, and she professed advanced political opinions. To her sister-in-law she wrote: "I am very much interested about the French, but I fancy you and I are on different sides, for I am quite a democrat and I do not think the King, after his treachery and perjury, deserves to be restored." Her son agreed with her and followed the events of the Revolution with passionate eagerness. Later he retained an adoration of Bonaparte, who to him always remained the Soldier of the Republic. He had brought to his school of Harrow a small bust of the First Consul and defended it against other schoolboys who, as English patriots, hated Bonaparte.

At the university it had been his hidden desire to become a leader of men, the center of great things. But surely Byron was not fit to lead British students of that time. Reading and culture, for which he had a sincere though haphazard taste, bored the other undergraduates. They enjoyed drinking and playing. Byron liked cards no better than he liked wine. He attached to women and to love a very un-English importance. So he felt out of it all. Later, when he came to live in London, he found himself alone, a kind of provincial squire, with neither family nor friends. By right of birth, being the sixth Lord Byron, he belonged to English society, yet his tastes, his ideas, his education made him unfit to live in that society. Very soon he realized that nothing remained for him but to leave England, which he did for the first time in 1809.

The Pilgrimage of Childe Harold was not exile, it was just travel. Byron went to Spain, Albania, Greece, Turkey. He loved these lands where he cared not about anybody and where none cared for him. He knew now that, in a strange way, he felt happy as an outlaw. Distance had taught him contempt of the English moral values. Henceforth he would always remember that, if things went askew with him in England, he need not worry. After all, a fortnight of sea voyage would bring him to white islands under a sky ever blue. Yet when the poems he had brought back were hailed in his own country as masterpieces, when he woke to find himself famous, when the most beautiful women in London flocked to him, when lovely, brilliant Caroline Lamb became his mistress, when the prince regent asked to see him, when he found himself in the spring season of 1812 the only subject of curiosity, of conversation and enthusiasm, then he forgot for a while his gloom and his resentment, his hatred of the Tories, and how he despised absurd womankind. He even thought of marriage and Childe Harold actually proposed to handsome, pious Anna Isabella Milbanke whom he called, because she was of a scientific turn of mind, "Princess of Parallelograms."

Had she then accepted him, perhaps he might have settled down in some lovely English country home. But she hesitated, asked time to think it over, as if Byron was not "a slave to impulse." In such cases his heart always "alighted on the nearest perch." It happened unfortunately that the nearest perch, at this time, was his half sister, Augusta Leigh. Incest? Well, was it incest? After all, she was only his half sister. He had not been brought up with her; in fact, he hardly knew her. But he took pleasure in finding himself guilty. It could almost be said that it was Byron, and Byron alone, who, by giving to this love the name of "incest," transformed a lapse into a crime. Then his friends became frightened. They pushed him toward marriage and he came back to the Princess of Parallelograms who, this time, was only too happy to accept him.

The marriage was a disaster. Being virtuous, his wife bored him and he treated her very badly. Very soon, he came back to Augusta and poor Lady Byron, terrified, horrified, asked for a separation. All London was whispering the incredible story. It was in 1815; Napoleon had just been defeated, and Byron, who still saw in him the symbol of freedom, openly lamented the victory of his own country: "Poor fellow," he said, speaking of Bonaparte, "I am damned sorry for him." His conjugal behavior had made him the whipping boy of London society; his political opinions completed his downfall. No one at the time was more unpopular.

Once more he felt and was an outcast. Once more he thought

that the only solution was to become a self-exile. Oh, to be gone, to go back to those white islands under the blue skies, to leave all the rottenness of the world behind, to find peace of mind in Greece or in Turkey! In fact, it seemed that life in England would soon become impossible for him. On his way into the House of Lords he was insulted by some bystanders and, in the House itself, none spoke to him, except Lady Holland. The Tory journals were comparing him to Nero, to Henry VIII, to the devil himself. Nor did the Whigs defend him. His private life was a public scandal. Not that the morals of the time were much better than his, but the trouble with Byron was that he added cynicism to laxity. Hypocrisy is a homage that vice offers to virtue. Byron offered no such homage and Virtue did not like him. When Byron and Augusta Leigh entered the ballroom at Lady Jersey's, the room emptied before them. The men were implacable and some of them stepped aside to avoid touching Byron's hand. He stood alone in a corner, folded his arms, and looked in disdain at the hostile crowd. He knew them well, these men and women, and he hated them heartily. They were no better than he was, yet they objected to him. He saw himself driven from his own country by a social ostracism far more definite and brutal than a legal decree. So he decided, if England declared it time for him to go, he would set forth again on his pilgrimage. A few days later, he was on the shore at Dover, writing a farewell poem:

> Here's a sigh to those who love me,
> And a smile to those who hate;
> And, whatever skies above me,
> Here's a heart for every fate.

The noise and flurry of departure sustained him until he was actually on board. But once there he looked very unhappy. Shortly after nine o'clock the gangway was pulled in. It was a rough sea with a headwind. When the vessel came past the jetty Byron raised his cap and waved it, in farewell to his friends.

II

Byron, as he was setting forth on his new pilgrimage, was gloomier than ever before. He had naught of hope left. He had tried to love and Love had been his undoing. He had tried glory and had found it disappointing. He knew now that action was no less futile than glory. Yet he remained at heart the passionate boy who had loved freedom and worshiped Bonaparte because he thought Bonaparte was a Soldier of Freedom. He called himself a liberal, partly perhaps because the English Tories had been so very hard on him; partly because he was a cripple and sided with all unfortunates; partly, at last, because there was in him a heroic strain and a desire to live and die a hero. And for what could he die, now that his country repulsed him, if not for liberty?

Shelley, who met him in Switzerland and became for a while his constant companion, found in this liberal Lord a fashionable and aristocratic tinge. Shelley loved mankind; Byron hated it, but all the same was ready to die for it if it could be done with a flourish, and become a theme for brilliant poetry. Madame de Staël, whom he visited, told him: "You ought not to have disputes with the world. The world is too strong for an individual." She had every reason to know, and she was right. Byron had wished to set aside all British conventions. The difficulty was that these conventions were solidly entrenched in his own heart. Of all his detractors, none was more severe than George Gordon, Lord Byron. Whether he liked it or not, Byron remained an English gentleman. His body was self-exiled; his mind was still in England. What the Swiss or the Italians thought of him, he did not care very much. They were just foreigners, part of the local scenery. What the English thought of him, this was what he wondered about all the time. When Hobhouse and Scrope Davies, both typical Englishmen, came to see him, they brought him English toilet powders, English drugs, and this essentially British product: an apparent contempt for sentimentality, but they also brought with them English prejudices, English ideas, English judgments. To be an exile would be easy if one could forget one's country. This, no decent man can do and Byron, in spite of his follies, was at the bottom a decent fellow.

When he left Switzerland for Italy, he plunged into politics again. The fall of Napoleon had once more subjected the unfortunate Italians to foreign domination. Spies were everywhere. Liberals and patriots banded in secret societies, and Byron immediately found himself in touch with Italian liberal circles. Was he not the archrebel and a persecuted radical? When he came to Venice, the Venetian Republic existed no more. An Austrian government ruled the province. But life was free and easy and, at times, he managed to forget entirely "that tight little island." Then suddenly he met some English friend, or someone brought him an English poem, and the exile again felt homesick.

> England! with all thy faults, I love thee still,
>   I said at Calais, and have not forgot it;
> I like to speak and lucubrate my fill;
>   I like the government (but that is not it);
> I like the freedom of the press and quill;
>   I like the *Habeas Corpus* (when we've got it);
> I like a parliamentary debate,
>   Particularly when 'tis not too late.
>
> I like the taxes, when they're not too many;
>   I like a seacoal fire, when not too dear;
> I like a beefsteak, too, as well as any;
>   Have no objection to a pot of beer;
> I like the weather when it is not rainy,
>   That is, I like two months of every year,
> And so, God save the Regent, Church and King!
>   Which means that I like all and everything.
>
> Our standing army, and disbanded seamen,
>   Poor's rate, Reform, my own, the nation's debt.
> Our little riots, just to show we're free men,
>   Our trifling bankruptcies in the Gazette,
> Our cloudy climate, and our chilly women,
>   All these I can forgive, and those forget,
> And greatly venerate our recent glories,
>   And wish they were not owing to the Tories.

The lines were humorous; the sentiment was sincere. Yes, he loved England dearly still and, like most Britishers, while he enjoyed the sun of Venice, he regretted the London fogs.

Of course, he was in love all the time. He liked the simplicity of Italian women. They deceived their husbands as a matter of course, and to the Calvinist Puritan, who was a confirmed sinner but felt so strongly about it, such innocent freedom was refreshing. At first he contented himself with minor adventures, but very soon, in Countess Guiccioli, he found a passionate Italian woman and she fell deeply in love with the beautiful English poet, who was such a success in Venice.

Loyal to the code of her society, Teresa Guiccioli was in search of no fleeting adventure, but of a permanent escort. It was a serious problem for a young Italian woman. One could take a husband in a moment, but to take a lover needed thought. Before long her husband would be taking her away to Ravenna, where he owned estates. Would Byron follow her? If he did not, she would lose face with her friends of the Venetian drawing rooms.

As a matter of fact, he did follow her. The weather was hot, the roads dusty. To ride, in such a climate, was no pleasure. "If I was not the most constant of men," he said, "I should now be swimming from the Lido." However, he was the most constant of men and, instead of swimming in the Adriatic, he was following a young woman as her cavaliere servante. Happily, he found in Ravenna a town made to delight him. Here Francesca had lived; hither Dante had been exiled. There was some sort of consolation in the fact of being an exile in the same town as Dante.

Teresa was ill; he installed himself at her bedside; he was enslaved and happy. He was growing attached to her. Was she not an honorable conquest? A Countess Gamba in her own right, pretty, and no fool; at least that was Byron's opinion. We agree about the prettiness; about the foolishness of the lady we have our own ideas. But what did it matter? She had fashioned a heroic image of him, which was exactly what he needed. Refusing to regard him as a cynic, she would have him chivalrous, tender, desperately in love, everything women have always wished their lovers to be. And he played up to this because, really, Countess Guiccioli's imaginary Byron was rather like the Byron he himself had loved long ago, the brave boy who wanted to fight the tyrants.

He could not help feeling a growing sense of the brevity of this life. He was thirty-one, and what was he doing? Making love? A mediocre occupation when what he wanted was action . . . action, action, action. But what sort of action? Should he busy himself in England with the reform agitation, then at its peak? What would be the use? He was far from England, communications were slow, and no one there took any interest in his thoughts and ideas.

At one time he thought of going to South America. He clipped from newspapers the offers made by the government of Venezuela to foreigners desirous of settling there, and Bolivar, the Liberator, was one of his heroes. "I might still be a decent citizen," he said, "and found a house and a family better than the former . . . There is no freedom in Europe, that is certain. Europe is a worn-out portion of the world . . ." Why not Venezuela? Why not Bolivar?

But his friends did not take his project seriously. This exasperated Byron and, to prove that he was capable of action, he became a member of a small group of Italian friends of liberty, and a source of anxiety to the spies of the government. There were all sorts of reports to the police about him. For the freedom of Italy he was ready to give his life, cheerfully, because he loved Italy and freedom, and also because he did not love life.

It was the year 1820 and Europe, stunned at first by the defeat of Napoleon, was beginning to recover consciousness. Everywhere there were riots against reactionary governments. In Ravenna, the walls of the city were scrawled with: "Long live the Republic! . . . Down with the Pope!" Byron was delighted, wrote to all his friends bidding them send him salt and gunpowder, and he organized an arsenal of one hundred and fifty guns at the Palazzo Guiccioli.

Count Guiccioli was ready to accept the fact that his wife had a lover; that was the custom of the country. He was even ready to take his wife's lover as a paying guest; that was another custom. But, surely, who ever heard of a lover piling up firearms in his bedroom and compromising a respectable house? Every drawer in Byron's sleeping quarters was cramped with explosive proclamations. In the end, the count ordered his wife to choose between himself and Byron. She chose Byron, of course, and from that moment he had Teresa on his hands. He loved her in his own way, but she bored him often. He did not want to fritter away his life at the knees of a woman. Oh, how he would have liked to show England, that had treated him so badly as a man, and was beginning to look away from him as a poet, that he was much more than a poet, that he was a great man of action! If he could show his friend Hobhouse, so exasperatingly patronizing, that he, Byron, had courage, physical courage, military courage! His greatest hope was now for an Italian revolution in which he might play a leading part.

All through the winter he conspired with the brother of his beloved Teresa: Pietro Gamba. Byron was ready to pay with his person and his purse. Did the Italian liberals need money? He would give it. Did they need arms? He would buy them. Yet he did not quite believe in the cause. It is a characteristic trait of Byron that enthusiasm, in him, always coexisted with an inexhaustible common sense. He was doubtful of the success of the Italians, if they could not achieve unity among themselves. And, unhappily, events justified his forebodings. All the minor insurrections were crushed. The people of Ravenna had to abandon their plans, and the police drew up lists of suspects. Of course, they did not dare touch Byron, who was an Englishman and a lord. But they banished the Gambas, brother and sister. As to Byron, he became an exile by proxy.

III

The Countess Guiccioli accepted exile, but not the loss of her lover. Where would he agree to follow her? After consultation with him she went to Pisa, where Byron found several friends, including Shelley, and a Greek prince: Mavrocordato. Another inmate of the house was a curious personage whose name was Trelawny. He had been a sailor, a deserter, a pirate, and he exasperated Byron by the tales, true or false (mostly false), he told of his life. Once more Byron would have liked to show this boastful braggart that he was capable of action.

When, in March, 1822, Prince Mavrocordato learned that there was a Greek insurrection against the Turks, and set off to place himself at the head of the insurgents, Byron envied him. With his friends Shelley and Leigh Hunt he was now publishing a magazine called *The Liberal*. He did not get on well with his coeditors and he was tired of the whole thing. Teresa Guiccioli had suddenly altered and aged. He began to tell everybody around him, and even to write to his friends in England: "I mean to return to Greece and shall, in all probability, die there."

Nobody in his group took any project of Byron's seriously, whatever it might be. How often he had veered from Venezuela to the United States, from England to Greece, his imagination landing for a moment on each of those dreams. "My heart alights on the nearest perch." So did his mind. So did his courage. Yet this Greek project seemed more enduring than the others; not that Byron had any hatred of the Turks. Indeed, he had rather liked them. But there was the prestige of Greece, the desire to show that he was something besides a poet, the will to be the first man somewhere, the Washington or Aristides of a movement, the leader in talent and truth. He had always regarded himself as a born soldier or statesman, who was deprived by bodily infirmity from the life for which he was intended. "If I live ten years longer, you will see that it is not over with me. I do not mean in literature, for that is nothing, but you will see that I shall do something that will puzzle the philosophers of all ages."

But he did not want only redemption in the eyes of the world. He wanted the salvation of Byron in Byron's own soul. In this Greek adventure everything seemed easy. In England, to be a revolutionary would have meant accepting strange bedfellows. In Greece, his prejudices as an English lord did not conflict with his desires for the freedom of a foreign race. He felt that, if he played this hand out, he would be, for reasons connected with classical education, supported by English public opinion. Hobhouse himself, his faithful English friend, was interested in the Greek adventure and so Byron proceeded with preparations for his departure.

There was one very serious opposition to meet with and it came from Teresa Guiccioli. She had given up everything to follow him; surely he was not going to give her up. "If he wanted to go to Greece," said she, "she would follow. It would not be the first time she would fight for her liberty." But he did not want her to go. Indeed, it was to a large extent to leave her behind that he wanted to go. He decided to take with him Trelawny, Gamba, and eight servants. He equipped a small boat, took along horses, arms, munitions. He really believed he was heading for death. But would not a soldier's death be for him the best and atone for all his sins? "I have hopes that the cause will triumph but, whether it does or not, still honour must be minded as strictly as milk diet. I trust to observe both."

He joined Mavrocordato in Missolonghi. It was a fishing town, built just above the level of the sea. Missolonghi was surrounded with marshes, yet it had a curious, inhuman charm. Half swallowed by the sea, it looked like a place cut off from the world. This was the exile of exiles. But Byron liked the silvery mirror of the lagoon and the dark string of islands.

The situation was not good. Mavrocordato was an honest man, but he had no authority over his men. Many of them were mercenaries who were not interested in a war for independence. Byron had to take them into his pay. The weather was frightful. Byron and Gamba discussed a scheme to take the neighboring town of Lepanto. Byron wanted to lead the attack in person: "Above all, these semi-barbarians should never entertain the least suspicion of your personal courage."

Curiously enough, this poet was much more of a practical soldier than the rest of his companions. In fact, they were all amazed at his kindness, courage, and good will. There was nothing left of his pedantry and affectation. Suddenly he showed what had always been in him: greatness of character. He knew the adventure would be neither dazzling nor picturesque. In fact, he had not come in search of adventures, but to do honorably an honorable and tedious task. Poet and soldier had triumphed over the dandy and the coxcomb. Would it be so for the rest of his life? Would he prove capable, if ever he went back to England, to remain the man he was in this last and worst of exiles? This was difficult to foresee. On the day of his thirty-sixth birthday, he wrote a few verses:

> 'Tis time this heart should be unmoved,
> Since others it has ceased to move:
> Yet, though I cannot be beloved,
>   Still let me love! . . .
>
> The sword, the banner and the field,
> Glory and Greece, around me see!
> The Spartan, born upon his shield,
>   Was not more free.
>
> Awake! (not Greece—she *is* awake!)
> Thy life-blood track its parent lake,
> Awake, my spirit! think thou *whom*
>   And then strike home.
>
> Tread those reviving passions down,
> Unworthy manhood!—unto thee
> Indifferent should the smile or frown
>   Of beauty be.
>
> If thou regrett-st thy youth, why live?
> The land of honourable death
> Is here:—up to the field, and give
>   Away thy breath!
>
> Seek out—less often sought than found—
> A soldier's grave, for thee the best;
> Then look around, and choose thy ground,
>   And take thy rest.

It had often been prophesied to him that he would die in his thirty-seventh year. Up to the middle of February he continued to keep a good face on things. The appointed date for the assault on Lepanto drew near. The mercenaries behaved so badly that Byron became angry and dismissed them. But he was sick at heart. This meant the end of the campaign he had prepared so carefully.

During the late afternoon of that day he felt ill, and collapsed.

When he came to, he heard the word "epilepsy" and began to fear for his reason.

"Do you suppose that I wish for life?" he said to Dr. Millingen. "I have grown heartily sick of it, and shall welcome the hour I depart from it. Why should I regret it? Can it afford me any pleasure? . . . Few men can live faster than I did. I am, literally speaking, a young old man. Hardly arrived at manhood, I had attained the zenith of fame. Pleasure, I have known under every form it can present itself to mortals. I have traveled, satisfied my curiosity, lost every illusion . . . But the apprehension of two things now haunts my mind. I picture myself slowly expiring on a bed of torture, or terminating my days like Swift— a grinning idiot! Would to Heaven the day were arrived in which, rushing, sword in hand, on a body of Turks, and fighting like one weary of existence, I shall meet immediate, painless death . . ."

For a while he felt better. On April 9th he received letters from England with good news of the Greek loan. Almost two and a half million pounds had been subscribed; he would be able to organize a new artillery brigade and an infantry corps of two thousand men. Given fresh heart by the news, he decided to go out riding with Gamba that day, in spite of threatening weather. Three miles out from the town, he was caught by the rain. On his way home, when they reached a fisherman's hut, Gamba remarked that it was rash to sit still in a boat with soaking clothes, and that for once he would be wiser to return on horseback. "I should make a pretty soldier indeed," said Byron, "if I were to care for such a trifle!" So they left their horses and came back to Missolonghi by boat across the lagoon.

A couple of hours after his return Byron was seized with shivering and complained of fever and rheumatic pains. In the evening Gamba found him lying stretched out. "I suffer a great deal of pain," he said. "I do not care for death, but these agonies I cannot bear."

A violent hurricane, with a howling sirocco, was sweeping over Missolonghi. Rain was falling in torrents. Parry had seen that Byron was seriously ill and wanted to send him to Zante, where he could have better attention; but he had to drop the plan, as no ship could be put to sea. For several days the doctors obstinately declared that Byron's illness was merely a chill, and in no way grave. His valet Fletcher's view was different. "I am sure, my lord," said he, "that you never had a cold of so serious a nature." "I think I never had," said Byron.

During the night the fever and restlessness grew worse. He was delirious. Millingen threatened him with brain troubles if he did not allow himself to be bled, and obtained his consent. He gave them one of those "under-looks" which, in the Childe Harold days, had sent tremors through the women in the London drawing rooms, and held out his arm, saying, "Come, you are, I see, a damned set of butchers. Take away as much blood as you will, but have done with it."

On the 17th he was twice bled. He begged the doctors not to plague him with their continual demands for blood. "Your efforts to preserve my life will be in vain," said Byron to Millingen. "Die I must: I feel it. Its loss I do not lament, for to terminate my wearisome existence I came to Greece. My wealth, my abilities, I devoted to her cause. Well: there is my life to her . . ."

During this Easter Day he was still able to read a few letters, and even to translate one written in Greek. In the late afternoon all who were at his bedside realized that the end was drawing near. Fletcher and Gamba had to go out; they were in tears. Tita remained, because Byron was holding his hand, but he turned away his head to hide his tears. Byron gazed at him fixedly and said in Italian, half smiling, "Oh! questa è una bella scena!" Immediately after that he fell into delirium, and began calling out, now in Italian, now in English, as if he were advancing to the attack: "Forward! Courage! Follow my example! Don't be afraid! . . ."

About six in the evening he said, "I want to go to sleep now," and turning over, he fell into a sleep from which he never woke. He seemed powerless to move a limb, but the on-lookers observed symptoms of suffocation, and a rattle in his throat. Every now and then Fletcher and Tita raised his head, but he seemed to feel nothing. The doctors applied leeches to dispel this lethargy. Blood trickled down his face. For twenty-four hours he remained in this condition. On the evening of the

19th, in the twilight, Fletcher was keeping watch beside his master and saw him open his eyes, then shut them instantly. "My God!" he said, "I fear his Lordship is gone . . ." The doctors felt the pulse. "You are right," they said. "He is gone."

A few moments before, a terrible storm had broken over Missolonghi. Night was falling; lightning and thunderclaps came one on the top of another in the gloom. Far off, across the lagoon, the fleeting gleam of flashes lit the dark outlines of the islands. A scudding rain lashed the windows of the houses. The fatal tidings had not yet reached the Greek soldiers and shepherds who had taken refuge indoors; but like their ancestors they believed that the death of a hero came heralded by portents, and as they listened to the prodigious fury of this thunder they murmured to each other, "Byron is dead . . ."

IV

It is a beautiful death scene. Beautiful because Byron died courageously and because he died for a great cause. Beautiful also because of the background of the silvery lagoon and of the moral solitude of the dying hero. He was a great poet; exile had turned him into a great man. Had he died "amongst silk and jewels," who, in Europe, would have mourned him? But because he had died in Missolonghi, all the young men of Europe cried when they heard of his death.

Alas! poor Byron! He was a fellow of infinite good faith and courage. Yet the events of his life had been such that, up to this last scene, he had never been given a chance to show his mettle. But did it matter? It is the last scene, and the death in exile, that remains in the memory of men. He who will lose his life will win it. Hamlet and Don Quixote had long fought in Byron's soul. Then they had both agreed to take a supreme risk. The reward was, and is, the Byron legend. To us the real Byron is no more the lover of Caroline Lamb, or the skeptic who scoffed at Shelley, but the dying hero at Missolonghi, and the poet remains, for ever, "such as in himself eternity changes him."

HEINRICH HEINE

by

H. E. JACOB

H. E. JACOB

was born in Berlin in 1889 and lived in Berlin and Vienna. He studied history, philosophy, and music. After the First World War—he had protested in one of his books against the stupidity of murder—he wrote several historical plays. His modern novels—*The Maiden of Aix, Jacqueline and the Japanese,* and *Blood and Celluloid*—were very successful and published in America. His *History of Coffee* made him known as a historian. Other books were published in ten languages. For several years he was on the staff of the *Berliner Tageblatt,* the great leftist German newspaper. As soon as the Nazis came to power they burned his books and for a year confined him in the concentration camps of Dachau and Buchenwald. After being rescued he went to America, where he finished his last book, *Johann Strauss, Father and Son,* published in 1940.

HEINRICH HEINE
by H. E. Jacob

I

EARLY in the nineteenth century a young man named Heinrich Heine was compelled to go into business. But he did not like the idea. At that time European youngsters did not want to become businessmen.

His parents, who were well-to-do but not rich, had sent him to good schools in Düsseldorf-on-the-Rhine. Here the young man learned who Alexander the Great was, read Vergil and the Bible, and committed to memory much of Homer and Shakespeare and the godlike Goethe.

In the morning, before leaving for his classes, the shy, blond lad studied. He learned that the mind had created the world and still held it together. The bun on the breakfast table was held together too, yet where the baker obtained his flour, and how wheat got from the field to the mill, he did not know and could not possibly know.

In Germany tradesmen were held in contempt, as they were in all of Europe. In order to rise socially a boy might become a landowner, an officer in the army, or a lawyer, but he might never become a merchant.

The Heine family were merchants themselves, however, and knew that their money had brought them what social standing they had. They made Heinrich go into business, but when they found that he cut his office hours short and kept notebooks full of poetry in his desk they only smiled. Their boy could afford to waste his time.

That was how Heinrich Heine spent his youth. Thousands of young men, also born in 1797, spent their youth in the same way in German middle-class homes. Yet there was a difference. The Heines were Jews, a foreign tribe in Germany, without full citizens' rights. Since their son could not become a landowner, an officer, or a lawyer, it was not such a bad idea to let him become a businessman.

But why should he not take up a free profession and become a writer? Why should he not write plays—and, backed by some money, even live on that? His conversation in salons was famous. He could imbue a single word with stores of meaning. He was a clever dialectician and remarkably fearless. His interests were in words and ideas alone, but the scope of his interests at eighteen was as wide as most men's at thirty. There was every reason to predict a highly gratifying future for him in the world of books, of the stage, and of the press.

Time itself favored his ambitions. The old curse of being a Jew lost its effect. On March 11, 1812, the last memory of ghetto life died away in Germany's most prominent state. Equal rights for Jews in Prussia! It was as if a tunnel had been broken through from two ends. At one end a great humanitarian had been laboring and spading, the philosopher Moses Mendelssohn. From the other end of the wall a hundred digging spades sounded their welcome. The Germans themselves dug the tunnel to meet the Jews. Their nineteenth century feeling had been awakened by Lessing, the dramatist, with his *Nathan the Wise,* and by Kant, the philosopher.

Enlightenment became the fashion. Whether people liked the Jews was not important. They liked the gesture of being enlightened and unbiased, of making the ghettos only a horrible memory. This gesture remains beautiful even though the German governments were in a hurry to make the Jews citizens before the final war against Napoleon. Napoleon had freed the Jews in France, and the Germans feared their Jews might take the French side with their money and sympathy.

All the circumstances worked together to foreshadow a bright future for all these "freed slaves of the European order" and also for Heine, who was one of them.

II

At this moment young Heinrich Heine was struck as if by a stone. (There is no better way to describe it.) He fell in love with his cousin without having his affections returned. To have his love not returned was an incomprehensible monstrosity: to feel that he possessed everything, wanted to give it away, and that this present was rejected.

Young Heine hungered for a response to his love. It was a hunger no less real than the hunger for bread. And there was something even worse: every unhappy lover temporarily loses his freedom. How would young Heine bear this—the man whose very watchword was: Freedom at any cost? Slavery did not suit him. This Werther catastrophe was something terrible to him.

Amalie, the daughter of a rich uncle, a frigid, haughty girl, lived in a castle in Ottensen, outside the gates of Hamburg. Heine was uneasy on his visits to Amalie, yet his tongue was eloquent with Homer, Shakespeare, and all his literary heroes. It was the wrong approach.

To change Amalie's indifference Heine would have had to be a more colorful and daring lover. But he suffered from migraine and indigestion. Every excitement affected his health. "A little man of dwarfish figure with a pale, uninteresting face," the student Eduard Wedekind, who admired Heine sincerely, called him a few years later, in 1824.

For the usual boy, unreciprocated love is like an influenza at worst, which confines him for a few months to the bed of Weltschmerz. After that he gets up as if nothing had happened. He becomes an economist, a preacher, a physician, or a lawyer of distinction. After a couple of years he does not even remember her name—was it Kaethe or Grete?

But for Heine the memory of having been repudiated was a serious sickness he could never forgive or forget. After forty years of struggle, of fame and other mental problems, that old wound still festered.

At the time, Heine began to hate the wealthy of Hamburg. This hatred, first directed against the merchants in his family, became a puerile anger against the entire Hamburgian Jewry. To the boy every Hamburgian, "Jew and Christian," appeared a chaffering dealer. It was almost the same scurrilous feeling the Byron held against the English or Hoelderlin against the Germans.

Heine's revenge upon his Amalie would be forgotten today had it not caused a by-product: his lyric poetry. Heine had been writing poetry long before, but only for exercise. Now he wrote the first "Heine poems."

> It is the same old story
> That ever seems new again,
> And when it happens to someone
> It breaks his heart in twain.

With these lines and this mood the revolution of German lyric poetry arrived.

III

A brand-new feeling, witticism mingled with sadness, characterized all the young Heine's work. Heine was a seeker of freedom. A desire for truth raged in his mind, directed not against emotionalism or religion, but against the position usurped by both in this world of realism. Heine, therefore, is greater when he shows no pity for himself or others—in poems of disillusion.

It is wrong to say that poetry must preserve illusions. Cynicism is as poetic as romanticism. If, in Heine's famous "Nordsee" poem, the dreamer, engulfed in his wistful fantasies, nearly topples overboard and is addressed by the captain: "Doctor, what the devil are you doing?"—this does not destroy the poetic mood but is a legitimate further expression of it. The Heine who is attracted by an illusionary water world and the realistic Heine who does not want to drown—they both exist, side by side.

Being a true romantic, he is too restless. Heine the poet emigrated restlessly from fashion to fashion, from philosophy to philosophy. He instantly dismissed what he considered untrue or inappropriate for him. Like a nomad he rushed through the different forms of art. Nothing could make him stay. He could not write songs of the forest like the great, timeless Eichendorff, so he visited the salons. He could not stand the salons either, the "smooth, polite shirtcuffs." He wanted to return to simplicity, to "folk poetry"—instead, he drew back the latch on greater complexity, he opened the door to politics.

From politics he emigrated to philosophy, from philosophy to religion, and from there to the only certainty—art.

Yet he never had the lordly feeling of being a traveler. He never relaxed on his travels, as Goethe did. And with his changing attitude toward everything he sought, with homelessness his only permanent attribute, he emigrated at the end of his life into the last homelessness—death. His eternal seeking and dissatisfaction reveal to us the first poet who was a truly modern character and the first truly modern character who was also a poet.

IV

Freedom! Freedom! Freedom! Long before Heine assailed the political slaveholders of this world he was shaking the iron bars of inherited faith. What the Jews and Christians had done was to put up large cages, "joy-killing systems," just to scare people, he said. The Jews were still lugging along their Moses, the father-god with the birch rod, who had saved them from the Egyptians in olden times and who now kept on cashing gratitude from the poor people as if it were a check.

And Christianity too seemed to Heine a failure. It ought to have realized long since that it could not govern human relations. Heine resented Christianity not only for this failure, but also for its tendency to make the world uglier wherever possible. The Jewish religion had banned the making of any likeness of God and this was a pity, because a Jewish Zeus would be much more beautiful than the Invisible. Christianity violated this law, but when making images of its god it depicted him as "an ugly sufferer, a crucified."

Yet Heine was a Jew and a Christian to a degree he did not realize himself, with a vigor that broke from deep within his heart into his outer life: He could not bear to see people suffering from injustice.

Long before the student Heinrich Heine had read a single line by Saint-Simon or heard of Fourier he had strong social instincts. One day in Goettingen he saw two of his fellow students, noble Junkers from Hanover, give a few dollars to a fellow to run a race on foot against them on horseback. It was merely a joke, and the runner could have given back the money— yet what a picture, what an image formed in Heine's mind. "The fellow ran, pale as death, wearing a red jacket, and the well-fed young nobleman galloped close behind him in the swirling dust on tall horses, whose hoofs repeatedly hit the panting man, and a man it was."

V

Out of this picture lightning struck the poet. Thunderstrokes followed. When he traveled in Poland he saw a Polish peasant standing before his squire, "a picture of obedience with only the wagging tail missing." This sudden realization of intolerable oppression, this dazzling, understanding compassion, never died as long as he lived. His blood and his mind inherited it from Moses, from the Prophets, from Christ.

And though he might for years not be aware of his Jewish blood and might ridicule his forefathers—he wanted instead to be a Greek artist and a worshiper of Hellenic beauty—he was something quite in line: a socialist. He may, of course, have been so intense a socialist because his aesthetic sense told him that Zeus, Athene, and Aphrodite were more beautiful than Moses and Christ. How could there be beauty on earth before justice for everyone had been established? He was furious that behind the frustrated happiness of the millions, behind the hunger of the starving, beauty and art had to wait in vain.

After being unsuccessful in business he gave it up to study law. But even the law disgusted him. He was horrified by the Roman principles, which, he said, had been "thought up only to furnish robbers with a legal title to their swag." Canonical law and the Prussian Land Law were just as bad. They all taught only how to justify having possessions. "Possess and you live within the law," the great Schiller scorned in his mighty trilogy,

Wallenstein. What more could be dreamed of and wished for than to give possessions to everyone so that all might live within the law? This, however, was revolution!

When, in the summer of 1830, Heine was lying on the beach at Norderney and watching the waves that rolled on vainly, the news of the French Revolution arrived. The French people had risen. The Bourbons had been driven out and a constitutional monarchy set up. It was again July and the world rejoiced as it had for the Revolution forty years before. With Louis Philippe, Paris had donned the Jacobin cap. Heine got up with a laugh and decided to live in Paris. . . .

"I had done much and suffered much, and when the sun of the July Revolution arose in France I had become very weary, and needed some recreation. Also, my native air was every day more unhealthy for me. . . . It often seemed to me as if the sun were a Prussian cockade; at night I dreamed of a hideous black eagle, which gnawed my liver, and I was very melancholy."

At this time Heine was neither attacked by German reaction nor forced into exile. He threw down the political gantlet of his own free will.

The culture of an epoch is characterized not only by its friends but by its enemies as well. The enemies of freedom in Germany were by no means barbarians. Heine met no Hitler or Goebbels. He would have been unable to think that such people existed. His chief enemy was Prince Metternich, a man of high personal culture, the founder of the Holy Alliance.

For forty years this Austrian premier had stifled democracy in any form. His tragic error was to see democracy as a kind of demagogism. Otherwise he had clear conceptions. After the Napoleonic bloodletting he wanted peace. Peace was guaranteed by the monarchies that had spread over Europe and made friends with each other. For this reason even *nationalism* seemed to be a crime "bordering on bestiality" (as the dramatist Grillparzer, Metternich's spokesman, put it). Metternich would have buried Hitler in the fortress Landsberg for life.

Unfortunately, however, there were not only rebels in Metternich's fortresses but Italian dreamers, Greek patriots, Poles who believed that "Poland was not yet lost," and German students who tried to present the bill for the battle of Leipzig to their princes. Yet the skeptic Metternich had ruled that nothing should be changed. Not because he found the status quo perfect but because he distrusted innovations.

Heine's biographers nowhere emphasize the unselfishness which Heine had already demonstrated in the fall of 1819 by taking the side of the German students. In their ranks were not only honest lovers of freedom but ruffians who expected from German freedom first of all a pogrom.

German students share with the middle class the doubtful credit of having started in 1817 the first persecution of Jews in the greater German Reich. It was supposed to be directed against the "war profiteer," Rothschild. In fact, it was directed against the rights granted to the Jews in 1812. Large parts of the population wanted to have them rescinded. But the government, headed by the Prussian reactionary, Chancellor Hardenberg, restored order. The mob was awed and entered into submission for another hundred years. But many of the Jewish intelligentsia went over to the conservatives.

Heine, however, was not to be blinded. As an undaunted foe of the German Police State and a fighter for the freedom of the people, he passed through the twenties of the century. He did not become a deserter, not even when some rowdies among the students—not knowing that he was a Jew—made up in his presence a "proscription list of Jews and Frenchmen." He regarded this as an infantile disease that someday would disappear in the fresh air of parliamentary government. Gentz, the writer of the conservatives, thought differently. "Any feudalism, even of a mediocre order, is welcome to me if it liberates me from the rule of the mob, the so-called scientists, the students, and the newspaper writers."

Heine belonged to the fourth of these categories. He answered the conservatives in pointed ripostes. His enemies, including Gentz, had long since been reading his skeptical poems with delight. Yet when he hurled his lances from Paris and parliamentary France—and they shattered what they hit—his enemies mobilized against him.

He had been living abroad for five years when they throttled his work. In December, 1835, the Frankfort Bundestag, on the action of denouncers, issued an edict which urged the governments of the German states to ban the works of great men like Heinrich Heine and Ludwig Boerne, and of minor writers like Gutzkow, Laube, Wienbarg, and Theodor Mundt. It also recommended persecuting the authors.

By one stroke the happily emigrated Heine had become an involuntary exile and a poor man. He had lived thus far on German royalties.

VI

It is very true that no Prussian government could ever have forgiven what Heine had said and written in Paris.

"Never," he wrote, "has a people been more cruelly scorned by its government. A handful of Junkers, with no better knowledge than that of fraudulent horse dealing, cardsharping, dice throwing and other boorish tricks, good only for duping peasants at the country fair: these Junkers fancy they can by such means fool a whole nation, a nation that has invented gunpowder and the art of printing." He lashed at the foolishness of the German princes of the Federation who, though their lands were already swallowed by Prussia, were still trying to snatch little pieces of territory from neighbor potentates. "They are like thieves who pick each others' pockets on their way to the gallows."

Austria, Heine explained, had always been an open enemy of German freedom. For three centuries she had remained true to herself: the same system that once had fought the Reformation now was fighting liberalism. But Austria was a foe that deserved human respect. Prussia was different and already brazenly planning—Heine wrote this prophetically in 1832—to grab the crown of the German Empire. "So far, however, the light-fingered Hohenzollerns have not succeeded in pocketing the crown of Charlemagne and adding it to their swag of so many Saxon and Polish crown jewels."

Heine had always been a good hater. In Paris he sometimes became clairvoyant about his own hate. He wrote: "It is with apprehension that I have always watched the Prussian eagle.

While others extolled its daring, looking toward the sun, I was the more observant of its claws. I did not trust this Prussia, this lanky, bigoted martinet. . . . I disliked this *philosophical-Christian soldiery,* this mixture of Berlin white beer, lies, and sand. Disgusting, most disgusting, sanctimonious Prussia, this Tartuffe among the states."

And again: "This Prussia, she knows how to make use of her people. She steals advantage even from her revolutionaries. For her political comedies she needs actors of every color . . . Thus she has used during the last few years her most zealous demagogues to preach all over the country that all of Germany must become Prussian. . . . It is outrageous and vicious, this using of philosophers and theologians, who are supposed to influence the plain people, and are now forced to disgrace themselves publicly *by betraying reason and God.*"

Is it not the intellectual and moral tragedy of today's Prussianism of which Heine speaks? But this was written in 1832.

In 1834 he wrote prophetically: "The German revolution will not prove any milder or gentler because it was preceded by the Kantian *Critique.* . . . Christianity has in some degree subdued the Germanic joy of battle, but it could not destroy it. And when the cross falls to pieces, then will break forth again the ferocity of the old combatants, the insane berserker rage whereof northern poets have said and sung. . . . When you hear the trampling of feet and the clashing of arms . . . there will be played in Germany a drama compared with which the French Revolution will seem but an innocent idyl."

Although Heine never witnessed the horrors of our time, he was, nevertheless, fighting for our kind of civilization, against the Germanic trend toward nihilism, Pan-Germanism, mysticism, and militarism—against Hitlerism.

And more than one hundred years before Warsaw's fall in 1939, Heine wrote about another collapse of Poland: "Finally, when Warsaw fell, the soft, pious cloak which Prussia had draped so beautifully around herself also fell, and even the blindest recognized at last the iron armor of despotism that was hidden under it. . . . The Poles! My blood trembles in my veins when I write this word, when I think how Prussia treated these noblest children of misfortune, in what a cowardly, mean, and murderous way." And he called for the *executioner* to avenge all these crimes.

From this position no retreat was possible, and when, during the following decades, the Prussian officials forgave many of their enemies but not Heine the reason was that he was a better writer than the others and that the scars of Heine's branding iron went deeper.

VII

In his exile Heine received no royalties from Germany. Yet his poverty was not so great. He lived in Paris, where successful writers were treated like kings. Genuine fame always has its own reward and Heine had won fame far beyond the German borders with his *Reisebilder* and *Buch der Lieder*. And since he was feared for his sarcasm the pamphleteer could once in a while succor the starving dreamer.

Paris—what a city! No place of refuge ever exerted such an influence over an exile. Paris did to Heine what Athena did to Odysseus in Homer's poems : "burnishing his hair and straightening his shoulders." It augmented tenfold his soul, his mind, and even his body. When he was banned from his homeland he was almost forty, and as described by the famous French writer, Théophile Gautier, "a good-looking man with rich blond hair." Thus he appeared to Paris and his new friends. While his enemies at home called him a Frenchie and a traitor, he represented Germany in Paris as no other German did.

He became both a Frenchman and a German. He welded these two disparate strains into a new unity: that of the European.

Heine may have belonged essentially to the humanists of the pre-Reformation era. Yet those men had the Latin language as a medium to put all of Europe within their reach. For Heine the European it was more difficult. If he described *Franzoesische Zustaende* to the Germans he could do it only in German; but if he spoke of *De l'Allemagne* to the French he wrote French. To be able to serve thus, he had to think in both languages.

And he knew how to serve! His thinking was deep and true.

He no longer indulged in the ephemeral and the witty, which formerly constituted a danger for his talent. He explained profoundly the development of religion and philosophy in Germany to the French readers. On the other hand, he explained with magisterial wisdom French politics in all their complexity to the Germans. In both cases his view was steadied by distance.

What he wrote was glowing with spirit. It was a torch of freedom—giving forth a resinous odor. Even today there is no better way of telling a German what a Frenchman is then by giving him *Lutetia* to read. *Romantische Schule in Deutschland* and *Elementargeister* still, after a hundred years, educate the French.

"I am all phosphor," the poet wrote from Paris because he felt himself mysteriously being consumed by flame. He was often homesick. But his art was never greater than in the years between 1831 and 1848 in Paris. Those were the years of his battle with Germany, whose state of affairs he never tired of criticizing in poetry and prose. He had the less pleasant necessity of also battling against his environment.

Unfortunately it often happens that refugees and voluntary exiles fight each other. There are, of course, always people who will tell their coemigrants, "We should stand united against the enemy." But the answer often is, "All right, tomorrow morning we will." And then, the same evening these fools crack each others' skulls.

Together with Heine, eighty thousand Germans had gone to France, the country of the July Revolution. They were mainly unimportant people, artisans and workers who fled the police and the German class state. Heine had coined wonderful phrases like these: "What is the great task of our time? It is the emancipation of the whole world—in particular of Europe, which has attained maturity and is now tearing itself loose from the iron lash of a privileged aristocracy."

Many thought that the man who wrote this should become president of a German Republic. Heine disappointed them thoroughly by asserting, "I am for a republic governed by monarchists or a monarchy governed by republicans." It was not necessary to be an antiroyalist at that time. A constitutional monarchy could be more democratic than any other form of government.

"Who is this fellow Heine anyway?" the tailor émigré from Baden said and the shopkeeper from Wuerzburg who had quarreled with the clergy. And they would slam shut the book by this man "who sold liberty for a joke." But Heine was really serious about it. He saw that France was governed by a bourgeois kingship, a mixture between monarchy and republic, and that the advantages of Louis Philippe's regime outweighed its disadvantages. There was no doubt that this regime brought economic happiness to many, and in Heine's opinion the arts and sciences thrived on economic happiness.

He wished nothing better for Germany than what he saw flourishing in France. The parliamentary system he wanted was that of the National Assembly of 1789. He did not want a one-party government. That laws should be made exclusively by workers was a horrible thought to him. "All for justice and all for the proletariat but not by the proletariat: this can be considered Heine's unspoken formula," writes Max Brod in his book on Heine.

VIII

Heine was not only a politician. He was a true artist and his life as an artist contained many mistakes. He drank champagne in public, not just secretly at home. He was a sensualist who never denied that for him emancipation was especially of the flesh. Grillparzer, who wished Heine well, once found him in the company of two grisettes. "He looks like the joy of living and with his broad neck like the energy of living."

Heine married into this circle of grisettes, a girl of nineteen who never grew up, and who enjoyed her parrot more than Heine's poetry. Mathilde Mirat became immortal through the thousands of tender jokes and allusions which her husband pinned to her. Sometimes he treated her like a child and a pet, but always he adored her body, to which belonged a noble and loyal soul, as was proved when hard times came.

And then, when death knocked on Heine's door, this "heathen poet" prayed the most touching of verses for Mathilde to his God:

When I in peace have laid me down,
Keep Thou my lamb, and do not let
A single thorn her bosom fret.
Oh, keep her fleece from thorn-hedge harsh
And all unstained in moor and marsh.
Above all, too, before her feet
Make Thou the best of pasture sweet
And let her sleep without a fear!

In politics and in love, many people distrusted the depths of Heine's feeling. They were wrong. As the great English novelist, George Eliot, pointed out, this mistake arose only from "the essential antagonism between keen wit and passionate partisanship."

Unreliable—this was the most flattering of the epithets fastened on Heine by his opponents. There was, first of all, Ludwig Boerne, the only writer who was his equal. He nourished an almost fraternal hatred for Heine. There was no question that this great German-Jewish man of letters who had emigrated from Frankfort was really "reliable." He was a republican and if he had lived longer (he died in 1837) he might have become the German leader Heine never could and never wanted to become.

Heine never was partisan. Boerne was. Ascetic and spiritualistic, Boerne despised the pure artist as lacking earnestness. "What did you do on your first day in Paris? Where did you go first?" he asked the poet impetuously, expecting the answer, "To the ruins of the Bastille." When Heine honestly admitted that he went to the library, "to look at an old German manuscript of Walther von der Vogelweide," Boerne soured toward him. From that moment Heine's so-called vanity and his "weakness of character" were pointed out.

Heine took revenge by publishing a pamphlet, *Ludwig Boerne,* after his adversary's death—an unpardonable book. In this way the exiled writers made life a hell for each other: because neither was enough of a revolutionary, in the opinion of the other.

The much-calumniated Heine—"who was interested only in himself"—never loved the oppressed German people as much as he loved them in France. Once he saw on the road between Paris and Le Havre peasant wagons piled high with chests and wardrobes of an old German type. On top of them women and children were sitting, and men were walking slowly beside the wagons. They were German emigrants to whom the French king had promised land in Algiers. "I was pierced by sudden emotion and my heart pounded against my ribs. . . . Truly it was the fatherland itself sitting there on the wagons. . . . I pressed the hands of these German emigrants and it was like shaking hands with the fatherland, sealing a renewed pact of love, and we spoke German. . . . It is this: *we ourselves are Germany.* And for this I became weak and sick when I saw these emigrants, like the blood of dear ones shed on foreign soil."

Was this the "unreliable" Heine? It was the *same* Heine who gave away new suits to people who knocked at his door and who, on request, underwrote debts he was unable to pay.

IX

As early as 1842 the special laws, imposed on literature six years before, were rescinded by Frederick William IV of Prussia. The emigrants were supposed to pledge "good behavior in the future." Gutzkow and Laube did, but Heine shook his head.

He would not bow in submission to the Prussian censor. He could not publish only what Berlin would allow. He had followed the four winds of the earth and he knew that the storm of free thought would finally reach Berlin. He could wait. And so he waited. When the March storm broke loose in 1848, Heine's dream of triumphantly returning to a liberated fatherland was impossible. He had become a very sick man. . . .

The Prussian and Austrian revolutions were preceded by the Paris revolution which cost the French bourgeois king, Louis Philippe, his throne. The slogan of Louis Philippe's regime, "Enrichissez-vous, messieurs!" had not been obeyed by everybody, it turned out. There were still the workers who did not cash dividends and the poor who tore up the pavement.

Those were unpleasant sounds for Heine—and when the people dragged into the open the sins of the regime it was found that since 1836 the Guizot government had paid an annual subsidy of six thousand francs to the exile Heinrich Heine. Had the government thought it could buy Heine's love for such an amount? He had always criticized Guizot. He was a writer who could use money, but did not allow money to use him. It was the same amount of six thousand francs that Voltaire took from the Prussian king; and the starving Schiller received a pension from a king who was certainly not a good German: the Danish king in Copenhagen.

That little sum to warm the body and please the soul was gone now. It was a hard year. While the French people rose, tried their muscles, and wrestled for freedom—and, alas, settled down again very soon—Heine was attacked by something embarrassingly private and yet tragic: spinal paralysis. The disease that had lurked in his body and not dared to come out was unchained by the bacchanals of the Parisian Venus grotto. Foreboding symptoms had warned him. But when he was dashed to the ground it was as if lightning had struck him.

The lover of freedom and free movement lay as helpless as a child. To recognize his visitors he had to lift his paralyzed eyelid with his finger. . . . Thus he was to lie, not for months, but for years.

The last time he stepped out of doors, he tells us, was in May, 1848. It was on a visit to the Louvre, "and I almost sank down as I entered the magnificent hall where the ever-blessed goddess of beauty, our beloved Lady of Milo, stands on her pedestal. I lay long at her feet, and wept so bitterly that a stone would have pitied me. But the goddess looked on me as if she wanted to say: 'Dost thou not see, then, that I have no arms, and cannot help thee?' "

He lay for eight years in his "mattress crypt," as he christened it—using a solemn word and upholstering it after his fashion with a bitter-ridiculous meaning—in his little apartment in the Rue d'Amsterdam. He was cared for by a nurse who changed his pillows and shirts, and also by Mathilde.

To leave Mathilde behind in this world was his anguish and his sorrow. And he asked her in a poem not to catch cold at his funeral—Paris streets were always so wet, and especially the cemeteries.

In the "mattress crypt" Heine wrote the truest, most profound, and most beautiful verses of his life. His thoughts and letters, too, were different from those he wrote in the time of his strength. "I am no longer a Hellenist, enjoying life and slightly corpulent, with a derogative, serene smile for the melancholy Nazarenes. . . . I am a poor Jew, sick to death, an emaciated picture of misery, an unhappy man."

He still had his wit but it had become milder. When a German visitor saw him being carried on the palms of his nurse to his bath and back to his bed, the exiled poet remarked, "Tell them at home that the people carry Heine on their hands in Paris."

"I wish I could die in Germany," he told another visitor. Yet when he applied in writing to be allowed to cure his spinal malady at a German spa, the answer was a cold No, and also a threat to arrest him for lèse majesté because he had called the predecessor of the present king "unfaithful to his given word." Then Heine knew that he would never see Germany again. He also never saw his mother again. She, strangely enough, survived him, and in his illness he felt a deep longing for her presence.

When his body had been soothed by opium after nights of terrible suffering, the air surrounding his bed seemed to become milder. There was the fragrance and the glow of Paris outside, the happiness of love and trees. His cursed bed that could land nowhere, like the ship of the Flying Dutchman, floated through eight French springs. Young Richard Wagner, in older Parisian times, Heine's admirer and drinking companion, had once received from the poet the gift of themes for his operas. The poet, who looked like Tannhaeuser and the Flying Dutchman, had now become a third Wagnerian character: the groaning Amfortas, looking forward to Good Friday . . . Will redemption never come? "The measurements for my coffin have been taken long ago and my obituary has been planned—but my death is so boringly slow."

A beautiful, mysterious woman of whom we know nothing except her name—Camilla Selden—came one day to bring the last earthly light before death to this sufferer. She came from the world of Heine's songs, the world of Mendelssohn, Schubert, and Schumann. Through her the thousands of women who sang and hummed his songs in Germany greeted him for the last time.

And then came death. When Heine was dead he resembled the greatest of the suffering Jews, the Rabbi Joshua whom the others called Jesus, and with whom he had not always been on good terms.

Where is it now, his death mask? Is it still in Duesseldorf? Or has it been broken to pieces, as was Heine's grave monument on Montmartre and as his ashes were trampled in 1940. This shame is on those Germans who conquered Paris and is not our concern. Neither was it the concern of Heine, Germany's greatest poet, when he wrote these lines:

> Where shall once the wanderweary
> Find his final resting ground?
> Under German limes, I query?
> On some southern palm tree sound?
>
> Shall I in the desert reaches
> Be interred by strangers' hands?
> Shall I rest on distant beaches
> Of the ocean, in the sands?
>
> Never mind! There will surround me
> God's own heaven everywhere,
> And at night the stars around me
> Hover as my death lamps there.

VICTOR HUGO
by
ROBERT de SAINT JEAN

ROBERT DE SAINT JEAN

author, journalist, and essayist, was editor in chief of *La Revue Hebdomadaire* in Paris from 1927 to 1934. He visited the United States in 1933 and 1934 and published a book, *The True Revolution of President Roosevelt,* which was awarded the Strassburger Prize, given to the book considered the best book of the year on the United States. He was chief of the London office of the *Paris Soir* from 1935 to 1937 and was sent by his paper to Vienna, during the "Anschluss," to Prague and to Munich. He obtained exclusive interviews with Mussolini, Ribbentrop, Schuschnigg, and others. During the war he became director of the North American Department at the French Ministry of Information.

Robert de Saint Jean was introduced to the American public through an article by André Maurois in 1933, in which he said: "He is the best journalist of his generation."

Among Saint Jean's books are *France, Which Way Do You Choose?* and *France Speaking* (1941). Since his arrival in America he has lectured at Hunter College, Kenyon College, The New School of Social Research and was visiting professor at the University of Buffalo.

VICTOR HUGO
by Robert de Saint Jean

ON A December day in 1851, a man passed hastily through the Gare du Nord in Paris and clambered into a train bound for Brussels. His cap was crammed down over his eyes, as though he intended its visor to cast a shadow over his face; and he wore the heavy blue denim shirt of the workmen of the day. His name was Lanvin, or that, leastways, was the name written upon his passport. But if Louis Napoleon Bonaparte's policemen had stopped this man at the gate and raised his cap in order to examine his face under a full light, they would immediately have recognized that Lanvin was none other than Victor Hugo.

As a matter of fact, the passport he bore told the truth, for Victor Hugo would never again be the man he had been. The Victor Hugo known to the public existed no longer; the moment he set foot in the third-class coach that was to bear him away from Paris, he gave up his identity in favor of Lanvin. *E cinere Phoenix:* from Victor Hugo's ashes Lanvin was to arise and grow. Yet the world at large would never heed any name but those four syllables, Victor Hugo, a name like a standard, a name sonorous with echoes which, to the French ear, spelled victory and gold, the blast of the hurricane and the power of pride. Victor Hugo . . .

Nothing had prepared Hugo for the lot that was to be his; indeed, save for his writings, he had until then been somewhat conventional. As a poet, he had played an active part in the political life of his country under several governments of very different character; he had managed to maneuver with both skill

169

and profit. Far from diminishing his reputation, the variance of his opinions had actually increased it. A royalist, he had hymned the birth of the Duke de Bordeaux and the coronation of King Charles X but, in his Ode *à la Colonne,* he had also touched and carried away such readers as retained a nostalgia for the bygone glory of Napoleon I. With each successive change, he may be said to have scored a coup, even at the very coup d'état. When, after the revolution of 1830, Louis-Philippe succeeded Charles X, Victor Hugo, a public character, rose in rank, while his literary renown kept shining ever more brightly. The French Academy elected the poet to its august body despite his originality and his youth. And, on April 13, 1845, a royal proclamation appeared, stating: "We, Louis-Philippe, King of the French . . . considering the services rendered to the state by Viscount Hugo (Victor), titulary member of the Institute, do hereby decree that he be raised to the dignity of the peerage of France." One evening when the poet had tarried late in conversation with his sovereign, Louis Philippe himself, candle in hand, accompanied him to the door of the palace antechamber.

When revolution again burst out in 1848, Vivtor Hugo was in the thick of events but sought to steer the wrath of the people in a special direction. He did his utmost to bring about the appointment as regent of the Duchess d'Orléans, who liked his works and would be likely to choose him as political adviser. But the people of Paris had not seen its sons fall upon the barricades merely to crown such a scheme with success; indeed, one workman actually had his rifle leveled upon the poet while the latter was pleading the cause of the regency.

In 1848, apparently, Count Hugo, peer of France, was for the first time vouchsafed the brutal revelation of the popular soul, with its sufferings, its violences, its long-standing and comprehensible rancor against injustice. Famous, happy and rich, Hugo had three reasons for knowing little about the wretchedness of the slums. Hugo's sudden discovery of the revolt frightened him but it also interested him passionately. He dared not accept a portfolio in the provisional government; he sensed how precarious this "new deal" of 1848 necessarily was. In principle he rallied to the new republic; but he believed in its early death from the ill that was gnawing at its vitals, the curse of demagogy.

In the elections on June 4, 1848, Victor Hugo presented himself at once as the people's friend and the enemy of anarchy. On that platform he was elected a representative of the department of the Seine, polling more votes—the fact is noteworthy—than another candidate, whose name was Louis Napoleon Bonaparte. Next, in his maiden speech, this "revolutionary" proved himself eager to assure the consolidation of order, property, and the family. During the riots of June 25, 1848, he again appeared at the barricades, wearing the scarf of the people's representative and adjuring the insurgents to drop all resistance. In so doing, moreover, he was risking his life and he knew it; but then he never hesitated to stake his all in the hour of danger, whether in 1848, 1851, or 1870.

From these early encounters with the revolution, Hugo gathered unforgettable memories which, in a man with a visual gift so highly developed, were translated into a series of prodigious pictures. (These memories were later to be set down and transposed in *Les Misérables*.) The experience was repeated in 1851; and the poet's work, especially that of the satirist who penned *Les Châtiments* was to profit no less than the novelist's. Hugo as a public figure, too, was to develop; he now turned to questions quite new to him, with the same ardor that he brought to everything. How could he forget the cry some of the insurgents uttered as they refused to surrender to the authorities: *"You cannot know, Monsieur Hugo; you have never gone hungry."* The echo of this heart-rending cry resounds in many speeches which Hugo delivered both before the Constituant Assembly (*On National Workshops; On the Death Sentence; For the Liberty of the Press and against the State of Siege*) and before the Legislative Assembly (*Poverty; Freedom of Teaching; Deportation; Universal Suffrage*). Again and again Hugo was to prove that his ideas were further "to the left," as the political jargon goes, than was indicated by the political label he bore.

Deeply stirred as Hugo was, at other times he remained the politician known to history. Thanks to his newspaper *L'Événement,* he commanded a certain authority and showed that he was prepared to collaborate with powers greater than his own, notably with Prince Bonaparte, who paid him a visit in October, 1848. Victor Hugo publicly upheld the future Napoleon III. Obviously at the time the poet believed he might play a leading role beside the politician who was, at the close of the year, to be elected by almost five and one-half million votes. Hugo experienced an increasing appetite for political power; Hugo dined at the president's palace!

However, by the end of 1849, the poet was suddenly at outs with the prince-president because of the Roman question. There was no longer any likelihood of his becoming minister of education. In 1850 things turned even worse, as *L'Événement* was haled into court. In 1851, Hugo denounced "Napoleon the Little" and, during the coup d'état of December 2nd, he was among the small number of those who sought to rouse the people. Indeed, he belonged to the committee of "The Five" which, between December 2nd and December 6th, changed refuge no less than twenty-seven times. The poet had become a revolutionary tribune; he harangued the crowd; he sounded the rallying call around the dying republic. Each night he must hide in a different place; early each morning, having scarcely slept, he set out to awaken Paris to resistance. The massacre of the Boulevard Montmartre, on December 4th, fired his indignation to the utmost; and a few days later, to all appearance, the game was up.

The fact was that Hugo had gambled and lost. But Hugo, unable to admit his antagonist's success, prepared to continue the struggle with the pen and beyond the frontier. Choosing deliberately to become an outlaw, he forfeited all chance of making his voice heard directly by his fellow countrymen. The latter, he thought, would always be able at least to read him, come what might. Primarily, then, Victor Hugo's departure into exile was an extraordinary act of faith in the temporal omnipotence of the pen. To be sure, the nineteenth century believed that the pen was far mightier than the sword. Did not Balzac vow that what Napoleon accomplished with the sword, he, Balzac, a novelist, would accomplish with the pen? Hugo, too, was undoubtedly convinced that what Napoleon accomplished with the sword, he, Hugo could achieve by virtue of the written word.

To vie with the *great* Napoleon, such was Hugo's secret thought, and therein lay one of the reasons for his hatred of Napoleon III, the "little," the "usurper." On December 11, 1851, on the point of leaving France, Hugo-Lanvin did not yet grasp the vastness and majesty of the part which exile held in store for him. Never dreaming that fate was to cast him in the role of a St. John of Patmos, Hugo sped to Brussels in order to continue the struggle by writing those books which were to overthrow Louis Napoleon Bonaparte.

Once the giant was felled, France could not but give herself wholly to the poet. . . .

A few weeks later, on January 9, 1852, Hugo's name appeared on the list of exiles published by the French government. This offered the poet an opportunity to repeat that matters would swiftly be righted again, that he would shortly resume his position in the capital, and that his hangman persecutor would be put in the pillory.

Thus Hugo at the outset shared the illusion all exiles entertain as to the brief duration of their exile. He differed from all exiles, however, by proclaiming that he loved his allotted fate and *cherished* his banishment. Was this mere bravado on his part? We shall have cause to return to this point and to measure Hugo's singular immunity to sorrow, doubt, and regrets.

By May, 1852, he had already finished *L'Histoire d'un Crime;* in his eyes, it was more than a book or a gesture, he believed he already had Louis Napoleon Bonaparte by the collar. Publication being impossible, Hugo immediately settled down to write *Napoléon le Petit,* which appeared in London at the end of July. Thereupon the Belgian government, apprehensive of trouble with the French, gave the poet to understand that his presence on Belgian soil was undesirable. Hugo then determined to go to London, from which he immediately sought the Channel Islands, the supreme refuge which he had chosen and which was to become the first setting for his legend. Alas, the poet's book had not overthrown the tyrant. And the French to a man answered the plebiscite call in the affirmative. Could it be that words exerted a greater sway than had been supposed over that people which of all peoples in the world was most sensitive to ideas clearly thought and clearly expressed? Hugo did not pause to ask the question. But from then on, he was to participate less directly in the struggle; the pamphleteer in him yielded progressively to other characters who had never yet made their appearance upon the French literary stage. Prophet, Prometheus, pope, visionary, mage? There is a little of all of these in the multiple Victor Hugo of Jersey.

On August 4, 1852, Hugo set foot on this island which he called "an idyl in mid-sea." To be deprived of the French countryside was apparently an ill he bore lightly, if we are to believe him when he wrote: "Exile is not a material but a moral thing. Every corner of earth is much the same . . . Any place to dream in is favorable provided the nook be dark and the horizon vast." Truly an amazing confession, which proved that Hugo was seemingly not endowed with the infinite capacity for suffering which characterizes the human condition, and above all the exile's. Here Hugo displayed the monstrous insensitivity of the gods. Little did he care for the countryside where he lived, provided he might make of it a convenient setting. Fate gave him a rock and the ocean; our poet took possession of them with all the assurance of a Neptune. Those innocent admirers who wrote to him addressing their letters "Victor Hugo, the Ocean" wrote not amiss. . . .

> Mon esprit ressemble à cette île
> Et mon sort à cet océan:
> Et je suis l'habitant tranquille
> De la foudre et de l'ouragan . . .

Ay, his soul was like that island and his fate like that sea, with himself the tranquil familiar of thunderbolts and hurricanes. . . .

One day Hugo and his son, François Victor, were discussing how they might best kill time. "What will you do?" the son asked his father. "I shall contemplate the ocean," said the poet. François Victor Hugo, who had not sat at the feet of the master for nothing, was anything but nonplused. "For my part," he said,

"I shall translate Shakespeare." Such was the tone prevalent at the court of King Hugo.

The poet discovered the compensating benefits of exile, renunciation and liberty, possessions dearly purchased. "Once banished, nothing can embarrass you any longer," he observed; "by taking everything from you they have given you everything; all is allowed him to whom all is forbidden; you are no longer compelled to be an academician or a parliamentarian." Here was a confession eloquent indeed, and ample proof that Hugo could himself scrupulously gauge the extent of his "academic and parliamentary" conformance during the years prior to 1848.

But was this exile sad? He himself answered the question: "He was sad in the sadness of public misfortune, yet at the same time he tasted the lofty joy of feeling himself to be an outlaw. Exile was a joy to this man because it was a power." Elsewhere Hugo tells us that during these nineteen years of exile, he was "content and unhappy, content with himself, unhappy about others." The most painstaking search can furnish but little proof that Hugo suffered from the chronic ill of exiles, an incurable nostalgia for his native land. Magnificent as it is, the invocation to Paris, with which he concludes his *Ce que c'est que l'Exil,* smacks too much of oratory to be convincing. Somewhat more convincing are a few gentle and subdued reminiscences in the poem called *Lueur au Couchant.* Here, across the mists of memory and regret, we glimpse the Panthéon, the Champ-de-Mars and "the great pensive trees of the old Champs-Élysées":

> J'entendais près de moi rire les jeunes hommes
> Et les graves vieillards dire: "Je me souviens."
> O Patrie! O Concorde entre les citoyens.

In point of fact—a circumstance which may provide the proper explanation—Hugo's exile was mild compared to that of our refugees today. Decidedly everything has deteriorated in these last few years, even the worst of things, including exile.

Both in Jersey and in Guernsey, when the weather was fine, Hugo could see the coast of France distinctly. Here alone was a mitigation to his trials. Again, both in Jersey and in Guernsey, every one about the exile spoke French. Hugo was also constantly receiving letters, newspapers, books, and visitors from the home-land. Many of the books he wrote could be sold in France; some of his dramas were revived. If he had lost considerable money by leaving France, he still possessed an ample private income and soon began once more to receive large sums from his publishers. For him, exile and need were never synonymous; nor did a pro-fession or craft force him to forgo any part of his leisure. In this respect, the recluse of Jersey and Guernsey remained a free man.

Hugo enjoyed the company of his wife, his children, his friends, and a little court. Both at Marine Terrace and at Haute-ville House he occupied dwellings which he was able to furnish and decorate according to his tastes. Even his mistress, Juliette Drouet, was available, for she had followed him to his island within twenty-four hours. On the first anniversary of the coup d'état which had changed their lives, she wrote to him: "Good morning to you, my life; good morning, my soul; good morning, my joy and my happiness; good morning to you! Dear, adored one, ever since yesterday and until the fourteenth of this month, there can be no day upon which I do not recall the dangers to which you were exposed a year ago, and the terror and inex-pressible anguish which I experienced during those ten horrible days." Well might Hugo remark discreetly of his own lot: "Amid all those shadows, he was well-beloved."

At the end of the year 1853 Madame Émile de Girardin came to visit the outlaw. It was Madame de Girardin who gave Hugo his taste for long spiritualistic séances in the course of which the tables vouchsafed amazing replies to questions pro-pounded by those present. During the first séance Léopoldine, the poet's dead daughter, addressed her father; those words from beyond the grave made an indelible impression upon him. Begin-ning on July 11, 1853, these séances were to continue for two years, with the most diverse shades appearing before the court. The minutes of these séances have been published; the text is eminently curious.

Charles Hugo was the most remarkable medium of the group; the oracle's speeches were written automatically either in the poet's presence (he limited himself to questioning, and never laid his hands on the table) or in his absence. Chateaubriand, Racine, Hannibal, André Chénier, Tyrtaeus, Mahomet, and Shakespeare appeared in turn, the last encountering Cervantes and Molière; other speakers were Jacob, Aeschylus, Marat, Anacreon, Galileo, Plato, Isaiah, and Christ. Abstractions, too, made themselves heard, as, for example, Criticism, Drama, Death, the Shadow of the Grave. Androcles's lion did not roar, but rather expressed himself freely and glibly; Tyrtaeus and Aeschylus used impeccable French, whether in prose or in verse. Before launching into the same language, Shakespeare observed, "The English tongue is much inferior to the French." Political events of the day were frequently discussed, as, for instance, in the following dialogue between Hugo and Chateaubriand:

CHATEAUBRIAND

I have read your book.

HUGO

Napoléon le Petit?

CHATEAUBRIAND

Yes.

HUGO

Tell me what you think of it?

CHATEAUBRIAND

It stirred my very bones.

Marat, when questioned as to an early restoration of the republic, replied, "Yes, in two years." The living were called to the bar of Hugo's justice as impartially as the dead. Here is an account given by Auguste Vacquerie, one of the faithful, of a "meeting" between the poet and—Napoleon III.

HUGO

Ha, scoundrel, I have you at last. Who sent you here?

NAPOLEON III

My uncle.

HUGO

Why?

NAPOLEON III

For my punishment.

HUGO

He is displeased with you?

NAPOLEON III

Yes.

HUGO

What are your feelings toward me?

NAPOLEON III

Hatred and respect.

HUGO

Speak.

NAPOLEON III

I read my duty in *Les Châtiments*. It was your heroism that destroyed my cowardice.

From these brief excerpts, the reader may judge that the hangman's repentance was nothing if not complete.

On another occasion, when Hugo was absent, Auguste Vacquerie asked the spirit to designate the great dramatic poets. Nothing loath, the latter cited Job, Tyrtaeus, Aesop, Aeschylus, Hugo, Shakespeare, Cervantes, Dante, Aristophanes, Molière, Rabelais, and—Nero! Victor Hugo subsequently asked the spirit to tell him something. "You have everything," the spirit replied. "Speak further," Hugo urged candidly. And the ever-docile spirit gave the poet the following portrait of himself: "Lover of the beautiful, lover of the noble . . . What wings! You create worlds; the very stars are jealous."

Literature was naturally the subject most frequently treated. Racine appeared, to make honorable amends and to concede to the author of the *Burgraves* that the author of *Phèdre* wrote somewhat superficial and skimpy plays. The shade of Criticism dismissed Mérimée as an old lady's lap dog and Dumas as a fashionable waltzer. The shade of Chénier dictated lines that were a mixture of Chénier and—Victor Hugo! Truth to tell, the invisible world echoed Hugo with unparalleled fidelity, *even when the poet did not attend the séances.*

In so far as Chénier's "answers" are concerned, something rather curious occurred. Hugo begged the poet to complete certain of his poems because in editions previous to 1840 (the only editions Hugo had with him) these were in fragmentary form. Unfortunately Hugo was unaware that these fragments had been published in full in editions which were printed in France after 1840. Chénier, completing at Hugo's request poems that actually lacked not a single comma, would seem to have "forgotten" what he had written.

It would be false, however, to utter the word "humbug" in connection with this incident or with the subject of table turning in Jersey in general, for then we should have to explain why the spirit's answers were as Hugo*esque* in inspiration and expression when the poet was out of the room. In truth, such was the phenomenal power of Hugo's moi—EGO HUGO!—that each and every inmate of Marine Terrace came to think and speak like the master. The soul of the divinity hovered everywhere, not only in the mind of the perfect disciple like Vacquerie, but in the minds of all with whom Hugo came in contact.

So tyrannical was Hugo's authority over his entourage that beyond the thoughts of his companions it dominated their lives. It was to take many long years before Charles Hugo, who abominated exile, determined to leave Jersey for Belgium; as for Adèle Hugo, thwarted at outset by her father in her love for an English officer, she was to lose her reason. When the poet arrived in Jersey with his family, Charles was twenty-nine years of age, François Victor twenty-seven, and Adèle twenty-five, but the liberty of a personal life was something they had to struggle for lustily. It was they who uttered the cry of every exile who has remained a human being:

"As for me," François Victor Hugo complained in 1858, "when shall I see that great city again which now seems to me to be but a dream?" And: "Suppose I was to return there an old white-headed man?"

Victor Hugo reigned as a tyrant over those about him precisely as he wished to reign over political and literary France— over those who read his name on the title pages of a book and those who write it in on a ballot—and precisely as he reigned by means of tables over the empire of the dead. Victor Hugo was determined to be omnipresent; Victor Hugo indulged in the divine prerogative of ubiquity.

From 1853 onward, exile brought Victor Hugo decisively into the intimacy of godhead. Now the poet placed himself as an intercessor chosen from among all men; now, in his boldest moments, he went so far as to identify himself with creation, and even with the creator of the universe. Undoubtedly if Victor Hugo was naturally drawn in this direction, exile first, and the spiritualistic séances next, could but emphasize his leanings.

In this respect, we find many texts that are revealing, as "I get on well with God my neighbor," or, in the poem entitled *To Her Who Remained in France,* the lines:

> Depuis quatre ans j'habite un tourbillon d'écume.
> Ce livre en a jailli. Dieu dictait, j'écrivais.

or finally, in a tone of quite natural confidence:

> J'ai dit à Dieu et Dieu m'a répondu.

The poet never considered these spiritualistic séances as a distraction or a fancy; they were, on the contrary, something serious, religious, and awe-inspiring. Did he not feel that he was encompassed by the fantastic? Did he not see visions which terrified him? Did not the "White Lady" make an appointment with him one night for three in the morning? To be sure, he did not keep it, but still he could not sleep and, at precisely three o'clock, he heard his front doorbell ringing.

Hugo went to the trouble of apprising us in a note that in his own work he never used such texts as he obtained from the questioning of spirits. Yet quite obviously the moving tables of Jersey exerted a profound influence over the last part of the *Contemplations;* quite obviously, too, poems like *Dieu* and *La Fin de Satan* owe a great deal to spiritualism. This spiritualism, if we may say so, is constantly showing its cloven hoof, as in the poem *Horror:*

> Esprit mystérieux, qui le doigt sur la bouche
> Passes . . . Ne t'en va pas! Parle à l'homme farouche
> Ivre d'ombre et d'immensité. . . .

or in the line written in June, 1855:

> Une nuit un esprit me parla dans un rêve.

This spirit bears another name in *Ce que dit la bouche d'ombre:*

> Le spectre m'attendait, l'être sombre et tranquille
> Me prit par·les cheveux dans sa main qui grandit,
> M'emporta sur le haut du rocher, et me dit. . . .

And yet if Victor Hugo explored the beyond he remained as deeply interested as ever in the happenings of our immediate world. That peculiar, unique mysticism of his did not quell his passion for politics. During his nineteen years of exile, from 1851 to 1870, almost no important political event took place without his commenting upon it.

Around him he gathered a strange circle of exiles from other European countries; they included a Hungarian, Colonel Sandor Telecki, a former Austrian officer named Wiesner; Dr. Frank, "a German refugee"; two Polish exiles Papowski and Zwietoslawski; and an Italian exile, Biffi. They formed a motley and melancholy assembly, a sort of anticipatory ghost of the League of Nations or a sketch of today's governments in exile.

Whenever one of these victims died, Victor Hugo was requested to utter the funeral oration. But he officiated in many other circumstances too: he celebrated the anniversary of the Polish revolution, of the revolution of 1848, of the Greek uprising; he participated from afar in festivals commemorating the births of Dante and Shakespeare, he sent his approval to those who sought to set up a statue in honor of Voltaire, and he saluted piously from his island the funeral cortege which transported Manin's ashes from Milan to Venice.

With inexhaustible generosity he appealed for the pardon of several men condemned to death (Tapner, the accused of Charleroi, the Irishwomen, Bradley). He implored Juarez to spare the Emperor Maximilian's wife. Whenever opportunity offered, he pleaded for the abolition of the death sentence, and his great voice resounded as that of the advocate general of the rights of man and citizen.

This was merely one of the roles he enacted. His voice could likewise rise in the fearful accents of the accuser. The poet haled the nations one by one before his public tribunal. He cursed "Nicholas of Russia" and later even adjured the Russian army not to crush Poland, a plea as chimerical as that he addressed in 1870 to the German soldiers invading France. He was opposed to the French war in the Orient, to the Mexican War, to Spain, to Austria, to the czar and to the Vatican. He was in favor of Poland, of Crete, of Mexico, of Ireland in its resistance, and of insurgent Cuba. At Mazzini's request, he lectured Italy and, in verse and prose, glorified Garibaldi.

Several times Hugo rose against the British government even though he was its guest on Jersey. But he could not bear to see Queen Victoria treating Napoleon III as she did; and, as he defended a companion who had sent the queen a coarse letter, Hugo had to leave Jersey for Guernsey in November, 1855.

In his relations with America, one episode dominated all others—that of John Brown. On December 2, 1858, Hugo wrote "To the United States of America" to beg them to grant John Brown a free pardon. "Ay, let America know and think of this: there is something more frightening than Cain killing Abel, it is Washington killing Spartacus." When he learned that John Brown had been hanged, the poet composed the epitaph of "Pro Christo sicut Christus," and made a fine drawing showing the condemned man dangling from his gibbet.

Ten years later Victor Hugo incidentally asked America to free Crete ("For America, this would mean her emergence from local politics, and her entrance into glory"). But on several further occasions he found cause to mention John Brown again. The man's name, with a few others, came automatically to the poet's mind whenever he thought of the United States. We may note in passing that, when Hugo was threatened with expulsion, he entertained for a moment the idea of seeking refuge in the United States. "As for me," he declared, "America suits me."

Long after the John Brown incident, Victor Hugo in exile still used to address America. When he learned that American workmen had formed a single organization, he drew up the following message: "I am of those who have made of the suffering classes the preoccupation of their whole existence. The lot of the worker everywhere, both in America as in Europe, arrests my most profound attention and stirs me to the point of tenderness. The suffering classes must become the happy classes, and man, who hitherto has worked in the shadows, must henceforth work in the light."

Hugo finally added these words, proof once more that he scarcely possessed the discretion expected of refugees today and that he scarcely denied himself the pleasure of giving advice to others:

"I love America like a motherland. The great republic of Washington and John Brown is a glory of civilization. Let her not hesitate to assume in all sovereignty her share in the government of the world. From the social point of view, let her emancipate the workers; from the political point of view, let her deliver Cuba."

At the beginning of 1870 some Americans, celebrating Washington's birthday, drank a toast to Victor Hugo "the friend of America and the predestined regenerator of the old world." Hugo replied from across the Atlantic: "Ay, beside the United States of America, we must have the United States of Europe. The two worlds should form a single republic; that day will dawn . . ."

To this universal republic Victor Hugo admitted all nations, all creeds, and all races. Had he not one day written to the editor in chief of *Le Progrès* in Port-au-Prince: "There are neither white nor black men in the world, there are only spirits; you are one of them. All souls are white." The success in Port-au-Prince of this phrase on the whiteness of souls, signed by the most glorious poet of the age, may be imagined.

On numberless occasions, the poet played the part of the forerunner of a new day. As early as 1853 he announced the dawn of the United States of Europe. He resumed the same theme in 1854; he repeated it ceaselessly in his appeals to youth; developed it in 1869 at the Peace Congress held that year in Lausanne and on September 4th, one year to the day before the battle of Sedan: "Let us turn toward the future," he declared. "Let us think of the certain and inevitable day, of the day soon to come, perhaps, when all Europe will be constituted like the noble Swiss people."

Destiny, as we know, replied to this invocation with a rain of fire and steel.

Thus during the exile Victor Hugo was Proteus himself: apostle, judge, pamphleteer, evangelist, revolutionary, seer, pontiff, demiurge, demigod. His glory which, after 1870, was to assume proportions vaster than any literary renown known before, began its flight from Jersey and Guernsey. The legend was born in these islands; the islands became the pedestal òf the Hugoesque statue.

Perhaps this was one of the reasons why Hugo proudly refused to return through the side door of amnesty. For the poet' realized how much remoteness and solitude added to the power of his voice. "He knew the excellence of the desert; it is in the desert that echoes dwell."

Exile not only added to his reputation as a writer, but helped his work. Never, indeed, did Hugo write as much and as easily as in his enforced retreat. To cite only his important works, the books which he produced, revised or completed during his nineteen years in exile include: *Histoire d'un Crime, Napoléon le Petit, Les Châtiments, Les Contemplations, La Légende des Siècles, Les Misérables, William Shakespeare, Les Travailleurs de la Mer, L'Homme qui Rit,* and, of course, the volume entitled *Pendant l'Exil.*

Posterity was not wrong; the picture most often produced in the popular, illustrated journals of the period and later in the textbooks of posterity is not that of the young, romantic poet, but rather that of the old mage with graying beard and pensive glance, the old mage who had himself photographed on his rock in contemplation of the ocean and who himself wrote at the bottom of the photograph "VICTOR HUGO LISTENING TO GOD."

LAJOS KOSSUTH

by

HANS HABE

HANS HABE

was born in Budapest in 1911. His great-grandfather was an artillery captain under Kossuth in the Hungarian war of liberation and followed the great patriot into exile. Hans Habe studied in Vienna and Heidelberg. At the age of twenty-one he was the youngest editor in chief in Europe. In 1932 he discovered Hitler's family tree and revealed to the world that Hitler's real name is Schicklgruber. In the last six years before the outbreak of the war he was well-known as a foreign correspondent. His first novel, *Three Over the Frontier,* was translated into eighteen languages and was publicly burned by Hitler. At the beginning of the war Habe volunteered for service in the French army. He fought as a front-line soldier against the Germans and was taken prisoner. He escaped after three months of imprisonment. Since 1941 he has been in America. His book, *A Thousand Shall Fall,* in which he relates his war experiences, was a best seller in England, America, and Russia. After completing a new book Hans Habe, for the second time in this war, volunteered for military service. He is at present a lieutenant in the American army.

LAJOS KOSSUTH
by Hans Habe

Lajos kossuth, Hungary's greatest fighter for freedom, lived to the age of ninety-two. Nearly half his life and more than half his maturity he spent in exile. From this exile he exerted a decisive influence on the future of his own country and the destinies of Europe. He committed the errors and endured the sufferings of exiled patriots of all times. He was betrayed, both by enemies, who considered no methods too base, and by friends, who grew weary of the struggle. He learned that prophets are crucified not only in their own country. And when he died after an exile of nearly half a century he had pushed the world forward by a hundred years.

Kossuth's first tragic error, which was committed in later years by so many other fighters for freedom, resulted from his blind faith in his generals.

On April 14, 1849, the representatives of the Hungarian nation, assembled in the Protestant church of Debreczen, the "Rome of the Calvinists," proclaimed that the House of Hapsburg-Lothringen had forfeited the crown of Hungary, and entrusted Lajos Kossuth, Hungarian minister of finance, with the formation of a free Hungarian government. Only one month before this, nineteen-year-old Franz Joseph I had erased the name of Hungary from the list of independent nations and incorporated the thousand-year-old country into the Austrian monarchy. This arbitrary act by the Austrian emperor, who had succeeded his uncle, Emperor Ferdinand, only a few months

187

earlier, in December, 1848, was his revenge for Hungary's resistance to all the reactionary measures instituted after March, 1848.

Emperor Ferdinand also had tried to break Hungary's will to freedom, which had grown ever stronger since the French Revolution. He had revoked all the liberal laws after having sworn to uphold them, and had sent sixty thousand Austrian troops to police the country on the pretext that they would protect Hungary against Jellachich, the Croatian leader. But whereas Emperor Ferdinand never gave up the hope of finding traitors from among the Hungarians to form a puppet government, Franz Joseph realized that to rule Hungary it was necessary to occupy it. General Prince von Windischgraetz marched into Pest. It was then that the free Hungarian government moved to Debreczen, the lovely town in the Puszta.

But the provisional government which appointed Lajos Kossuth Governor of Hungary, the first government-in-exile in Hungarian history, was no fata morgana. The Hungarian army, under the military command of General Arthur Goergey and led by Kossuth, achieved victory after victory. General Windischgraetz was put to flight. Emperor Franz Joseph implored Czar Nicholas to help him. The invasion of Hungary by the Russian general, Prince Paskevich, decided the fate of the free Hungarian state.

At this point Kossuth committed his first important mistake. Unlike Clemenceau, who wisely asserted his authority even in military matters, Kossuth did not realize the dangers involved in entrusting the fate of his country to professional soldiers. He thought it proper to give Arthur Goergey not only military, but also civilian power, General Goergey chose to lose a war rather than lose a battle. He had more respect for the discipline in the army of his enemies than for the fire of freedom which burned in the hearts of his own soldiers, and he preferred a general's gold-braided collar to a civilian frock coat even if that collar topped off an enemy uniform.

One day after his appointment to office Kossuth's commander in chief offered the "unconditional submission" of the Hungarian army to the enemy. His refusal to capitulate to the defeated Austrians, and his insistence upon handing over his soldiers only to "the army of his Majesty the Czar of Russia," was a piece of empty bravado. The dream of a free, independent Hungary vanished.

Thus began the exile of Lajos Kossuth.

On August 13, 1849, the Hungarian army headed by Arthur Georgey, traitor and short-lived dictator, laid down its arms on the battlefield of Vilagos, near the town of Arad. On that day for the first time Lajos Kossuth had to answer the question he was later to ask himself so many times during his exile, a question which has always burdened the conscience of political refugees: Did I really have to go, was I justified in leaving my native country?

Refugees have always been asked that question because it is characteristic of human nature to be generous with the lives of other people. Lajos Kossuth did not treat this question lightly. There was no doubt that he had to leave Hungary. Emperor Franz Joseph was even more intent upon destroying him than upon disarming his army and executing his generals, who were to go down in history as "Hungary's thirteen martyrs." Two full years after Kossuth's flight, on the day his ship approached the Rock of Gibraltar, straw effigies representing Kossuth and thirty-two other Hungarian patriots were hanged in a Pest prison. Kossuth had to flee or suffer the fate of these straw puppets. It is true that he could have become a martyr. But the world which loves martyrs, because dead men can cause no unpleasantness either to their fellow men or to their government, has a habit of quickly forgetting them in order to ease its own bad conscience. Kossuth was compelled to leave his native land to escape certain death. He was right to leave it because it was his duty to cause unpleasantness and arouse the world to fight for freedom. A dead man cannot perform this task.

On that August night of 1849, however, Kossuth was not yet thinking of flight. With his companions—five generals, numerous civilian officials, and the leaders of the Polish, German, and Italian volunteer groups fighting for the liberation of Hungary— he arrived at the small frontier settlement of Orsova. Here, at

the lower end of the Danube where the river makes a sharp bend
to the south, old Hungary touched the ancient Ottoman Empire;
on the other side fluttered the Turkish flag.

At the little village inn, Kossuth and his companions waited
for last-minute news from the army. Kossuth carried with him
a large iron box and many whispered that the governor had
"provided for himself." Suspicion, the mother of dissension,
lurked in every corner of the wretched smoke-filled inn even during these first hours of exile. But the mystery of the iron box
was soon revealed when a messenger from Goergey reached
Orsova with a brief message in the form of an order. "The
fugitive Lajos Kossuth," it ran, "is hereby enjoined to surrender
to the bearer of this message the crown of Hungary which he
has illegally carried off."

A murmur of amazement ran through the inn. No one knew
that Kossuth had taken the crown. But Kossuth confirmed it.
The fleeing patriot had taken with him the symbols of Hungarian
independence—and these were the only treasures locked in the
strongbox: the crown of St. Stephen with the coronation insignia,
the scepter and the orb. According to the thousand-year-old constitution of Hungary no king can legitimately rule over the country who does not wear the crown of Hungary's founder, St.
Stephen. Kossuth replied, "Tell your master that the crown of
St. Stephen will never adorn the head of a Hapsburg."

The messenger departed. For Kossuth and Hungary the
crown was a symbol, not an object of vulgar amusement. Only
with a heavy heart did he agree to show it to his companions.
Bertalan Szemere, the Hungarian premier, who was an irresponsible rebel and Kossuth's rival, grabbed it. A cracked and dusty
mirror hung over the bar. Szemere placed the crown on his head,
and contemplated himself in the glass. "The Turks will pay us
a handsome sum for it!" he cried. Many joined in the laughter.

Kossuth turned away from this ribald scene in horror and
disgust. He snatched the crown from Szemere. Outside the inn,
on the banks of the Danube, he found a rowboat and rowed down
the river. On a piece of land densely covered with wild under-
brush he dug a hole with his bare hands. It took him more than
an hour to bury St. Stephen's crown under an old willow. He

returned to his companions believing that it was safely hidden. But even in this he was betrayed; a few years later the crown, orb, and scepter were unearthed, and later adorned the heads of two Hapsburgs.

While Kossuth was engaged in this task several Hungarian battalions who were fleeing from the Russian army entered Orsova. Five thousand men were now gathered—enough to form the nucleus of a new army for freedom.

For the last time he spoke to his soldiers on Hungarian soil. The soldiers wept. Only Bem, the commander of the refugee army, muttered under his breath, "This is simply play acting." And in a sharp voice he gave the order to march off.

To the Turkish officer on guard at the frontier Kossuth showed an identification card bearing the name of James Bloomfield of Manchester. It was an affidavit from Count Casimir Battanyi, the Hungarian foreign minister, to the effect that this James Bloomfield had lost his passport and was now returning through Turkey to England.

The officer politely refused to read the paper. "I know you, noble lord," he said. "Luck has turned against you. But you will find peace under the protection of the powerful padishah. I salute you in the name of Allah"; and he added, "Your sword, Excellency!"

This sounded like a command. A few minutes later Kossuth, the refugee, stood disarmed on the soil of the Ottoman Empire.

He was forty-seven years old.

When Kossuth promised the five thousand men who went into exile with him that "the freest of the free nations" would hasten to the aid of the heroic little nations, he was convinced that England would liberate the Hungarians from the Hapsburg yoke.

He had good reason to believe this. Since 1830, when the Holy Alliance had come to an end, Austria and Russia, the two absolutist powers, had competed for the domination of the Continent. Kossuth knew that Czar Nicholas I had not put his troops at Emperor Franz Joseph's disposal out of unselfish love. The czar had sent Paskevich into Hungary in order to use this op-

pressed country as a springboard for the conquest of Turkey.
On that August day of 1849 the well-informed exile knew that a
Russo-Turkish war was inevitable. He knew that Turkey was
granting him asylum only because she could not afford to miss an
opportunity of testing France and England's promise of aid
against the Russian threat. He knew that England was only
waiting for a chance to block Hapsburg imperialist ambitions.
What Kossuth did not suspect was that four years would pass
before the world was ready for the Crimean War. His dream
had far outstripped reality.

In this, too, Kossuth's fate, on the very first day of his exile,
was typical of the fate of all exiles. So profound was his knowledge of Eastern European problems, so intimate his acquaintance
with plans of the Hapsburgs, so keen his understanding of Czarist
Russia, that he simply could not see why the Great Powers should
not oppose the designs of the two dictators at the earliest possible
moment. But he was soon to realize that the Turkish government
was much less clear-sighted than he himself, and that it hoped for
a compromise with Russia and Austria even at this eleventh hour.
The age-old fear and shortsightedness which make nations save a
hundred men today only to lose a thousand tomorrow brought
about a pacifism of which Kossuth was the victim. A few days
after he crossed the frontiers of his own country he learned that
a seeing man among the blind is no less lost than a blind man
among those who can see.

Kossuth was no dreamer. As a lawyer, a journalist, and a
provincial official he had gone through the hard school of reality.
He had experienced the malice of petty bureaucrats, the rivalries
of provincial politicians, and the brutality of prison guards. He
was convinced that there is no contradiction between idealism and
realism. He knew that the absolutism of the Hapsburgs and the
despotism of the czar were neither "ideologies" nor the personal
expressions of evil characters, but political realities. Yet from this
true insight he drew a false inference. If the ideology of absolutism implied a threat to the world, he thought, the world would
necessarily oppose this absolutism. But the "realists" of that time
did not share Kossuth's opinion. Only the soil of a country was a
reality, they thought. Only the earth that can be touched is real—

and freedom cannot be touched. Why defend something that you cannot touch with your hand.

The leading statesmen of Europe thought this—and Turkey thought it too. The czar's soldiers had not yet crossed the Turkish frontier; the aggression had not yet begun. An idea is not an act of aggression. Sultan Abdul-Medjid refused to allow Kossuth to continue on his way to Constantinople. He confined the Hungarian leader and his five thousand men at Vidin, on the Turkish side of the Danube; in a small dirty village, separated from the rest of the world by the wide river and the dark high mountains of the Balkans, at the foot of a ruined fortress.

Here, for the first time, Kossuth felt the deep solitude of exile. Sitting alone on the riverbank, he seemed to himself "the loneliest soul in the world." The gloomy landscape, the still yellow Danube, the shut-in valley, the ruins of the Baba Vida fortress, and the dilapidated clay huts—all evoked the passage of time.

"This is the end," he said to one of his officers. It was the beginning.

But much time was still to pass, and Kossuth would have to undergo all the humiliations, disappointments, and ordeals of exile before it was given to him to bear the torch of freedom throughout the civilized world.

In Vidin the physical discomforts of emigration were hard to bear. "What dirty streets!" wrote Bertalan Szemere, Kossuth's premier, in his diary. "Oh, what a miserable life! Is the East everywhere so dirty? Our beautiful dreams are falling to pieces. There is no lock to this room, the windows are broken, there is not a single chair, only a wooden plank which serves as a bed and on which we must lie dressed, eaten by bugs and ill from nauseating stench."

Thus was housed the premier of the Hungarian Republic. But his lot was enviable compared to that of the five thousand brave Hungarian soldiers. They lay without blankets, in their thin summer uniforms, on the damp bank of the Danube. They never received warm meals. They lived on melons. Cholera broke out in their camps and three hundred men died in a few days.

Every day Kossuth saw ox-drawn carts laden with his dead soldiers pass under his window.

Even worse than cholera was the disease which raged in the camp of Kossuth's generals, a disease which every group of exiles knows and which might be called "refugee psychosis." It is the spiritual cholera of the uprooted. Its two characteristic expressions are betrayal and opportunism. Seeking to escape from their own responsibility, exiles often do not content themselves with shifting responsibility to their companions. They try to avoid the reality of their exile by a flight into the past or a flight into the future. Flight into the past, that is, compromise with the enemy, attempts to conciliate him, return, betrayal. Flight into the future, through bargaining with the masters of the asylum, careerism, securing of advantage and new positions, selfish opportunism. These two symptoms of a destructive disease manifested themselves around Kossuth at the very first stopping place of his exile.

By mid-September a messenger from the sultan arrived at Vidin. He was a colonel, the aide-de-camp of the war minister. "The Emperor of Austria," reported the colonel, "demands your extradition, Excellency! Yours and your companions! And the czar demands the surrender of General Bem and his Polish soldiers. The emperor's demand is an ultimatum. If we refuse, it means war."

"And what are the intentions of the Sublime Porte?" asked Kossuth.

"The Christian emperors are without mercy," answered the messenger. "But Allah is great, Sultan Abdul-Medjid is merciful, and Aali, his foreign minister, is as wise as a serpent. There is still a way out. According to our treaties no refugee can be handed over to another power if he accepts the Moslem faith."

Kossuth was given only a few hours to make up his mind. For days his generals had not honored him with a word. General Bem, when asked for a report on the provisioning of the troops, had answered in two lines: "I have the honor to report that I have not a penny." Now the generals gathered around Kossuth.

"I do not presume to dictate the attitude of any one of my fellow countrymen," he said, after informing them of the new danger and the way out of it. Then he added, "For myself, I prefer the gallows to abandoning the faith of my fathers."

Kossuth still believed in his companions in exile. But only one hour later General Bem declared that he was ready to accept the religion of Allah. Many followed his example. Baron von Stein, the German general, and the Hungarian Georg Kmety could not resist the temptation to become Turkish officers. Sixteen hundred soldiers became Moslems; the Turkish inhabitants of Vidin now opened their homes to their new coreligionists. Thus the disease of opportunism corroded sixteen hundred fighters.

The first deserters from the flag had not yet departed when an Austrian ship entered the port of Vidin. Was Kossuth to be kidnaped? For the moment nothing like that was contemplated. General Hauslab, the envoy of Emperor Franz Joseph, brought a pardon for every private who would join the Austrian army. He brought food and clothing. The first thousand freshly bathed, well-fed, warmly clad soldiers enticed another two thousand. When the ship left Vidin three thousand former Honveds waved their caps and cheered for the Emperor of Austria. Betrayal had done its work. Only four hundred men had withstood this new ordeal. Four hundred men gathered around Kossuth still symbolized a nation. Human greatness was now indeed on trial.

Kossuth reviewed the situation. Working day and night he wrote a document which Hungarian history would later proudly name the "Vidin Letter." It is a masterful exposition of the history of the Hungarian insurrection against the Hapsburgs; above all, it is a convincing exposition of the Hapsburg danger to the world. It concludes with the words: "I refuse to be a Turkish prisoner. I would rather die than accept such protection. I hereby put myself under the protection of England."

He was under England's protection. Lord Palmerston, who had helped to create Belgium as an independent kingdom, represented the liberal English middle class. And for liberal Britain the refugee of Vidin had long been a symbol. When the Turkish diplomats wondered whether it was worth while to risk the lives of Turkish young men for the sake of this "refugee," Sir Stratford Canning, his British Majesty's ambassador to the

Sublime Porte, announced that if Kossuth were handed over to the emperor the British fleet would force the Dardanelles. That very day a British squadron approached the Straits.

France, too, made it difficult for Turkey to adopt a spineless attitude, and supported England's threat. Soon it became clear what enormous power one man can wield when he succeeds in mobilizing public opinion. Kossuth, although unable to avert treachery and opportunism in the ranks of his followers, avoided the most dangerous plague of exile—sterility. Not for a moment did he allow himself to become absorbed in the petty squabbles of his unfaithful henchmen. His "Vidin Letter," his instructions to his envoys in London and Paris, his political manifestoes, exerted their magic influence even from that lonely room in a dirty one-story house in a Turkish frontier town.

Vidin became the center of the world. From London arrived the leading foreign correspondent of the day, Carl Frederic Hennigsen, and the letters of this noble democrat to the Manchester *Guardian* stirred all England. Poles, Serbs, Rumanians, Italians, and the representatives of all the free movements of the time met at Vidin. The Hapsburgs, too, were active. Hired murderers, spies, and secret agents transformed the clay huts of the little settlement into thriving hotels. Turkey was forced to put an end to this show. Kossuth and his four hundred followers were ordered to move into the interior.

The sultan's carriage was waiting. As Kossuth was leaving, a woman threw herself at his feet. She was the Polish wife of one of his former generals and extremely beautiful. Her name was Emilia Dembinsky, née Hogl. Kossuth took her into his carriage. She was an Austrian spy. When the carriage bearing her and Kossuth vanished in the dust of Vidin the Austrian consular official in the town reported to Vienna: "Chief rebel in my hands. Send agents. Emilia."

In the history of emigrations those exiles have rendered the greatest service to their country and to the world who did not reconcile themselves to their fate. There are politicians whose happiness is not rooted in their native soil; they quickly succumb to the temptation of irresponsibility. Shumla and Kutahia symbolize a dangerous period in Kossuth's life, the most dangerous in his forty-five-year exile—the period of temptation.

The first temptation confronting Kossuth was of the classical-Biblical kind—woman. His wife and three children remained in Hungary. Confident that he would soon return he had left them under the protection of the Hungarian nation.

Emilia Dembinsky, the agent of the House of Austria, knew her business. The seductive Polish beauty carried out the orders of her Vienna employers to the letter. However, in the stage-coach era political murder had not yet achieved the simple brutality it was to attain in the age of the conveyer. Just as flirtation at that time was more discreet and nuancé, though its results were the same as today, political murder in the 1850's was surrounded by an aura of romanticism. Since 1535 Turkey had been subject to the so-called "capitulations" according to which citizens of the Austrian monarchy on Turkish soil were under the jurisdiction of the Austrian consulate. If Kossuth could be lured to an Austrian consulate he could be "sentenced" there, and the crime would acquire a semblance of legality.

A whole organization consisting of numerous Levantine agents, Austrian consuls, and fourteen hired bravos was set in motion; trap doors were built and subterranean passages dug leading from Kossuth's house to Madame Dembinsky's love nest and thence to the Austrian consulate. But just as all the stage sets arranged with the cheap fantasy of Oriental brigands and the sadistic imagination of Austrian policemen were finished, Madame Therese Kossuth arrived in Shumla. She appeared to Kossuth not only as a loving wife but also as the incarnation of legitimacy. Thus Kossuth escaped the first temptation of his exile.

But his wife, who had disguised herself as servant and as a beggar, who had hidden in the Puszta during many weeks of sickness, and had finally become the guest of wild Serbian mountain chieftains, in order to make her way to her husband, soon became Kossuth's second temptation. The ambitious woman soon tired of her existence as an émigré, and built an unreal world around herself and Kossuth. Forgetting the purpose for which her husband had fought, she tried to establish herself as a queen in exile. The social opportunities which now opened up before

her blurred her sense of reality. She isolated Kossuth from the
outside world; she gave irresponsible interviews to the press and
official personages, and failed to realize that the loving Byzan-
tinism with which she surrounded her husband had become a
farce in the narrow circle of Shumla.

This second temptation, symbolized by Therese Kossuth, was
fundamentally the universal temptation of exiles to overestimate
their own small world. Kossuth was not proof against it. In
Shumla he continued organizing and reorganizing the four-
hundred-man army which he considered the nucleus of Hungary's
army of liberation. But the Turks, under constantly growing
pressure, quickly deported him to Kutahia, in the interior of
Turkish Anatolia. Only fifty-four companions were permitted to
go with him. But even then he was not cured. In Kutahia he set
to work to found a Hungarian "colony," which was to be the
germ of a new Hungary. But The Sublime Porte forbade the
entire project. Kossuth was furious. He did not realize that his
"colony" without national roots was stillborn anyway. He did
not know what service Turkey had rendered him and the world
by unwittingly preventing his struggle for freedom from shrink-
ing into a provincial Hungarian utopia.

Thus Shumla and Kutahia were the purgatory of Kossuth's
emigration. No sooner had he escaped the two temptations than
he awakened once more to the realization of his own worth. His
horizon widened. He realized that what was at stake was not the
fate of Hungary but that of Europe; and he realized that even
the fate of Europe cannot be separated from that of the rest of
the world, that there is something greater than frontiers, nations,
races, even continents. He realized that geography divides mankind, while ideas unite it. He wrote his "Address to the People of
the United States."

His spirit soared across oceans although his frail body was
still in Europe. But, for Europe, this pale man with the well-
groomed beard and transparent features still embodied the principle of freedom. Mazzini sent his friend Lemmi to confer with
him; a short time afterward Cavour, through his envoy Regaldi,
tried to win over the exile. The Serbian princes, the oppressed
Poles, the "Democratic Committee" of the Italian Mazzini, the

Frenchman Ledru-Rollin, the Polish leader Darass, and the German Runge, the Rumanian Prince Ghika—all thought of him what an Austrian police agent reported to Vienna, "The man is not broken. Every European rebel sends him his respectful admiration and assures him of his solidarity. Kossuth will never rest. . . ."

The "European rebels" were not the only ones who showed their interest in Kossuth. Lord Palmerston assured the British ambassador in Constantinople, "We have compelled France to follow our example." Socialists and liberals in France, fearing a putsch by "Napoleon the Little," thrilled to Mazzini's description of Kossuth as the "torch of freedom." In England and the United States immense popular demonstrations demanded the liberation of the Hungarian leader from Turkish "imprisonment." Baron Huelsemann, the Austrian ambassador to Washington, bombarded the State Department with protests. Secretary of State Daniel Webster replied haughtily, "The fact that the government of his own country describes someone as a rebel cannot prevent the United States government from granting him that recognition which is due to the merits and talents of all those who wish to win fame and freedom for their fatherland."

Finally, on February 28, 1851, the American ambassador to Constantinople requested free passage for Kossuth and his companions. On September 1st of the same year the Sublime Porte acceded to the American request. At the same time the exiled governor of the Hungarian Republic learned that the American frigate *Mississippi* had entered the Dardanelles and was waiting for him.

On September 10, 1851, he boarded the *Mississippi*. All the plagues of emigration were behind him. None of his generals was with him now On the day when the world of freedom opened to him he informed his friends in Sardinia of two things: "First, Austrian money, the insidious work of spies, broken promises, and human frailty have reduced to eight the number of exiles willing to follow me; and second, my hands are not tied by any kind of political pledges, not even to the power which has freed me."

In a pouring rain, on that early fall morning, Kossuth briefly addressed the crew of the *Mississippi*. Captain Long tried to make a speech in reply, but the old sea dog was so moved that thick tears rolled down his beard. All he could say was "Sir . . . you are . . . Three cheers for Governor Kossuth !"

The American ship set out to sea to bring to the United States the man who symbolized the forces of freedom in Europe.

Kossuth had, however, decided not to leave Europe without "interesting British public opinion in the cause of Hungary." He wanted to spend a few weeks in England before saying farewell to the Old World.

In those days Kossuth was convinced that his mission was far greater than Hungary. He understood that nationalism and internationalism are not contradictory. Earlier, in his *Address to the People of the United States,* he had demanded freedom, not only for Hungary but for all the nations which formed part of the Austrian monarchy. Now he went one step further. "As lovers of freedom," he wrote, "we would not ask liberty for ourselves alone : we would not boast of privileges that others do not enjoy, but desire to be free in fellowship with other free nations around us." He was so deeply imbued with the idea that civilized mankind was "one single body" and that freedom was an indivisible good that he believed each nation must fight not only for itself but for all other nations.

His trip to England seemed to confirm him in these ideas. When his ship put in at a Portuguese port his mere presence sufficed to conjure up a revolt in the town. In Gibraltar the British sailors feted him for three days. In France, Napoleon Bonaparte, president of the Second Republic, forbade him to disembark. But the inhabitants of Marseilles learned that his ship had cast anchor in their port and they went out to meet him in hundreds of boats. The Hungarian flag flew next to the tricolor. And while Kossuth leaned over the rail, bands in rowboats played the "Marseillaise" all night long. All over France a pamphlet was distributed, signed by Kossuth, which contained the words, "Monsieur Bonaparte has betrayed the French Revolution."

Kossuth boarded the British ship *Madrid* at Gibraltar and sailed to Southampton. Two years of exile and imprisonment were behind him; the climate of Asia Minor had affected his health. But in the free air of hospitable England he soon became himself again. Justus MacCarthy, a laconic English historian, wrote: "Kossuth is five feet eight inches tall. Bearing and clothing, those of a romantic character. His face, fascinating and beautiful, emanates natural dignity . . . He is doubtless the greatest orator who ever spoke to an English popular meeting . . . His English is not the language of the streets or saloons, but that of Shakespeare."

Official receptions, speeches, honors, solemn meetings at Winchester, Manchester, Birmingham, and London, followed the ecstatic welcome at Southampton.

Amid this exuberant acclaim Kossuth might have forgotten his purpose. But he sensed the dangers which lurked for him in England. England was a kingdom; he was a republican. The struggle between the Whigs and the Tories was in full swing; Kossuth belonged unequivocally to the Whigs. Now that the differences between Turkey, on the one hand, and Russia and Austria, on the other, had been readjusted, Lord Palmerston did not wish to reopen and exacerbate the old conflict; the distinguished Hungarian guest embodied the idea of armed intervention. And Kossuth, whose whole life was devoted to politics, proved that he was fundamentally no politician. He did not worry about whether it was "proper" for a foreigner, who in addition was an official guest without a native country, to "meddle" in the affairs of the country that gave him hospitality. In Birmingham he openly admitted this. "England," he said, "has only two alternatives. If the coming events align the European states in two hostile camps and if the conflict is decided without England, England will cease to be a European power. Moreover, if in this struggle reaction and despotism triumph, England's freedom and independence will cease to exist. Then Europe will be one big barracks, and foreign, barbarian horsemen will water their horses in the Thames."

Kossuth himself was surprised at the incendiary effect of his words. Truth seemed to be on the march. He did not know yet that the Tories were about to conclude a pact with the rulers of Austria. He did not know that Queen Victoria was more akin to Austria's young emperor than to the Hungarian republican. He did not know that eight years later he would leave England forever with the words:

"I could not call even a lodging my own . . . Not a bite of bread could I earn. England grew cold. But I cannot live without the warmth of freedom. Thus I shake the dust of England from my feet."

For the time being England had not yet grown "cold." The idea of freedom and the man who embodied it enjoyed a season of prosperity.

Kossuth's reception in the United States surpasses all the honors ever accorded an exile. The American people had followed Hungary's struggle for liberation with sympathy for many years. The deep democratic instincts of the American people, their natural feeling for fairness and justice, their touching tenderness for the weak, their profound spiritual repugnance to every form of oppression, all contributed to their enthusiasm for Kossuth. His *Address to the People of the United States,* which Horace Greeley, champion of the abolition of slavery and publisher of the New York *Tribune,* reprinted in toto although it comprised twenty-six book pages, enhanced the foreigner's popularity.

This manifesto by Kossuth has more than sentimental value. "Citizens of America," Kossuth wrote, "to you I declare that my aim in the federation of Hungary with smaller nations was to secure the nationality and independence of each, and the freedom of all." And—more than sixty years before the First and almost ninety years before the Second World War—he outlined the plan of a Danubian Federation. Thomas G. Masaryk, Woodrow Wilson, and Henry Wallace later took up Kossuth's idea and popularized it in America, but it was this exiled Hungarian who first prophetically realized the great and dangerous problem of Central Europe.

Kossuth's journey across America was a triumphal procession. Cannon thundered to salute the *Humboldt,* which the government had sent to bring him from Southampton, as she approached Staten Island. An Indian chieftain adopted the exile into his tribe as "the great man of freedom." The "Commodore" sent his own ship, the *Vanderbilt,* to meet him. Since 1824, when a similar honor was granted to Lafayette, no foreign statesman had spoken before Congress. Now both Houses assembled together in Washington to hear Lajos Kossuth. It was in this speech that the Hungarian Kossuth enriched the English language with a word which it had not possessed before—the word "solidarity."

The city of New York, the Bar Association, the eastern universities, the press clubs, the Protestant Church, the states of Maryland, Pennsylvania, and Ohio gave him jubilant receptions. On the soil of New England, in Massachusetts and Connecticut, he found the living spirit of the Pilgrim Fathers and more understanding than anywhere else. State Secretary Daniel Webster, who always supported Kossuth but regarded him as a wild rebel, was spellbound by the foreigner's "mild, melancholic, and dignified behavior." The enthusiasm for Kossuth which the isolationists of that time disapprovingly called the "Kossuth frenzy" at first swept aside the resistance of certain political circles. The "Kossuth hat," a round, black hat with ostrich feathers, became a national industry. "Never before had the city of New York," wrote the New York *Tribune,* "seen such a fervent reception, which was also brilliant in its outward manifestations."

Kossuth responded passionately to America's love. During the six months he spent in the United States he not only laid the foundation stones of a free Hungary but also of a Danubian Federation without the Hapsburgs, and of a democratic Europe. During those six months, surpassing all his earlier work, he made those speeches which were to become not only the Bible of Hungarian liberalism but also an organic part of American thinking. "Either the continent of Europe," he called out to the assembled representatives and senators, "has no future at all, or this future is American republicanism."

In a New York speech, he declared, "One may profess the principles of democracy or the system of socialism—the fundamental question remains: Where does a country stand when the task is to unite in the common fight against tyranny?" And at a great banquet in Washington, at which the army and navy spokesmen declared their adherence to Kossuth's liberalism, he said: "Your fundamental principles have conquered more in seventy-five years than Rome by arms in centuries. Your principles will conquer the world. . . . Upon this basis will we get rid of the mysterious questions of language and nationalities, raised by the cunning despotism in Europe, to murder liberty, and the smaller states will find security in the principles of the federative union, while they will conserve freedom by the principles of sovereign self-government; and while larger states, abdicating to the principle of civilization, will cease to be bloodfields to sanguinary usurpation and a tool to the ambition of wicked man, municipal institutions will assure the development of local particular elements."

A few months passed before Kossuth realized that the hot ground of American politics could be no less fatal than the "cold soil" of old England. As is the case with all political geniuses, Kossuth's historical sense was faulty. The fire of fanaticism within him magically inflamed his people, but it consumed his own objective understanding of political and economic facts. So convinced was Kossuth that the principle of freedom was a universal law, that all the peoples of the earth were fighting for the same thing, that he disregarded the rule which always ties the hands of the refugee: the rule that foreigners must not interfere.

He did not suspect into what a risky affair he was plunging. At that time America's principal problem was the abolition of slavery. The shadow of the Civil War already loomed. The slaveholders felt that this foreigner was dangerous, despite his assurances that he "did not intend to interfere in the domestic problems of the country that gave him hospitality." In St. Louis he succeeded in transforming the public's hostile mood into enthusiasm, but New Orleans definitely cold-shouldered him. His tour of the southern states was a failure. He was forced to break it off abruptly. He hastened back to Boston.

But the slaveholders were not the only ones who considered this "man of destiny," as Ralph Waldo Emerson called him, a living threat to their existence. For the Catholic clergy, Kossuth embodied Protestantism, and the revolution which threatened the big church estates in Hungary. In vain did he protest: "I am a humble member of a nation the majority of which is Catholic, and it is not the least glory of my nation that in all times we have fought and bled for religious liberty—the Catholics as devotedly as the Protestants." The Roman Catholic Church in America did not forgive him for his having sought admission to the Masonic Lodge in Cincinnati, and for having filled out the application blank with the classical answers:

Residence: Being in exile for liberty's stake, he has no place of fixed residence.
Age: 49½ years.
Occupation: His occupation is to restore his native land, Hungary, to its national independence and to achieve, in community of action with other nations, civil and religious liberty in Europe.

The Irish, too, turned against him. They charged that he, who claimed to be fighting for the freedom of all the nations, had done nothing for Irish freedom and had "wooed England for opportunistic reasons."

But all the resistance was insignificant beside the enmity of the isolationists. He could not meet them halfway. He had never fought against the Catholic religion. He was able to answer the Irish with the declaration that "whoever fights for freedom fights also for Irish freedom." But he could not and would not take a conciliatory attitude toward the isolationists, for he was convinced that American intervention was of decisive importance not only for Europe, but also for America itself. He picked up the gauntlet hurled at him by the isolationists. He was for intervention—and he "intervened."

Five days after his arrival in the United States he declared, "Let anyone show me even one single word in the eleven volumes of Washington's works that advocates indifference to the violation of human rights." A few months later, in Massachusetts, he said, "You should not say 'American liberty.' Liberty should not be either American or European—it should be just liberty. God is God. He is neither America's nor Europe's God. He is God. So must liberty be." He wrote an ambitious essay in which he showed that the ocean does not separate the continents, and that Europe and America form one close economic unit. This work concluded with the words: "Air is not more indispensable to life than freedom and constitutional government in Europe to the commerce of America."

Even then he had a premonition that he had come "unhappily, in a bad hour." How bad the hour was he learned only when he ventured to come out early with the demand that had brought him to America: the demand for armed intervention. Already in Cincinnati he felt a cold atmosphere spread around him when he said, "If oppression is a perpetual aggression against mankind, America's war against the European tyrannies would only be a justified defensive war."

He was considered a real foreign warmonger when in New York he let himself be carried away to such an extent that he declared: "There have been wars which arose from the insane greed for power or the selfishness of individuals, even from the whim of a woman. Why should not the world be shown the magnificent example of a war waged by a great nation, unselfishly, without egoism, for the exclusive purpose of defending the eternal rights of truth, the eternal human and divine laws? This would be the greatest glory ever achieved by a nation. And this would be the greatest blessing for mankind, for it would be the last war." This declaration could well serve as a motto for the Holy War of 1939.

With this speech he definitely violated the laws of hospitality. Slaveholders, isolationists, Irishmen, and Catholics all combined against the man who was a master of the "gentle art of making enemies." They were joined by emissaries from Austria. What most grieved Kossuth was the attitude of his own countrymen in America. They split into camps, formed groups "for" and "against," wrote anonymous letters, and confused the newspapers with their "expert opinions"; in the end Kossuth was left with no alternative but to avoid the Hungarians in the United States.

Now the enemies of the exiled leader felt that the wind was beginning to blow their way. Kossuth had floated a loan, which he called the "Hungarian Fund." The bond certificates carried the pledge that the loan would be repaid with four per cent interest "from the date of the actual formation of an independent

Hungarian government." This was a highly dubious "loan," and no one who subscribed to it could consider his contribution anything but a gift to the cause of a free Hungary. From all over the country a total of $100,000 was collected—not enough to pay for Kossuth's first armaments order, which amounted to $117,000. But unscrupulous politicians always try to accuse their opponents of base crimes. Kossuth was accused of having misappropriated the Hungarian Fund. The accusation was absurd. Kossuth accounted for every penny of it to the United States government, and Daniel Webster declared that "no slander could touch his person." Nevertheless, rumor and slander did their work.

"Good friends" advised Kossuth to "disappear from America." The government did not keep him back. It was known that Austrian and Russian secret agents had been hired to murder him. Barely six months after the governor of the Hungarian Republic had been welcomed with cannon salutes, a mysterious "Mr. Smith" quietly left the port of New York. "In addition to his wife only two companions followed him to his European exile; only seven persons knew of his departure." The London *Times* spoke of the "complete failure" of his American trip.

Aboard the ship, which this time was not a luxurious private steamer, Kossuth read the words addressed to him by the great American writer and philosopher, Ralph Waldo Emerson: "Far be from us, sir, any tone of patronage;—we ought rather to ask yours. We know the austere condition of liberty, that it must be reconquered over and over again: yea, day by day, that it is a state of war; that it is always slipping from those who boast it to those who fight for it; and you, the foremost soldier of freedom, in this age;—it is for us to crave your judgement; who are we, that we should dictate to you? . . . You may well sit a doctor in the college of liberty; you have achieved your right to interpret our Washington. And I speak the sense, not only of every generous American, but the law of mind, when I say that it is not those who live idly in the city called after his name, but those who, all over the world, think and act like him, who may claim to explain the sentiment of Washington."

Kossuth smiled. He knew that the future belongs only to him who sacrifices the present. He knew that his triumph was only an

incident, and that solitude was his fate. In the great night of the
Atlantic Ocean he knew that many cities await the exile. Many
cities but no haven.

More than once in the course of the following years of exile
Kossuth thought he would live to see the liberation of his country.

When he returned to England his friend Lord Palmerston
was out of power. Queen Victoria had reproached her minister
for "having treated Austria and the emperor in so unworthy a
manner." But the Crimean War soon offered a new opportunity
to Hungary. England and France were at war with Russia.
Austria could easily have become involved in this war. The
Hapsburg now had an opportunity of paying his debt of gratitude
to Russia. But the emperor uttered the historic words: "We
shall surprise the world by our ingratitude." Austria feared Hungary more than she feared Turkey. Franz Joseph now occupied
Bosnia, Herzegovina, and Rumania.

The ingratitude of the emperor united Russia with the Western powers. In 1914, and later in 1941, they would fight on the
same side in the wars against tyranny. This was a triumph for
Kossuth—too late for him to enjoy.

After the Crimean War, England did not wish to become
involved in a conflict with Austria. Lajos Kossuth, the political-
minded "lecturer" at British universities, he whom Palmerston
had called the "ferment of revolution," began to be an uncom-
fortable guest for England. Emperor Franz Joseph seized the
opportunity of rendering his adversary harmless forever. He
accused Kossuth of counterfeiting money, and demanded the
confiscation of the bank notes of the Hungarian Republic stored
in London and earmarked for future distribution in Hungary.
It was a political trial, which once again showed Kossuth at the
height of his juridical and rhetoric genius. But the court and
the lord justice of appeals decided against him. Kossuth lost the
case against Franz Joseph.

After a six years' stay he left England. But he was still far
from a retired rebel. Two rulers awaited the lonely man: Napoleon III in Paris and Cavour in Turin. The war which would
find France and Italy fighting against Austria was inevitable.

Napoleon III and Cavour would not miss the opportunity of playing the "Kossuth card" at the right moment.

Kossuth's greatness lay in his refusal to learn from his experiences. If he had learned from them he would have laid down his arms. But his memory lives because he did not lay down his arms. He never learned that the part of the exile is to be a card, not a player. He asked Cavour for an army of fifty thousand men which was to land in Fiume and thence advance toward Croatia. Strategically the plan was magnificent: such an army would have involved Austria in a two-front war. But to protect a landing in Fiume, a considerable fleet would have to move into the Adriatic. "England would not tolerate such a movement," said Cavour. "She does not want any shift in the balance of naval power."

There remained France. In Paris, Kossuth's plenipotentiaries, with the consent of the French government, formed a "Hungarian National Council," presided over by Count Laszlo Teleki. On May 5, 1859, Emperor Napoleon III who, several years earlier, as president of the Republic, had refused permission to land in Marseilles, received Kossuth in a two-hour audience.

"It was a superb night," wrote Kossuth in his diary—the night of May 5th, when the three men sat in the emperor's study: Jerome Bonaparte, Kossuth, and the emperor.

Events now hurried, one after the other. On June 8th the allied Franco-Italian troops entered Magenta. Kossuth's Legion distinguished itself in the battle. He himself hastened to Italy. Flowers were strewn in his path. "Evviva Ungheria! Evviva Kossuth!" resounded at every station. In a few days the troops of Hungarian liberation were to march into Hungary. On the same day—so ran the project—Kossuth was to proclaim the independence of his country. It was agreed that the emperor and the governor would meet at Valeggio.

The emperor was in a good mood. The battle of Solferino was another victory. France held both Austria and Italy in her grip. Only Kossuth seemed impatient. "Will your Majesty order the French army to march into Hungary?" he urged.

The emperor looked out the window. "C'est entendu . . ." he

said. And he added in a low voice, "If I am not compelled to make peace before."

Eight days later Napoleon met Franz Joseph at Villafranca. He betrayed Italy. The Kossuth card was no longer worth anything. Instead of the emperor, Jerome Bonaparte received the exile: "The emperor expresses his regrets. He wishes you good luck. The war is over. If the emperor can do anything for you and your family his treasury is at your disposal."

"Tell your emperor," replied Kossuth, "that the cause of Hungarian freedom is not for sale."

On his way to Turin, where he was to die, he wrote in his diary: "There are no words to express the tragedy of my fatherland. But the struggle for freedom begins anew every day."

In Turin, Kossuth was as alone as a man can be. To earn his bread he wrote his memoirs; he occupied his leisure by cultivating roses. During his stay in Turkey he had written a profound work, the *Hungarian Doctrine of War and Defense*. Now he worked at an equally fundamental botanical treatise. He escaped into nature. The last companions of his exile left him. His wife and daughter died young. His two sons adapted themselves to the machine age, becoming mediocre engineers in the employ of the Italian government.

He himself could have returned years before his death. In 1867 official Hungary reconciled itself to Austria. This was the "Ausgleich," the final settlement—a fatal compromise. Three Hungarian districts elected Kossuth as their deputy in Parliament. A hundred delegates from the city of Czegled came to urge him to return home. "I am the guardian of a holy relic," he answered the delegates. He refused to recognize the compromise. He did not return.

In 1879 the government of Count Kalman Tisza introduced a law which shows Franz Joseph's constant fear of Kossuth. According to this law every Hungarian "who has not crossed the frontiers of Hungary for more than ten years loses his citizenship." It was a "lex Kossuth." The recluse of Turin could no longer be re-elected. The greatest Hungarian was no longer a Hungarian. He was then seventy-seven years old.

But he remained faithful to himself to his dying breath. When his writings were put in order after his death his last note dated March 20, 1894, the day of his death, was found. In a trembling hand he had written: "The hand of the watch does not determine the course of the time; it only marks it. My name is only a hand, but it shows the time that will come."

Hungary understood these words. The emperor could no longer resist the wish of Hungary: the mortal remains of the recluse were immediately brought back to his native land. For this trip Lajos Kossuth needed no Hungarian passport.

During the first years after his death Hungary erected more than eighty monuments to Kossuth. In more than three hundred towns and villages streets and squares were named after him. By a singular irony a Hapsburg archduke laid the first wreath at the feet of the dazzling white monument erected to his memory in Budapest sometime between two world wars.

But a somber destiny twice plunged Kossuth's beloved land into the tragedy from which he had striven to preserve it. Against the feelings of a people which has always felt like Kossuth, the Hapsburgs in 1914, and Admiral Horthy, a spiritual descendant of the treacherous General Goergey, in 1941 drove Hungary into war on the side of the despotic forces. As for the free nations, they are now waging for a second time the bloody struggle which could have been avoided if Kossuth's contemporaries had learned three lessons of history:

That an idealist is not necessarily a fool.
That a war today is not always worse than a war tomorrow.
And that an exile is not always wrong.

GIUSEPPE MAZZINI

by

COUNT CARLO SFORZA

COUNT CARLO SFORZA

is a descendant of one of the most famous Italian houses. After having been a career diplomat, he entered the Italian Parliament in 1919 as a young man. In 1920 he was foreign minister of Italy and the first postwar statesman who concluded with Yugoslavia, Turkey, etc., treaties of cordial co-operation. When Fascism came into power Count Sforza refused Mussolini's offers and fought him as leader of the opposition in the Senate and later as voluntary exile in France and the United States. His books of this period have been translated into nearly all languages. In 1942 a Congress of the Italians of Latin America proclaimed him leader of all the Free Italians throughout the world.

GIUSEPPE MAZZINI
by Count Carlo Sforza

W<small>E HAVE</small>, all of us, a recollection of our childhood or of our adolescence which became, later on, sometimes a
premonition, sometimes a ray of light.

This happened to Mazzini when he was sixteen. Born in 1805
in Genoa, during his earliest years he was delicate and fragile
but with a mind precociously active. The young dreamer was
walking on a Sunday of April, 1821, through one of the narrow
streets of old Genoa with his mother, Maria Mazzini, who remained all her life his most intimate friend. At a turn of the
street they encountered a group of men, evidently not Genoese,
all with fierce and at the same time sad expressions on their
weary faces. Suddenly one of them approached Maria Mazzini
and the lad; with natural dignity he held out a white handkerchief
and said, "Please, for Italy's proscribed." The mother understood
and, silently, gave all her money; the other passers-by gave, less,
after her. The gentlemen-beggars were the defeated fighters of
the Piedmontese insurrection of 1821, men who had believed
that Charles Albert of Savoy was ready to lead the revolt of
Italy against the Austrians. Charles Albert, at the last moment,
had changed his mind and the unlucky mutineers had flocked
to Genoa hoping to be able to sail for Spain. That nation had
turned liberal and by taking refuge there they hoped to escape
the trials which eventually were to condemn so many of them
to death.

"That day," Mazzini wrote years later when he began his
short autobiographical prefaces to the successive volumes of his

Scritti, "that day there was confusedly presented to my mind
for the first time—I will not say a thought of country and
liberty—but a thought that one might and therefore ought to
struggle for the liberty of one's country. . . . The idea that there
was in my own country a wasting evil against which one must
fight, the idea that in that fight I might have to take my part,
flashed before me that day, never more to leave me. The image
of the proscribed, many of whom afterward were my friends,
followed me everywhere by day and was before me in my dreams.
I would have given I know not what to follow them. I sought to
gather names and facts. I studied as best I could the story of
their generous attempt and the causes of their defeat. They had
been betrayed, abandoned by those who had sworn to concentrate
all their forces on the endeavor. The Italian king, Charles Felix
of Savoy, had called in the Austrians. . . . The sum of all these
details I was acquiring led me to think: would it have been
possible, then, if each had done his duty, to have conquered?
Why, then, not repeat the attempt? This idea took almost constant possession of me, and the inability to perceive in what way
I might endeavor to translate it into deeds darkened my soul."

Romantic style, style of the generation, but sincere. Mazzini
never lied. These thoughts—his parents confirmed later on—continued during his stay at the university to haunt the young student
who had dressed in black for his country.

Mazzini wrote, in the sixties, of these days: "My mind was
full of visions of dramas and novels which I felt I could write;
but the shame of our national abjection stood in the way."

Of his later formula, "Pensiero e Azione" (Thought and
Action), he chose action and he entered the Carboneria in 1829.
Initiated through the dramatic ritualism of the secret sects, he
obeyed, he worked; but his soul remained unsatisfied. He wrote of
this period: "Our chiefs were floundering around without a clear
aim, hoping for freedom even from a Louis Philippe; we, the
young ones, we experienced pleasure only in buying rifles and
making ammunition, waiting for some inevitable conflict."

The government had its spies among the Carbonari. One of
them, a Frenchman, betrayed Mazzini, who was arrested. The
police had suspected him for some time. "What on earth—" the

governor of Genoa had asked Mazzini's father, a worthy professor of anatomy at the university—"what on earth has your son to think about when he walks alone at night? We do not like people to think without our knowing their thoughts; we do not like young people walking alone at night."

Mazzini was taken to the fortress of Savona, where he consoled himself by reading Dante, the Bible, Tacitus, Byron, and by taming sparrows who came into his cell through the gratings. His case came before the Senate of Turin. He was found guilty, but the prosecutor had only one witness, while two were needed, and the court had to acquit him.

(In this year of grace 1943, in the light of the original records of Fascism and Nazism, we must not forget that it is most unjust to compare, as sometimes is done, these regimes with those which Mazzini fought in Italy. In Turin the Savoys, in Naples the Bourbons, in the duchies the Hapsburgs-Estes were intolerably cruel, but cruel according to their laws; they almost never violated them. Of course Bourbons and Savoys violated the constitutions which they had sworn to uphold, but princes always do so, for they have confessors to absolve them.

(The Duke of Modena was the most intolerant of all those princes. When my great-grandfather, however, suspected of being a liberal, felt in danger, he went to Modena, saw the confessor of his Royal Highness and asked him, "Am I safe in my lands or must I go into exile?" The confessor inquired and told him that the duke was highly dissatisfied with him but that he would be safe for the time being if he confined himself to his country home and never came to the capital. My great-grandfather knew that he could rely on the word of the priest. For us under Fascism and under Nazism no word was sacred. We lived in constant and extreme peril.)

Once Mazzini was acquitted, Charles Albert and his Piedmontese police made their gravest error: they allowed the young conspirator to go into exile. To them he was a romantic dreamer, and they were glad to get rid of him. In reality, most of the future events of Italy were a consequence of Mazzini's long exile. It was in Switzerland, in France, in England, that the

Genoese "dreamer" became the greatest teacher of civic dignity the Italians ever had.

Just before Mazzini was released from Savona an insurrection organized by the Carbonari had broken out in the duchies of Modena and Parma and in the northern provinces of the States of the Church. In three weeks the Pope and the two dukes began to tremble for their thrones. Yet the revolution was at the mercy of an Austrian attack; the liberal leaders had naïvely counted on a French pledge of support to ward off invasion. "Nonintervention"—then the British and French equivalent of the Monroe Doctrine—seemed the main principle of King Louis Philippe's foreign policy. The French Cabinet had assured the Italian Carbonari that if the Austrian Empire violated the principle, France would declare war against it.

But Louis Philippe at the last moment, with truly Bourbon disloyalty, let Metternich know that "nonintervention" stopped at words. A few weeks later, despite the gallant resistance of the Italian levies, the Austrians entered the valley of the Po and quelled the insurrection.

The main fault of the Carbonari leaders had been their reliance on France rather than on the Italian masses. They were honest patriots, but they still had in their hearts a warm admiration for Napoleon, who during his Elba "reign" had told many of them that he was sorry not to have been more "Italian." Like the whole Carboneria they believed in princes, in diplomacy, in foreign help. Was not Lafayette, in France, an ardent Carbonari? What they lacked was religious inspiration. That is why Mazzini substituted for the Carboneria, which was a political system, the Giovine Italia (Young Italy), which he created as a religious and moral system.

The whole Mazzinian school never deviated from this conception. In order to act quickly for Italy's sake, Mazzini preached: What better propaganda than insurrection crowned my martyrdom? What nobler fate than to give one's life for Italy and humanity?

And, from a practical side, he promulgated a creed: All for the people and with the people; for the unity of Italy, for the

Italian Republic, without compromises, without reliance on help from abroad.

It was in the years that preceded the great explosion of 1848 that from his hiding places in France and England, and with the aid of his Giovine Italia, Mazzini was the moving spirit of all the significant events and of the noblest concepts in Italy.

Mazzini's moral generosity—so rare in political leaders—allowed him to discover that the only way to persuade men to risk life and to die was to appeal to unselfish motives. Mazzini offered to the Italians a "religion," a "creed and an apostolate." He told them that victory, permanent victory, comes only by "reverence for principles, reverence for the just and the true, by sacrifice and constancy in sacrifice." And he added his eternal warning: "As individuals and as a nation you have a mission given you by God."

Contrary to the Carbonari, he saw and proclaimed the social side of the Italian problem. "Revolution," he wrote, "must be made by the people and for the people, and as long as revolutions are, as now, the inheritance and monopoly of a single class, and lead only to the substitution of one aristocracy for another, we shall never find salvation." The cry of the poor was always with him, which cannot be said of Cavour, nor even of Cattaneo. (It is true that Cavour said in 1858 that if he had not the national problem of Italy in his hands he would have devoted himself to the conditions of the working classes, recognizing in this way the close link of succession existing between freedom and social justice.) "I see," Mazzini wrote, "the people pass before my eyes in the livery of wretchedness and political subjection, ragged and hungry, painfully gathering the crumbs that wealth tosses insultingly to it, or lost and wandering in riot and the intoxication of a brutish, angry, savage joy; and I remember that these brutalized faces bear the fingerprint of God, the mark of the same mission as our own. I lift myself to the vision of the future and behold the people rising in its majesty, brother in one faith, one bond of equality and love, one ideal of citizen virtue that ever grows in beauty and might; the people of the future, unspoilt by luxury, ungoaded by wretchedness, awed by the consciousness of its rights and duties. And in the presence of that vision my heart beats with anguish for the present and with exultation for the future."

It is impossible not to feel that these lines are inspired by a love which Karl Marx felt through his somber prophecies, mainly dictated by hatred. But it is almost as impossible to pretend that the social (or socialistic) thought of Mazzini is marked by a deep intellectual originality. Indeed, one might easily assert that most of the formulas of Mazzini's political philosophy derive from previous sources. The idea of the republican unity had been felt, before him, by the Italian Jacobins disgusted by the cheap and selfish diplomacy of the Directory and by the frauds of Bonaparte. The concept of nationality had already been formulated by German historians, and for Italy herself by the first of our modern thinkers, Machiavelli. In the formula which Mazzini frequently proclaimed, of "Italian primacy," he did not himself believe. Even to him—if not to naïve and emphatic Gioberti— the "primato" was mainly a myth, necessary to encourage a nation which needed to rise from a long dark period of servitude; while it was also, to him, a way of discarding the hopes, existing then not only among the Carbonari but even among Neo-Guelphs, for a French "initiative," which meant French hegemony.

His socialistic views, natural as they were in a mind as generous as his, he took from Saint-Simon. But he was greater than all the thinkers or apostles whose works he had studied because his was moral greatness—the greatness of a man believing, writing, performing. That is why he rose from his poor lodgings in Tottenham Court Road, London, to a unique position of intellectual, moral, and political influence in Europe. Of him, and of him alone, said Metternich, when still the most powerful man in Europe: "I had armies which fought heroically although composed of different races; I succeeded in uniting kings and emperors, czars and sultans—and the Pope. It was sometimes difficult. But no one caused me more difficulty than a brigand of an Italian, thin, pale, shabby, but as eloquent as the storm, as shining as an apostle, as cunning as a thief, as indefatigable as a lover—and his name is Giuseppe Mazzini."

It is true, that a growing European consciousness helped Mazzini's preaching, just as from 1926 to 1940 a moral depres-

sion or cynicism hindered the efforts of a new wave of Italian
exiles—fighting this time not against foreign invaders but against
a national disease, Fascism. It was during this time of Europe's
growing consciousness that Lamenais wrote to Mazzini: "Do not
lose your faith, sir. Europe's mothers bear children for you."
A truth which Giusti repeated from Florence in his less solemn
style:

> . . . Il campanil del Duomo
> E'la che parla a chi lo sa capire:
> A battesimo suoni o a funerale,
> Muore un brigante e nasce un liberale.

(The campanile's bell is there to speak for those who
have ears to hear. Each time it tolls for a christening or
for a funeral a brigand dies and a liberal is born.)

At such a time it was natural that a man like Mazzini should
become a myth to all the Italians; the popular poet Dall'Ongaro
interpreted the murmurs of all the streets of Italy when he sang:

> Some say He is in Germany, or in England once again,
> Some swear He is in Genoa, some are certain He is in Spain.
> Some place Him on an altar, some wish Him underground,
> But none among his hunters know where He can be found.
> O stupid men who seek Him, once more look wildly around;
> There is only one Mazzini, and can He not be found?

The great period of Mazzini's Italian activity ended with the
events of 1848-1849. After that Mazzini's Italian fortunes no
longer ascended. Not only had Cavour come into power in Turin,
creating new prestige for the Savoy kings, but Louis Napoleon,
the man most despised by Mazzini, had become emperor of the
French. And many in Italy began to believe that the old Car-
bonaro of the Romagna revolution in 1831 might someday remember his oath to work for the freedom of Italy.

In 1849 an event took place, however, which showed to the
world Mazzini's personality in a new and unexpected light: the
conspirator, the schemer, the idealist transformed into a practical
statesman, into a farseeing head of a government, as the First
Triumvir of the Roman Republic.

Mazzini had left Milan at war—where his presence had not been happy—for Tuscany, where he found it difficult to get on with a demagogic dictator, Guerrazzi. Meanwhile Rome had proclaimed the Republic, heading its acts with the Mazzinian "Dio e Populo" (God and People), and Mazzini left Florence for Rome. He arrived there on the evening of March 5, 1849, slipping through the Porta del Popolo unobserved, "awed and like a worshiper, but feeling," he wrote, "a spurt of new life," after the disillusionments of Milan and Tuscany.

He was right: without doing anything for it, he was at once elected a triumvir, and soon became the head and master. He built a government that should be worthy of his lifelong ideal. He warned the Assembly: "Here we may not be moral mediocrities." He suppressed intolerance, wars of classes, attacks on property, attacks on churches and priests. His attitude toward the Catholic Church gave the lie to the legend that declared him to be a fanatical anticlerical. Was it the necessity of removing any pretext for intervention of foreign Catholic powers, or was it his innate respect for Christianity? The fact is that he soon succeeded in winning many priests and monks over to the Republic. With the money derived from the nationalization of church property he improved the stipends of the poor clergy. Under his rule religious services and processions went on uninterrupted. Confronted by the meanest of nineteenth century crimes—the expedition which the French Catholics imposed on Louis Napoleon against the Roman Republic—Mazzini succeeded in fighting the French but suppressing any anti-Catholic outburst.

One day during the siege, fearing an imminent French advance into the city, the Romans, near Porta San Pancrazio, had fetched a few confessional boxes from the churches to make barricades. Mazzini, who happened to arrive on the spot, said, "Remember that from these confessionals came, for generations, words of comfort to your mothers and the mothers of your mothers." And the confessionals were taken back at once.

To a nun who had written him, fearing the suppression of her convent, he answered, "Do not be afraid. Pray God for our country and for men of good will." With the Pope himself—who had fled to Gaeta—Mazzini showed how ready he was for any decent compromise. Anticipating what Visconti Venosta did in 1870 and 1871, he tried to persuade the Assembly to define the guaranties to be offered to the pontiff and declared himself prepared to consider any suggestions for them that the Catholic powers chose to make. "Our duty," he said, "is to distinguish the Pope from the Prince and claim our Italian rights without any violence to the Catholic faith."

Of his diplomatic notes to the foreign governments and even to General Oudinot, the disloyal head of the French expedition, Lord Palmerston said that they were "masterpieces of reasoning and dignity." Numerically the French expeditionary force was twice the strength of the Roman army and was armed with the most powerful artillery of the time. Mazzini soon realized that a long resistance was impossible, but he decided to leave a great example—and he and his volunteers fully succeeded.

He who studies all the acts of the Roman Republic may criticize the generalship of Garibaldi or the demagoguery of a few leaders like Sterbini. But there is not one decision, not one speech of Mazzini which does not arouse admiration for a man who had never before been tried in practical politics. When the end of the Republic appeared imminent, after a siege where a few thousands of heroes resisted and frequently repulsed the attacks of a well-organized modern army, Mazzini succeeded in the final miracle of persuading all, patricians and plebeians, saints like father Ugo Bassi and sinners like Ciceruacchio, to fight and die side by side, moved by a common love for Italy and Rome.

In the last days, when Rome's private houses were shelled by the French, six thousand women offered their services for the wounded. And when popular Trastevere was partly destroyed by the bombs of the besiegers, Mazzini ordered the modest families of the Trasteverini to be lodged in the gorgeous palaces of the Roman princes, on their simple promise that there should be no theft and no vandalism. The promise was given in the name of "Dio e Populo" and was scrupulously kept.

When the French entered Rome, Garibaldi began his famous retreat to the Adriatic with three thousand who had disdained to surrender; but Mazzini remained in Rome, hidden, for a few days. He hoped to be killed by the French. At last his friends persuaded him to leave; eluding the French police, he escaped again to England.

The steamer whose patriotic captain had dared to take him on board, at Civitavecchia, called at Leghorn, where the Austrians had arrived. They searched the vessel but they passed unnoticed a gray-bearded old steward calmly washing the glasses in the pantry and now and then staring idly at the white-coated sentries on the quayside. He was Mazzini, whose beard had become white in the few months of the Roman Republic.

Mazzini's second exile lasted almost uninterruptedly until his death—March 10, 1872.

The life of Mazzini is so full of events, his biographers are so many, and some so good, that here, in a book consecrated to the great exiles of history, I think I should study mainly the influence of almost forty years of exile on Mazzini as an Italian, as a writer, as a thinker.

"Ugo Foscolo diede all'Italia una nuova istituzione—l'esilio" (Ugo Foscolo gave Italy a new institution—exile) wrote Cattaneo, himself later a noble exile. The poet of the *Sepolcri* was the first to escape an Italy enslaved by the Tedeschi. He landed in London on September 11, 1816. After the revolutions of 1821 many other Italians followed, among them Santorre di Santorosa, who died four years later in Sfacteria fighting for the freedom of Greece, and who had been one of the unhappy young Italians Mazzini had seen in Genoa on that day of April, 1821. Another of that group, Gabriele Rossetti, when escaping from Naples where the king had betrayed the Constitution, wrote in his *Addio alla Patria:*

> Ahi l'amor della sua terra . . .
> Infelice! Il cor gli dice
> Che mai piú non tornerá.

(Alas, the love of his own land, his heart tells him that never again shall he see it.)

Indeed, he died in London in 1854. He had learned to like and respect England, however, and he wrote in his late *Dimora in Inghilterra:*

O Britannia venturosa . . .
Triste nebbia e' ver t'ingombra:
Ma quest'ombra orror non ha;
Sii di luce ancor più priva,
Pur ch'io viva in libertá.

(O happy Britain . . . True that sad fogs becloud you,
But this shadow has no horror. Even more deprived of
light you may be, on condition that I live free.)

He was a mediocre poet but honest and warm like all the
exiles of the Turin and Naples revolutions of 1821, of the
Bologna and Romagna revolts of 1831, of 1848, of 1849, of
1853. . . . Many of them were not only ardent patriots but men
of high literary value and political vision, like Berchet. Rossetti
himself gave England three most gifted sons, one being the true
poet Dante Gabriele. Mazzini, however, is the exile par excellence,
the exile who would rather remain in exile than compromise with
any of his ideas, and at the same time the exile who works
incessantly, day and night, in order to go back to his country
which he serves from abroad according to his own ideas of her
dignity and of her future. In this sense Mazzini is the greatest
exile of the nineteenth century.

To understand Mazzini, to understand the meaning of his
actions in Italy and of his actions in exile, we must never forget
that there are two Mazzinis: one who worked for the Italy of his
time and one who worked for posterity and for the world.

As I have said before, Mazzini ceased after 1849, so far as
Italy was concerned, to be an important political factor. He did
not even take satisfaction in the independence and unity Italy
reached ten years later, because he was afraid that the monarchy
would vitiate the good that had been achieved. He wrote to Daniel
Stern: "Little it matters to me that Italy, a territory of so many
square leagues, eats its corn and cabbage cheaper. Little I care
for Rome if a great European initiative is not to issue from it.
What I do care for is that Italy shall be great and good, moral
and virtuous, that she come to fulfill a mission in the world."

Italy had disillusioned him in the practical field of politics, following a Cavour who—looking at Europe as it was—used to say
(and his was an indirect answer to Mazzini): "I am resigned.

There are on this continent three powers interested in undoing the status quo: France, Russia, and Prussia. And two interested in preserving it: Austria and England. I regret that the former are not more liberal; but what is to be done? I cannot stand with the other two."

The rest of Europe ended by disillusioning Mazzini just as much.

In the Hungary which had meant so much to him and to his plans of revolutions, his friend Kossuth was forgotten in his Italian exile, and the approximate independence of the Hungarian nation was achieved in 1867 by Deak, Kossuth's enemy, with the consent and help of the Austrian emperor.

In Germany, not the old liberals of Frankfort but the King of Prussia and the cruel genius of Bismarck made an iron unity. And the old liberals bowed to the new masters like satisfied courtiers.

The Poles were still enslaved. So were the Czechs. The Yugo-slavs—for whom Mazzini had written a series of eloquent "Letters" *(Lettere slave, 1857)*—were still divided even more by old hatreds than by frontiers and flags. (And, unfortunately, the old history repeats itself today.)

Mazzini's idealistic socialism was more and more discarded by masses and leaders looking only for material conquests, precious of course, but not sufficient, as it was proved, when the Fascist storm came. Because men die for ideas, not for wages.

If only Mazzini had tried to win to his movement the Italian peasantry, as Bakunin suggested to him once, in London! But he had answered, "For the time being, nothing can be done in rural Italy." It was his main tactical error, as it will be, if they are going to be guilty of it, the main error of those who will succeed in Italy to Fascism. Only vague promises to our peasants, instead of facts, may mean disaster for Italy, for Italian freedom, for social progress in peace.

Materially speaking, Mazzini's direct political career may seem a failure. He admitted it himself, implicitly, in a moving letter he addressed on April 5, 1853, to one of his disciples, Emilio Visconti Venosta, who had indicated to him, after the vain uprising of March, 1853, in Milan, that he no longer believed in Mazzinian tactics. The letter is tragic reading even today. Probably Visconti was right. But I well remember the old Marquis Visconti Venosta, pride of European diplomacy, telling me in 1906 in Algeciras, where I was his young secretary at the Morocco Conference: "This letter, its four pages, I still know them by heart. And frequently do I remember the pang of having been obliged to part with Mazzini."

Yes, Mazzini's abortive uprisings, after 1849, did perhaps more harm than good. But even the old Visconti, by then a great historical figure of official European diplomacy, had to agree with me in 1906 when I said: "Who can measure harm and good? Who can say what has been Mazzini's regenerative influence in the hearts of millions of Italians, even when his attempts not only failed but proved utterly futile? What is true is what Swinburne said in one of his most inspired poems:

> But this man found his mother dead and slain,
> With fast-seal'd eyes,
> And bade the dead rise up and live again,
> And she did rise.

Anyhow, Mazzini's message is immortal in that he addressed it not to Italians only but to men and women everywhere, not to Italy only but to all the nations which in his time were struggling for independence. After the First World War, in 1919, his message was still a living force to Poles, to Czechs, to Yugoslavs, to Rumanians, to Greeks, and so it will be again after this war.

The French Revolution had magnified the Rights of Man. Mazzini preached the Duties of Man. He purged patriotism of the selfishness which, in spite of too many fine words, the French had attached to it. He was the first to project moral considerations into the rising struggles between capital and labor.

If we compare Mazzini with his contemporaries we see how he surpasses them in significance. It is not only Ledru-Rollin, Lassalle, Louis Blanc, and others like them, who are now mere names. Even Victor Hugo, sublime rhapsodist that he is, is distant from us. And Karl Marx appears to us, as Mazzini said of him, "with a greater element of anger than of love in his heart."

When Mazzini's action became less essential for an Italy

which had found Cavour, the Genoese was helped by his exile in his new work. His Central Democratic European Committee and the appeals it issued to the "peoples of Europe" after 1850, as to "individuals of humanity," exhorting them to elect democratic assemblies from which was to come the "representative congress of the free nations," seemed then utopian. But they are today the very issues which practical statesmen should try to bring about in the world. Mazzini, after all, was no more a utopian than Lord Clarendon when this British statesman tried in vain at the Congress of Paris to impose on Europe the institution of mediation before resorting to war. All these are the same old utopians, transformed by two criminal wars into imminent realizations, at least if our "statesmen" have an ounce—I'll not say of generosity —but of creative imagination.

Even the foolish attempts which have been made in the United States, by irresponsible people, in 1942 and 1943, to revive the possibilities of a Hapsburg Central European Empire prove that most of Mazzini's pages might still be usefully meditated by "leaders" of opinion in the world. For example, his pamphlet *Italy, Austria, and the Pope,* where, in 1844, he replies to the British home secretary who had opened his letters in order to communicate the plans of Giovine Italia to Vienna. In this inspired tract Mazzini defined Imperial Austria as "the Chinese principle of immobility." And in order to describe the Hapsburg rule as it was to the free Englishmen he simply reproduced from the Austrian catechism for the children of the Italian schools:

Q. How ought subjects to conduct themselves toward their sovereigns?
A. Subjects ought to behave toward their sovereigns like faithful slaves toward the master.
Q. Why ought they to behave like slaves?
A. Because the sovereign is their master and his power extends over their property, as over their persons.
Q. Is it a blessing that God bestows in giving us good and Christian kings and superiors?
A. Yes, it is one of the greatest blessings the Deity can bestow when he gives us good and Christian kings.

The only excuse an irresponsible young gentleman may have when, from a pleasant refuge in the United States, he offers himself as the Lord "by grace of God" to millions of Central Europeans who do not want to hear his name is that he naïvely thinks, with mixed Hapsburg and Bourbon conceit, that "subjects ought to behave like faithful slaves toward their master"—as his august uncle, Emperor Franz Joseph, wanted it to be stated in his catechism.

Mazzini's private life, the sacrifice of his forty years of exile, were the noblest testimonials to his teachings. Born for love, for art, for happines, he renounced home, family, marriage, for the task of the apostolate to which he dedicated himself. During his long exile in London he awakened the admiration of the noblest spirits of England and at the same time the filial love of the small Italian organ grinders, then still existing, victims of a white-slave traffic.

How did he appear from 1830 to 1850 and after to his friends and contemporaries?

Alexander Herzen, the Russian revolutionary leader, saw Mazzini and wrote: "Even in Italy a head so severely classical, so elegant in its gravity, is rarely to be met with. At moments the expression of his face was harshly austere, but it quickly grew soft and serene. An active, concentrated intelligence sparkled in his melancholy eyes. There was an infinity of persistence and strength of will in them and in the lines of his brow. All his features showed traces of long years of anxiety, of sleepless nights, of past storms, of powerful passions, or rather of one powerful passion, and also some element of fanaticism, perhaps of asceticism."

Psychologically, the main characteristic of Mazzini's mind was probably this: a strange coexistence of a deep moral pride and of a winning, almost childish, personal modesty. When, in 1864, Garibaldi came to London where he was lionized by the aristocracy and idolized by the populace, he proposed a toast to Mazzini at a banquet: "Today, I have a duty to fulfill. Here in the midst of us is a man who has rendered both my country and the ideals of freedom the greatest service of all. When I was a young man

I looked for a leader. I sought him as a thirsty man seeks water. I found him. He alone was on guard, he watched alone, when everyone around was still sleeping. He became my friend and will always be my friend. In him the sacred flame of love for our Fatherland and for Freedom has never been extinguished. This man is Giuseppe Mazzini, my friend and master—I drink to him."

Herzen was sitting beside Mazzini. He saw him deeply moved and heard him whisper, "No, no, it is too much."

If only because of the criminal war Mussolini and his gang waged against England, I should like to close by remembering that if Mazzini has been the exile par excellence he has been also the "Italian in England" par excellence.

At first he liked neither London nor the "sunless and musicless island." He resented the fact that in England "want, especially in a foreigner, is a reason for a distrust which is often unjust and sometimes cruel"—a thing unheard of in Italy. But gradually, especially after he became friends with the Carlyles and a group of admirable Englishwomen, he felt at home. Carlyle was impatient with some of Mazzini's "Rousseau fanaticisms," as he used to say with his bitter sarcasm. But when at the time of the letters concerning the Bandiera brothers, letters opened by the British police, the Tory press spoke with disrespect of Mazzini, Carlyle wrote to the *Times*: "Mr. Mazzini is, if I have ever seen such, a man of genius and virtue, a man of sterling veracity, humanity, and nobleness of mind, one of those rare men, numerable, unfortunately, as units in this world, who are worthy to be called martyr souls."

By chance, as an adolescent boy, I received a testimony of Mazzini's ultimate feeling toward England, a testimony which seems tremendous to me, even if to some it may appear trifling. Nowhere in Italy had Mazzini more devoted friends and religious disciples than among the old sailors and captains of merchant vessels of the small ports around Spezia, like San Terenzio and Lerici, the place whence Shelley went to his death. Whenever I went there as a boy between the ages of ten and fifteen I escaped at once to the tiny quays and held interminable conversations with the old lupi di mare watching from morning to evening the sea that had been their life. Frequently Mazzini was the topic of our conversation: how he had hidden in "the hold of *Maria My Goletta,*" said one, "when the carabinieri heard that he might be there." And another: "When he came to Genoa and here in 1857 to prepare Pisacane's expedition to Il Napoletano he spent a whole night with me. Since I asked him about London he answered me that not only did he like the place but that he was discovering that he did not like any more the voices of Italian women, but only the voices of the Englishwomen."

And later he said, and this is well known: "Italy is my country, but England is my real home, if I have one."

These are things the Italians ought not to forget, especially after Fascism has tried, in vain, to create anti-British legends in enslaved Italy.

But loving England as he did, when Mazzini felt that a new and irrevocable death sentence was being imposed upon him—replacing an old revoked sentence of death of Charles Albert's tribunals—he came to Italy to die.

The end came after a few weeks, on the morning of March 10, 1872, in Pisa, in a white-walled bedroom, surrounded by a few of his faithful friends. His wandering speech was hard to follow. But in the last moments his voice became clear again.

He suddenly sat up, stared at his friends, and cried out: "Sì, sì, credo in Dio" (Yes, yes, I believe in God).

He fell back—and expired.

GIUSEPPE GARIBALDI

by

COSTANTINO PANUNZIO

COSTANTINO PANUNZIO

was born in Molfetta, Italy, in 1884. His grandfather, for whom he was named, was killed in the Montefusco dungeon for his leadership against the Bourbons; his father was a political and social reformer. Like Garibaldi, Panunzio ran away to sea and later came to America. Cofounder of the Mazzini Society, he is active in the Free Italy movement. His written works include *Deportation Cases, The Soul of an Immigrant, Immigration Crossroads, The Self-Help Cooperatives,* and a forthcoming volume on present-day Italy. The New York World's Fair of 1940 named him as one of 500 American-minority persons who, in the entire history of the United States, have made "outstanding contributions to American culture."

GIUSEPPE GARIBALDI
by Costantino Panunzio

GARIBALDI's *pursuit* of freedom started early in life and ended only with his death. At fifteen years of age, breaking the fetters of school life, he "borrowed" a boat, provisioned it, and with some other boys set sail from Nice, his native place, for Genoa, some eighty nautical miles away. At Monaco, a few miles out, he and his companions were overtaken by a corser sent by his father in hot pursuit. This was the first in that long series of events in which Garibaldi was again and again stopped short of his immediate goal by forces far beyond his control. His ultimate objective, however, never altered.

That objective was well-formulated in young manhood. On board a small trading vessel commanded by his father, Garibaldi touched Fiumicino, the port of Rome. One day he journeyed to the Immortal City, with his father. He was eighteen. While his father attended to a business matter, he went about the city. That visit made a profoundly disturbing and never-to-be-erased impression on him. To his dying day, he never forgot it. "When I thought of her misfortune, of her degradation, of her martyrdom, to me she became holy and dear beyond all other things." At twenty-five, on a voyage to the Orient, he met Barroult, a Saint-Simonist exile from France, who unfolded to him the ideal of social and economic equality and spiritual freedom. On another voyage, at Taganrog in the Black Sea, he came upon another exile, a young Genoese named Cuneo, who revealed to him the plight of the whole of Italy under foreign and domestic yokes. Cuneo also told him about Mazzini and his secret organization,

Young Italy, whose youthful members were conspiring to drive the tyrants out of Italy. The liberation of Italy, with Rome as its capital, became the ruling passion of his life.

On his return to Marseilles, Garibaldi first set eyes on that slender, frail body, that unquenchable spirit called Giuseppe Mazzini. Mazzini, though only two years Garibaldi's senior, was already recognized as the "soul" of the Italian movement. Banished the year before by Charles Albert, ruler of Piedmont, for his revolutionary activities, he was living in exile. Mazzini was just maturing plans for a revolutionary expedition, when Garibaldi appeared on the scene. The two young men foresaw each other's future possibilities, as subsequent events clearly indicated. Soon after that Garibaldi joined the Young Italy society under a nom de guerre, enlisted for service on a Piedmontese frigate under that name, and devoted himself to fomenting revolution among the crew. When the time for the outbreak came, Garibaldi was ashore, lying in wait for action on land. But the Genoa outbreak—as it came to be known—was premature, as most early outbreaks must necessarily be. Garibaldi escaped; traveling under cover of darkness, he dodged the police for twenty nights, was arrested twice, but managed to reach Marseilles. There the first thing he read in the paper was that as a rebel and deserter he had been condemned to die before the firing squad.

At the age of twenty-seven, therefore, Garibaldi was an exile for the first time. First times are always important in man's life: first job or loss of job, first love or loss of love, first upholding or rejecting of principles. What men do on those occasions determines the course of their lives: some turn to further "deeds of daring rectitude," others revert to "man's meaner joys"; and in some cases what they do has a bearing on the destiny of whole nations. What Garibaldi did at the time of his first exile had a direct effect on the future of at least three nations.

During the next year Garibaldi went on with his seafaring, perhaps wondering where to throw his lot next. On returning to Marseilles on one occasion, we catch a glimpse of a characteristic that marked his whole life. Finding the city swept by a cholera epidemic and greatly in need of hospital attendants, he volunteered as a helper. His broad sympathy for the suffering and the oppressed never faltered.

Garibaldi was not a philosopher or analyzer of systems such as Mazzini was. Yet he seems to have vaguely realized that there was no hope for the time being for any decisive action on the Continent. Europe after the Congress of Vienna was one vast Hapsburg occupation area; discontent did prevail, literally everywhere, but for the moment it could not be made sufficiently articulate; the Pentarchy of the Great Powers and the un-Holy Alliance were in the saddle; the forces of reaction-restoration were too overwhelming. As in the Europe of 1940-1943, so then: free spirits must possess their souls, use their heads, patiently nurse the plant of freedom in hidden places, and wait. And wait they did, for three decades, till 1848. Mazzini, like many others, stood by, schemed and plotted, waited patiently, on the ground. Garibaldi, man of action that he was, took a different course, not by deliberate choice but only because, as with most exiles, one step led to another.

Across the Atlantic, on two continents, the struggle for freedom was in its primary stages. Thousands of political refugees were making their way to those shores. In North America the issue had already been joined and the path well-laid by the American Revolution. But in South America the struggle was still in its elemental phases. There where nature's open spaces made for simplicity and directness of life, people were all the easier prey for oppressors. Many young Italian rebels were going there and taking part in the local fight against tyrants.

Chance often lifts a man from one setting and places him in the very spot where he is most needed. It was mere chance that led Garibaldi to Brazil, a focal point in the struggle for freedom in South America; and even more of an accident that he stayed. He himself states that he decided to remain not because he knew anything about what was going on in South America, but only because he was much impressed by the beauty of Rio de Janeiro. But a series of circumstances sent him into the fray. For one thing, Mazzini had seen to it that his representatives in Rio were informed that Garibaldi was coming. Then, too, Garibaldi's mind kept dwelling on the European situation, on Italy's enslavement, on the events that led to his exile and his death sentence.

In January, 1836, a few days after his arrival in Rio, he published a fiery attack on Charles Albert of Piedmont in the local newspaper, *Paquet de Rio*. From that his fellow Italians in exile learned he was in Rio; and when, soon after that, Rio Grande do Sul (a Brazilian state) rose in revolt against Imperial Brazil, they saw to it that Garibaldi was used to good advantage. It was Livio Zambeccari, another Italian exile and a moving spirit in the Brazilian revolutionary movement, who introduced Garibaldi to the republican leaders. The young skipper was put in command of a ship, which, significantly enough, he renamed the *Mazzini*. Presently he was in command of the whole tiny fleet of the revolutionists.

For six years (1836-1842) Garibaldi gave his best to the republican cause in Brazil. That this was not his native country did not matter; his love for freedom exceeded the bounds of nation, race, or creed. When the little fleet he commanded was destroyed, he fought on land. He seems to have been everywhere, in every important action. The events of those years, though corroborated facts, read like romance: a series of daring raids, the seizing of a Brazilian prize of war, help coming from the most unexpected sources, some betrayals, periods of buoyancy and depth of mental depression, shipwrecks, imprisonments, indescribable privations, and torture! The torture was severe. It considered of having his hands tied behind his back and his being suspended by them. His shoulders were dislocated and he suffered from that injury more or less the rest of his life. Tyrants seem incapable of learning that torturing brave men's bodies does not subdue, it strengthens, their souls. Garibaldi's determination to fight for the liberation of people, anywhere, did not diminish. He seems, in fact, to have realized that such punishment was part of the day's work, an inevitable element in the never-ending struggle for human freedom. For liberty like life, like love, is never permanently won, it must ever be won anew.

On one occasion during the Brazilian campaign, greatly depressed over the loss of many of his dearest comrades in a shipwreck, he felt an inexpressible longing for intimate human companionship, especially that of a woman. Arriving at Laguna to occupy the port against the imperial forces, he turned his binoculars on the shore. His eyes fell on a beautiful woman drawing water at the village fountain. With the swiftness that marked his whole life, Garibaldi went ashore, met the woman face to face. She was Anita Riberas (some sources give Riveivo) eighteen years of age. How was he to know that she was already promised in marriage by her father? After a moment of poignant tenseness, he whispered in her ear, "Thou shalt be mine!"

Two months later she did join him, on the ship *Rio Pardo*. That was an event of far more than personal significance. It was the instantaneous fusing, the mutual reinforcing of two lives in the struggle for freedom. She became an inexhaustible source of strength to him. Two spirits were never more suited to each other, or more firmly fused, and yet more free in their mutual fetters. During the tumultuous events of the following years she was almost constantly at his side: on board ship, on horseback, fleeing over mountains and plains, in victory and in defeat. Even when her first child was born, she had a pause of only twelve days, to be followed by a flight, pursued by enemy forces.

In the depth of winter Garibaldi, Anita, and tiny Menotti made a harrowing retreat, through forests and wild countryside. On reaching Montevideo, for a moment, Garibaldi entertained the hope of a breath of peaceful existence for his loved ones and himself. He attempted to make his living by teaching arithmetic in a private school.

But Manual Rosas, the Argentine dictator, was pushing on to Montevideo and threatening the independence of Uruguay. Forgetting the peacefulness he had planned on, with incredible speed Garibaldi raised his famous Italian Legion, consisting of some eight hundred Italian emigrants. It was then that he first used the famous *red shirt* which thenceforth became the symbol of Garibaldian soldiers, dreaded like Satan by enemy forces and always a source of inspiration to his followers. His leadership was so outstanding that he was made commander in chief of all land and sea forces. At the long siege of Montevideo, Garibaldi came to be known as the "Hero of Montevideo." Then in the spring of 1846, Garibaldi and his Legion accomplished a prodigious feat; overwhelming far superior forces, they won the two memorable battles of San Antonio and Deyman, which ended the campaign and assured the independence of Uruguay.

Garibaldi's actions after the Uruguayan war showed the simple greatness and fixed purpose of the man. He had now been in South America twelve years and had come to love it. He had contributed to the cause of liberty on that continent, had been successful by all common standards, and his fame had spread far and wide. Why not rest on those laurels and enjoy life? Most men would have done precisely that. The Uruguayans were so grateful that they offered him the rank of major general with the pension that went with it; and offered also to supply him and his legionaires with such land as they might need.

But Garibaldi intuitively knew what that would mean. Throughout his life, again and again, he unhesitatingly shrank from wealth: he knew how easily it can undo a man, sap his ideals, destroy the very foundation of his larger objectives. His heart was in one thing and one alone. And he knew that a person can attain any large end only as he himself keeps free. It is questionable whether he would have clung even to Anita had she proved to be a fetter. That Rome visit of twenty-two years before, those lessons he had learned from exiles Barroult and Cuneo, the recollections of his first encounters with tyrants, all burned within him like living flames. He would not, could not be one of those émigrés, who, going to lands of refuge and being well-received, find life in the refuge so pleasant that they forget why they came and leave the struggling people in their homelands to their own fate. He had every opportunity to remain in South America, honored and comfortably situated. But the epic battle for the conquest of elemental freedom in South America was over; the need for him, leader of armies, no longer existed; the people must now struggle by and for themselves, consolidate the gains, forge new institutions, seek adjustments, in their own way. Garibaldi's work there was done.

Meanwhile, his native country kept calling him, across the distance; Mazzini kept his representatives constantly reminding Garibaldi that he was needed in Italy: Europe was beginning to stir; Italy was awakening. He must push off. So he graciously but firmly declined Uruguay's generous offers.

The years between the Congress of Vienna, 1814-1815, and the uprising of 1848 must have seemed endless to all lovers of freedom. Oppression seemed to hang ever heavier on men's souls. But even the most fortified oppression cannot sustain itself indefinitely: there are the mills of the gods! As the years passed, discontent became increasingly cumulative, articulate, pointed. Hope pierced the overhanging clouds. Italy's heart leaped when Pius IX initiated a liberal pontificate in 1846: his famous words "Great God, bless Italy" even led many to believe that the Papacy had at last seen the light and would now lead the liberation movement. When that news reached Uruguay, Garibaldi, with typical spontaneity and eagerness to serve the cause, wrote the Pope offering his services. We now know that the Pope did reply, rejecting the offer, but Garibaldi never received the answer. Yet he could not wait. He knew that significant events were bound soon to transpire in his native land. He must move.

In December, 1847, anticipating his leaving and with typical affectionate consideration, he shipped Anita and their three children to Nice, to be under the protective care of "my adored mother." Then he proceeded to make preparations for his own departure.

He left Montevideo in April, 1848, with sixty-two legionaires, the surviving remnant of his Legion, and with eight hundred rifles and two decrepit cannons which the Republic of Uruguay had given him. They renamed their ship the *Speranza* (Hope). Touching the Spanish coast to take on water, they learned that Charles Albert had in February (1848) granted his subjects a constitution. Garibaldi and his legionaires could not believe their ears. They went wild with joy. They improvised a red-white-and-green flag out of anything they could lay their hands on, hoisted it, and let themselves loose in frantic rejoicing. When they reached Nice, in June, the little city too knew no bounds of excitment and joy. The whole town turned out to welcome its "native son" whose fame had preceded him.

Once more Garibaldi's actions showed the mettle of the man. Though no longer an unknown entity or a mere junior seaman, though now known as a daring soldier and an able commander, still he was ready to go begging, so to speak, for a chance to do his part in the liberation of his country. No sooner was he on the mainland than he borrowed money—from the city of Genoa, mind you—and made straight for Roverbella, near Mantua, where the Piedmontese royal headquarters were located. Although Garibaldi was ill when he arrived (on the way he had contracted a fever, probably malaria, which plagued him for a long time) he proceeded to the royal palace to offer his services to Charles Albert, the very ruler who fourteen years before had condemned him to die. The king received him, but with cutting coolness. Like most persons in power, Charles Albert had a long memory: seldom forgave, rarely forgot. How could he forget that Garibaldi was a deserter and rebel? That Charles Albert himself now professed to be fighting for the same cause that Garibaldi had upheld years before did not matter. The king despised the rebel; more, he feared the revolutionary power of the man. So he sent him to Ricci, his minister of war, whose headquarters were in Turin. Ricci also, of course, would have nothing to do with the outlaw and his gang. He told Garibaldi to betake himself and his men, pirates that they were, to marauding around the waters of Venice.

There was Garibaldi, then, still an outcast, still an exile, in his native country, for whose liberation he had come across an ocean. It was at that time that Ricci made himself famous by sarcastically referring to Garibaldi as the "Hero of Two Worlds."

What Garibaldi did from that time, June, 1848, to the end of the siege of Rome, June, 1849, does not fall within the scope of this account, which deals mainly with Garibaldi in exile. Rejected by the king, Garibaldi immediately made his way to Milan. That city had only the previous March driven out the Austrians in a furious uprising lasting only five days, the famous Cinque Giornate. The Milan Provisional Government made Garibaldi a lieutenant general. During the next few months he and his legionaires fought in every important engagement: first in guerrilla action in the north, at Gergamo, Luino, Morazzone; then, confronted by far superior forces, escaping into Switzerland; next in Genoa, then in Leghorn; and lastly in the thick of the fight in the great siege of Rome, April 30 to June 20, 1849. When that city fell to the French, Garibaldi escaped with a force of some three thousand men and tried to get to Venice.

It was in the course of that harrowing march that, near Ravenna, he lost his adored Anita. "My good Anita, disregarding my requests that she should remain behind, was determined to go with me. My calling to her attention that I would have to undergo tremendous hardships, privations and dangers surrounded by so many enemies [four armies of them] was that much more of an incentive to the courageous woman and in vain was my stressing that she was pregnant. At the first house we came to she asked a woman to clip her hair, she dressed herself up in men's clothing, and mounted a horse. . . . After long days and nights of forced march, through Tivoli, Terni, across the Apennines, our soldiers deserting us by the hundreds, we reached the protection of the small, independent republic of San Marino. There I begged my Anita, well-advanced with child and suffering, to stay in that land of refuge, where at least she could be assured of a shelter, since the inhabitants had shown us so much kindness. In vain! . . . That virile and generous heart scored my every suggestion and forced me to cease my pleadings by saying, 'You want to leave me!' . . . We took to sea at Cesenatico . . . I was much distressed over the condition of my Anita—she was in a deplorable state and suffering greatly . . . We followed the Adriatic coast . . . But the night unfortunately for us was too beautiful: the full moon proved to be our undoing . . . The Austrian battleships spotted us and drove us toward land, while on the shore Austrian and Bourbon soldiers were lying in wait for us . . . One may well image my state of mind in those miserable moments, with my woman mortally ill . . . We made a forced landing . . . I took my precious companion in my arms, left the ship and deposited her on the shore. We managed to escape and finally found shelter with some friends. While I was placing my beloved on the bed, I seemed to see the expression of death on her face. I took her pulse . . . it beat no more! I had before me the mother of my children, whom I loved so dearly, a cadaver . . . I wept bitterly over the loss of my Anita! she who had been my inseparable companion during the most adventurous circumstances of my life. I begged the kind people who surrounded us to bury her and I moved on."

He moved on. The soldier leaving the dearest thing in life. He moved on, retempered in his master objective. The Piedmontese authorities ensnared him into Genoa, made him a prisoner, and deported him to Tunis on board a battleship. But Tunis, being under France's influence, would have none of him. Next the Piedmontese deposited him on the small, highly fortified island of La Maddalena, a naval base on the north coast of Sardinia. Though he was their prisoner, the authorities claimed he was fomenting revolution on that island. And so he was. His very presence anywhere was enough to give despots trouble. So they pushed him on, to Gibraltar. The English governor at that station gave him six to fifteen days to get out. "That kick . . . given by a representative of England, land of universal asylum, hurt me to the quick." The Spaniards, across the strait, also would have nothing to do with him.

So he went on to Tangier where he remained for six months, hoping the clouds would break and he be able to return to the battle in Italy. He was treated royally by two very human persons: Carpenetti, Piedmontese consul, and Murray, English vice-consul. Still he was restless, chafing, pawing like a horse craving for the battle, "yearning to turn [his] prow Italy-ward." He tried to visit Gibraltar, "just for the exercise and to look over the harbor." What authorities would believe that? He made cigars, ground lenses, just to wear down his uneasiness. He frequently went hunting and fishing, both of which he found "very good." But even the Tangier hosts seem to have been uneasy over his presence. So, when a Genoese friend offered to raise some money so that Garibaldi could have a ship of his own and thus become independent, he left.

For the second time he turned his face toward America. Hundreds of Italian political refugees had gone to the United States, especially after the fall of Rome in 1849, and had been received with open arms. For the youthful republic, with its buoyant, throbbing westward movement, its abundant resources, democratic government, was indeed a refuge for free spirits.

Among others who went there was General Avezzana, who had taken part in the defense of Rome; New York gave him a rousing reception.

Garibaldi arrived in New York, on July 30, 1850, *alone.* "Finally, after a voyage of 32 days, I have reached this land of liberty." When the New York *Tribune* spread the news that he was in the city, interested personalities planned a parade, and a banquet at the Astor House. But he knew that such demonstrations usually only serve the interests of the promoters, almost never the cause which they profess. Even in the days of his greatest triumphs, Garibaldi frowned on public demonstrations. Giving his poor health as a reason—he really was suffering from rheumatism—he politely declined. He found shelter with some simple Italian lovers of liberty, living on Staten Island. His Genoese friend had succeeded in raising only three thousand lire (roughly $150) for the ship project. Since that was far from enough to build a ship, as they had planned, or even to buy a broken-down one, Garibaldi had to find other means for a livelihood.

For about a year he lived with the famous Florentine scientist, Antonio Meucci, reputed part inventor of the telephone, and worked obscurely in Meucci's candle factory. He was forlorn, sad, and broken. On one occasion he even ran away, like a boy, in despair. He filed a declaration of intention to become a citizen of the United States, but did not reside in the country long enough to take out final papers.

His restless, unquenchable spirit pushed him on. He traveled far and wide, not propagandizing, not in dramatic and regal splendor, but obscurely, often under privations, his yearning always with him. He went to Central America in 1851; thence to Peru, to China in command of a trading vessel. He mentions having sighted the Sandwich Islands, Formosa; he speaks of touching the Philippines and taking on a cargo at Manila. He went to Canton, to Australia. In 1853 he was back in the United States, went to New York, Boston, Baltimore ever chafing, ever yearning to "see once more my promised land," to be at his task. He shipped back to England. At Newcastle the miners touched him profoundly by presenting him with a sword of honor and acclaiming him the hero of oppressed peoples everywhere.

In London he met Mazzini again and they quarreled, as they had before. Garibaldi held that Italian liberation and unification should come first, while Mazzini maintained that the establishment of a republic must be the master objective of the liberation movement. The strain of exile is always so severe that even the greatest of refugees often pitch against one another, often wasting their powers in controversy. This fight between Garibaldi and Mazzini lasted until death. Garibaldi won in the end and in that he perhaps showed himself far more realistic than Mazzini.

In December, 1855, with a small sum he had saved, plus a few lire inherited from a recently deceased brother, Garibaldi purchased a few acres of land on the tiny, mile-long island of Caprera on the northeast tip of Sardinia. He also bought a small cutter which gave him considerable freedom of movement. We know he did some reconnoitering with his *Emma*. Just why he came to this particular spot remains an enigma. We know that Caprera is connected by a bridge with La Maddalena, the naval base where he had been held years before. Did he entertain the hope of somehow gaining possession of that base or perhaps of winning the support of the naval people on the island for his side? Then, too, Caprera is also almost exactly west of Rome and a midway point between the tip of Sicily and the northernmost seacoast point of Italy. Did he foresee the significance of all this? Or was it merely an accident that led him to that spot?

Whatever it was, that little island became an unofficial headquarters for the liberation aspirations of both Italians and other peoples in Europe and overseas. One cannot read his Caprera correspondence without being impressed with the very great importance which that tiny crag assumed in the history of freedom in the nineteenth century. It is to the lasting credit of a group of English sympathizers that, nine years after Garibaldi had settled there, they purchased the rest of the island and gave it to him, that he might be that much more free, that much less likely to be molested. Isolate by nature, he loved the peace and freedom of the tiny rock; he even wrote verses extolling its peacefulness and contrasting it with the crass intrigues of courts and courtiers. From the moment he set foot on that island to the day of his death, except for relatively brief intervals, he remained virtually a prisoner, often an actual prisoner, and at all times an exile on his own property.

But what a prisoner! What an exile! Even the 'mightiest dreaded his power. To the east he could easily trace in his mind's eye the coast, the hills, the plains of his native country, his beloved Italy, still writhing beneath the tyrants' yokes, its people downtrodden, bowed, and yet aspiring. That land, whose "fatal gift of beauty" had enticed many foreign powers and led them to desire her, pulled at Garibaldi's heartstrings with an inexpressible pull, a pull that was as inevitable as life itself, as inescapable as death. His daily labor, bending over the hoe, trying to eke out a meager existence, even the fearful winds, could not stop that pull. In the open fields, in the silences of nature, he was ever mapping out his next move.

In August, 1856, eight months after his settling on Caprera, his first real opportunity came. He went to Turin for a secret meeting with the mighty Cavour. Cavour, the state department of the Piedmontese Kingdom, made a great contribution toward Italian unification; but he often played with Garibaldi as a big tomcat will play with a lively mouse. Two and a half years later (February, 1859) Cavour invited him to lead the volunteers in the war with Austria. Garibaldi rose above all the humiliations of those years, held steadfast to his purpose.

The northerners, infected with the racial superiority idea (prepotendi, they called them), had no faith in the Sicilians. Garibaldi was himself of the same mind at first. But he soon foresaw that it was the Sicilians who would take the first real steps toward the emancipation of Italy. So he mapped his moves. There is some evidence that Cavour gave Garibaldi some secret aid, and by diplomatic maneuvers succeeded in preventing foreign intervention. Still that aid at best makes one think of those who with frozen calculation sit on the fence and at the opportune moment lend aid to the winning side. Perhaps what tipped the scale was that England declared itself in favor of Garibaldi. The general, still wearing the shirt he had worn at the siege of Montevideo, at once launched

thát legendary Sicilian campaign which came to be known as
"Garibaldi and His Thousand" (1860).

Though conducted against tremendous odds, that campaign
took the first real steps toward the liberation and the ultimate
unification of his country. At the head of his Thousand, passing
from victory to victory, onto the mainland, up through Calabria,
fighting against political as well as military difficulties, Garibaldi
drove the Bourbons out of the Two Sicilies, established himself
a temporary dictator and became virtually a master of half of
Italy.

But again he showed his realistic sense. When Victor
Emmanuel, then king of the Sardinian State, who was leading
the liberation movement from North Italy, appeared on the
scene in Naples, Garibaldi cried out, "I salute the King of Italy."

It was the greatest page in the life of Garibaldi. Rising above
all personal considerations, he took the only step that could unite
his country and avoid civil war. In the moment, when all honor
was his, he turned away from the political theater, back to his
little fortress. But as he left the small band of comrades who
came to see him depart, he said quietly, but firmly, "We'll meet
again, on the way to Rome."

That was late in 1860. From that time the aspirations of
thousands of liberty-loving people, literally on three continents,
focused on little Caprera like so many transmission waves. Garibaldi's correspondence contains items dealing with Russia, Poland,
France, Hungary, Prussia, England, all parts of Italy, and many
other places. He corresponded with William H. Seward, Abraham
Lincoln's secretary of state, regarding his going to the United
States to take part in the Civil War. But the turn of events made
it clear that Italy needed him at that moment.

And when no one was suspecting it, in August, 1862, he
showed up on the Calabrian coast intending to march on Rome.
But the appeasing Italian authorities must not offend France;
must not permit Garibaldi to drive out the French forces out of
Rome; they were protecting the Papacy! So the government
turned its troops against the very man who had largely made
possible such success as the Italian liberation movement had had
to the moment.

At Aspromonte, the government forces seem to have concentrated on the very person of Garibaldi. While, above the din of battle, he kept cursing "this civil war" and commanding his own men to cease firing, he was wounded in the calf of his left leg and in the ankle joint of his right leg: nicely placed wounds . . . not mere accidents! Apparently they dared not kill him outright. Again his realism stood him in good stead. "I salute the King of Italy!" he shouted.

Once more to his exile, on Caprera, in December, 1862. There he remained for the next four years, suffering greatly from his wounds and his ever-present rheumatism, seeing scarcely anyone except his family and a few friends. In April, 1864, he made a short trip to England, where he was received with great acclaim. Seeing Mazzini in the crowd he pointed to him as his master, the true liberator of Italy.

In 1866 the new royal government of Italy called on him to take part in the war with Austria. Forgetting the betrayal of Aspromonte, he fought under its standards. But in the midst of the fighting, politics made it necessary to call a halt to the campaign. Always keeping in mind his central objective, the unification of Italy, he uttered the famous, "Obbidisco."

But his "I obey" was like the obedience of a lion momentarily recoiling in his lair! In fact, he did look like a lion, with his roundish face and reddish hair, worn long and encircling his face. Almost next moment, as it were, he leaped to the mainland again, and started recruiting volunteers. The authorities arrested him and locked him up in the fortress of Alexandria in Piedmont. Later they transferred him to his little island. At first he was watched by one ship, then by two, and so on, until eight battleships (some historians say as many as twenty) were guarding every inch of the tiny island, as if tiny Caprera were a whole continent and Garibaldi a whole army. The authorities were not far wrong.

For when, in 1870, he learned that his followers, including his sons, had actually entered papal territory, nothing could hold him in check. Although no longer a young man, although crippled from wounds and rheumatism, he ran the blockade in a small boat, singlehanded, reached the land safely and was at the heart of every engagement of that year. But that was a disastrous undertaking. Defeated by the French, once more the Italian government arrested him, once more placed him in the fortress of Varignano, once more returned him to Caprera. From there, with eagle eye, he watched the events which in the end did bring about the unification and liberation of his beloved Italy. Surrounded by a corps of friends who came and went, he lived relatively at peace.

But like all really great personalities, he had become a bone of contention. Men argued and still argue about him, the while reflecting their own frailties, their own loves and hates, their own bewilderments and agonies. Some saw in Garibaldi's great deeds mere flashes of accidental greatness, the accidents of time and place. They repeated over and over d'Azeglio's saying that Garibaldi had "the heart of gold and the brains of an ox." In that too they reflected their own values.

Garibaldi's heart was of an utterly different species. He had an elemental sympathy for all who suffered, all who were bowed, all the oppressed, literally the world over. Forlorn causes were his meat and drink. Nor was it great causes alone that moved him. All kinds of persons: mothers of children lost in his campaigns, mothers of those whom he had never known, orphans and widows, people in high and low places who had suffered wrongs—all commanded his sympathy.

In one case he took pains to employ an attorney in Nice to see to it that a person whom he did not know in Montevideo had justice done to him in collecting a few lire from an inheritance left him in Italy. People in trouble all over the world turned to Garibaldi as a matter of course. Even in the midst of his campaigns he had time to write to these. In his correspondence with the United States regarding his taking part in the Civil War, the one condition he kept reiterating over and over was that the slaves be set free.

As to his brains: if such brains were of oxen, what furrows of freedom could oxen beat! His mind was like a powerful ray that instantly germinated nobility of deed, deeds of daring, of rectitude, in all who had capacity to understand him. His simplicity, directness, almost naïveté, endeared him to all who came in direct contact with him. Part of his power lay in his personal appearance, his candid face, his long, reddish-gold tresses hanging over his shoulders. His power lay also in the quickness of his movement and action and in that inexplicable, native fascination which fairly hypnotized all who came under his influence.

The staid and calculating, those concerned with the safe-guarding of their own preserve, their position, their power, shrugged their shoulders. "He's an idealist, an inconsistent fool, hard to get along with." No doubt he was some of all these. What rugged peak does not jut above "our low content?"

In many respects, however, Garibaldi was exceedingly practical and consistent. His first and supreme aim was to free Italy from the enslavement of the multitude of oppressors that thrived like vermins on its soil. He subordinated everything, everybody, including himself, to that objective. The establishment of a republic was always of great concern to him, but liberation and unification came first. To mix the two issues might mean losing both: it might mean serious internal difficulties, possible civil war, antago-nizing friendly foreign powers, such as England.

Garibaldi was practical in another respect: he wanted to see concrete evidence that people themselves were willing to fight for liberty and unity, before he himself would do anything to help them. When Mazzini, back in 1854 in London, urged him to un-dertake the Sicilian campaign, he replied that he would do nothing of the kind until he had certain proof that the Sicilians were them-selves going to do something about it. Further, he was sufficiently practical to see that Mazzini's Dieppelike raids, such as those of the Pisacane and Pilo, amounted to nothing but the loss of some of the finest Italian youth.

On one point even Garibaldi's warmest friends take issue with him. He argued with Mazzini against the establishment of a republic in Italy on the grounds that the deplorable conditions of the South, the political corruption and the irresponsibility of all classes in that region, were positive proof that the Italian people were not ready for a republic. A republic would mean nothing but license and looting, violence and crime, he maintained.

Had Garibaldi been better versed in history he would have known that that is a familiar refrain; that that argument has been used times without number, everywhere, wherever any downtrod-den people have aspired to liberty and to some measure of democratic government; he would have known that that contention had been employed even in his own yesterday of the French and American revolutions. And were he living in this year 1943 he would hear the Fascists, the Nazis, and other principalities and powers in and out of Italy using that same "old saw" with reference to the Italy of tomorrow. Italians have had almost three-quarters of a century of quasi-democratic rule, still there are those who with diplomatic unction lift their eyes to the heavens and proclaim to all the world that the Italians are not yet ready for self-government.

Italy and the world remember Garibaldi, are inspired by the memory of him, wherever his life is known. His profound sympathy for suffering mankind, his great reverence for the teachings of Christ, his eagerness directly to aid the distressed and the oppressed, were among his mastering qualities. He was resolute, quick in action, decisive; he loved candor as he hated subtlety, resoluteness as he abhorred temporizing, directness as he despised finesse. He was fundamentally open, generous, honorable. It was these characteristics that entwined men's hearts and through them made possible, at least in part, the unification of Italy; these characteristics that make him a lasting influence in the minds and hearts of men, wherever his name is heard, his life is known.

He shunned honors, emoluments, prestige, power. To those who followed him, as to himself, he offered only "thirst and heat during the day, and cold and hunger at night, danger always; and as a simple compensation to free and generous hearts, the independence of Italy."

Foolish? Vain talking? That is the stuff that makes enduring, ennobles all that is worth preserving in this brief human existence and worth transferring from age to age. No less a sober historian than Trevelyan, referring to the very subject of this sketch, puts it thus: "With our eyes fixed on realism and the doctrine of evolution [we] are in some danger of losing faith in ideals, and of forgetting the power that a few fearless and utterly disinterested men may have in a world where the proportion of cowards and egotists is not small." The rash will need to learn that they cannot dispense with wisdom. But the prudent should learn that "in the uncertain currents of the world's affairs there come rare moments, hard to distinguish but fatal to let slip, when caution is dangerous, when all must be set upon a hazard, and out of the simple man is ordained strength."

As if the whole world were his country, Garibaldi was now to take one last stand on the field of battle. He had fought from the pampas of South America to the southernmost tip of Sicily; he had sponsored or was to sponsor the cause of liberty in Greece and Crete, Rumania, Serbia, Herzegovina and Montenegro, in Switzerland, Hungary, Poland, Bohemia, Prussia, in Spain and Mexico. Far ahead of his time, he had repeatedly pleaded with the rulers of Europe to give up their futile fracticide, to organize a European Federation and live in peace. He had often urged men to learn from America, "apostle of liberty to our fathers, harbinger of progress," as he had written to Lincoln. But it was not enough. He must take one last stand, perhaps it would be the last chance he would have, actually to wage battle in behalf of human liberty. After Sedan, though he was over sixty, he offered his services to the provisional republican government of France and he fought in his usual vigorous manner, in the Franco-Prussian War, in command of the Army of the Vosges.

His return to Caprera in February, 1871, was to be his last. When the census blank reached him that year, he scrawled "profession agriculturist." Free and united Italy elected him to its Parliament and voted him a pension. First he refused, but when progressive elements came into power he accepted. He lived in Rome off and on, actively engaged in any and all causes that promised improvement for the masses. Caprera, however, continued to be his real home. There he remained, constantly sending out "short waves" of his passion for liberty, in every direction, till one evening in June, 1882, at the age of seventy-five he passed on. In his will he had requested that his body be cremated and the ashes strewn to the winds and the waves of the sea that he had loved so long, so dearly, that he might be free, in death. But the powers decreed otherwise. Forces far beyond his control interfered, to the end. Beyond the end. There still rest his remains, on his beloved little island, which now again looks upon troubled Italy.

There lie his remains. Yet his spirit is still at large, unfettered. And wherever the least flicker of aspiration burns in the human heart, wherever men fight for a breath of freedom, the spark known as Giuseppe Garibaldi still burns, still inspires, still leads men on.

KARL MARX

by

PIERRE COT

PIERRE COT

born in 1895 in the French Alps, spent his youth in the Savoie mountains. He loves their men and beasts and flowers, he owes them his joy and his habits and the molding of his mind.

After serving in the First World War he studied at the universities of Grenoble and Paris and became professor at the University of Rennes. In 1928 elected deputy from his native Savoie, he was a member of the French Chamber of Deputies for twelve years. In the same year Pierre Cot was appointed by Aristide Briand member of the French delegation to the League of Nations. Subsequently he was, at various times, minister of air and minister of commerce.

Up to 1932 the French reactionaries attacked him because he championed close relations with democratic Germany. After 1932 they attacked him because he favored a Franco-Soviet alliance and because he was one of the founders of the Popular Front.

Pierre Cot, who is a prolific writer, believes in collective security and in the traditions of the French Revolution. He came to America in 1940. He recently said: "Had I my life to live over again I should change nothing in its general course, but I should like to be granted even more power against my enemies: the Fascists."

KARL MARX
by Pierre Cot

Day in, day out, for thirty years, from 1850 to 1880, a period embracing the greater part of the Victorian era, the attendants at the British Museum were wont to observe the same familiar figure dart across the threshold as the doors swung open. It was a very dark man, with a luxuriant beard, a high majestic brow, a piercing glance, and a rough boorish look about him. He was so swarthy, and looked so fierce, that his family and intimates had dubbed him "the Moor."

Always, he carried an old brief case, which grew more worn year by year and was crammed with papers and manuscripts. He was poorly clad, and obviously a foreigner. Truth to tell, he had been banished from Germany for political reasons and was now pursuing a course of exhaustive research in the library.

He would sit fast at his table until nightfall, going through the documents he had called for, and taking voluminous notes. Then, having cast the glance of a vexed prophet over the city, he would fade away into the rainy mist, bound for the most modest of lodgings in some wretched quarter of Chelsea or Soho. There a smiling wife and the happy cries of many children welcomed him. After a scant meal, consisting often of but bread and potatoes, the Moor would jest with his daughters for a while and give his youngest sons pickaback rides. After which he would closet himself in the nook which served him as study and bedroom, to spend a considerable part of the night meditating upon the history and evolution of human society, pacing up and down like a caged lion, smoking incessantly to the point of nausea, and

pausing only to jot down in his small nervous writing the ideas
which stormed his brain.

These ideas were destined to turn the world topsy-turvy, for
the man was Karl Marx, Doctor of Philosophy.

Most of Marx's life was spent in exile. He was not yet
twenty-five when he left his native Germany in 1843 to go to
Paris. Fifteen months later, expelled from France, he found a
haven in Belgium. When, in 1848, the Belgian government in
turn banished him, he went back to Germany where, for the
moment, a certain current of liberalism was in the air. Nevertheless, the following year, after attempting to have him condemned by the courts, the Prussian government banished him
again. Marx thereupon left for London and there he spent the
rest of his days in labor, dignity, and poverty.

In the first place, the chief characteristic of Marx's life in
exile was his intellectual activity. This activity extended to
philosophy, history, the political and economic sciences; it revealed a store of knowledge few human beings have ever accumu-
lated. In his immense work, his harshest critics have never been
able to unearth one error in fact, figure, or date. Indeed, he carried
intellectual probity so far that late in life he studied Russian in
order not to be wholly dependent upon a more or less faithful
translator.

Secondly, this life of work was spent in the dignity of the
family circle. When still young, before leaving Germany, he had
married his childhood friend, the beautiful Jenny von Westphalen. There was something romantic about the marriage. The
union of a young philosopher of Jewish origin and the descendent
of an old aristocratic Germany family had roused much opposition, less on the part of the parents than on that of kinsman and
friends. Yet this marriage turned out to be the happiest in the
world; never a cloud darkened their horizon. Jenny shared both
the privations and the thoughts of the man she loved. Numerous
children were born to them; and Marx proved to be an attentive,
indulgent, and tender father. This man, generally irritable and
sometimes violent, was capable of deep affection and of warm
friendships, as, for instance, his long relation with Friedrich
Engels.

Finally, Marx's life in exile was spent amid poverty. A formidable polemist and, when he wished, a brilliant writer, he could readily have followed a lucrative career in journalism. But to do so he would have had to forego his scientific activities. He preferred poverty, one which the hatred of his political enemies soon turned into actual want. For long years, to meet the needs of his large family, he was reduced to the sum of one pound a week, the price of his weekly article for the New York *Tribune* —and to the generosity of his friend Engels, himself often short of money.

Pursued by their creditors, Marx and his family experienced all the suffering and humiliation of indigence; they went hungry and they were cold. Three of his children died partly for lack of adequate care. "I could not and I cannot fetch the doctor," Marx wrote to Engels, "because I have no money for the medicine. For the last eight or ten days I have fed my family on bread and potatoes, and today it is even doubtful if I shall be able to obtain these." At the death of little Franziska, her parents had not enough money to pay for her coffin. When poverty reaches such tragic limits.and is voluntarily accepted as the ransom of freedom of spirit, it becomes downright heroism.

Indeed, of all who bore the torch of liberty in exile during the last century, Marx was surely among the greatest. His influence after his death never ceased to grow; the significance of his thought may be gauged as much by the enmity it aroused as by the enthusiasm it created. Hitler, Mussolini, the Fascists and reactionaries of the whole world have always posed as champions of anti-Marxism; but the construction of a "new civilization" in Soviet Russia pursued its course under the sign of the doctrine evolved by Marx in long years of obdurate labor.

I do not seek here to present even a summary picture of the work Marx accomplished in exile. I would simply show how much the fact that he spent so many years outside his native land contributed to the formation and enrichment of his mind. If he was among the geniuses of his age, it was because, a citizen of the world, his activity extended to the frontiers of humanity. He was at once a philosopher, a political thinker, an economist. If it is permissible to define so vast an intellect within the limits of one simple line, I should venture to say that he owed his philosophical culture to Germany, his political culture to France, and his economic culture to England. Thus his doctrine would have been less complete if, first, the Prussian government and then the French had not, by their decrees of expulsion, driven him to follow lifelong the cycle of his intellectual formation.

When he reached Paris in 1843, Karl Marx was in no sense a political agitator, let alone a professional revolutionary. He was a youthful doctor of philosophy, passionately interested in the discussion of ideas. He possessed, at that period, the tastes, the serious aspect, and I dare say, the professional deformities of the German scholar of the romantic era: a certain pedantry, a certain ponderousness, but great intellectual honesty.

He was born at Trier in 1818. His father, a liberal lawyer of Jewish origin, had become a convert to Protestantism, less, it would seem, to embrace the Christian faith than to cast off the Jewish. Marx's childhood was a happy one, passed in a beautiful country of hills, vineyards and song, its graces heightened by the majesty of the Rhine. At seventeen he was sent to the University of Bonn; the following year he registered at the University of Berlin.

Berlin was then a gloomy and cheerless city; a young student from the South could find little to do there outside his academic studies. Marx plunged headlong into his work, and, discovering that his true vocation lay in the realm of pure ideas, he soon transferred from the Law School to the Philosophy.

Like all German universities, that of Berlin was then particularly interested in abstract speculation. After a long period of torpor, due to the exhaustion that followed the Thirty Years' War, German thought, reawakening at the call of Kant, Fichte and Goethe, had begun that extremely brilliant cycle which was to run for more than a century. In 1836, when young Marx arrived in Berlin, Hegel's philosophy formed the mainspring of this renaissance. As it developed, Hegelian philosophy gave birth to two currents: the one clearly reactionary, the other tending from liberalism to radicalism. Marx was gifted with too much temperament not to take part in the struggles which aligned the rightist Hegelians against the leftist Hegelians; he was gifted with too much intellectual curiosity not to join the liberal ranks. Soon he was admitted to the Doktor Klub, a group of young philosophers headed by Bruno Bauer; nor was it long ere he became one of its most active members. Thus his youthful years were devoted to study and to doctrinal controversy; and his mind was inured to the use of Hegelian dialectics to such an extent as to bear out Lenin's judgment when he observes that it is impossible to understand Marx's works "without having mastered thoroughly all the Hegelian logic."

In 1843 Marx was graduated doctor of Philosophy of the University of Jena. His ambition went no further than teaching philosophy in a small German university. But the Prussian government prevented him from fulfilling this dream, modest though it was. Subject to Metternich's influence, Prussia one of the most reactionary states in Europe, fully realized the perils to which liberal doctrines exposed a social order established upon religion, the police, and the principle of hierarchy. A member of the Doktor Klub thus had no chance to make his career in the professional world.

For want of anything better to do, Marx accepted a position as editor on the *Rheinische Zeitung,* a liberal organ which some Rhenish manufacturers had founded in order to defend their interests against the bureaucracy in Berlin. He took up residence in Cologne and was soon appointed director of the gazette.

His career as chief at the *Rheinische Zeitung* was as brilliant as it was brief. Thanks to his talent as a polemist, the circulation of the periodical rose rapidly; but its success invited the ire of the Prussian governor. In April, 1843, after frequent differences with the censorship, the *Rheinische Zeitung* was suppressed. Finding himself once again without employment, Marx made the most of his enforced leisure by marrying Jenny von Westphalen and spending a few months at Kreuznach. It was then that he decided, in concert with his wife, to leave Germany. "The atmosphere here is really too intolerable," he wrote to one of his friends. "I am tired of the hypocrisy, stupidity, and boorishness of officials. In Germany there is nothing I can do . . . in Germany one can only be false to oneself."

At this period of his life Marx believed that the progress
of human thought must result in some sort of union between
German and French thought. With another "young Hegelian,"
Arnold Rüge, he resolved to publish a Franco-German review,
the *Deutsch-Franzoesische Jahrbuecher*. Rüge gathered the necessary funds and the two friends set out for Paris, armed with that
solid philosophical culture which Germany alone could then supply to young minds.

In November, 1843, Karl and Jenny reached Paris where
Rüge was awaiting them. Paris was then the intellectual capital
of the world. French thought, first bound hand and foot by
Napoleon, then stifled by the Restoration, was now enjoying its
new-found freedom and burning with a new flame. Romanticism
had extended the boundaries of the public mind; France admired
Shakespeare, grew passionately fond of Byron, waxed enthusiastic over Goethe, and devoured the historical novels of Sir
Walter Scott. If the constitutional monarchy of Louis Philippe
lacked grandeur, it was at least tolerant. Paris had become the
refuge of exiles, rebels, freethinkers, and revolutionists; in a
word, of all those who dreamed of adding something to the
common treasure of humanity.

The contribution of Paris to the intellectual progress of the
world was as great in politics as in literature. France was then
the cradle of socialism. The period and place abounded in systems, plans, and doctrines which were sometimes ingenious, often
childish, but always generous. Moreover, it would be a mistake
to reduce French socialism during the romantic period—socialism
in blossom—to unworkable dreams and mad chimeras.

To measure the importance of this effort, we must recall
what a low and backward station the historical and economic
sciences occupied during the early part of the nineteenth century.
Romantic socialism strove to prolong the doctrines of the French
Revolution along economic and social lines and to apply to modern
society the spirit of the Declaration of the Rights of Man. If
"journeys into the land of Icaria" were proposed, scientific and
philosophical works were nevertheless being drafted. Before Marx,
Saint-Simon had been the first to point out how important the

economic factor was in the development of society and to show the part played by class struggle in the process of history. Fourier had forcefully criticized economic liberalism and denounced the illusions of laissez faire. Proudhon had launched vigorous attacks upon the dawning capitalism, while others, like Barbès and Blanqui, had concentrated their efforts upon political action and the organization of workers. All this was far from negligible; indeed, it had placed the France of 1840 as the leader in the renewal of European political thought.

Paris was not only the cradle of socialist thought, it was one of the vital centers of modern economics. A new world, that of finance and the manufacturing industries, had come to birth and was in process of organization. The technical and industrial revolution was taking shape and following the same pattern in France and England, while Germany, hampered by its internal custom barriers, had not yet been swept into that vast movement which was to overturn at once the economic, the social, and the political orders of the world. Thus France was the great industrial and financial power of continental Europe and the characteristics of capitalistic society, in process of formation, were more clearly marked there than anywhere else.

Moreover, France had adapted its political institutions to the needs of the new economics. The revolution of 1830 had substituted the power of the bourgeoisie for that of the traditional aristocracy. Banking and manufacture, under the constitutional monarchy of Louis Philippe, had taken the place occupied by the Church and the nobility under the "restored" monarchies of Louis XVIII and Charles X.

In brief, a somewhat exceptional combination of historical circumstances enabled Marx to find in Paris, the intellectual capital of the world, the stammerings of socialism and the realities of capitalism, or, in other words, all the fundamentals of modern society.

How was the young German philosopher to react against these new conditions so different from those which he had known?

The youthful couple settled down in a small apartment on the left bank of the Seine and established their first contacts with the German émigrés, then numerous in Paris. One of their earliest and dearest friends was Heinrich Heine, the poet; through his good offices they soon knew everyone worth knowing both in Parisian society and in the foreign colony.

In the early days of his sojourn in Paris, Marx was much absorbed in preparing to launch his review. The first number of the *Deutsch-Franzoesische Jahrbuecher* appeared in February, 1844, in the form of two volumes. But the review soon found itself at grips with such financial difficulties that this first number was also its last. Marx was again without employment but, the master of his time, he had ample opportunity to pursue his studies and to extend the field of his knowledge.

It was at this period that he met Friedrich Engels, who was to play Pylades to his Orestes. The two young men discovered that albeit through different channels—the one through philosophy, the other through political economy—they had arrived at similar ideas and conclusions. From this rose one of those perfect friendships which death alone can dissolve and which Cicero defined for all time when he wrote: "Idem velle, idem nolle, id demum est amicitia."

It was in Paris too that Marx met Proudhon. He spent long evenings initiating the famous polemist in the beauties of Hegelian dialectics, which Proudhon, a former workman in a printing shop and a curious self-taught man, wished to acquire. These conversations resulted in a work called *The Philosophy of Poverty* which he submitted to Marx. The latter then perceived that his pupil had understood absolutely nothing of dialectics. The great irritation he conceived at this was to vent itself a few years later in a reply Marx called *The Poverty of Philosophy*.

Meanwhile, to occupy his leisure moments, Marx had become interested in *Vorwaerts,* a German weekly of radical tendencies which existed thanks partly to a subsidy from the musician Meyerbeer. The Prussian government requested the French government to suppress this periodical. At first Guizot resisted; then, in January, 1845, he agreed to banish the collaborators, including Marx.

Marx then repaired to Brussels, where the police and government observed his arrival with some dread. Though only twenty-seven, he was already considered one of the leaders of radical thought in Europe. To obtain permission to reside in the country, Marx was forced to sign a statement whereby "he agreed on his honor not to publish in Belgium any work on the politics of the day."

He kept his word. Engels came to join him and this period of his life was devoted to scientific labors which were utterly alien to the "politics of the day." These labors enabled him to complete the evolution which led him from liberalism to communism.

In 1847 he went to London with Engels to attend the Congress of the League of the Just, which was subsequently to become the Communist League. The two friends were appointed to draw up a program which became the celebrated *Communist Manifesto*.

Published on the eve of the revolution of 1848, this document remains the most important monument of communism. It was a flaming torch that Marx cast at the old world. "A specter is haunting Europe, the specter of communism," said the manifesto. "All the powers of old Europe have entered into a holy alliance to exorcise this specter : Pope and Czar, Metternich and Guizot, French radicals and German police spies . . . It is high time that communists should openly, in the face of the whole world, publish their views, their aims, their tendencies, and meet this nursery tale of the specter of communism with a manifesto of thè party itself."

After sketching a vast picture of social evolution, showing the contradictions of capitalism and exposing their own doctrines, the authors of the manifesto launched their famous appeal to the union of workers to free humanity : "The proletarians have nothing to lose but their chains. They have a world to win."

Thus Marx's exile in Brussels completed his Paris exile, for his philosophical and political thinking had come to maturity. His influence continued to grow. Barely thirty years old, he terrified the conservatives and the timid by the boldness of his ideas, but aroused the enthusiasm of the workers by the generosity of his feelings, and earned the respect of all true men by the rigor of his reasoning and the purity of his convictions.

He fared poorly, moving from furnished room to garret, in order to escape from his creditors. He boasted some devoted friends and many desperate enemies; his pride as a prophet and his scrupulousness as a scholar frequently threw him into violent controversies with men who had been his dearest friends the day before. When the revolution of 1848 broke out, the Belgian government seized the first available pretext to banish the young "revolutionary." The youthful French republic, which had just driven out King Louis Philippe with gusto, offered him its welcome; but Marx left for Cologne, where new tasks awaited him.

In the course of this first period of exile, which includes his sojourns in Paris and Brussels, the German philosopher and professional dialectician had become the most active animator of the workers' movement in Europe; he had, in brief, founded scientific socialism. This transformation in him occurred not by great leaps and bounds nor by a sort of sudden conversion but by a lengthy and continuous deepening of the philosophical doctrine which he had acquired during his years of study in Germany. In the homeland, he had passed gradually from the dialectics of Hegel to the philosophical materialism of Feuerbach; he himself, in 1859, in the preface of his book *The Criticism of Political Economy* told how, subsequently, in the course of his early years of exile, he was to reach this second stage in the development of his thought:

> In 1842-1843, as editor of the *Rheinische Zeitung,* I found myself embarrassed at first, when I had to take part in discussions concerning so-called material interest. The proceedings of the Rhine diet in connection with forest thefts and the extreme subdivisions of landed property; the official controversy about the condition of the Moselle peasants, into which Herr von Schaper, at that time president of the Rhine province, entered with the *Rheinische Zeitung;* finally the debates on Free Trade and protection, gave me the first impulse to take up the study of economic questions. . . .
>
> The first work undertaken for the solution of the question that troubled me was a critical revision of Hegel's *Philosophy of Law.* I was led to the conclusion that legal relations as well as forms of state could neither be understood by themselves nor explained by the so-called progress of the human mind, but that they are rooted in the

material conditions of life, which are summed up, by Hegel, under the name of civil society; the anatomy of that society is to be sought in political economy. The study of the latter, which I had taken up in Paris, I continued at Brussels, whither I emigrated on account of an order of expulsion issued by M. Guizot.

And here are the conclusions to which this study of "the anatomy of civil society" led him:

> In the social production which men carry on, they enter into definite relations that are indispensable and independent of their will; these relations of production correspond to a definite state of development of their material power of production. The sum total of these relations constitutes the economic structure of society—the real foundation from which rise legal and political structures, and to which correspond definite forms of social consciousness. The mode of production in material life determines the general character of the social, political, and spiritual processes of life. It is not the consciousness of men that determines their existence, but on the contrary, their social existence that determines their consciousness.

This long quotation shows us how Marx arrived at the conception of "historic materialism" which was to dominate his work and which remains his most important contribution to the advancement of the social sciences. Applying Hegelian dialectics to his materialistic conception of history, he saw in the movements and contradictions of contemporary society reasons for hoping in a society in which man, freed from class opposition and class struggle, might emerge "out of the prehistoric stage of human society" to attain liberty. Thus it was that Marx arrived at socialism and communism.

What part, then, did exile play in this intellectual evolution, and what contribution was Paris to make to Marx's doctrine?

In the first place, it was in Paris that Karl Marx was first exposed to the spirit of the Declaration of the Rights of Man, to the spirit of the French Revolution. He grew conscious of the value and dignity of the individual, the supreme end of all civil-

izations. Indeed, he intended to write a history of the Convention.
What interested him in the French Revolution was not so much
its initial success as its ultimate failure. He wondered how the
Convention, which had represented "a maximum of political
energy, political power, and political understanding," had been
powerless to dominate "social anarchy" and to impose its views
upon its opponents. His expulsion from France prevented him
from carrying out the project; but his research and his reflections
led him to believe that the Convention's failure rose from the
fact that the French Revolution had aimed not at the total liberation of the people, but rather at the liberation of but one part of
the people—the bourgeoisie of city and country. "The Terror,"
he wrote some years later, "served only to cause the magnificent
disappearance, under its powerful hammer blows, of the feudal
ruins on the French territory." Thus the revolution had abolished
a political order corresponding to a social order beyond which the
new economic conditions had gone. It had done nothing more.

On the other hand, Paris afforded Marx the opportunity to
observe the reciprocal reactions of the social and political orders.
Looking observantly about him, he understood that the forms and
movements of political society are determined by the forms and
movements of economic activity. From this he concluded that in
society the "infrastructure" is economic and that the modifications
of the infrastructure inevitably, after a short time, involves the
modifications of the political "superstructure." He discovered that
after the French Revolution the infrastructure of France had
become modified: wealth had changed form and hands; and the
economic power, instead of belonging mainly to the great landowners, the nobility, and the clergy, was now mainly in the
hands of the new class of bankers and manufacturers. Marx
realized that the political superstructure had fallen into line with
these changes. In one of his works that examine French history,
he explained the revolution of 1830 and its consequences not by
"rivalry between the house of Bourbon and the house of Orleans"
but by "the opposition between the class of big landowners and
the capitalists born out of the industrial revolution." Thus the
sudden leaps and bounds by which French politics progressed
facilitated Marx's analysis of the mechanism of the state.

Lastly, Marx discovered the proletariat of Paris, which was then the most intelligent and cultivated of all proletariats. During the social and political upheavals which gave birth to modern France—the revolution of 1789-1793 and the revolution of 1830 —the workmen of France had attained a surprising political maturity. They constituted the truly clear-sighted, generous, and dynamic portion of the French nation; their attitude offered a glaring contrast to a bourgeoisie already marred by the taints which recent events in our day have bared to the world. It was by becoming intimate with the French workman that Marx learned to understand the important historical role which the proletariat was called upon to play in the evolution of modern society. In the workmen he saw brave men, conscious of social realities yet oppressed and sometimes degraded by the material conditions of their lives, and by the economic servitude that weighed, ever more heavily, upon their shoulders.

From this he concluded that the liberation of the proletariat, "wretched and conscious of its own wretchedness," would be the liberation of humanity itself, since "the proletariat as proletariat" remained the last class that was enslaved and exploited. Marx was ever ready to offer the French workers to others as a model. "When the communist artisans band together," he wrote, "their aim is, first, instruction, propaganda, etc. . . . But at the same time a new need stirs in them, the need to have intercourse with their own kind . . . The brilliant results achieved by this practical movement may be seen in the association of French socialist workers; on their lips the brotherhood of man is not a phrase, but a truth; and in their faces that labor has scarred shines all the beauty of humanity."

Marx's second political exile, his exile in England, lasted longer than his exile in France and Belgium but calls for less comment.

When he reached London in 1849 he was just thirty, but his personality was already so rich and so powerful that exile and contact with other men exercised little hold over him. He was no longer, as in Paris, a student seeking out his way; he was a man with a vigorous and masterful brain. The traits of his character were strongly and clearly marked; he was already armed with his own method of work, his own general conception of the world, his own political doctrine, and his own will to participate in the march of the world. In other words, he had nothing more to acquire; he needed but to verify and to apply his ideas.

Again, London possessed no such educative values as Paris. The London of his day was more remote from the rest of Europe than Paris and Brussels; it was even more remote than the small town of the Rhineland. "Insularity" was more than a word; it was a fact governed by difficulties in travel. Further, Marx was too much a citizen of the world to adopt the current British code of thinking. What London did supply him with was that sense of intellectual and moral liberty which England assures alike to its own nationals and to those foreigners it shelters. Such a climate accommodates a strong personality, and Marx was quick to sense its value. He mingled little in the life of London, he had few English friends. But he appreciated the qualities and the institutions of the British people. True, he often blamed their policies; but he was convinced that of all Europeans the British alone were capable of avoiding violent revolutions and of shaping their political institutions in accordance with economic transformations and social evolution.

What manner of life did he lead in the British capital?

I have already mentioned his work and his privations, his long sessions at the British Museum, his financial troubles, and his penury. A spy of the Prussian government, detailed to watch him, supplied a police report that covers the background of Marx's existence:

> He lives in one of the worst and cheapest neighbor-hoods in London. He occupies two rooms. There is not one decent piece of furniture in either room; everything is broken, tattered, and torn, with thick dust over everything . . . manuscripts, books, and newspapers lie beside the children's toys, bits and pieces from his wife's sewing basket, cups with broken rims, etc. . . . Here is a chair with only three legs, there another which happens to be whole, on which the children are playing at cooking. . . But all these things do not in the least embarrass him or

his wife. You are received in the most friendly way and are cordially offered pipes and tobacco and whatever else there may happen to be. Presently a clever and interesting conversation arises which repays for all the domestic deficiencies, and this makes the discomfort bearable.

Marx was no Bohemian, but rather a highly studious man; he suffered from this squalor, physically and, even more, mentally, for himself and for his family. In 1856, when he lost his son Edgar, this infinitely proud man wrote letters to his friend Engels betraying a kind of infinitely touching despair:
"I have suffered every kind of misfortune but I have only just learned what real unhappiness is."
His work and his wife's love supported him in his effort. As the years passed, his influence spread, his renown increased, and political work added its burden to his strictly scientific labors. In 1862, when the French workers' delegates came to visit the London Exposition, it was decided to create the Workers' International. Two years later this organization came into being. On this occasion Marx made an *Inaugural Address* which, in importance, matched the *Communist Manifesto;* and, flanked by faithful Engels, he assumed the direction of the new movement. In Marx's hands the International was destined to grow rapidly until it became a political instrument powerful enough to worry the governments of Europe. Thus Marx was placed in direct contact with representatives of the workers of all countries: people came from everywhere to consult him, visitors flocked to his lodgings, he laid down directives, framed policies, and set the keynote to vast movements.

To this political activity Marx brought all the uncompromising ardor and ruthlessly strict principles that characterized his thinking. He would brook no error, tolerate no ignorance, countenance no disloyalty. Thus he found himself engaging in resounding quarrels worthy of the great intellectual disputes of the Renaissance. It was Proudhon he fell afoul of, and Lassalle, and Bakunin, and all those who seemed to him to be themselves going astray or, worse, leading astray the masses of the proletariat. The publication after 1920 of the German and czarist government archives established the fact that Marx's fulminant excommunications were, in the main, uttered deliberately against such would-be doctrinaries as were "flirting" with the enemies of the proletariat.

Despite his intolerance and irreconcilability, Marx as a man was not only just but kindly. His door was never closed to the refugees and exiles who sought him out; indeed, he welcomed them as brothers sent to him by destiny. The Russian sociologist Kovalevsky, who visited Marx, was touched by his courtesy. "Marx," he commented, "is usually described as a gloomy and arrogant man who flatly rejected all bourgeois science and culture. In reality, he was a well-educated and highly cultivated Anglo-German gentleman, a man whose close association with Heine had developed in him a vein of cheerful satire." His intellectual pride was only a reflection of his passion for truth. There was nothing of the pedant in him. One day when a flatterer spoke of a "Marxian concept" he broke in, observing that "in so far as I myself am concerned, I am certainly no Marxist."

His joys and distractions were as healthful as his work. He loved reading and poetry. Thanks to an inexhaustible memory he knew by heart long passages of Aeschylus, Dante and Shakespeare, and his wife often gave him his cue. His intellectual curiosity was boundless. When, in the evening of his life, he had learned Russian, he plunged with delight into Pushkin and Gogol, just as he had plunged into Balzac in his youth.

He loved physical exercise, and used to go to the outskirts of London for long walks on Hampstead Heath. Sundays, when the weather was fair and money not completely lacking, the Marx family spent the day in the woods. His son-in-law, Liebknecht, has described these days of relaxation, when the great Marx was no more than a child among children.

"On Hampstead Health, we would sometimes play 'cavalry.' I would take one little daughter on my shoulder, Marx the other one, and then we would jump and trot, outdoing each other; now and then there would be a little cavalry engagement, for the little girls were wild as boys and also could stand a bump without crying."

After which, they would pick flowers and return homeward afoot, singing old German or French folksongs.

Marx's earliest works found no more than a limited public, consisting of philosophers, historians, and political men. The publication of *Capital* spread his fame throughout the world. No other book was to earn such success; the first volume was speedily translated not only into French and German but into Spanish and Russian.

This success enabled Marx to emerge not from embarrassment, since he died a poor man, but from extreme want. Now he could at least assure his family a modest and decent if not comfortable existence.

Simultaneously he became a target for attacks and persecutions by men who feared his doctrine without having studied it or who presumed to criticize it without having understood it. Fame won him more than his share of insults and anonymous leters; yet he never seemed surprised, much less irritated, at such treament. In the eyes of the public at large he had become "the red terrorist doctor," and invested, by its imagination, with Machiavellian designs. When the Commune broke out in Paris in 1871, opinion credited him with having instigated it. In point of fact, if he was later to rise to the defense of the communards, in the beginning he had offered drastic counsel against an insurrection which he knew was doomed to failure. His increasing confidence in the workers of the entire world and the esteem in which scholars and thinkers held him were hundredfold compensation for the misunderstanding and brutality of his opponents. Marx moved forward through life, his eyes set upon a future which he devoutly hoped would be a better one; such a prospect made him immune to the bricks and stones that beset his path.

What was this doctrine which aroused at once the fright of governments, the terror of the "haves," and the enthusiasm of the masses, the "have-nots," whose thinking had progressed beyond that of any other class?

To summarize Marx's views here is pointless. Certain of his ideas are dated, others have stood up with difficulty to the lamination of critics. But the body of Marxist thought has generally been subjected to such conscious efforts of deformation that Marx's life in exile cannot be described without lodging a protest against the obvious absurdity of certain attacks. To establish this absurdity we need not consider either his economic theories or his political doctrines; it is sufficient to discuss his general conception of the world and of history, or, in other words, the very crucible of his thought. Sedulous to discredit this thought by falsifying it, his antagonists generally affect to assimilate Marx's historical materialism to vulgar materialism and to fatalism. Marx is amoral, people say, because he demands no effort of man; he expects a spontaneous evolution, at once mechanical and brutal, whereby the so-called "capitalistic hell" will be transformed into a so-called "communistic paradise." More, they continue, in his general interpretation of history he neglects the most noble aspirations of man. Right, a sense of justice, the notion of liberty, all these fade out for Marx before the vulgar satisfaction of material interests and the search for economic ends.

The truth is quite different.

To begin with, Marx's philosophy is a philosophy of effort. Were his works wanting, his life would amply prove this. If he professed that man is a product of history, he knew that history is made by men, that history results from the activity of men, and that history may be reduced to the efforts of men. "History," he wrote, "wages no battle; it is the real man, the living man who acts, who possesses, and who struggles. It is not history that, like some independent person, uses man to achieve her ends; for history is no more and no less than the activity of man pursuing his ends." In his reply to Proudhon he made a point of the fact that "all history is but a transformation of human nature."

The plain truth is that Marx expected this transformation to result from a change brought about in the social milieu in which the human being develops. As we have seen, he believed that our ideas, our feelings, our judgments are *conditioned* or *determined* by the sort of existence we lead, that is, by the society we live in. Marx was a determinist; he had every right to be so. However, we need not revive the somewhat vain debate over free will in order to remark that the most apparently abstract notions, such as law, justice and liberty, change in value and content when "social relations" are modified. These notions do not mean the same to the real man living in Washington in 1943 and the real man who lived in Byzantium in the age of Theodosius; nor do they mean the same to the primitive man in the˙ heart of the equatorial forest as they do to the man living in London, or to a Harvard professor, a Wall Street banker, a Moscow worker, and a Hindou untouchable.

Further, Marx's materialism is historical: he sought to interpret not the actions of the individual as such, but rather the great movements of history. Now, history is subject to the law of great numbers; it results rather from collective currents than from isolated acts. The acts of an individual are nothing in this process of history if they are not integrated with the more or less conscious action of peoples. It has become trite to remark that Napoleon I, born twenty years earlier or twenty years later, would have been no more than an obscure soldier. As Antonio Labriola noted about the Marxist conception of history: "Martin Luther, like the other great reformers who were his contemporaries, never knew, as we know today, that the whole movement of the Reformation was but one moment in the gradual growth of the Third Estate and a rebellion of German nationalists against papal exploitation."

If Marx in his interpretation of social evolution lent so much importance to the economic factor, it was not through prejudice but because the observation of realities had directed his thought. "In the materialistic conception of history," Labriola added, "there is no question of retranslating into economic categories all the complicated manifestations of history, but simply of explaining, in the last analysis [Engels], all historical facts by *means of the subjacent economic structure* [Marx] which requires analysis and reduction, then meditation and composition."

In what, I ask, is this conception more shocking than Taine's, which explained history by means of the milieu? In what is this doctrine more vulgar than that lately made fashionable by the geopoliticians, which emphasizes the importance of continents and seas in the conduct of states and in the lives of nations? If Marx's thought had perforce to be rejected as scandalous heresy, I much fear that, by the same token, we should have to reject the most masterly works of our historians and sociologists. After all, the theological approach to history cannot possibly satisfy the curiosity of modern science.

Finally, we must note the noble ideal which inspired Marx's life and his work. "Even the faults of his prophecy," Harold Laski writes, "may be pardoned to an agitator in exile, to whom the cause of the oppressed was dearer than his own welfare." If he plunged headlong into action, regardless of self or possessions, if he bore indigence so admirably, and if he braved the cruelest insults, it was because, through the mists of the future, at the end of great efforts and long struggles, he foresaw a classless society. This society would be a more equitable and brotherly one, in which man would cease to be "a wolf toward man," in which "partnership" would take the place of "competition," in which "the realm of necessity" (i.e., the time devoted by each of us to material labor) would be reduced in favor of the "reign of liberty" (i.e., to the profit of disinterested culture).

For Marx, indeed, modern man is not free, he is the prisoner of his social condition and of his job; class divisions and the implacable class struggle are obstacles to the liberation of man. Man will recover, or rather find, his liberty only by creating conditions of liberty, a creation which presupposes the abolition of classes. The end Marx sought was not the liberation of one class at the expense of another, but the liberation of humanity by the abolition of all classes. "Communism," he wrote, "is the return of man to himself, but as social man, or with all the riches originating in the earliest development [of humanity]. . . . Communism coincides with the humanism of tomorrow."

What in all this smacks of vulgar materialism? Where is there one note of hatred? Where is there the slightest suggestion of demagogy? If Marx was, as has been said, the prophet of proletarianism, he did not supply the world of workers with the charter of its rights, he preached to it the gospel of its duties; he indicated the mission it should accomplish, he never concealed either the sternness or the grandeur of its historic task. To Marx the proletariat of today was the creation, condition, and ransom of capitalism, just as slavery had been the creation, condition, and ransom of society in the days of antiquity. This appeared to him as a degradation of human nature and spelled a loss of wealth for humanity. The abolition of the proletariat ("intellectual and physical misery conscious of its misery, inhumanity conscious of its inhumanity"), the end of all economic servitude, and the suppression of the rule of classes seemed to him to be both the end of a long evolution prepared by the work of centuries and the condition of humanity's emancipation. "Once these are accomplished," he wrote, "then humanity will emerge from prehistory."

Accordingly, we must not hesitate to place Karl Marx among that handful of humanists who, in the course of history, strove constantly to speed man along the path of progress, and who sacrificed themselves to the noble teaching of ideas.

His glance leveled upon the future, Marx advanced through life without ever suffering the wickedness of man or the rigor of events to divert him from his task. Age whitened his beard and head without modifying his habits. He was seen less frequently at the British Museum; but, rising before seven o'clock every morning, he continued to devote the major part of his time to endless study, reading, meditation, and writing. He now lived almost entirely in his study, which was piled high with books and manuscripts; no one was allowed to touch these, since he alone held the secret of the apparent disorder that startled his visitors. His distractions remained the same: long walks, readings of his favorite authors, and highly skillful games of chess. His grandchildren now took the place of his dead or married children; like Victor Hugo, he was supremely gifted in "the art of being a grandfather." His alert mind still lay in wait for discoveries and novelties; when death called him, he was passionately studying the works of the scientist Marcel Deprez on electricity.

At sixty, his health declined. Throughout his life, he had suffered from divers ailments, which, for want of money, he had been unable to have attended. Toward 1880 he began to walk the way of a bitter Calvary. His wife, whom he cherished as deeply as he had the first day, was stricken by an incurable and horrible malady, cancer. With true stoicism, worthy of the nobility and love which had stamped the lives of this perfect couple, each hid his suffering from the other. In 1881 they made their last journey to Paris to visit their daughters. Frau Marx returned exhausted; Marx, for his part, was affected with bronchitis and pleurisy. In December, 1881, Jenny Marx died; according to Engels, her death killed her husband. To be sure, he survived her by a year, but it was a year of prolonged agony, for he could not resign himself to his loss. The doctors ordered him to spend the winter far from the London fogs; in the Isle of Wight, then in Algiers. Spring brought him back to Europe, first to Paris and then to Vevey on the Lake of Geneva, where he spent six weeks. By September he was back in London. His condition having improved, he set to work again, but he still mourned his wife's absence.

Engels was right: the mainspring of Marx's life broke when his wife died. On January 11, 1883, the death of one of his daughters dealt him a final blow. His bronchitis returned, complicated by pleurisy and laryngitis. Unable to swallow without pain, he had only milk for nourishment. He grew gradually weaker, but his spirit retained its lucidity and power, and he continued to work unceasingly. On March 14th, alone in his study, ensconced in his armchair and following the trend of his meditations, suddenly he died.

On March 17th, his family and a few faithful friends accompanied him to his last resting place. His old comrades, Engels, Liebknecht, Longuet and Lafargue were in attendance. He was buried with his wife in order that this pair, so intimately joined in life, should not be parted by death. Engels spoke very simple words: "As Darwin discovered the law of evolution in organic nature, so Marx discovered the law of evolution in human history. . . ."

Around his grave they planted rosebushes imported from Germany.

No man inspired more hatred and more enthusiasm. No man went so far in consecrating his entire life to work and to disinterested action. No man lived so perfectly with the wife whom he had loved since earliest youth. In a word, no existence is worthier of being held up as exemplary.

In 1845 he had written: "The philosophers have only interpreted the world in various ways; the point is, however, to change it." Having attempted to understand and to interpret the world, Marx strove to transform it. He sought for a better society in which man, freed of all prejudices and servitude, "might at last emerge from prehistory." He went on to say that "science must not be a selfish pleasure; those who are so fortunate as to be able to devote themselves to scientific studies must also be those who put their knowledge at the service of mankind."

He lived up to his word, he kept the faith. He placed his knowledge at the service of humanity. Today we have gone beyond certain of his theories. But if we survey the struggle now being waged in defense of the dignity of man against Fascist barbarity, then Karl Marx looms as one of the great torchbearers of humanity, and the light he kindled will long guide all men of good will.

FEODOR DOSTOEVSKI

by

ALFRED NEUMANN

ALFRED NEUMANN

was born in West Prussia in 1895 and grew up in Berlin. During the First World War he won the rank of corporal (the only similarity between his and Hitler's career). In 1915, in a field hospital, he wrote his first poems. After the war he lived partly in Munich, partly in Florence, Italy. In 1933 he left Hitler Germany, where his books had been banned and his possessions confiscated, to retire to his house in Fiesole. In 1938 he left Italy for Southern France. After the collapse of France he was rescued and brought to this country through an emergency visa granted to a group of endangered European writers by the State Department under the auspices of the President's Advisory Committee on Political Refugees.

In 1926 he received the annual German literary award, the Kleist Prize, for his novel *The Devil*.

His books have been translated into practically every language. Ten of his novels were published in the United States, among them *The Devil* (1928), *Another Caesar* (1935), and *The Friends of The People* (1942). His play, *The Patriot,* was staged by Gilbert Miller in New York in 1928 and subsequently filmed by Paramount.

FEODOR DOSTOEVSKI
by Alfred Neumann

I

Twice Fate came to young Dostoevski at night not like a thief in the dead of night but with resounding footsteps and a legitimate right to disturb the peace.

The first time it came as good fortune . . . out of the white Petersburg night, storming up the wooden stairs to the proletarian lodgings of the twenty-five-year-old Dostoevski, and it personified itself in two men—Nekrasov, the poet, and D. V. Grigorovich, a man of letters. To them, on the previous day, and with fast-beating heart, Dostoevski had submitted the manuscript of *Poor Folk*, his first novel. They came in Russian ecstasy, with embraces and jubilant superlatives that quickly turned into endless comments. What a book! It took them until morning to enumerate and praise all the virtues of *Poor Folk*. And Dostoevski sat there, his face stone-gray, the heavy Slavic cheekbones protruding above his sparse, colorless beard—a face as bleak as the Russian steppe. Only the mighty dome of his forehead shone in the first rays of the confirmation that his life had a meaning.

But for the time being it was no more than Fame's tiny night bell, a mere private excitement, a night-weary affair between the discovered and his two discoverers. Now the professional bell ringer would have to be found, the official voice, the trumpet of literary judgment.

Nekrasov, whose annunciating zeal did not diminish with the sobering approach of day, rushed to the great critic Belinski, brandishing the *Poor Folk* manuscript like a furled flag and calling, still in the throes of the white night's enthusiasm, "A new Gogol has risen!"

Pronouncements of that sort are rarely appreciated by literary high priests, and the relentless Belinski immediately parried, "Your Gogols seem to spring up like mushrooms!" However, when he had read *Poor Folk* he summoned Dostoevski at once.

"Young man," he shouted into the author's shy face, "do you realize what you have achieved in this?" The intuitive secret of artistic value! Truth in art! The artist's service to truth! Truth as endowment and talent! "Take care of this precious gift. Remain loyal to it, and you will be a great writer!"

Dostoevski himself tells us how he felt when he was out in the street again, in front of Belinski's house, looking up to the sky, into the bright day, at the passers-by, at everything. With all his being he felt: this is a solemn moment, this is the great turning point in my life, greater than the most passionate dream of the passionate dreamer. "Can it be possible, can it be true that I am so great?"

When Fate struck out of the night the second time, barely three years later, it came as misfortune. The steps that rumbled up the stairs to the writer's flat in the early morning hours of April 23, 1849, were different from those of the literary enthusiasts—heavier boots and metallic clattering: police officers and Cossacks. Author Feodor Mikhailovich Dostoevski was being arrested for participating in the Petrashevski Circle. The government called it the Petrashevski Conspiracy.

It is wrong, according to Dostoevski's own words in later years, to call this Friday gathering of reformistic liberals a more or less harmless debating society of intellectual idealists. In these years of blackest reaction, Czar-dictator Nicholas I shielded his Holy Russian Empire with Cossacks and special courts against the 1848 flame of revolution darting out from Western Europe, while out of the tobacco-beclouded discussions about Western social theories, about Proudhon and Fourier, there rose the Russian revolutionary activism with Bakunin's label.

Petrashevski himself was a snobbish atheist rather than an

agitator, and he was more important as host of the Circle and owner of an extensive library of forbidden books than as a subversive spokesman. He and the Circle majority identified themselves with Fourier's theory, that is, they favored his evolutionary method by peaceful means and rejected only Fourier's religious tolerance. But before long this led to secession of the radical minority, who formed an inner circle of revolutionary activism, with the immediate, atheist-communistic program for the emancipation of the serfs. They, too, named their circle after their host, writer Sergei Durov—calling themselves the Durov Circle.

Dostoevski was one of the seven radical secessionists. The same man who had introduced him to the literary world had brought him into politics—Belinski, "Western" reformism's propagandist and the Petrashevski Circle's spiritual leader. Thus, Dostoevski's youthful radicalism may have been literature, "truth in art," rather than political conviction. And thus the destiny of a literary association rounded itself out. For it was Dostoevski who read to the Petrashevski Circle Belinski's famous contraband letter, which was an attack on a reactionary book by Gogol and, beyond that, the revolutionary accusation against the state and the church. And it was the reading of this letter that provided the authorities with the reason for exploding the conspiracy which had long been closely watched.

Dostoevski was taken to the Fortress of Sts. Peter and Paul and brought before the czar's much-feared special commission of inquiry. His defense may seem wretched and depressing to us, but he had become convinced that the authorities accused him only of participating in the Petrashevski Circle and of reading the contraband letter; that they knew nothing of the Durov Circle, nothing of the secret press and the revolutionary program. Therefore he confined himself to the petty arguments, to the cheapest form of political apology: that he, loyal subject of the czar and faithful son of the Russian Church, was merely an idealist; that, as far as he was concerned, any possible reforms could be carried through only by means and ways sponsored by the legal government; that despite all his desires for world betterment he was not even utopian enough not to smile at the social theory of gentle Monsieur Fourier.

He was not the only one to use this defense. All the other suspects used the same technique, with the exception of Speshnev, leader of the Durov Circle. The latter was a handsome, mysteriously attractive man of authority and determination, both a rich landowner and a communist, who frankly professed his credo, and whom Dostoevski resurrected as Stavrogin in *The Possessed*—twenty years later, when in violent hate-love Dostoevski placed the possessed, the nihilists, the terrorists before the judgment of his Russian god.

Whether his defense was mendacious or more truthful than the twenty-eight-year-old prisoner could realize, whether he recognized how threadbare his Western socialism was and how strong his Russian faith, the professed "loyal idealism" did not do him any good. The verdict of a system that has to terrorize and has no part of justice is influenced neither by the courage nor by the cowardice of the defendant. The verdict against Dostoevski was death by the firing squad.

What happened next, on that ice-gray December morning of 1849 in Semenov Square—the government-sponsored reviling of the death terror, the official atrocity campaign exploiting the condemned man's last hour—shocked the more civilized nineteenth century more than it does us callous contemporaries of the New Apocalypse. The gray dawn, the place of execution, the death shirt, the body tied to the post, eyes blindfolded, the reading of the verdict, the roll of drums . . . and then, instead of the volley expected by the wildly rearing and then prostrated heart—the announcement that the czar's "infinite mercy" had changed the death sentence to penal servitude in Siberia.

But the monstrousness of such a sham intrusion by death upon life was to become more than a heart convulsion for Dostoevski. Within him there already slumbered the "holy disease"—epilepsy. Now it had been awakened by the death mockery of the "execution" and forthwith, with its dreadful raptures, its falls and resurrections, it became part of the disease-ridden man and his work. Forthwith he lived with a body which, with each attack, gained a more profound death experience; forthwith he lived with an intellect which, owing to the affliction, praised the intermittent periods of life.

II

I believe that we, the exiles of today, in trying to call upon the great exiles of the past because of the similarity of our destiny, and to receive from their hands, for our comfort and support, the eternal torch of the joint idea—I believe that we shall face Dostoevski's phenomenon in forlorn helplessness unless we have the courage to realize that, as a fate-bearer, he had something which we do not have and, perhaps, must not have.

Dostoevski had *amor fati*—love of fate. We, at best, have the courage for fate, the defiance against the great wrong, a will to live that gazes rigidly at the enemy and wants to outlive him—a will, therefore, fighting for survival. We will have to hold sacred our resistance, our permanent opposition, our belief in survival. There can be no live-and-let-live for us. The alternative is suicide, and there is enough desertion already.

Dostoevski, however, had a holy meekness. For all his corporal experiences with death he never thought of suicide, always of life only, which is precious because it is hard and full of trials and threats. He started the katorga—his prison term in Siberia—with this deep gratefulness for being alive or, as he put it, for being reborn for a new form of life. His affliction acquainted him with rebirth after each epileptic attack, it gave him in the midst of his suffering the strangest kind of confidence in life: a curiosity for the new stretch of life ahead, up to the next fermata—a curiosity for life and a deep-seated willingness for spiritual transformation. Thus we must not search in convict Dostoevski for the courage to live as we need it, nor for the courage of conviction held by the torchbearers who let themselves be flogged and crucified in the concentration camps of our time. We must look for something altogether different, something no longer, incomprehensible or even disloyal: the courage for transformation of the Russian servant of God.

The czar's "infinite mercy"—which we have to put in quotations, not because we are mocking it or repeating an official phrase, but because we are quoting Dostoevski and his gratitude— the czar's mercy placed him in the prison at Omsk. It put chains on his feet (and on his epilepsy) and it made him count the fifteen hundred oaken posts of the prison fence, the round number of days comprising the four years' imprisonment, his sentence. Every day he carved a notch in one of the posts. He lived with felons who hated him because he was a nobleman; it grieved him that they hated him, and it was his aim to make them love him. He lived with lice, bedbugs, a broken-winged eagle, and a mangy dog, this last the only one who loved him, without reserve or coaxing. The convicts' work was firing alabaster, carrying bricks, and shoveling snow—he did not mind doing it. The foot chains required a new technique of walking—he learned it. The only book allowed him was the Bible. Since it was a new life it knew no other teachings than the Holy Scriptures. The period of teaching and learning was as severe as the Old Testament, and as promising as the New.

Since it was a new life there was neither remorse nor complaint, neither courage of conviction nor criticism of society. All this was part of the past and might interfere with the great transformation. Dostoevski's immortal report about the four prison years at Omsk, in his *The House of the Dead,* showed an impersonal objectivity which took the avenging and punishing moral laws of society for granted, accepting them as being as immovable as the fifteen hundred posts of the prison fence. With this impartiality he went so far as to disavow his own case and his possible position of preference as a political prisoner with a term of only four years, and to describe himself in his report as a wife-slayer serving ten years. But perhaps he deliberately made himself a criminal to escape any risk of coming to terms with society. For guilt and atonement, as old as the original sin, are not up for political debate; they are subject to God's wrath and God's mercy. And mankind's duty for transformation runs between guilt and atonement, between wrath and mercy. Whoever is destined to set the human example and, simultaneously, to interpret the human parable—here the compassionate and recreating writer finds his eternal subject. Here Dostoevski gained his eternal subject.

As all guilt must be atoned for, and as the prison at Omsk was God's place of atonement on earth, each convict at Omsk had a right to God's mercy. Thus, convict Dostoevski became the spokesman for the prison inmates who were entitled to rebirth and whose souls were not condemned but worthy of mercy. Being the advocate before God of their great claim, he occupied himself with them, studied them, lived with them, lived in them, and arrived at the mighty result—at God's reward as such—that they, the murderers, thieves, robbers, and poor sinners were worthy not only of theological mercy and the love of Christ, but worthy of love as a matter of course, as people, as members of a nation—as Russians.

In the incomparably magnificent chapter in *The House of the Dead* describing the convicts' steam bath, Dostoevski experiences on his person the Maundy Thursday mystery of the washing of the feet. That, to him, is experiencing Russian mercy, God's nationalization in the Russian Church, and God's election of the Russian man. Now, as apologist for the Russians-in-Christ, Dostoevski voices the only protest he raises against society, a powerful protest against flogging, a blunt report of the procedure, an unforgettable analysis of the sadistic floggers; and we find this shocking sentence: "We are a whipped people—everything in us is shattered, that's why we cry so at night." Now, too, he remembers the power which ruined his life that he may be reborn as a Russian, the power which is Russia and the Russian essence, the personal union of state and church; and Dostoevski writes his hymn of thanks to the czar of all the Russias for his "infinite mercy."

After serving his four-year term in prison Dostoevski was not free, far from it. The czar's mercy made him drain the cup of misery to the dregs—the prescribed measure and not a drop less. He had to remain in Siberia for another six years, first as a common soldier in a regiment of the line—imagine the poor emaciated epileptic as a soldier—then, after his discharge with

the rank of officer and his rehabilitation as a member of the
nobility, he continued living in the Godforsaken Siberian garrison,
strictly and expressly forbidden to carry on any kind of writing
activity.

He married a widow, a victim of tuberculosis. It seems to
have been a marriage dictated by the duty of compassion,
prompted by the obligation inherent in Christian charity—consistent, therefore, with his great trial. He never spoke of his
motives or of the burden of living with his sick wife, who was a
strange, unloving woman. And he, the pauper, had to provide for
her son and her family as well. But in *The Insulted and Injured*
we find something about the meaning of this sacrifice.

Though not allowed to write he was allowed to read. That
he was mentally starved and longed for books, that he had his
brother send him not only the Church Fathers and the Koran, but
also books on history and economics, on the Greek and Latin
classics, on Kant and Hegel, is proof that the tried and transformed man was ready to come to terms with the world. He was
ready to draw the sum total of his new experience.

As with every great intellect, it was a cyclic development
toward the fulfillment of life, not toward resignation in death—
death, after all, could have stood in wise finality at the end of his
path of trials—not even toward religious mysticism. The cycles
he traversed had the deep significance of the creative, therefore
of the living. The fact that the katorga brought him to God as
well as to Russia and, in close interrelation with his experiences,
to the Russian man in God, the Russian god—this fact carried
in it the prevalence of life, or the return to life via the detour of
belief.

But it was more than that. It proved the human, the
wonderful, earthly fact that his entering into the Russian man
was more complete, and had to be more complete, than his
entering into the Russian god. Thus there was for Dostoevski—
the man possessed with the tremendous vitality of the Russian
people—no resting in God, no mercy fulfilled; there was only
the national right to mercy; and that is and always will be the
search for God in the rhythm of guilt and atonement, of good
and evil in the Russian man. Thus there is and always will be the

doubting of God, the eternal struggle of Jacob with the angel. His credo from this period of trial is: to believe that there is nothing more beautiful, more profound, more worthy of love, more human, and more perfect than Christ, and that, if one were to prove to him Christ's existence outside of truth and truth outside of Christ, he, the Russian, would stay with Christ, not with truth. Such thoughts contain all the beauty and all the doubts of divine knowledge.

Added to the national right to God's mercy was the earthly prerogative, Dostoevski's other credo: his conviction of Russia's historic mission, the fulfillment through Russia of the European destiny. And Dostoevski the writer, still forbidden to write, felt within him the harvest of the years of trial, the stored-up Russian destinies he was to fashion and create.

In 1859, ten years after the "execution," he was allowed to return to Petersburg, a free man, a poor man, a forgotten man.

III

The katorga had been no "Schulungslager," to use the abominable misnomer applied by the Nazis to one of their coercive institutions, and Dostoevski did not serve his term to change from a revolutionary socialist into a reactionary nationalist. The phenomenon that was Dostoevski, especially as viewed from our own exile and in the reverential intention of enlisting his spiritual patronage, does not admit of our approach via the pontoon bridge of our nimble and facile terminology. We shall hardly be able to claim him as a protector of the expatriates; but we can claim him as the promoter of the Russian destiny—and that has become the world's destiny, our world's.

Dostoevski's *amor fati,* after his katorga transformation, had become the *amor fati* of the Russian, whom he created in a dozen immortal novels and in ever-new variations during the twenty remaining years of his life. It might be said too—and this holds true for no writer of world literature with greater justification

than for Dostoevski—that he transformed or split himself into
the numberless characters of his Russian world, that he was in
each of his characters, on either side of the gigantic dialogue
of his novels, on both sides, in both extremes.

With himself he fought out the great struggles over good and
evil, guilt and atonement, Westernism and Slavophilism, socialism
and nationalism, nihilism and czarism, revolution and reaction—
the struggle over the great hatred and the great reconciliation. He
was the pro and the contra, he had within him the two poles of the
Russian existence, the nihilistic and the messianic. But the struggle
did not go according to his will, it went according to his strength
on either side. More often than not, that part of his struggling
self won out which he wanted to be defeated, for the sake of
God, of the Russian god, and of Russian mercy.

After his return to freedom, in the early eighteen-sixties, it
appeared for a time as though Providence wanted to reward him
for his ten years of purgatory. The publishing of *The House of
the Dead* not only retrieved him from oblivion but made him
more famous than he had ever been. The czar himself, heading
a galaxy of beautiful souls, wept bitter tears over the magnifi-
cently sober report from Hades; but the name of the czar was
no longer Nicholas I, it was Alexander II who, at least in the
beginning of his reign, was an extremely liberal man. He abolished serfdom and brought a shower of reforms to the dictator-
withered country.

Dostoevski founded a successful periodical in which he published *The House of the Dead* and *The Insulted and Injured*.
Besides, he expounded in its pages an Alexander-tempered conservatism and a somewhat unripened synthesis of Westernism
and Slavophilism.

But synthesis was not Dostoevski's field, and his political
significance was to be found not in his journalistic programs but
in his epos of the Russian man, in his own destiny. Peace did not
come to his epoch because an initially liberal czar propagated
belated reforms. The epoch had just experienced the disaster of
the Crimean War. Belinski was dead and the revolutionary development had rolled beyond him, beyond him as well as the gentle
Fourierism of the forties. A tremendous political consciousness

was rising in the new generation. Herzen and Chernishevski were stirring up the young proletariat. Marx and Bakunin were making themselves felt as spiritual inciters of unrest. Positivism had arrived, materialism, scorn for everything emotional and spiritual, hatred for belief, atheism. Secret societies sprang up like mushrooms, for terroristic action, and Turgenev gave them their name: nihilists.

How was it possible for Dostoevski to be serene and to work with amicable syntheses when the scope of the Russian destiny within him extended from the Russian god to the nihil, from the holy irrationality of life-in-Christ to organized terror? How was it possible for Dostoevski—this sufferer of all human and political passions, this servant of God, Christophoros and exorcist, this boundless embracer of misfortune, suffering, and disease—to be granted the same independence of life and work enjoyed by the gentlemen farmers, Tolstoy and Turgenev, whom he envied so much?

His wife died after years of suffering, ending the agony that had been her dowry to this strangely veiled Samaritan marriage. That same year also witnessed the death of his brother Mikhail, his best friend and helper, manager of the periodical, which went bankrupt soon afterward. The support of Mikhail's large family, yes, even of his mistress and her child, fell to Dostoevski. His debts mounted sky-high. He fell into the clutches of a publisher who forced upon him, for the granting of an advance, the most monstrous contract ever to be imposed on a great writer: unless he delivered his new book on the date agreed upon Dostoevski was bound to hand over to the publisher, without remuneration, his entire work of the next nine years.

He went abroad—not, as on former occasions, to strengthen his antipathies to the West for the Slavic side of his Russian struggle and destiny, or to take home for vehement and extravagant argument the three reasons for the decline of the West: capitalism, socialism, and Catholicism. He went abroad to visit the gambling halls of Wiesbaden and Baden-Baden, for the purpose of winning in order to redeem his literary independence— and to meet again a young Russian girl, who was as beautiful as she was sophisticated, and who had cleverly tortured and betrayed him before. He loved gambling because it was an epileptic sensation, so to speak, with ups and downs, a typically Russian passion, and he loved the Russian girl for nearly the same reasons. He lost all his money in Wiesbaden, and together with it he lost ruthless Polina Suslova, which was the girl's name. He also conceived his book, *The Gambler,* whose heroine is Polina Alexandrovna—the change in name is negligible. In order to return home, he borrowed money from Turgenev, and from that day the two were enemies.

The deadline of the publisher's Shylock note drew nearer and nearer; but what did it mean as compared with the new Russian destiny which Dostoevski imposed on himself? He was working on *Crime and Punishment.* He was Raskolnikov. He had to commit a murder and pay the penalty for it. He had to redeem himself, Raskolnikov, from intellectual nihilism and bring himself to meekness, to salvation-in-Christ. He had to drag Satan's dialectician before God. Did he achieve it? The fact that the reader puts this question, just as Raskolnikov does a thousand times, keeps the Russian struggle for God on this earth where we dwell, and drives that struggle into the life we are fighting for today.

The deadline for the Shylock contract was only thirty days off. Raskolnikov was still deeply entangled in the chaos between crime and punishment. Not a line of *The Gambler* had as yet been written. And how could the Raskolnikov problem be solved within thirty days, how could Raskolnikov be brought to redemption-in-God, when Dostoevski, exhausted from his Sisyphean task and epileptic fits, was already standing at the gates of his literary prison? Under all these circumstances, he dictated *The Gambler,* without notes and in twenty-six days, to a young girl secretary— and was saved. This helper-in-need was twenty-year-old Anna Grigorievna Snitkina, to whom he further dictated the last part of *Crime and Punishment* from his manuscript. She became his wife, the wonderful companion for the balance of his life.

But his financial worries were not over. The literary acclaim he won with *Crime and Punishment,* even the fact that this book was valued more highly than the other two publications of this astounding year of masterly achievement, Tolstoy's *War and Peace* and Turgenev's *Fathers and Sons,* did not alleviate his situation. Everything he wrote was paid for in advance; invariably the money for a finished manuscript was "eaten up" before he was entitled to it. Again the horde of creditors was on his neck, this time joined by the horde of family dependents who trembled for their "pensions" in view of Dostoevski's new marriage. Again he was threatened by court action and the debtor's prison. So he saved himself and Anna by flight abroad, by flight into voluntary exile.

It may strike us as odd and quaint that exile, our fateful word, can have a motive so light and so slight. We went into exile because we neither could nor would continue to live in the Germany, the Italy, the France, the Europe of the antichrist. Dostoevski went into exile because he had debts—exile in the West which was anti-"Christ-Russian."

But right here, in the very concept of the word "exile," a century that is, on the whole, urban clashes with our downright barbaric times, for Victor Hugo, the nineteenth century's classical example of the writer in exile, was allowed to publish his empire-shaking works in France, gaining fame and wealth.

But perhaps, after experiencing the katorga, Dostoevski could not be spared the exile, the fate of the Russian expatriate that was to prove so important for Russia and for his work. And no matter how cheaply he slipped into exile, he had to live a life on alien soil as harsh, as merciless as ever any exile had to live. And if, in his passion for suffering, he also accepted the cross of exile, only to let his love for Russia mount to hysteria and madness, then he achieved this absurdity too: exile in the enemy's camp.

He hated the Germans, the French, the English, the Italians; he hated their language, their country, their cities, and their monuments. He was in Baden-Baden, not to enjoy the gentle landscape of the Black Forest—he was there to gamble. He went to Geneva, not to gaze across the lake at Mont Blanc—but to meet Russians. He went to Florence, not because of the eternal honeymoon of the Tuscan countryside and the beautiful architecture of a perfectly harmonious city—he went because he could buy Russian papers there, and to write *The Idiot.*

His was the exile of unrest, of humiliation, of poverty, of

begging letters, of illness, of suffering—a typically Dostoevskian succession of scenes: passion for gambling and bad luck, epileptic fits, Anna's pregnancy, birth and death of the child, birth of another child, no money, never any money and a never-ending obsession for work. . . .

In Geneva he attended a meeting of the League for Peace and Freedom. He heard Bakunin's disciples outline the road leading to this goal, via fire and sword, revolution and terror, destruction of the old world. Again he had to ge to battle to save the Russian god and the Russian Church. He no longer cared to be Raskolnikov whom he must drag before the Redeemer. He wanted to be a truly good man, the Russian-in-Christ, Christ as embodied in the meek Russian who, by delivering and reconciling society, will eradicate the poison of the West's revolutionary idea from the young Russian generation, thus saving the universe instead of destroying it. He wrote the story of Prince Myshkin, *The Idiot*.

But Myshkin, the angelic man, is not even a Don Quixote-in-Christ; he is a Parsifal of passivity. And if, with his intricate theory about the Christ-Russian meekness and its necessary victory over the West's Roman Catholic and socialistic "doctrine of violence," he wants to convince the nihilistic youths, he succeeds only because, hurriedly and unconvincingly, the author turns these youths into candidates for easy conversion. No, Myshkin achieves nothing; and in the end he passes into the hopelessness of a waning intellect. And Dostoevski could not be satisfied in having created or lived in one of the most touching figures of a failure in God—for he had wanted exactly the opposite.

The fight went on. In November, 1869, he read in a Moscow newspaper—during his exile he read only Russian papers—of the murder of Ivanov, a Moscow student, by nihilistic fellow students whose leader was a Bakunin disciple. Here, then, was the fight which Dostoevski had to carry through to victory. Here it was, in black and white, the crime of the terrorists, of the West fanatics, the revolutionary demons. And he wrote *The Possessed*, labored at it under the torments of disease, financial distress, a mounting feeling of responsibility, and a zeal for truth. His health grew steadily worse; his hatred for Europe weakened him.

He felt suspended in the air, a Russian Antaeus who had to touch the Russian soil again before he could finish the book and win the fight.

For the book's sake the publisher came to his aid by sending him the fare home. In July, 1871, after four years of self-imposed exile, Dostoevski returned to Petersburg and immediately resumed his work on *The Possessed,* happy to be home, strong again on his native soil. But once more the same thing happened: no matter how fierce his hatred for the demons, no matter how violent his distortions of the revolutionaries, how unfair his travesties and caricatures of them—in the great fight between left and right, between the Eastern god and the Western devil, it was not Shatov, the servant of God and searcher for God, who was the victor; no, it was the book's central figure, Stavrogin, the demon, the Russian demon.

The fight went on. Dostoevski, at the pinnacle of his European fame, stormed into battle with *The Brothers Karamazov;* and he was both Dimitri, the arch Russian, who cried, "I hate harmony!"—and Alyosha, the servant of God. And once again, in the famous chapter "Pro and Contra," it is Dimitri, the doubter of God, who wins out. For he tells of the torturing of innocent children—of a general who let his dogs tear a slave boy to pieces. If God permits that, then what is to be done with the general? And Alyosha, the servant of God, knows no better answer than brother Dimitri: the general must be shot.

IV

The rebel in Dostoevski and in his work always prevails over the servant of God, and the Russian destiny goes its grand way. Dostoevski shaped it powerfully, but he does not hold a torch which we, the exiles of today, might be considered worthy of carrying on in the relay race of the history of the mind. He is himself the torch, the torch of the Russian man; he burns forever and is in good hands.

Stavrogin hammers the relentless question against Shatov—the man who had said that truth is God and Russia the only God-bearing nation destined to save the entire world through belief—ever again the relentless question, "Do you yourself believe in God?" And Shatov, at last, groans the answer, "I believe in Russia!"

The fight goes on.

CARL SCHURZ
by
EMIL LUDWIG

EMIL LUDWIG

was born in 1881 in Breslau. His first writings were entirely in dramatic form, much of them in verse. He was strongly in favor of the Weimar Republic, and the murder of Rathenau, in 1922, stirred him deeply. Since his middle twenties, Ludwig has had a home at Ascona, on Lake Maggiore in Switzerland. After the Nazis came to power, this voluntary expatriation became compulsory. From Switzerland he set out on his incessant journeys in search of material for his biographies. His biographical style is modeled on Plutarch and Carlyle. His books on Goethe, Napoleon, Bismarck, Kaiser Wilhelm II, Lincoln, Cleopatra, Hindenburg, Roosevelt, Masaryk, and others, have made him the best-known modern biographer. His latest books are: *The Germans; Bolivar; The Mediterranean; Stalin; Beethoven.*

CARL SCHURZ
by Emil Ludwig

IN A comfortable room an enormous peasant is sitting in his armchair, giving milk to drink to his three-year-old grandson. The child wants his cup filled and refilled, till the old man loses patience and calls out to a farm servant working in the yard to go and get a tubful of milk. When it is brought the old fellow undresses the boy, puts him into the tub so that the white liquid is close to the child's mouth. "Now drink till you're full!" The boy drinks and splashes happily in the milk, and granddad has a good laugh.

This scene, told by Carl Schurz as the first thing he remembered of his youth, took place in a German castle on the Rhine where his grandfather was the tenant of a Catholic count, harvesting the fruits of the estate for his boss with the work of his giant hands, his peasant cunning and energy, while the count lived the leisurely life so many of his forefathers had led.

It was a patriarchal life. The grand old tenant gave his son, who was a teacher, a position on the estate, and the noble family lived at peace with these peasants who, like most Rhenish folk, combined Western gaiety with a certain feeling of liberty. Here, at the French border, where government and nationality have shifted continually, the best German types have arisen.

Carl Schurz—like most eminent men—felt more akin to his grandfather than to his father. He has given a vivid picture of the old farmer, governing his small realm as a dictator of gigantic strength, a hunter who always shot the best birds, the first to enter the barn when the corn was brought in on the wagon, sitting astride one of his four fine horses decked with flowers, a man who in a quarrel broke a chair to attack his opponent. Daily Carl saw him standing at the head of the table saying grace for the farmhands, who were obliged to turn away as long as the prayer lasted. Then, when the old man banged his big knife on the table, all could turn round and begin their meal.

This old fellow was in love with his grandson, he took him for rides in front of his saddle, he let him hold the leather sheath of his big slaughtering knife when he killed a pig.

His father, the teacher, taught the boy reading and music, and so he had a good and useful education in and out of doors.

But it was not long before he came to know the first clash of the classes, of rich and poor, in his own German home. About 1835 the old, good-natured count died, and his son and heir was of a different mold. He had been educated in Prussia, which twenty years before had taken possession of the Rhineland. The smart military spirit of Prussia took hold of this old noble family.

The young count disliked to see his rich tenant, an ordinary peasant, keep hunting grounds of his own. He began to vex the old fox, who had handled and increased the fortunes of his forefathers, he played humiliating tricks on him, just as half a century later young Emperor William did with his servant Bismarck.

So in the end old Schurz was fired and a deep resentment gave birth to the first germs of revolt in his grandson's heart. Fifty years after this happened, Schurz still remembered the dirty jokes of the auctioneer when he was selling the farm tools of his family. It was this hour that made a revolutionary of Schurz. The injustice of the count against his peasant grandfather excited this young mind that by nature was inclined to be peaceful and loyal.

The position of the family steadily declined. The father had to give up his profession as a teacher and began to trade in hardware, an uncle lost his fortune speculating in grain. The terrible moment came for the seventeen-year-old student when he was called home because his father had been put in jail, for failing to pay a draft. Carl succeeded in earning the money owed and saved the honor of his family; but the power of the nobles, the hard spirit of the government, the threat of Prussian military rule had cut deep wounds into his heart.

He was a poet and not a politician. A handsome youth, an idealist, with dreamy eyes, long straight nose, a clear forehead surrounded by black hair; he looked like a musician. He was one in his youth, and remained an amateur all his life. Only his resolute chin foretold the man of action God intended him to be; long before the dreamer and poet was conscious of it.

Imagination and energy combining in this young man were united by a trait of character that governed his whole life: by nature and education Schurz was an eminently honest man, and this was of importance to him in all the ups and downs of his later life; it was decisive in his political and military career in America.

It was his mother, a quiet religious woman, who in his early youth trained him to regard honesty as the foundation of all human relations. This simple woman—as her letters prove—took life, and God, and her duties seriously.

How the boy combined moral sensitiveness with a sense of dignity he tells us at the age of sixty when he reports the sin of having hidden a bad school-note from his father:

"You have tried to hide the truth from me—says the father—you deserve a beating."

"Okay—but let's have it done in the stable where no one will see!"

These experiences were much more responsible for his revolutionary career than general ideas of liberty. The strange career that made him an emigrant and later an American statesman was formed by those happenings in his youth. This German boy had not gone in search of government and politics. He intended to live as a poet and scientist in the service of beauty, art, philosophy.

"You ask me what has become of my poetry," he writes at the age of fifteen to a friend. "It forsakes me when I am alone, but also at other times. Come soon—I am so lonesome."

Why does he want to be a poet? Why does he write drama?

"Because it can influence so many people. In this way you get the greatest audiences. . . . Pardon me for my vanity—but I would like to become a playwright."

Here already we see his creative talent mingled with the will to success. In those years he began to write a novel, but, like most young authors, he never finished it. He wrote verses, and tried his imagination on the piano and the organ. But he also loved to roam in the woods, where his grandfather had been a hunter, and his whole life long he preferred them to the ocean and any other landscape.

A child brought up in the country has an advantage over the city youngster that can never be overtaken. These childhood days in woods and fields bring us nearer to God and our fellow men. Silence and observation are better for a growing mind than amusement and gossip. Poverty and the craving of knowledge, the best educators if working in harmony, accompanied his high school years. But the holidays when he returned to his parents' home in the village were always the joy nothing else could replace. Schurz was fortunate that he grew up as a poor boy and learned to have no pretentions but those he demanded of himself. He laid the foundation of a character that in many ways resembles Lincoln's, who later became his friend.

He expressed his early resentment against Prussian arrogance in a school composition. In those days public opinion timidly expressed itself against the Prussian king and his aristocratic governors for not having kept their promises to the people, who had helped them to drive Napoleon from Germany. Schurz dared to write down these thoughts in his paper and got the following note from his Rhenish teacher: "That's all very brilliant. But remember, you should never write such ideas on the bench of a Prussian high school." (Almost the identical words were said to the present author, fifty years later, when he, as a boy of seventeen, tried to write some of his advanced political ideas in a school paper.)

At that time a growing wave of unrest and dissatisfaction swept over the students along the Rhine. They were not subjected to a dictatorship, but were in opposition to Prussian military rule. Schurz, then a student in Bonn, was drawn into this movement. Shy by nature, always silent, he was often made fun of by his boisterous comrades. But suddenly his public talents were discovered, when in their tavern one of his friends disclosed that Schurz was the author of the best song hits and articles appearing in their paper.

This humanitarian youth disliked force even if it went for liberty, and yet, although he declined to fight duels, all his comrades respected him because he was finely built and had a strong physique. He had given his measurements when he was twenty, at five feet ten and three-quarter inches. He was one of those rare cases that continue to grow after they have "grown up." After an attack of scarlet fever in America, at the age of twenty-three, he grew several inches. An amusing symbol, that the German who came over here put on height.

The will to action that was to be the governing force of his later life now suddenly came to the fore. A speech he improvised, "For Greater Liberty," before the fraternities made him an honored board member and soon he became president and leader. This was shortly after the Paris revolution of 1848, when the French king was done away with and the Republic reconstructed. The young generation, especially those close to the French frontier, believed the time had now come to rise against Prussian autocracy. The dismissal of his beloved grandfather, whom the young count had turned out of his home, rose in Schurz's mind as a sinister recollection, and the general demand for greater liberty urged him on to join the rebels. He wrote to a friend:

> On the eve of these great happenings I have come to understand how stupid it is to retire from this stormy world to a life of academic quiet. But I also grasp how often service in a small circle can become important and have wide influence. I wish every one of us would come to this same conclusion in his special sphere.
>
> We are all republicans, but with deliberation and moderation. Public life brings pleasure and satisfaction, but it also contains poison. We have had the privilege of a colorful youth; this should lift us for our whole life above the realm of commonplace . . . We are approaching a general revolution of the people.

Such thoughts were rampant among the youth of Europe in those days; ambition and idealism interwined then as today. In

Hungary, Poland, Italy these same revolts of the masses and the students took place. The same young men who in our day are labeled "communists" because they stand up against the prerogatives of wealth, in Schurz's time combined against their autocrat kings, thus preparing a social and political revolution. At a distance, these revolutions have a more picturesque aspect; in the year 2000, the Soviets will be romanticized by our grandchildren. Like Schurz and his friends, two older and more celebrated men rose as leaders in their countries: Kossuth and Mazzini, who were both to cross Schurz's path in later years.

In the beginning the German students limited their efforts to an attempt to activate the hesitating Frankfort Parliament. To tell the truth, they themselves did not seem to get out of the atmosphere of speeches and protests. Schurz as a writer and orator in a limited circle, now found a poet and prophet to look up to, a man seventeen years his senior yet young enough to rouse the enthusiasm of an idealistic youth.

Kinkel, professor of philosophy and literature at Bonn, attracted Schurz by two traits they shared: handsome looks and poetic imagination. Kinkel's broad forehead and the passionate look of his eyes attracted the students. They honored him for keeping away from the women, who adored him, and for being true to his clever though not at all lovely wife. Schurz, it seems, at that time had no time for girls. But Kinkel had talents his admirer did not possess: eloquence, a fine voice, and the art of oratory. In his youth he had made himself a name as the author of a romantic epic, was universally admired as an orator, and filled to the brim with Greek and Roman ideals of liberty. He soon changed from a teacher to a friend of young Schurz. Both were ambitious.

"Vanity," Schurz writes as an old man, "is the most common and the least dangerous of vices if it is controlled by ambition. Exaggerated vanity, however, is ridiculous and self-tormenting, as the experience of a long life has taught me."

Kinkel, as an orator, with his knowledge of art, was a more vivid and humorous entertainer than Schurz, who had more depth of character and energy. A wish to compete with his idol and teacher seems to have bound the younger man to Kinkel, and later urged him to do a heroic deed in his favor. Both friends were driven into the rising fever of revolution, and being poets were attracted by the dramatic side of the movement.

In his memoirs the colorful description and his constant self-analysis show how much of a poet Schurz remained in spite of his will to action that later drove him into the adventures of the revolution.

Could anything be more romantic than to ride up to the Wartburg under the golden autumn foliage of century-old beeches to meet some hundred delegates from German universities at this venerated center of German poetry, and with flaming songs and solemn oaths swear death to tyrants? In those days, revolution had a more colorful aspect than in our present iron-gray time. Long feathers swept from the boys' broad-rimmed velvet hats, clattering swords hung from their belts, colored sashes and high riding boots—perhaps also one or two unloaded pistols—made up the picture of noble pirates. Wine and beer united the singers until morning.

Young Schurz, among the others, enjoyed his speeches filled with quotations of Brutus and Anthony. Verses and community singing filled the woods and halls where the delegates met, and in the distance they all saw rise the fiery image of the Revolution.

But nobody seemed to realize that the guns were in the hands of the Prussians, and that the Junkers and soldiers, who had so easily suppressed the Berlin revolution for the King of Prussia, were waiting for the moment to advance all over Germany and crush every movement in favor of self-government and liberty. On the one side were fiery hearts, romantic minds, and fine, colored sashes; on the other side were guns, cannon, and the military discipline of two hundred years.

When the citizens in Southern Germany, in the Rhineland and in Baden, began to arm and when some of the regular troops went over to their side, the time seemed ripe for Prussia, the old reactionary autocracy, to send her soldiers all over the country as safeguards of the world of yesterday, and to suppress the elements that clamored for new laws and liberties.

A fortress in Baden—Rastatt, where the rebels had found ammunition—became the center of the fight. The Duke of Baden, who in his fear had almost given way to the rebels, in his last emergency called to the King of Prussia for help—and now those iron regiments, forerunners of the Nazis, came marching along, led by the same type of aristocratic generals that are leading the Germans today. They came as they come today, to tread out every bit of liberty that may have dared to raise its head.

In the fortress of Rastatt, Carl Schurz, a lieutenant in the rebel army, was besieged with his friends. The circle closed down on them, no assault could be made, the commander saw he was lost. He negotiated with the Prussians; they demanded unconditional surrender, tomorrow at midday. It was clear that the political leaders would be shot. Carl Schurz belonged to them.

An idealistic young poet who wrote plays and studied the ancients was now to lose his life for a liberty he could well have done without. The Germans had always liked to leave their freedom to the poets, they loved to hear it proclaimed in their songs, but they were never really ready to die for it. In a thousand years' history they never found the enthusiasm that drove other nations to rise against tyrants. Luther risked his life for his religion, but when princes and government were to bend to his new code, he quickly drew back and gave them more power than they had had under the Pope's supervision.

Some hundred citizens fell before the royal castles of Vienna and Berlin, because they had dared to advance against the king's soldiers. Some poets who could not hold their tongue fled to Switzerland, Paris, and America. But the idea of liberty did not arouse the German nation. They liked to obey their princes and preferred to dream about liberty on a secluded isle where they wrote songs of freedom and developed utopian systems for the future.

In the whole of Germany after five hundred years there is not a single monument of a hero of liberty at whose feet young idealists might collect to raise their hearts and hopes. The first martyrs of freedom were Robert Blum and the radicals of 1919. Karl Liebknecht, whom the Nazis shot down from behind, and some of his friends who fell later, are the only exceptions of a slave empire of a thousand years.

Twenty-year-old Schurz had to prepare himself to be shot on the morrow. In this night before their fortress fell, he wrote the two finest documents of his life. They breathe that virile idealism and steadfastness that since the time of the ancients has been the real hero's stamp. In his memoirs he gives only two words to these documents, but they were printed after his death.

To his parents and sisters:

I can hardly describe the agitation I am in the moment I begin to write this letter, for I do not know if these will be the last words I ever shall write, or—what really would mean the same—if I shall cease to be a free man tomorrow. In this hour of extreme importance, which is perhaps the last one giving me a chance to regard my past and future with a clear mind, before my fate will be ultimately decided, great problems weigh down my soul —so many of them that I shall not be able to answer them all, although I know full well what I owe to you.

I know how much worry I have brought to you. I know what hopes you had—I know your pain and disappointment. I should stand before you as a penitent, but my pride and principles forbid such resignation. Am I just a violent young man following the impulse of a moment in childish ambition—without reason and deliberation? . . .

Listen, this is the day of decision. Now is the moment when I must die for my ideas or be imprisoned for life. This moment finds me quiet and self-composed—as a man. The annihilating reality of this moment has swallowed all my romantic illusions: I see more clearly than ever that I must do my duty honorably and intelligently. I was never more sure of myself and feel I never had more reason to be so.

In happy days gone by you recognized my vanity— rightly or wrongly. I tried to understand the spirit of great situations, although I had seen none—and because I had not seen them I wanted to take part in great happenings, although I was not wholly convinced of the necessity of wide organizations.

If I was wrong, I am suffering the general state of Man and will have to pay heavily for a small mistake.

I foresaw most of this. I knew my life would be full of storm and dangers as I was too proud to evade them. But I always imagined I would die as a man looking back onto a life rich in action and success. The knowledge that I have accomplished so little is grievous. If a longer life had been given me—I might have fought for the good of many. The only consolation I can give you is that in life and death I was worthy to be your son. Believe me that I love mankind more than myself and that I shall continue to do so to my death.

Kinkel is condemned to death, he will die as a man—he lived so. If I could say the same of myself I would carry my head higher. But I am glad that weakness is as foreign to me as cowardice, that my heart is strong enough to bear these blows of fate and the burden of my own thoughts.

Good-bye—on the day of capitulation.

To his friends:

You will say: he was too rash, else he might have become someone. True: I didn't want to play second fiddle where I thought I might be first. I didn't care to serve, where I saw I could give orders. But I have always bent to Providence when it approached. And yet I have kept my pride and will not bow down to others. I feel I am worthy of life since I know I can expect death with a clear and unperturbed conscience.

Think of me sometimes as a friend who gave his life for the realisation of an idea before he knew how to carry it out, whose greatest error was—against his better knowledge—not to have thought enough of himself—Once more: good-bye.

Two marvelous documents of a loving son and a proud comrade, night confessions of an idealist whose sense of dignity bears him up above the fear of death. They alone would be enough to conserve the memory of his name.

But even in this very night Schurz's energy did not forsake him, he was still hoping, still thinking "perhaps!"—still trying to save himself.

The next morning he tried to escape. He had once noticed a big sewer pipe leading from the fortress, and now he and two comrades, while the others were preparing the military capitulation, crawled down the pipe in the hope of escaping at the other end at nightfall. Two terrible days they spent in that sewer pipe, half filled with rain and blocked by bricks and grates; then, after they succeeded in breaking through, they found a Prussian guard at the outer end. They had to return and hide in a stable loft, while the Prussians were already masters of the town. They managed to signal a friend, who secretly brought them food. Then they tried a second time. This time they escaped, found their way to the Rhine and to a boat which took them across—to France, safety, and liberty.

This story—a common one in our world of today—shows the active, practical side of Schurz's nature. After having secretly crossed the Swiss frontier, he earned his living as a teacher, then went to Paris with a false passport, wrote articles, and studied languages and art—more than politics. As a whole, he thoroughly enjoyed life as an emigrant, because for the first time the world opened out to him.

But suddenly he halts—his friend Kinkel has not been shot but withers away in a penitentiary. All intellectual Germany was indignant at this treatment of a political prisoner, yet no one lifted a hand to help him. Mind and action—as always in Germany—did not combine to liberate the poet from his prison. Freedom of speech and press were more suppressed than they were before the revolution; it was all a great failure, and no one tried to make up for this failure. While in Hungary and Italy revolts followed one after the other, Prussia and Germany brooded in sullen silence.

Prussian militarism had decided on Kinkel's fate. His sentence by a civilian court had called for several years in a fortress, where he might have continued his studies and writing. But the Prussian generals—against the law—revoked the sentence and put him into jail like an ordinary criminal, with shorn hair and no right to read, forcing him to clean and spin wool; just as a hundred years later the Nazis treat men who do not share their opinions.

Kinkel's wife, who had tried all possible ways to rescue her husband, after many failures turned to Schurz in Paris. Perhaps, she thought, the friend who was in safety cared to venture his freedom. After reading her letter, Schurz at once started for Germany, where a warrant had been issued against him and where he might have been recognized any moment as a convicted rebel and been thrown into jail like his friend. This he ventured only a year after his miraculous escape.

For months the exile traveled in Germany, hiding behind a forged passport but with an undisguised face. One night he arrived on foot in his native village. As he still carried the latchkey to his father's house he entered the back door and his parents' bedroom. They were asleep. Patiently he sat down on a chair, and waited. At last his father woke. The parents recognized their son: joy, excitement, fear, and again joy.

It took him many weeks to prepare Kinkel's flight. No one knew his plans, not even his nearest friends. They believed he was in Germany to prepare new revolts. With the caution of a burglar he approached his aim. By the help of a friend he became acquainted with one of the guards of Kinkel's prison in Spandau, won his confidence never mentioning his real object. The smallest details were prepared for the attempt, every noise, every shadow in the street was foreseen—and yet on the decisive night the plan did not succeed because their guard friend could not find one important key. The coaches, the relays, the private lodgings they had ordered for their drive to the coast waited in vain.

The next night, with no preparation, they ventured the escape with the courage of despair. Kinkel, a shortsighted scholar with no physical training, and weakened by prison life, succeeded in letting himself down from the loft of his prison—sixty feet high—by means of a rope, while tiles from the roof kept passing his head and shoulders.

He arrived in safety, another carriage had been prepared. They started for the Prussian frontier and the coast. They managed to put the pursuing police on the wrong track—by Schurz's ingenuity. They arrived and halted in a German port, and a rich friend sent them off in a trading vessel to England.

This courageous escape and flight was admired, sung, and

related all over the world; the Germans put it into verse, made songs about it, and published cheap prints showing the whole story. Schurz's letters of this period show that he was in no way responsible for this adulation.

But he was too much of a poet not to feel the symbolic importance of his deed, he was too religious not to regard the whole thing as a task set him by his own conscience. He explained it to his parents in a letter from England as an obedient son trying to excuse his rashness:

"Is Kinkel not of great importance to our party, is he not a friend? I had to take a risk for him. Judge such things by their success. I am glad I did not sacrifice my plan to the doubts that came to me. Don't let me know how much you've worried about me. Now we are safely rescued I would not have a shadow on our joy. But I should like to hear all about the joy of your friends on hearing of Kinkel's deliverance."

Schurz again became a refugee, living as a journalist and a teacher in Paris and London. He was arrested by the French secret police as a dangerous foreigner, was set free but had to flee France and live in England. In London he met Kossuth and, above all, Mazzini, who filled him with enthusiasm.

But when Louis Napoleon made himself emperor and suppressed the French republic and her liberties, Schurz at once understood that Europe, and particularly Germany, was lost to the revolution. With bitter sarcasm he later described the political circles of German and French refugees, meeting in the cafés of London or in the drawing rooms of some political hostess, how they discussed their utopias and exaggerated their merits in the coming revolution. It was easier for him to evade such illusions; he had never totally believed in the possibility of an immediate liberal government in Germany. Now, at twenty-two, Carl Schurz really emerges as the man of politics, for only such a man could come to this conclusion:

"When will the day arrive? . . . The spirit of History does not trouble about what men wish—it reckons with their weaknesses and talents. Here we have the free will of nations! Be it today or tomorrow, we are all young enough to learn from the run of History that you cannot bind the tempest with ropes. Let us wait. We have done it honorably. We are at a point where silence means action. And the New Year?—It will be dictated by the logic of events. I am very tranquil. The study of the past gives me greater patience to await the future. I deem it my fortune to be connected with the fate of suffering nations."

Do not these words seem to have been written yesterday by one of our contemporaries? And what did they mean?

On the day of Napoleon's coup d'état Schurz went for a walk as was his habit when he had to think things out. The will to action, always stronger than his passion for liberty, rose in his mind and made him feel useless and unmanly, sitting about for years and waiting for a time when perhaps some of his youthful dreams should come true.

Terrible news reached him from home. When it became known that he had been the man who rescued Kinkel from prison, Prussian soldiers marched to the house of his parents with drawn swords, entered by force, and smashed everything that was breakable, leaving a mass of wreckage behind them.

This act, without trial, one century before the Nazis, shows a cold efficiency of revenge, an anarchy of civil morals that other nations have had in times of revolution but never when they possessed the power of government.

These general and personal reflections passed through the young man's head as he was sitting on a bench in Hyde Park, and he came to the conclusion that he would leave Europe and migrate to the country that seemed to offer him more liberty and greater opportunities. He remembered that as a boy he had watched a neighbor's family in the Rhenish village pack their stuff onto a wagon and leave their home to emigrate to America. Later, in his emigration, many reports of other emigrants from across the Atlantic had reached him and now encouraged him.

He made up his mind to cross the ocean, but not like Kossuth and other republicans to collect money for his party or for a suppressed country. No, he wanted a new free field of action only for himself, he wanted to begin a New Life. That was all.

About this time he fell in love, for the second and last time of his life. And he married the pretty blonde German girl who later became the mother of his children.

Schurz went to America because he felt all revolutionary attempts had failed in Europe. He could not return to Germany before a great upheaval had taken place, and he did not believe it was coming. He could not go to France as long as Napoleon reigned there. In England, Lord Palmerston's friendship with the French tyrant had disappointed him deeply. He was bored by the never-ending repetition of refugee discussions, by their inactivity, their contentment to wait and feel superior because they had been unjustly persecuted.

He saw how Kossuth after his triumphs was soon forgotten in England and America. Mazzini, who recognized the values hidden in Schurz, tried to persuade him to remain in Europe. In a dramatic conversation he promised him a new revolt in Italy and constructive work. But Schurz had made up his mind. "I had found out that life as an exile was empty and enervating. I felt an irresistible urge not only to take up a regular work, but to do something constructive for the benefit of mankind. The ideals I had dreamed of, for which I had fought, I saw realized in America and—if not completed—yet on the constant road of development. There—I thought—I might help to speed the way. A new free world with great ideals and aims. There I might find a new home and country. Instantly my mind was made up. I would have to remain in England till I had made enough money by my teaching—and then off to America!"

On a morning in September, 1852, the two young people, Schurz and his wife, stepped from a sailing vessel onto the docks of New York. That was the end of Carl Schurz's emigrant life, for here he found a new country and stuck to it for half a century.

Exile to him was on the other side of the Atlantic. More and more he disliked life and events in Europe, more and more he believed in things American. He became the best example of a European who never forgot the language, customs, education of his youth, but was utterly given to the new country of his choice.

Schurz's long life in America is better known in this country than his short youth in Germany. Here the children learn in school how in the eighteen-fifties this young German who knew little English first gave his speeches for the Republican campaign in German, in the German-speaking districts, how no one impressed him so deeply as Lincoln, whose campaign he shared. Lincoln was the sort of man to fill Schurz with enthusiasm; he was struck with the same natural shyness and silence. Schurz tells that Lincoln's influence on an audience was so great that Schurz knew his own speech would be a success if he sat down next to Lincoln on the platform.

What he appreciated most over here were the things he had fought for in vain in Prussia. He marveled to see the public so developed that the audience in a stuffy assembly hall quietly started to vote on its own initiative if he—the orator—should take off his coat or not.

His German experiences were of no use to him over here. They only embarrassed him now and then. Once he rather hesitatingly presented a countryman to Lincoln, a German count who wanted to fight in the Civil War. When this fellow began to enumerate his ancestors, Lincoln interrupted with the words: "Never mind, you won't be made responsible for your ancestors, if you only turn out to be a good soldier." When Schurz later became a general, he met two German officers who once had been his superiors and treated them with superior tact. Once, when a private on guard omitted to salute him, his Prussian education thought this impossible—and he jotted down in his diary the explanation the soldier gave when blamed: "The general had not been presented to me."

Schurz tells of another soldier who saluted him with his right hand, and taking off his cap with the left, expressed his respect for some good campaign speeches Schurz had made.

Belonging to two countries, he took every occasion to say that all nations were worthy of one another, that there existed no pure and no superior races. After the Civil War he wrote this fine word: "No race or class ever changed from slavery to freedom with less feelings of revenge than the Negroes."

Twenty years after his flight from Germany he returned there as an American diplomat and therefore immune to arrest. He was deeply moved when he saw the Rhine, the Cologne cathedral, and other places of his youth, and he gave poetic vent to these feelings.

But the great event of his German trip in 1868 was his meeting with Bismarck, who in 1848 had passionately fought against the revolution. He was superior to Schurz in age, position, and fame, and yet, when he heard of Schurz's arrival in Berlin, he at once invited him for the same afternoon. He did something that was unique in Bismarck's professional life: he had wine and cake offered to the stranger in his office.

As Bismarck was neither a poet nor a romantic and not at all inclined to forgive old trespassers, this reception given to Schurz was something extraordinary. The old dictator was so charming that afternoon that Schurz said he had never had so brilliant a conversation since his interviews with Mazzini.

Bismarck's interest and respect were roused for a man who h:. ı escaped so courageously from the Rastatt fortress and for the ɟdventurous way he had rescued Kinkel. He said he would have liked to go with Schurz to Spandau to hear the tale from his own lips on the spot.

With the candor of greatness, Bismarck told his runaway countryman that he soon would be at war with France, and that he hoped—through this war—to unify the German people, a plan Schurz and his friends had vainly tried to achieve in the revolution.

"Why will you not take over the plan of the constitution worked out by the Frankfort Parliament?"

"My plan," answered Bismarck, "is not so very different. But it cannot be just coldly made a law." He explained, as he later did on several occasions to others, that he needed the heat of a victorious war to blend together the ever-quarreling German tribes.

After he had thus won Schurz's sympathy by showing him his confidence, he threw out a challenge over a glass of Rhine wine. He told how Lothar Bucher, the youthful friend and co-revolutionary of Schurz, had returned home from exile and was now in a high position in the government. In this comment

Bismarck hid an invitation to Schurz to return to Germany and work with his government: A great temptation for so ambitious a man and for one so German in his feelings.

But Schurz simply replied that he had found so great a field for his activity over in America, was so indebted to his new country that he would never leave it. That this new-made American would not for anything return to be a German is of significance. He had traveled through the country of his fathers with deep emotion, and the leading man of the government indirectly offered him a high position. This might have had the power to tempt Schurz.

But he remained firm. The only man to whom both Bismarck and Lincoln made offers preferred the side of liberty and humanism to the powerful politician in an unfree Prussia.

This decision must be recorded as a victory in the moral history of the United States of America.

EMILE ZOLA

by

HEINRICH MANN

HEINRICH MANN

the elder brother of Thomas Mann, was born in 1871. His numerous novels, plays, and short stories are either satirical or poetic and have been translated into many languages. *Der Untertan* (*The Subject*) and *Die Armen* (*The Poor*) attacked the bureaucracy and militarism of Germany under the Kaiser. *Zwischen den Rassen* (*Between the Races*) was the first great novel on the racial problem.

Heinrich Mann has written extensively on Zola. His first essay was written at the request of Zola's family when Mann, who went into voluntary exile in Paris in 1933, was fighting against Nazism. Mann liked the theme because it showed an intellectual fighting the physical powers of this world. Zola in his time had the same opponents he would have were he living today. Fascism, in Mann's opinion, was no mere response to the Russian Revolution; it existed always.

In 1907 Heinrich Mann portrayed a Fascist in one of his novels with an Italian background. In 1914 he portrayed the Nazi type in one of his novels with a German background. Mann thinks he was something of a prophet; his warnings, of course, went unheeded. His latest novel tells the life story of King Henry IV of France. Here, too, he is interested in the problem of power against the individual. After the fall of France, Heinrich Mann came to America and now lives in California.

ÉMILE ZOLA
by Heinrich Mann

Any man who becomes an exile has been pre-destined for this fate. Remaining aloof from politics does not help such a person avoid his destiny. It makes no difference what he has striven for in life; every path ultimately leads him across a border which closes behind him. The longer he is united to his country the more certain it is to evict him one day. Even though he carries the essence of his country wherever he goes and though he personifies it more convincingly and in greater measure than his adversaries who suppress him, yet it is they who hold the positions in the community at home, positions that are forever lost to him.

Émile Zola, novelist and revolutionary of the novel, was without demagogical ambition. The proclamation of new truths through the medium of powerful characters was an effort that was its own reward, but it was only after ten years' time that it enabled him to reach a large audience. Another ten years and the twenty volumes of his outstanding works were completed, and Zola was the most famous Frenchman in the whole world.

When he conceived the plan of his colossal work and drew up the family tree of the terrible family Rougon-Macquart in 1869, he had in mind a regime that actually existed and was very much alive. Speculation as the most important function in the life of the Second Empire, the unbridled amassment of wealth, the huge gratification of the pleasure seekers—all three aspects were theatrically glorified throughout an entire epoch in exhibitions and festivals which gradually assumed Babylonic proportions.

However, the masses too awakened during this period. Their appearance on the scene, their independent demands, hark back to the time of Napoleon III, who himself had vague ideas regarding socialism. Few, however, realized the events that were in progress; only one person gave expression to this progress in palpable form, anticipating its irresistibility.

Quite remarkably, this novelist from the very beginning built up his cause with a blind faith in the masses. He demonstrated this in his novels long before it became evident that the masses someday actually would rule. The world which he created for himself granted the masses a position such as they actually still had to fight for in the future, in the world of reality. The fact remains, however, that he observed nothing but defeats of the masses for a long time, and particularly toward the end of this period. Only to his inner vision did they appear as victors. The uprising of the miners in *Germinal,* which took place during the Third Empire, ended unsuccessfully, and even later, under the Third Republic, while Zola was still writing this same novel, such uprisings were doomed to frequent failure. Nevertheless, the light which the poet has to shed shines into these mines. With each volume the future reveals itself to him more clearly; it is governed by the impulse of the masses and can only be socialistic.

Scarcely thirty years of age, Zola proceeded with a plan he had been preparing for three years: he wrote the natural and the class history of a family under the Second Empire. This was, he realized, the scope of a historian. Historically it was necessary that the family perish along with the empire. In reality the empire in 1869 stood as firmly as ever, just having been confirmed by a plebiscite, and no one foresaw its impending demise. Zola, who knew all the symptoms of the end, was filled with anxiety. "For my book and its logic, I require the downfall of these people! As often as I think the drama through to its conclusion, the conclusion is always their downfall. The way things are in reality, it is not probable that this will occur soon. Nevertheless, I require it." That was the alternative: the further continuation of the empire would make the Rougon-Macquarts impossible.

Suddenly the empire collapsed, completely and suddenly, to the astonishment of all, and particularly to that of Zola, who needed this downfall for his purpose. He was possessed of a sound sense of moderation which prevented him from making much of the fact that he had been right in his prophetic requirement: it was henceforth never mentioned. Still, the fact is that this work of his was born of a prophecy and that he had conceived as historical past that which suddenly became full-fledged present.

Yet, what is past is not altogether vanished. The famous Dreyfus affair did not take place in the authoritarian empire—no, it occurred in the most broad-minded of all republics. It could have taken place just as well in the "Century of Enlightenment." Then Voltaire would have been the one to take a stand against the obscurity of mind, the obduracy of heart, just as Zola did later.

Zola considered this affair as representing the depth of human baseness and evil. Embroilment in it cost him a great deal: his most evident sacrifice was an eleven-month exile. A mild century, moderate even in its disgrace! A man of that day, with his earnestly acquired convictions as to the perfectibility of life and the world, would have thought incredible the extent to which events repeat themselves, would have been astounded at the resemblance between matters concluded and matters current. The course of the twentieth century, of the two wars, of the interval between them, as well as their consequences—the French as well as the universal succession of events—these could not be comprehensible to the man of that time as we know him. They could, in fact, occur only after all of his sort had become extinct or isolated.

THE AFFAIR

I have herewith presented the hypotheses of the political struggle that Zola took upon himself, his literary efforts themselves having been a continual struggle during this period. To the very end they gave no promise of a peaceful course.

His literary work was perpetually characterized by dangerous exposés of the powerful, the rich. What was still more dangerous, the masses were portrayed in the most sympathetic, heroic roles. Even their defeats occurred in the sign of their eventual victory.

At first this was overlooked, but it could not remain unrecognized. The truth invariably is disturbing and social truths are bound to give rise to bitterness. It is not literature alone that the author revolutionizes thereby.

When the Dreyfus case came to light, the skeptics in particular were in no easy position, since they had a high regard for justice and truth—perhaps too much so. They believed the world unsuited for these virtues. Some had become reconciled to the existence of fraud and lawlessness even before the Dreyfus case and merely interposed the opinion that mankind could not exist a single day without a lie.

A young officer was sentenced to deportation by a court-martial in 1894. For three years afterward it seemed that this procedure had been fair, and the matter was forgotten. In times of protracted peace, when army service becomes too dull, espionage, counterespionage, and sometimes even the betrayal of military secrets furnish the only interesting activity for officers of high rank. The nation, which has no share in all this except that it pays the bills, learns to its mild dismay that something is amiss. A man who by reason of his standing is supposed to be the personification of national honor has permitted himself to be "bought," by a "foreign power"—actually a prospective enemy.

This, of course, should not be, but everyone who is worldly-wise reckons with such accidents and puts up with them. It would have been less painful if the General Staff and the "Second Bureau," to which Captain Dreyfus belonged, had washed their dirty linen at home. Unfortunately the matter was aired before the whole country and as a consequence the story reached foreign ears. According to the latest dispatches the wrong man had been deported, while the real culprit, in spite of tangible proof, had been shielded by his superiors. He continued to play the man of honor, the man of the world in the nation's capital. Meanwhile, on Devil's Island in the distant ocean, someone was substituting for him, someone who had nothing to do with the whole thing. No, this most certainly should not be.

Why, then, had it happened? All things considered, the General Staff, which had committed such a grave error, held just as high an opinion of the army as did the nation itself, an opinion wholly inapplicable. It was for this reason that it involved itself in the affair, forging documents, setting free a convicted man, and stubbornly persecuting a harmless creature who had no idea what was going on. For "the army," that is to say, certain military personages who had rendered a false verdict, must not be exposed under any circumstances. "The army" is pure and must remain so. To do wrong is permissible, because it is unavoidable. To be in the wrong would be more pernicious than the treason itself, and "the army" had the power to put across its falsifications as the truth. The nation was at stake: but strange to say, it was the nation that suffered disgrace when certain gentlemen of high rank and distinction were not able to bear the truth.

These gentlemen were not alone by far in treating the matter from this point of view. Every one of the Cabinet ministers who was forced to resign and was replaced during the course of the affair was filled with the same conviction. Even the last president of the chamber, who finally had to settle the case, by no means acted out of a higher sense of justice. He was merely making a concession to the defense, for, owing to a Zola, a Clemenceau, and many of their kind, the land had long been engaged in a civil war—no favorable circumstance in the event of an attack by a foreign power.

The opposing party—the self-styled patriots who sided with the General Staff—was doubtless superior in numbers to the group of intellectuals and their followers, with all their passion for justice. The cause of injustice makes its adherents no less belligerent. The army could not afford to be caught in a lie, and since all that had happened was that a Jewish captain had committed treason this same army could well afford to parade along the open highways with flags and music.

¹"The army" is the noble outward representative of the Fatherland and is essentially a business, designed to maintain the conflicting social forces in a delicate equilibrium. How important, then, to preserve its flawless luster, its unsullied reputation! Obviously, people only imagined that a court-martial had rendered a false verdict, that a General Staff, merely to prove itself in the right, was defending the real traitor while it condemned an

innocent man to the searing climate of the tropics! One must not forget that the so-called innocent man was a Jew, not a Frenchman, while the other, Esterhazy by name, was a genuine compatriot.

Today it is quite evident, although it was then asserted in vain, that the blunders and even the crimes of a few high-ranking officers never determine the reputation of an army: the rank and file alone will uphold and preserve it, as long as the soldier deems the land and its institutions worth defending. Since then we have witnessed the prompt execution of a Marshal Tuchatschevsky. The treachery initiated by him failed to be carried out, and the People's Army of the Soviets continues to fight on to ultimate conquest. It would, however, neither conquer nor fight if it were not a people's army but a "class" army.

The French army, a class army, finally has met the fate that the Dreyfus case foreshadowed. A marshal has betrayed the Republic which failed to remove him from office despite the fact that it knew him well. Himself of the upper class, he wantonly came to terms with an enemy that to him seemed to be of his own caste. The unscrupulousness and blind inconsideration with which a people were disarmed, with which a country was played into enemy hands, are astounding. The consequences daily prove to be more terrible: no marshal could have foreseen them.

It may be regarded as the glory of the intellectuals of 1897, however, that they knew in advance what it would lead to if the ruling class, as represented by certain saber wielders, began to treat justice and truth with contempt. These farsighted individuals declared, and meant it sincerely, that they were not against the army. The army is the people: they could never be against the people, whose champions they were.

No, what they were fighting was the arrogance of the privileged in uniform, who falsely called themselves "the army," and who were twisting the nation about their fingers, imposing their notorious lie upon the people, obliging them as a whole to accept the blame for the crime committed by a single clique.

The Dreyfus Affair was the first sign of treason against the people, in a quarter where treason is the most dangerous: the army.

The intellectuals of the fin de siècle fought with worldly understanding, a highly desirable attribute when one is pursuing a spiritual goal such as Truth. They did not wander into generalities, they kept silent about the character of the class army. Zola, at least, by reason of the experience gained in his work, was prepared for the revelation that a class army was no reliable defender of either this or any other nation.

At the same time the question remains as to how much of later events he immediately would have comprehended had he not died four years after his noble deed. What would startle him, what would horrify him, were he to return to see the present outcome? He could say, "This is just what I foresaw in my worst dreams"—for on the whole he had seen and portrayed mankind in a gloomy light. He could also say, "No; I did not anticipate such an abyss of depravity." For he had painted the gloomy aspect as a friend of man, whom he believed destined for a constant ascent. The thoughts of the dead are difficult to fathom.

In those days the menace to human rights in his own country was not so great. The institutions of a bourgeois republic permitted an open fight against corruption, with at least a hope for a just settlement.

The most dangerous course, he often said, is to suppress scandal and keep up a front. This admonition subsequently became applicable to the case of the German Marshal Hindenburg. Defeated in the war, but placed at the head of his republic for the sake of a false front, this incompetent, corrupt marshal betrayed his unfortunate land, sold it into bondage to the new warmonger.

"When one buries the truth underground," said Zola, "one prepares the way for the most frightful disaster."

THE DEED

When the affair occurred Zola was in Rome. As usual he was looking for documentary evidence for a book, which in this case was to deal with the Church. The Church was a greater social factor than the army, whose débâcle he had dealt with in a tragic novel five years before. In the fall of 1897 he learned that the army once more required his full attention. He had probably never imagined that any military affair ever would claim more of his energy and passion than had the collapse of the Second Empire on the battlefield of Sedan.

The records he examined immediately convinced him beyond any doubt that a great crime was being committed. Yet it was, as he himself later remarked, primarily the expert novelist who was "fascinated, nay enraptured" by the great dramatic possibilities of the plot. Mercy, faith, and the desire for truth and justice followed later. The same fertile enthusiasm that stimulates the creative power of the writer also tends to aid the innocent man.

One must, however, not neglect to pay tribute to another person who was first to fulfill his human obligation and did so without hesitation, though the misfortunes of Captain Dreyfus were not to him a potential plot for a novel. That man was Scheurer-Kestner, a senator from Alsace whose name lives on, not on account of the laurels won in the performance of his duties, but because of this single deed. He proclaimed what he knew and what he would have abhorred to conceal. The unwritten law of his class required his acquiescence, since the army was unassailable. His class, the rich bourgeoisie which at one time had seized power by means of its idealism, has always preserved its fundamental strength through the actions of upright individuals. "He did not realize what storms he was to create; truth and justice come first and are the sole guaranties of the greatness of nations."

These were Zola's words; Scheurer-Kestner could not speak as expressively as one who had made the fashioning of words his lifework. Zola, the fashioner of words, wrote the motto. This time events were to follow mere words and human destinies were to be decided by a single sentence.

This was the type of action for which Zola felt himself qualified. Everything seemed so complete, like material gathered for a novel, ready to be molded. And like a novel, it called for an introduction, suspense, and a logical conclusion. One could foresee that the plot would have its heights and depths, but finally there would be a solution and a happy ending. To be sure, matters took quite a different course, but probably he had anticipated the above well-ordered succession of events. After all, one must consider all the possibilities before risking one's name and splendid career for a cause. He was certain the truth would prevail, for truth had assured the triumph of his works. Whoever has trained himself to be truthful thinks the world and mankind also can be thus educated.

As a true educator, he first appealed to youth. It was his first failure, for the newspapers refused to publish the appeal. This admonition came unexpectedly to one accustomed to nation-wide attention whenever he raised his voice. Yet nothing was to deter him. The appeal was published—only the young people to whom it was addressed failed to respond, for they were more strongly biased by class consciousness than their elders.

The determined stand of the Alsatian senator forced the army to put the real traitor on trial, the outcome of which was a fore-gone conclusion. The court-martial acquitted Esterhazy. This was the first act, thought Zola; the second was to follow. His slogan, "Truth is on the march," has lived to describe the incident as well as the age. Convinced of the mathematical certainty of every step to follow, he took the next one, which was far more revolutionary. He proclaimed the truth that many knew and no one dared to utter, even though by this act he endangered both himself and the country.

The name of the paper was *L'Aurore,* and its editor was Georges Clemenceau. Later Clemenceau gave sufficient proof that he did not hate the army. He won a war with the same army, an army whose General Staff he had cured of the habit of betraying it.

On January 13, 1898, he printed three hundred thousand copies of a letter written by the well-known novelist, Zola. This epistle was addressed to the president of the Republic, a former tanner, now a polished gentleman who had introduced the use of outriders in order to enhance his dignity. Small-minded men love such trappings of state once they have reached the top by recognizing and upholding all sorts of privileges, injustices, and profitable untruths. In those days such men did not have a thousand bodyguards, for dictatorship was beyond their reach. This tanner was by no means the proper addressee for the novelist's letter.

Nevertheless, it reached him: so did it reach the man in the street.

Only one phrase of the letter became immortal, but its fervor is as everlasting as that of the words "Écrasez l'infâme," "Eppur si muove," or "Hier stehe ich, ich kann nicht anders." The phrase was "J'accuse!" These words immortalize a gesture. Posterity sees him as a man who professed the truth without concern for his own welfare: "I do not wish to be an accomplice. The specter of the innocent man who suffers torment for a crime he never committed would haunt my sleep."

It is highly significant that among the great number of persons who knew the true state of affairs there was only one who seemed predestined to profess this knowledge. No one was surprised when Zola raised his voice: he would have been the natural choice for such a task. He justified the message of truth his writings had manifested. Four years later, Anatole France concluded his eulogy at Zola's grave with the words "He was a moment in the conscience of mankind."

President Faure, the highest official of the Republic, learned from this letter the fact that he had neglected an opportunity to prove his own superiority. A novelist had been able to render a brilliant analysis of a judicial matter, while the president, who had access to all the records of the case, had kept silent. The executive head of the state had unscrupulously allowed the perpetration of a horrible crime. To safeguard the imperiled authority of the state, as well as his own, the chief executive had preferred a perversion of justice at a time when the true facts could no longer be suppressed. The president of the Republic was Zola's real opponent, although the writer did not accuse him by name.

The mature intelligentsia never fails to attack a form of government that neglects to function in the interest of mankind. The Third Republic will always preserve its reputation as having promoted, in general, the welfare of humanity. Within the given limitations of class consciousness it demonstrated an understanding for the rights of the individual as well as of the underprivileged masses. Up to that time the Third Republic had stood out as the most successful attempt to apply human knowledge to the problems of life. Its final vindication was brought about by the revolt of the intelligentsia, by their "affair"—the case of Captain Dreyfus. For this affair was definitely "theirs."

J'accuse did not stop at generalities; every offense was specifically cited. Zola called his defendants by name: "I accuse, I accuse—" he said, appending a long list of names. The whole Dreyfus case was the invention of a madman. When this lunatic began his "investigation," he was only an army major. He was promoted to the rank of lieutenant colonel as a reward for his cock-and-bull stories. Not only did he invent these wild tales, but he also made them ring true. Promoted in rank instead of being placed in an asylum, he was protected by his superiors, the generals, out of either stupidity or esprit de corps. Even the minister of war, who was personally disinterested in this affair, deemed it necessary to shield the fraud.

The manner in which the entire clique maintained the hoax to the very end is astonishing. At least at the beginning of the affair it was much simpler to limit the disgrace to a few subalterns. The forger of the document which had been the cause of the Jewish captain's misery finally committed suicide. His accomplices never admitted their participation in the crime. They were "the army," which could do no wrong. One wonders if Dreyfus himself would have dared to stigmatize "the army" in a case like this had he not himself happened to be the innocent victim. Most of the guilty ones were respectable family men; their only fault was their blind faith in authority.

When it comes to a crisis truth will hardly find more than a single, stanch supporter among those who have debauched it. Surprisingly enough, even among this General Staff, there was such a person. Lieutenant Colonel Picquart was proud enough to desire to maintain his integrity and pressed his superiors to such a degree that they finally sent him to Africa. Their secret hope that he might perish there never was fulfilled.

"I am waiting," Zola had concluded in his letter. He did not have to wait. On the very day his accusation was launched the Chamber of Deputies voted to bring him to trial. The majority of 312 votes to 122 was a clear indication of the general sentiment, shared by political factions and the people alike. On February 23rd, after fifteen stormy sessions, the jury reached the expected verdict. The testimony of the witnesses had brought no surprises. In court, both jurors and jurists were influenced by noisy demonstrations of popular sentiment. There were riots on the street. The authorities were careful to protect the troublesome writer from possible assassination, but did little to protect him against the hostile demonstrations of the crowd.

The time was not ripe for political murder until sixteen years later, when Jaurès was assassinated. At least, such extreme violence would have been considered out of order at the close of a century that had held a firm belief in the constant progress of human decency. Even minor offenses were scorned as unworthy of such a progressive century. Many shouted, "Down with Zola!" but were ashamed in their hearts. The twentieth century never displayed such self-assurance: there has been no basis for such pride.

The point had been reached when the foremost personage of the country in the eyes of the world could not express the most credible, the most authentic of facts without risking his entire career. He said to his jurors: "I swear by the reputation which I may have gained through forty years of effort that Dreyfus is innocent. I swear by all that I am proud of, by the renown I have won through my writings, which have contributed to the dissemination of French literature, that Dreyfus is innocent. May all this go to ruin, may all my works perish if Dreyfus is not innocent! He is innocent!"

The disgrace and decline of an age did not begin with his being condemned to one year of imprisonment and a fine of three thousand francs, nor when the incapable or dishonest handwriting experts each demanded five thousand francs: these were minor consequences. The significant and fatal symptom was the fact that one of the intellectual leaders of the time had to sacrifice himself. For the climax of the century had been marked by the implicit trust of the people in their galaxy of intellectual leaders. These prominent spiritual leaders had been the real rulers of Europe.

We owe it to Zola and his followers that these days of grace were at all extended. The final collapse of moral standards came about when the rabble set themselves up as leaders of nations.

Zola exacted of himself the utmost sacrifice: he did not go to prison, he went into exile. Labori, the name of his lawyer, lives on in a symbolic sense: this was the last labor of European conscience before the catastrophe. Labori did all in his power to protract the legal proceedings. On July 18th the appeal was referred back to the same court and the decision was upheld. This time the judicial sentence was based on three lines of a so-called defamation, twenty pages long. Sentence was pronounced upon an absentee who knew that the outcome was inevitable. He left for London the same evening.

THE APOTHEOSIS

Zola went into exile because the sentence of the court was not valid until he had received the writ. His friends and he were eager to keep the affair alive in hope of an ultimate deliverance, even if this seemed remote at that hour. Zola believed as firmly as ever in the logical conclusion of his deed. He felt certain that the complications and discords of his novel would result in the final solution he had anticipated. While he was forced to live in solitary exile he wondered only how much will power it would take to maintain this confidence. Compared with exile, life in prison would be festive with visits, homage, and the daily bustle of publicity.

Suddenly transplanted from the excitement of a successful career into the rural solitude of another land, he worked on his next book. He had trained himself to become thoroughly absorbed in the lives of his characters, but this time all his art and training could not help him forget that his own life had reached its crisis. His voluntary exile gradually would begin to appear as an escape, as his enemies already had maliciously called it. The dangers of exile were grave. Living permanently abroad, this successful author would soon become a forgotten man, a failure.

Zola's faith in the beloved country which had fostered his fame, as well as his belief in himself and in his knowledge, was shaken. At the most critical moment of his entire career his own work, the discovery of the masses, the prophetic bluntness with which he had pictured their primitive desires and struggles, turned against him. His country resented the universality of his fame and regretted that it had ever allowed him to become great.

The change for the better which he had long awaited occurred as effectively as it had in any of his novels. The forger killed himself. The scene changed rapidly. There was a shake-up in the government and incidentally the Republic inaugurated a new president. His predecessor, to whom *J'accuse* had been addressed, died suddenly, poisoned by drugs he had taken as a stimulant in anticipation of a feminine visitor. Everything was proceeding smoothly thus far. The Chamber of Deputies, however, now took six months to rectify their errors, although it had taken them but a few hours to condemn Zola in the first place. The military court required an additional period of ninety-five days for the reversal of its verdict of 1895. In their opinion, three more months could not matter to an innocent man who had spent five years on Devil's Island.

One may rightly assume that Zola had no illusions as to this delay in a case upon which divine judgment already had been passed. His faith in the irresistible march of truth was justified, but it was erroneous to expect that everyone would welcome this truth with open arms. No one seemed eager to acknowledge it. The old clique was embarrassed rather than relieved at this belated airing of the truth. Amid much gnashing of teeth they bowed to the inevitable, but they were as ready as ever to deny their guilt and to defend their evil actions. The most broadminded rulers ostentatiously welcome the truth but are afraid actually to touch it.

The rapid turn of events came forty-five days after Zola's departure from France. Though he had a chance to return then, he remained in exile for a total of eleven months, a short time if one considers that exiles in other eras have lasted half a lifetime and have ruined the victims' careers. Often they have died in exile, innocent of all wrongdoing. There is always the question of just what a man loses thereby. If Zola had died in England it would have spared him the sight of what was to follow. Dreyfus was widely acclaimed when he arrived in France. His case was reviewed and the original verdict upheld. Such gross injustice seemed unbearable to a writer whose faith in life was based on the experience of his own perpetual fight for improvement. For him, the world seemed to come to an end.

"I am shocked" was all he could say. He had considered the retrial as the fifth act of his tragedy. If this was not to be the final act, then fate itself would have to shape its course. A man who is no longer able to comprehend, who is merely shocked, leaves the final outcome to the Unknown. Ingenious fate had decided to add a final, improbable, and monstrous touch to the living work of art in order to heighten the glory of atonement and redemption.

Zola had named this final act the "apotheosis," a word which is properly used with regard to the stage or to religious paintings. It does not apply to the reality of life. The author of the "dreadful" Rougon-Macquart surely was aware of that fact. After he returned to his native city, and to the life and people he had analyzed for forty years, he realized only too well what was to take place. Everything possible was done to hush up the entire scandalous affair by silence and subterfuge.

The retrial of his case was repeatedly postponed, and although it never was held, neither was it canceled, for it did not fall under any statute of limitations. Dreyfus was pardoned. Fifteen months later a general amnesty was declared. Zola called it a disgrace to the law.

In his eyes the pardon which was forced upon him was a "loi scélérate." It deprived him of his well-deserved right to castigate those who were responsible as well as of the chance for retribution for all he had suffered. To add insult to injury, it was the same ruling which protected the real culprit from further prosecution. The minister consoled him with the hope that history would pass the judgment he deserved. What about the present? If only the law might be administered differently, if only it consisted of something besides legalized special privileges! There were some who should have been expelled from the army, others who should have been removed from their posts of command. But they had to remain, in order to keep up the pretense of law and order.

The fact that the World's Fair was held in Paris in the year

1900 should not be overlooked. Such an exhibition not only serves to promote commerce and trade, it also represents the greatness of a country, which it enhances. It was imperative that the nation be pacified and united at a time when it played host to the world. The exhibition displayed the power of a country which required that its General Staff remain intact. It also heralded its glory, of which the name of Zola was an integral part.

Yet the nation committed the gross blunder of failing to restore Zola's name, best known of all French names to every foreign visitor, to the role of officers of the Legion of Honor. One year later Zola commented on this fact. Two years later he was lost to his country, his death caused by poisonous fumes from his fireplace. Posterity was quick to pay the tribute which his contemporaries had denied him although they had realized his greatness. The body of Zola lies in the Panthéon as an eternal monument to truth.

The "affair" of the French intelligentsia was brought to a conclusion at the very end of the century, but its shadow still looms over the present age. It had served to outline the criminal complacency of not one particular country, but rather of all countries. It foreshadowed the plight of all intellectuals who battle the forces of evil and it demonstrated how nations reel helplessly into catastrophies of injustice. The First World War as well as the present one are the catastrophic results of a disregard for justice and the suppression of knowledge.

Zola has set an example for us by his full recognition of the hour, "when the pernicious powers of the past will fight the decisive battle against the forces of tomorrow." What he then proclaimed still holds true:

"The decision must be made whether mankind is to regress and is to be engulfed by the resurgent forces of injustice and slavery—perhaps for a century to come."

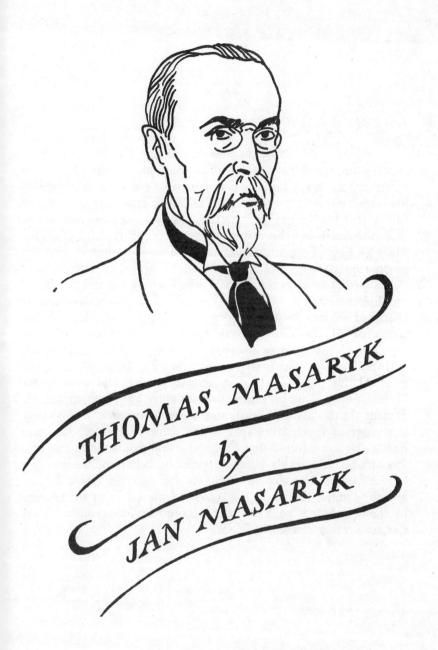

THOMAS MASARYK

by

JAN MASARYK

JAN MASARYK

foreign minister of the Czechoslovak government in London, was born in 1886 in Prague. From his American mother, Charlotte Garrigue of New York, he inherited his humanitarianism and love of the arts, especially music. His father was the founder of the Czechoslovak Republic. When he was mobilized by the Austro-Hungarian army in 1914, Jan Masaryk had an opportunity to see the Prussian militaristic spirit at close quarters.

Immediately after the First World War, Jan Masaryk entered the diplomatic service of his reborn nation. His first post was as chargé d'affaires in Washington. From 1922 to 1923 he was counselor of the Czechoslovak legation in London. Later he represented his country as minister plenipotentiary and envoy extraordinary at the Court of St. James's. In 1938, Masaryk resigned this post as a protest against Munich and went to the United States. But he returned to London and inaugurated his famous short-wave broadcasts to his people at home. In his opening program he declared that in the name of him whose name he bore he was assured that Czechoslovakia would again rise as a free nation. Masaryk's latest activities on behalf of the struggle of the United Nations has been divided between Great Britain and the United States. In the course of his last visit to America in the winter of 1941 he was appointed vice-premier of the Czechoslovak government in exile.

THOMAS GARRIGUE MASARYK

by Jan Masaryk

How can democracy be most speedily brought about? Follow
your convictions. Do not merely talk your politics. Live them.
Tell the truth and do not steal. And, above all, do not be
afraid to die.[1]

I AM WRITING these lines from London, the same
inspiring capital of a great empire from which my father organized Czechoslovakia's first struggle for freedom during the First
World War. In many ways that struggle and the present one are
similar. The enemy is largely the same, and the objectives are
almost identical. We strive to secure individual and national freedom for those who have been deprived of both by the enemies
of humanity.

The impact of the present war upon our social, national, and
international institutions will undoubtedly be more penetrating
and, I hope, more enduring than was the case less than a generation ago. Had the world accepted and realized some of the fundamental ·principles which T. G. Masaryk upheld throughout his
life, many an error in judgment and in action might have been
obviated. Through many mistakes during the interbellum period
we have grown wiser and are better prepared to make the peace
become a real thing.

Thomas Masaryk was born in 1850 at Hodonin in Moravia.
His father was a Slovak coachman on the royal estate. His
mother was a cook.

[1] T. G. Masaryk, in 1933, when interviewed by Edgar Ansel Mowrer.

He has been called the "President Liberator of the Czechs and Slovaks." His name represents the culmination of the centuries-long struggle of our people for independence. Continuing in the tradition of Jan Hus, Comenius, and Palacky, Masaryk secured for the Czechoslovaks the honorable place to which they were entitled by their achievements in the spiritual and material fields, and by their constructive co-operation as a member of the family of free nations.

The Czechs and Slovaks were united in the ninth century in the Moravian Empire. In the tenth century the Magyars invaded Central Europe from Asia and conquered the Slovaks. The Czechs, however, maintained their independence for six more centuries. It was in 1620, after the battle of White Mountain, near Prague, that the Czechs' independence was destroyed.

During the Thirty Years' War the Czech population was reduced from three million to eight hundred thousand and it was believed that the Czechs as a nation were finished. But thanks to their vitality, they regained their strength in the next three centuries, while waiting for the first opportunity to regain their independence.

They rose against the Hapsburgs in 1848, but ever since the end of the eighteenth century, when the spirit of nationalism began to grow, they had been recuperating from the blows of the past. The national revival was progressing rapidly and was taking inspiration from art and literature and from the works of Jan Hus, Comenius, and other Czech spiritual leaders of the past.

In 1914 there were seven and a half million Czechs and two and a half million Slovaks. They made up one-sixth of the population of Austria-Hungary, under the Hapsburgs.

Thomas Masaryk, a university professor, writer, and political leader, was an antimilitarist until the outbreak of the First World War, and for some years he still hoped that Austria-Hungary would solve the problem of its nationalities on the basis of equality and equal opportunities. But when the Vienna government attacked Serbia he became convinced that the Czechs and Slovaks could no longer look toward the Hapsburgs for the solution of this problem and that the only way to secure social, cultural, and national freedom for his people was through separation.

For that reason Masaryk urged the Czechs and Slovaks to fight the Hohenzollern Kaiser and the Hapsburgs.

The name of Masaryk is identified with faith in the ultimate victory of the best in men. His motto was: "Truth Will Prevail." He dedicated his life to the struggle for freedom: freedom from alien oppression, from social exploitation, from prejudice. Like most true fighters for a better world he often found himself avoided by those on whose behalf he labored. He was deeply national in the sense that he believed in the right of every people, large or small, to live according to its conscience. His nationalism, however, was tempered by his humane approach to the problems of group relationship. A nation was to him not an end but a means toward a better way of life. He was a realistic humanist, rooted deeply in the soil from which he came and struggling onward in the firm belief that the people would follow him.

He never courted popularity. He valued objective truth more highly than any comfortable illusions. This brought him often into conflict with his contemporaries.

It was in 1877, during his stay in Leipzig, Germany, that Masaryk met a turning point in his life.

A young American music student, Charlotte Garrigue, came to live with the German family with whom Masaryk boarded. Masaryk, a tall, distinguished-looking man, and Miss Garrigue found many intellectual interests in common and soon became engaged. But shortly afterward Miss Garrigue had to return home to Brooklyn.

Masaryk went to Vienna and tried to secure a teaching position. In February, 1878, he received a telegram from Miss Garrigue's father: Charlotte had been injured in an accident. Masaryk immediately started for America. On his arrival he found that Miss Garrigue had recovered from her injuries, and, still in his impulsive mood, he decided that they should marry immediately. The wedding took place in March, 1878, and the following month Masaryk was back in Vienna, but now accompanied by his young wife. As a symbolic gesture he now adopted Garrigue as his second name. For almost fifty years they lived together in a most happy marriage.

Born a proletarian, and later the "ruler without a country" of twelve million people, Masaryk looked like an intellectual aristocrat. He was proud of his dark-brown beard. In later years the white mustache and goatee of the "grand old man of Czechoslovakia" became dear to all Czechs. In Vienna he was called the "best-dressed man in Parliament."

In April, 1887, at the age of thirty-seven, Masaryk visited Russia and went to see Tolstoy. His general impressions were favorable to the Russian people, but he was repelled by the spirit prevailing among the officials and the intellectuals. Nor did he find Tolstoy altogether to his liking. There was about the man and his surroundings an air of pretentiousness which ran counter to the fundamental qualities of Masaryk's mind. In particular, Tolstoy's theory of nonresistance to evil proved quite unacceptable to Masaryk, who insisted upon the need for resolute defensive action against an aggressor.

Masaryk was a true democrat. In later years he told the Czech poet Čapek: "True democracy, founded on love and respect for one's neighbor and toward all neighbors, is not only political but social and economic. Communism I reject . . . I base democracy on love—on love and the justice that is the mathematics of love, and on the conviction that we should help the world toward the realization of God, toward synergism with the divine will. . . . Humanity does not exclude, or weaken, the love for one's nation. I must love my nation positively, but because of that I need not hate other nations. True love is proved not by hatred but only by love."

Masaryk's philosophy stemmed from Hume and the logic of John Stuart Mill. He was also influenced by Locke, Spencer, and Comte, but he rejected Kant and the whole German school of philosophy. He was one of the keenest critics of Marxism, and believed that the world was working its way toward universal humanism. No wonder he rejected Richard Wagner's religion and philosophy.

As a revolutionary, fighting for his oppressed people, he had sympathy for the Jews. He once said, "He who chooses Jesus as leader cannot be an anti-Semite. You can be either for Christ or for anti-Semitism."

In 1899, Masaryk became involved in the famous "Hilsner case." The dead body of a girl was discovered in a wood near the small town of Polná in Bohemia. From the very outset the crime was assumed to have been a Jewish ritual murder, belief in which was still rife among the superstitious peasantry and was fostered by their spiritual guides. As a result, a young Jew, Leopold Hilsner, was brought to trial, found guilty, and condemned to death, although the evidence against him was extremely weak.

Hilsner's counsel appealed the case and at the retrial in 1900 the original indictment was extended to include a new charge of murder. Hilsner's second alleged victim was a servant girl who had disappeared in the summer of 1898. So flimsy was this particular charge against Hilsner that the court acquitted him of it, although the proceedings were conducted in the same spirit of gross prejudice as the original trail had been. The acquittal, however, did not help Hilsner. The previous conviction was upheld and he was sentenced to death.

Masaryk made a close study of "ritual murder" in general and the Hilsner case in particular. The result of this research was embodied in several essays and pamphlets, urging a revised verdict. In the end, Masaryk's efforts led to a commutation of the death sentence to penal servitude for life. Hilsner remained in prison until 1918, when he received a pardon.

Masaryk's activities on Hilsner's behalf were prompted not by any great regard for Hilsner himself but in defense of a principle. As he emphasized, he wanted "to free the Czechs from the bonds of superstition." He was, of course, denounced as "a hireling of the Jews" and suffered a vast amount of abuse.

Another incident illuminates Masaryk's courageous stand for truth. During the first decade of the present century the situation in Austria-Hungary became increasingly ominous. A symptom of this unrest appeared in 1908 when Count Aehrenthal commemorated the sixtieth anniversary of Franz Joseph's accession to the throne by annexing Bosnia and Herzegovina, two provinces in which ninety-six per cent of the inhabitants were Serbs and Croats.

Aehrenthal had prepared a press campaign to justify his high-handed action. It denounced a Pan-Serb revolutionary movement for allegedly spreading disaffection to Hapsburg rule. Wholesale arrests followed and ultimately fifty-three persons were in jail. In the middle of January, 1909, five months after the arrests had started, the public prosecutor indicted the accused for high treason.

The trial opened at Agram (now known as Zagreb), the capital of Croatia, early in March. The proceedings, which frequently lapsed into a blatant travesty of justice, dragged on until October. All except twenty-two of the accused were sentenced to prison terms.

Meanwhile, Masaryk had paid several visits both to Agram and to Belgrade, where he succeeded in obtaining material which revealed the anti-Serbian intrigues of the Austrian Foreign Office. Masaryk made two speeches in Parliament. There was no doubt that the trial had been engineered.

In March, 1909, the *Neue Freie Presse* had published an article, "Austria-Hungary and Serbia," which repeated the charges contained in the Agram indictment. Dr. Friedjung, a well-known historian, had been used by Aehrenthal to bolster up his case against Serbia. In due course the members of the Serbo-Croatian coalition in Austria-Hungary brought an action for libel against Dr. Friedjung. Masaryk, who appeared as a witness for the plaintiffs, gave evidence which helped to discredit Dr. Friedjung's material. After a fortnight's hearing the Austrian Foreign Office contrived to get the prosecution withdrawn.

Masaryk's further inquiries at Belgrade brought to light the startling fact that the documents which had figured so prominently in the Friedjung trial were forgeries emanating from the Austro-Hungarian legation at Belgrade. Masaryk started a parliamentary campaign against Aehrenthal, and the foreign minister was compelled to make increasingly damaging admissions. He went on leave, never to return.

Aehrenthal's successor, Count Berchtold, soon showed that the errors of the past had taught him nothing. He displayed a remarkable capacity for mischief during the Balkan War of 1912. Masaryk felt convinced that, with Berchtold directing Austrian foreign policy, a European conflagration was inevitable.

He expressed this view openly at the congress of his party executives in January, 1913, hinting that the Czechs would have to decide upon their course of action in case such a disaster occurred. Significantly enough, his last speech in the Austrian Parliament, in May, 1913, was a protest against the incompetence of the government's home and foreign policy.

When the First World War broke out, Masaryk was sixty-four. He was spending his summer vacation with his wife and children at Schandau, a Saxon health resort near the frontier of Bohemia. He at once decided that there must be Czech resistance to Austria, and he realized that the Czechs could assert themselves only on the side of the Allies.

In the autumn of 1914 he paid two visits to Holland, where he met Dr. Seton Watson. He handed Dr. Watson a memorandum on the reconstruction of Central Europe, with special reference to the Czech problem. This memorandum was brought to the attention of Sir Edward Grey, and was carried out almost to the letter in 1918.

On his return to Prague, Masaryk and a small group of his associates, including Dr. Eduard Beneš, began to meet in secret to discuss a plan of action.

From these meetings developed the Mafia, that underground intelligence service which played so important a part in the Czech liberation movement. Thus that old name, which had been rather contemptuously applied to Masaryk and his followers nearly thirty years before, was revived under conditions that imbued it with renown.

By December, 1914, Masaryk's plans were complete. He was to go into voluntary exile. Dr. Beneš would act as a link between him and the other members of the Mafia. After having made arrangements to protect the interests of his family as best as he could, Masaryk left Prague, accompanied by his daughter Olga, and proceeded to Rome. His chief object in visiting Italy was to establish contact with his Southern Slav friends.

On January 11, 1915, he went to Switzerland, hoping to get back into Prague, but his Czech friends informed him that his movements in Italy had already been reported to Vienna and that he was to be arrested the moment he set foot on Austrian territory. Masaryk faced what might well be lifelong exile.

His task of pleading Czechoslovakia's cause before the leading Allied statesmen was burdensome and hazardous, and his funds were limited. He himself said: "The plain truth is that throughout the war we were short of money. I fancy that no revolution in history was ever engineered with so small an outlay . . . But we all had our hearts in our work, and that is why we were able to manage with so little money."

The four years of Masaryk's creative political effort in exile which followed were unique of their kind. They involved changes of scene that would have proved a considerable strain even under normal conditions and for a younger man. Masaryk was sixty-five years old and undertook all the hardships and dangers of wartime travel. His vast itinerary may be summarized as follows:

January-September, 1915	Geneva
September, 1915-May, 1917	Paris and London
May, 1917-April, 1918	Petrograd, Moscow, Kiev, Vladivostok
April, 1918	Tokyo
April 29-November, 1918	Chicago, Washington, New York
December, 1918	London, Paris, Prague

While in Switzerland, Masaryk took steps to utilize to the utmost all the resources at his disposal. In March, 1915, he distributed among the Czech organizations abroad a circular, in which he indicated how their work could most effectively be carried out. In the middle of April he paid a short visit to Paris and London to acquaint himself with conditions there. He traveled with a Serbian passport in his own name, and while in London, he drew up a second and more detailed memorandum for Sir Edward Grey. He also met Count Benckendorff, the Russian ambassador, and got the impression that Czarist Russia had no special interest in the aims of the other Slav nations.

Before taking this trip to Western Europe he had assumed that the leading statesmen there had little knowledge of the Czech cause and he discovered that his assumption was correct. He decided to take the earliest opportunity of making his position clear on some public occasion. He did this on July 6, 1915, when a lecture was delivered at Geneva by Professor Ernest Denis, the famous French authority on Czech history, to celebrate the five-hundredth anniversary of the martyrdom of Jan Hus. At the conclusion of the lecture Masaryk made a speech in which he emphasized the need for every Czech to make up his mind in favor of Czech principles or of Austrian principles.

The Viennese newspaper *Neue Freie Presse* described this speech as the "first Czech declaration of war against Austria."

Before long, the technique of secret communication between Masaryk and his friends in Prague reached a high standard. As time went on, the devices for outwitting the Austrian authorities became more ingenious. But in May, 1915, Kramář, the leader of the national front at home, was arrested and condemned to death.

In August, 1915, the Austrian police in Prague proceeded against Masaryk on a charge of high treason. A joint military and police "commission" raided Masaryk's house. But Masaryk had removed all his important documents before leaving, and the commission discovered only a few periodicals and books which were not of the slightest value to the authorities.

A few days later, Masaryk's wife and his daughter Alice were cross-examined at Prague police headquarters. The military officer in charge of the proceedings decided that Mrs. Masaryk could be set free, but that Alice should remain in custody until further notice. In due course she was removed to Vienna, together with the wife of Dr. Beneš, and was kept in prison until July, 1916.

Masaryk left Switzerland for Paris, where he was joined by Dr. Beneš, who remained in Paris as general secretary of the "Conseil National des Pays Tchèques" (afterward the Czechoslovak National Council) while Masaryk proceeded to London.

London proved to be a congenial working center for Masaryk, who was deeply attached to English culture and had already made important contacts in England. He soon became a member of the Slavonic department of King's College, London, and started his chief political work, *The New Europe*.

During his stay in London, Masaryk lived at Hampstead, first in rooms, and then in a furnished house at the now historic address of 21 Platt's Lane. Here, with his daughter Olga, he made himself as comfortable as circumstances would permit. He did a great deal of writing, mostly articles for the English press. He drew up numerous memoranda and had a heavy correspondence to attend to. He also worked on a book describing his activities—*The Making of a State*.

As regards propaganda, in his conversations with Karel Čapek, he explained that his principles were ". . . not to abuse the Germans, not to underestimate the enemy, to distort nothing and to refrain from boasting; not to make empty promises and not to beg favors . . . And, one other thing, not to be a nuisance."

A vital point in the Czech liberation movement was reached in November, 1915, when the first joint manifesto of the main Czech and Slovak colonies abroad appeared. It was signed by Masaryk and the leading Czech and Slovak representatives in Great Britain, France, Russia, and the United States. The style of the manifesto reveals Masaryk's authorship. After outlining the historical background of the struggle, it draws attention to:

> . . . the appalling terrorism which throttles the slightest expression of the genuine sentiments among the people in the Czech regions. . . . Today the chief Czech politicians are languishing in jail, and the gallows have become the favorite device for furthering the purpose of an incompetent administration. The rights of the Czech language have been mercilessly trampled under foot. An unrestrained soldiery is running riot in Czech, non-German and non-Magyar territories, as if in enemy country. . . .

This led up to the climax of the manifesto which was the following terse declaration of purpose: "We are striving for an independent Czechoslovak State."

On November 21, 1916, Emperor Franz Joseph died, and Prince Sixtus of Bourbon, the brother-in-law of Karl, the new emperor, made an attempt to obtain a separate peace for Austria. Masaryk's anxiety was great, for Sixtus, owing to his ability to approach influential persons in France and Great Britain, had a by no means negligible chance of exploiting the pro-Austrian sentiments which existed in certain Allied circles. Fortunately Sixtus delayed his action until the spring of 1917 when two factors substantially changed the general outlook: the outbreak of the Russian Revolution on March 14th, and the entry of the United States into the war less than a month afterward.

By the spring of 1917 the number of Czechs and Slovaks who, while serving in the Austro-Hungarian army, had been captured by the Russians exceeded fifty thousand, and it became urgent to organize them with a view to future contingencies. Masaryk went to Russia. He traveled on a new passport made out to Thomas George Marsden, and spent ten months there. His chief task was to transform the many thousands of soldiers on Russian soil into an independent military force which could be placed at the disposal of the Allies.

Finally he signed a contract with Albert Thomas in Petersburg, according to which forty thousand men should be brought to the German-French border. It was the first contract signed by a nonexistent state. Masaryk's influence on the Czech and Slovak soldiers was great, although he was a civilian and wore no uniform. The soldiers recognized him as their leader and followed his orders with blind confidence.

In July, 1917, the Czechoslovak brigade, numbering thirty-five hundred went into action for the first time as a separate unit and defeated a combined force of twelve thousand Austrians and Germans at Zborov. Masaryk obtained the approval of the Russian General Staff for the establishment of a self-governing Czechoslovak army corps in October, 1917.

The outbreak of the Bolshevik Revolution and the separate peace with the Germans, however, confronted Masaryk with a new problem. French military circles wanted to have the Czechoslovak troops transferred to the Rumanian front. But after a brief visit to Rumania, Masaryk concluded that the country was about to collapse. He therefore decided that the Czech army must be sent to the Western Front. The only route by which the bulk of it could be conveyed there was across Siberia to the Pacific coast, and then westward by way of the Indian Ocean and the Suez Canal.

On March 7, 1918, his sixty-eighth birthday, Masaryk left Moscow for Vladivostok in a British Red Cross train. Before his departure he made all possible arrangements with the Allies in Russia to safeguard the interests of the Czechoslovak troops. It was Stalin, then a commissar, who telegraphed from Moscow to the local soviets, instructing them to allow the Czechoslovaks to proceed on their way as free citizens.

Masaryk's journey from Moscow to Vladivostok took three weeks. He worked very hard on this trip, and spent most of his time composing *The New Europe,* a careful presentation of the Czech case for independence.

As it proved impossible to sail directly from Vladivostok to America, Masaryk traveled by the Manchurian railway via Mukden to Korea. From there he took a steamer to Japan. The voyage from Yokohama to Canada lasted ten days. Masaryk started at once for Chicago and on his arrival there was welcomed by a crowd of more than a hundred thousand, representing the Czech population of Chicago. It was the beginning of his triumphal progress across the United States.

His duties were urgent and onerous. American public opinion had to be made familiar with the case for Czechoslovak independence. Masaryk addressed meetings, delivered lectures, and wrote articles.

The Czechs and Slovaks in America numbered two million. Masaryk aimed at a closer understanding between Czechs and Slovaks. He also wished to define the position of the Slovaks in the future Czechoslovak State. This was necessary in order to counteract Count Károlyi's efforts to persuade official circles in America that, after the war, Hungary must be left territorially intact.

On June 30, 1918, an agreement was signed at Pittsburgh, the chief Slovak center in America, by a representative group of Czechs and Slovaks. The agreement, although it could be only of a provisional character, contained a series of stipulations on the subject of Slovaks in Czechoslovakia which, whatever adverse criticism may allege, were fulfilled when the Republic came into being.

On June 19, 1918, Masaryk had been received by President Wilson, to whom he handed a memorandum on Russia. The conversation lasted forty minutes. Masaryk urged the Czechoslovak claim to independence and pointed out the precarious situation of his soldiers in Siberia.

Three months later Mr. Lansing informed Masaryk that the United States now recognized the Czechoslovak National Council in Paris as a de facto government. Masaryk had founded a new state.

A month later a German and Austrian peace offer reached Washington, and, as a sequel to President Wilson's reply, Austria accepted the principle of the Fourteen Points on October 15th.

The fact that President Wilson had not replied to Austria-Hungary caused Masaryk some uneasiness. There were good reasons for supposing that Emperor Karl intended to reorganize the Dual Monarchy on a federalistic basis.

Masaryk, therefore, at once set to work upon a "Declaration of Czechoslovak Independence." The document, which ran to about fifteen hundred words, was written in Czech and English.

On the morning of October 18th a copy of the English version was handed to Wilson and Lansing, and that same afternoon it was published in full by the American press. It was cabled to Dr. Beneš at Paris and to Štefanic at Vladivostok, who signed it as foreign minister and minister for war of the "Czechoslovak Provisional Government." Masaryk signed it as premier and finance minister.

The effects upon the policy of the United States were immediate. Wilson transmitted his reply to Austria in a note which bore the same date as the declaration itself. He said that he could no longer accept a mere "autonomy" of the people of Austria-Hungary as a basis of peace.

Events now developed with bewildering speed. Eleven days later Count Andrássy replied to President Wilson's note, asking for a separate peace. Masaryk was unaware of the bloodless revolution in Prague resulting in the proclamation of the Czechoslovak Republic on the previous day; and he suspected that the Austrian willingness for a separate peace might be a German ruse. He was reassured when November 4th brought news of the armistice with Austria.

His vision of the times to come was clearly shown during his conversations with President Wilson, when he warned of the danger of Prussian militarism to European peace. It is unfortunate that his warnings were not heeded. He wrote later:

> When the peace offers began and the question of arranging an armistice arose, I expressed to the President my conviction that the war ought to be continued until the Allies had compelled the German army to lay down its arms and that, if necessary, they should enter Berlin. I argued that this course would not cost more lives than would be lost by an indecisive peace. . . . As I knew how strongly the masses of the German people believed in the invincibility of the Prussian-German army and its commanders, I feared that German public opinion in general would not be convinced that Germany and Austria had been strategically defeated.

On November 10, 1918, a memorable date in the annals of Masaryk's struggle, he received a telegram from Geneva, signed by Dr. Kramář and a number of Czech politicians. It was the first open message from home since his departure in 1915, the first greeting the exiled revolutionary had received from his people in Bohemia, Slovakia, and Moravia. And on the same day a telegram from Dr. Beneš informed him that he had been appointed president of the Republic. He was asked to return immediately, and ten days later he sailed from New York.

In London both official and private welcome awaited him. A luncheon, attended by Mr. Balfour and Winston Churchill, was given in his honor. Paris, where he stayed for a week, was equally appreciative and enthusiastic.

Yet during these days of triumph he did not lose sight of realities. During a talk with Dr. Beneš in Paris he said, "All that we have done is mere child's play compared with what still awaits us . . . To win was a problem, but it will be a greater problem to maintain the results of victory."

On December 21st he arrived in Prague, amid celebrations unparalleled in the history of the Czech capital. But his mind was centered upon what, with prophetic insight, he knew would be an uneasy future.

In his very first speech in Prague, at the railway station, at an unforgettable moment when the reunion with his old friends had brought him to the verge of tears, he emphasized that the battle was not yet won. "I know, and you all know too, that much labor still awaits us. I know, and you all know, that we still have many difficulties to overcome."

From the station he drove through Prague to the Hradčany castle, which was to be his presidential abode. Even now, during this triumphal progress, he did not shake off the preoccupations which might well be called misgivings. "What were my feelings," he wrote later, "and thoughts amid that magnificent welcome by Prague? Was I glad, did it make me happy? As I gazed upon all that splendor, upon that wealth of colors, costumes, banners, and decorations . . . I constantly had in mind the difficult tasks now looming ahead of us."

He visited his wife, whose health had broken down under the strain of her wartime anxieties and who was in a sanitarium. Then he withdrew to the Hradčany. On the next day he delivered his first presidential message to the Czechoslovak people. He urged the need for genuine democracy, and heralded social and legislative reforms which would remove all remnants of unhealthy Austrianism. In conclusion he appealed for the maintenance of order.

This appeal was heeded, and during the critical period following the end of the war the Czechoslovak Republic was spared all those upheavals which impeded a return to normal conditions in most of the neighboring countries.

In the spring of 1920 the first general elections were held in the Republic and the first Czechoslovak National Assembly came into existence. Masaryk was elected president of the Republic.

His wife died in May, 1923. Masaryk, accompanied by his daughter Olga, left Prague and traveled as far as Algiers and

Tunis. On his return he took up residence in the castle of Topolcianky, in Slovakia, which he subsequently occupied every summer.

Masaryk's third term of office as president expired in May, 1927. He spent the two months preceding the presidential election in Greece, Egypt, and Palestine. On his return to Prague he was re-elected.

When, on March 7, 1930, Masaryk celebrated his eightieth birthday the National Assembly passed a special vote: "T. G. Masaryk has deserved well of the state." This quiet praise of his achievements, which is as unrhetorical as his own way of speaking, was carved in stone in both Chambers.

Masaryk's health seemed to be better than ever. On October 28, 1933, the fifteenth anniversary of the Republic, he made his appearance on horseback at a public parade in Prague. But within a few months the physical effects of old age began to make themselves felt. He doubted whether he ought to seek re-election in May, 1934, but in view of political conditions he was induced to do so and was again re-elected. In the following year, however, he was to resign in favor of Dr. Beneš, so as to avoid any possibility that the Republic might even for a short period lack a president. The resignation ceremony took place on December 14, 1935.

Masaryk lived on for nearly two years after his retirement. During this period he devoted himself to the scholarly pursuits which had always been closest to his heart.

The end came on September 14, 1937, in his country mansion at Lány, near Prague.

By what must surely be regarded as something more than a coincidence, the book that was read to him to the very last was Konrad Heiden's *One Man Against Europe,* for within eighteen months this "one man" overthrew the results of Masaryk's long and patient endeavors.

The funeral oration was delivered by President Beneš, who, in conclusion, said:

"President and Liberator, we shall safeguard the legacy which you placed in our hands."

This legacy has been snatched from us by the Germans, but side by side with the United Nations we are now striving to recover it. Our whole nation, whether at home or in exile, is certain that the legacy of Masaryk will be restored to us.

SUN YAT-SEN

by

HENRY B. KRANZ

HENRY B. KRANZ

belongs to that group of young Viennese authors who—like Arthur Schnitzler—are typically Austrian and combine it with an international viewpoint. He has traveled in Spain and Greece, England and Siberia, America and Africa, and met his first Chinese in Manchuria. Having won his literary laurels with a romantic comedy *Heart Is Trump Again* in 1930, he wrote plays, novels, short stories, essays, poetry, and he adapted the works of twenty American and English playwrights for Austrian audiences. Among them were plays by Robert Sherwood and Elmer Rice. At one time he was Viennese theater correspondent for the New York *Times*. His historical play *Garibaldi* was in rehearsal in Berlin when Hitler came to power in 1933. This was the beginning of the end of Kranz's literary career in Europe, as it was of all those who fought with the pen against Nazism. He learned soon that *Garibaldi* was *personna non grata* even in Austria, and when a friend told him he had seen his name on the list of the first five hundred Viennese to be arrested by the Nazis he left the City of Waltzes—three months before Hitler marched in.

SUN YAT-SEN

by Henry B. Kranz

IN THE happy clime of the south, in Kwantung Province of the vast Celestial Empire, lies the small village of Choy Hung. Here then, the matter of warm clothing was of no concern to the young peasant boy. Early dawn found him toiling in the rice fields, beside his aged father. As the sun rose higher in the heavens, he trudged off to school, barefoot. At night his head did not rest on a cloth-covered brick according to village custom. Nor did he recline on a bed of tender tea leaves. Mindful of the teachings of the great Confucius, he chose the "golden mean": he slept on a sack of beans.

Tai-cheong—"He Who Serves the Gods"—his gentle mother called the young boy, who found contentment in sailing his kite from among bamboo and sugar cane, banana trees and rice stalks. His father would tell strange tales of Canton, the wealthy city at a distance of a day's journey, or of Macao, the haunt of gamblers, opium addicts, and dancing girls. The boy longed to visit far-off lands. But he did not run away from home as had his older brother and two of his uncles. Gold had tempted them, mountains of gold in California, in the land of the "white devils." He remained. All happiness is to be found in the lap of the family; so said the wise men. He did not, as he later explained, "wish to be unfaithful in my duty toward my people."

This accent on duty is perhaps a shade too strong for one so young. Actually it serves as a poignant reflection of the boy's character, who as a devout student of the classics learned the significance of sincerity, humaneness, and knowledge.

The prevailing spirit, however, was in direct contrast to these ideals. He saw a stranger on the sacred throne of the dragon: a Manchu. He saw eunuchs, corrupt officials, venal women, and ruthless tax collectors to whom one must kowtow. He saw ignorance, poverty, filth, disease, coupled with superstition and indolence.

In his youth, his father had taken part in the abortive revolt of a Ming brotherhood against those Manchus. But long since, he had reconciled himself to wearing pigtails; his mother hobbled about on bound, deformed feet. The Sun family worshiped the wooden gods at the ancient village shrine. It is true that in school young Sun Yat-sen learned the doctrine of "San Tse Chin." Filial affection, brotherly love, uprightness, sincerity, charity, and loyalty: these were its precepts. Yet he felt that, in spite of this, ignorance was threatening to stifle the ancient, time-tested moral code.

Was there no remedy? His teacher told him, "No. Such is the will of the Son of Heaven, of the emperor."

No letters or notes are extant of Sun Yat-sen's childhood but we may safely assume that the boy would have become a coffin-maker, in accordance with his father's wishes. Fate intervened, however, turning his footsteps toward distant fields, far from the homeland. He was to study abroad, he was to become a wise man, wiser in many ways than those whose tenets he so admired.

Ah-mei, his brother in far-off Honolulu, brought the thirteen-year-old boy to Hawaii in 1879. There young Sun attended the "Bishop's School," and learned English. Three years later, from the hands of King Kalakaua, he received a coveted award for "Excellence in English Literature."

Well-to-do as a result of his activities as a merchant, Ah-mei frowned upon his young brother's submission to Holy Baptism. He viewed with growing alarm the change that was taking place in the boy. He saw that he was unable to answer the lad's many questions. "Tai-cheong," he wrote to their mother, "has become quite foreignized." And with that, he sent the boy home.

Sun Yat-sen returned to the village, a Bible under his arm. Nineteen years old, he married. Lu Sze was his bride, a young girl of the neighboring village. It was at the wedding that he saw her for the first time, but he did not mind this, for it was his father's wish.

The Bible furnished the answer to many of his questions, but not all of them. The great philosophers in his homeland taught that there is no need of commandments when it comes to judge between good and evil. Did not Confucius declare, when a pupil asked him to explain his teachings in a single sentence, "Do not do unto others whatsoever ye would not have done unto you"? Had the young boy not read that "The truth cannot be proved; it can only be interpreted"? Was it not written there that the meaning of life is not to be discovered in the world to come, nor may it be found in success or mere striving? That one must live simply, enjoy this world, practice kindness, and hark to the wisdom of one's elders? No, the young man said to himself, one does not need mediators, supernatural beings, or saints in order to find the path of righteousness. That lies in one's own heart.

Yet he had seen that in Hawaii his countrymen were free, while at home they lived in bondage and poverty. Over there they had justice; here, the Manchus. Yet how could he arouse this superstitious, illiterate people?

He is said to have consulted a friend in this regard, receiving the following answer: "Perhaps you were born to become the Napoleon of China."

One day the youthful Sun accompanied his friends to the village shrine and saw them fall on their knees before the idol Buck Dai. He grasped one of the god's fingers, broke it off. The divine image remained silent. His companions rushed out of the temple in horror.

The young man's father, who had secured him a position in the village pawnshop, strongly suspected that his own blood had begun to manifest itself in the veins of the precocious young rebel. He did not punish his son, but he decided that the lad must not remain there any longer. The whole village was seething with indignation. Ah-mei, however, did not care to have his Christian brother in Honolulu. So this time the youth was sent to Hong Kong. There were schools there that would accept him.

Sun Yat-sen had become an outcast. This affected him grievously, for he had gone home to tell of the strange events recorded
in the books of the world outside: of Cromwell, of the French
Revolution, of a world that was better because it was ruled by
enlightenment rather than ignorance, because it cherished pride
above any other considerations that might lead to subservience
to foreign rule. They had sent him away before he could speak
of any of these things. But, he reflected, if it was possible to
dethrone an idol, why not dethrone the old empress in Peking?
China must be free, not only from internal tyranny, but also from
the grasping clutches of the foreigners who had settled in every
seaport.

The people of China are known for their realism, sobriety,
conservatism, love of freedom, and democracy: there are no aristocrats in their midst. They are persevering, tolerant, and bear a
great respect for the law: they have no policemen. Sun Yat-sen
manifested all these qualities, but he was also a dreamer. And, like
many dreamers, he eventually became transformed into a revolutionary. Like Moses, Luther, and Mahomet before him, he was
destined to a great deal of suffering. His burning desire, his uncompromising sense of justice, and his deep distress over the
poverty of his four hundred and fifty million countrymen made
him destroy a thousand-year-old yoke, but he was shown no gratitude. Hailed at first as liberator, he was soon forced into exile.

Attending medical school first at Hong Kong and later at
Canton, his earliest confidant was Cheng Shih-liang, member of
one of the secret societies which bound the sons of the Celestial
Empire in brotherhood wherever they might be. Sun Yat-sen
unfolded his plans to his schoolmates. Immature, aimless, boyish
plans, they were; but there were many who listened, and heeded.

He became a physician and he became a father. And soon he
was the recognized leader of a small group of students. They felt
that the man who nightly addressed them was destined to play a
decisive role in the history of China. Many years later an American journalist commented on Sun Yat-sen's personality:

"Sun is a solemnly disturbing fellow. I gave up trying to

understand him long ago. But there was something lovable about him that could not be disregarded or forgotten."

Probably it was his veracity as well as his fanatic, impersonal devotion to his ideal that brought these first friends, and later an ever-increasing host of adherents, rallying around him. They sensed his innate courage and kindness, qualities that make for a successful leadership.

His appearance invited confidence. Stocky, of medium height, he had a high forehead and his eyes barely showed a Mongolian "slant." His nose, protruding above a bushy mustache, was rather long for a Chinese, his cheekbones were softly rounded. Like his master, Confucius, he seldom smiled; in that all who knew him agree. He did not incline to be humorous. In company he was silent. But when he stood upon a lecture platform his dark eyes would light up and he instantly became the prophet.

When Dr. Sun Yat-sen settled in Canton it was not so much in order to practice medicine as to give talks. The nights were passed in heated debate with his friends over the political situation. The first task at hand was to rouse the national spirit of the people. Social problems were then of little concern to the young physician.

During this period, early in 1895, China was at war with Japan. It seemed, however, the intention of the Great Powers to take advantage of this conflict in order to partition China among themselves. The French had already seized Annam, the English Burma, Nepal, and Tibet, the Russians a part of Mongolia, while the Japanese had taken Formosa, Jehol, and Manchuria. Now they added Korea to the booty.

How was it possible to prevent the collapse of the great empire? First of all, so thought the young physician, it was necessary to put one's own house in order. With this in mind he worked out a memorandum which he presented to the powerful viceroy of Chihli. It proposed the following reforms: free trade, utilization of the soil on a scientific basis, free schools, and the alleviation of poverty. It contained but a single indirect indictment of the widowed empress at Peking. For the time being, Sun Yat-sen wished to adhere to the golden mean.

Only when he received no reaction did he resolve "to overthrow the Manchus," and he began to prepare the revolution. Ten other revolts were to follow, however, before the Manchus abdicated.

He was on a "propaganda" trip to Hong Kong when his friend Soong, a wealthy young merchant from Shanghai, urged him to return to his homeland: the time was ripe. Little did Sun dream that one day he would take Soong's daughter, Ching-ling, now five years old, home as his wife.

Military preparations occupied a half year's time. Resolute men had to be recruited, arms smuggled into the country, soldiers and officers of the imperial army won over to the audacious plan of a revolt.

But on September 9, 1895, before the time to strike had arrived, Cantonese customs officials discovered six hundred pistols in one of the conspirators' ships. Scores of arrests followed. Sun Yat-sen, however, succeeded in concealing himself in a basket, which coolie revolutionaries hung over the city wall. Crouching within this basket, suspended in mid-air for three days and nights, he finally managed to escape. (Later, whenever he saw a wall, he had it torn down.) When his poet friend Lu Hao-tung was beheaded Sun Yat-sen had long been safe in Yokohama.

Thus began his exile, spent in years of vagabondage in many lands, with a price on his head, beset with adventure and peril.

In order to remain incognito in Japan, and also as a protest against the Manchus, Sun Yat-sen clipped off his pigtail, donned European clothing, and later secretly brought his mother, his wife, his son and two daughters to Honolulu. But he continued his travels.

Confucius was no longer his sole mentor or he would have resigned himself to a fate which to most Chinese would have seemed inevitable. He knew there were many wealthy Chinese in America. He decided to solicit funds there. Arms and munitions are essential for an uprising. A revolution "from below" was unthinkable, for the people could scarcely read and write and had never heard the word "democracy." They were enervated, sluggish, and fearful. What a task for a young surgeon!

Soong, his merchant friend from Shanghai, provided him with traveling funds. In Honolulu he happened to come across Dr. James Cantlie, who had been one of his English medical instructors at Hong Kong. The missionary doctor invited Sun to look him up in London should he ever go there. This accidental meeting and a purely social invitation were shortly afterward to save his life. In the career of every revolutionary there are extraneous developments that tip the balance between life and death.

From Honolulu, where Sun Yat-sen on an earlier visit had founded the Hsing Chung Hui, or Advance China Society, his path led via San Francisco to New York. Here he lectured to small groups. Distrust met the fugitive from the distant homeland. The Chinese envoy in Washington, however, paid special attention to him. He hastened to dispatch a cable to London, warning the legation of Sun's arrival there.

On October 1, 1896, Sun Yat-sen came to London. He went to see Dr. Cantlie, who was surprised to see him. Sun was lonely, he was looking for friends. A few days later a countryman approached him on the street, another joined them and a conversation developed. Suddenly Sun Yat-sen was dragged into a doorway. Before he realized it he found himself a prisoner at the Chinese legation on Portland Place.

On October 17th, at midnight, there was a knock at Dr. Cantlie's door. A woman handed him a hastily scrawled note, which read:

I was kidnaped into the Chinese legation on Sunday, and shall be smuggled out from England to China for death. Pray rescue me quick. A ship is chartered by the Chinese legation for the service to take me to China, and I shall be locked up all the way without communication to anybody.

The messenger explained that she was the wife of an English servant at the legation. The doctor rushed to Scotland Yard, but received no co-operation there. Next morning he visited Downing Street, where he was put off with empty phrases. A reporter of

the *Globe,* however, thought he was on the trail of an international incident. Was it possible to kidnap a person from the
freedom-loving British Isles? This would mean conceding too
much rights to a foreign legation. Moreover, this Dr. Sun Yat-sen,
on whose head there was an enormous price, had been educated in
an English college. Also, he was a Christian. These factors set
the stage for an effective newspaper crusade.

The *Globe* front-paged the kidnaping of the Chinese rebel,
and other papers followed suit. Threatening letters poured into
the Chinese legation and finally Prime Minister Lord Salisbury
sent a personal protest to Portland Place.

A week later Sun Yat-sen was free once more, just one day
before the arrival of the £6,000 payment for the chartered ship
by which he was to be returned to China. Those days of prison
aroused him completely. He wrote to a friend:

> . . . I prayed six days in great agitation but on the
> seventh God gave me peace . . . The Manchu govern-
> ment has lost its reputation over this, and I am put in
> touch with the best people . . . I feel favored as the
> Prodigal Son or the Lost Sheep. Truly, this is the bless-
> ing of the Fatherly God . . . Now I believe in God more
> than ever.

Never before had he revealed that he really believed in the
God of the Christians. Never again did he show such devout belief.
But he did not become a churchgoer. From that moment on he
merely believed that his destiny was in the hands of a Higher
Power. That gave him the strength to fight. It did not matter to
him that he was extremely poor during the next few years, that
for many months he had to live on rice and water, that in
London he was compelled to tramp many hundred weary miles
on foot. He had come to learn, from out of the history and the
wisdom of the West, the construction of the new nation, which
had up to then been only vaguely and generally conceived.

When China would be free, he now meditated, what then?
A republic? That was only a means, but not a solution. What
form should this republic take? What were the fundamental principles of a free commonwealth? How would the customs and

traditions of his people assimilate the new ideas of the West? Was such an assimilation possible? Had the European democracies proved their worth? Were there other methods? It was necessary to test, to choose, to weigh and consider, and to make vital decisions.

He read extensively during this period: Rousseau, Marx, Henry George, Lincoln, Jefferson, Bismarck, Bakunin. He studied books on unemployment, industrial and agricultural development, military science, mining, ethnology, and geography. Yet he was not in the least surprised by what he found in these volumes. Much of it seemed oddly familiar to him; it was as though these authors had made a study of Chinese history.

There was anarchy, for instance. Had not Lao-tzu described the "Kingdom of Huan Hsu" of a thousand years ago? There, according to the historian, people lived in a natural state, without any government, and their law was the law of free social life.

Then there was socialism. Had not the Emperor Shen Tsung, a long time ago, granted the social philosopher Wang the privilege of trying out a new order for a period of ten years? The state forthwith had taken commerce, industry, and agriculture in its own hands. Ceiling prices were set. The land was partitioned and taxes established according to the yield of the soil. Old-age and unemployment insurance were introduced. Neither was universal compulsory military service an invention of the West, any more than was antimilitarism or democracy. To be sure, tyrannical rulers had later replaced popular government in China with autocracy while in Europe it was the other way around. There it started with theocracy and arrived, via autocracy, at democracy.

Later, in reporting his Continental experiences, he wrote:

> I liked political equality as practiced in Europe, but was disturbed at the manner in which economic inequality and class distinction grow in industrialized society.

Above all, he was impressed with one thing: Europe, although rich and powerful, was unable to make its people happy. For that reason they desired not only political but also social reforms.

All that he read and saw, in London, in Japan, in America, and on the European continent, helped him to formulate his system of "Three Principles." Sun Yat-sen called them: Nationalism ("Our doctrine of Nationalism corresponds with the French Revolutionist's idea of Liberté"); Democracy ("Our doctrine of Democracy corresponds with Égalité"); Socialism ("Our doctrine of Socialism corresponds with Fraternité").

Of course, there was much that remained unclear, that remained more vision than actual knowledge. These principles, however, known as "Ming Sheng," became the fundamental political tenets of the Chinese people.

From Europe, Sun Yat-sen proceeded to Singapore, disguised as a beggar. There he found many disciples, particularly among women. His ascetic mode of living—he did not smoke or drink—brought him many followers of both sexes all his life long.

In Japan he gathered about him a strong community of partisans. He chose as headquarters the only vacant house in the neighborhood of the Chinese consulate in Yokohama. In London he had learned not to fear his fellow man and he wanted to prove that courage to himself and others.

Meanwhile, he learned that in his homeland the political situation was growing acute. The British had seized Weihaiwei, the Russians, Port Arthur, and the Germans, Kiaochow. Furthermore, another revolutionary party had dedicated itself to the establishment of a constitutional monarchy. Its leader, Kang You-wei, stormed against the exiled Dr. Sun, but later was converted by him.

Better news followed. A group of secret societies in Fukien and in the Yangtze Valley announced themselves ready to cooperate when it was time to revolt. The Boxer Rebellion had led to armed intervention by the Western powers, leaving a disordered and dissatisfied Chinese people in its wake. The caldron of revolt was boiling over—but how could one destroy a throne with empty pockets?

Had Sun Yat-sen not been a man of imagination, he would not even have attempted it.

At the beginning of 1900 he went to Formosa, and from there gave his friends and followers in Kwantung the order to attack.

The revolutionists actually held out for a whole month. In a number of southern coastal cities they raised the new flag of China. It had five stripes: red, yellow, blue, white, and black—representing the Chinese, the Manchus, the Mongols, the Mohammedans, and the people of Tibet. But in the end the revolt was suppressed.

Sun Yat-sen was far from discouraged. On the contrary, he felt himself much stronger. Though up to now he had been regarded as a bandit, the conquest of Peking by the eight powers had opened the eyes of the masses. A new patriotism arose and its path led directly toward Sun Yat-sen. An English journalist wrote at this time:

> When I went through southern China in October for the purpose of seeing something of the Rebellion, which was in progress, I was perpetually hearing of Sun Yat-sen. He was the organizer, the strange, mysterious personality whose power was working it all. Yet no one could tell his exact whereabouts. He has a good following of modernized young Chinamen, who have been educated in England, in Honolulu and in Japan, and among them men who are wealthy.

From Formosa, Sun Yat-sen went to San Francisco, where he addressed a gathering as follows:

"The Chinese nation will rise and overthrow the Manchu dynasty. Then the republic will be erected, for the great provinces of China are like the States of the American Union, and what we need is a president to govern all alike."

The Chinese consul of that city begged his countrymen: "There is a revolutionary leader in our midst, who is arousing the people by his false statements . . . His aim is to collect money which he will afterwards squander." In vain. The number of Sun's followers grew daily.

For two years his travels continued, across America, via Singapore to Japan, always from platform to platform. He preached, demanded, entreated. A person not of his peasant, robust make-up and temperament would probably have broken down under such a strenuous life. Little has been recorded of him during this period. In his scanty autobiography he avoids

everything that is personal, intimate. In all likelihood he lived
alone and every minute was consecrated to the one, the only idea:
the winning of friends for China's cause. He actually found thousands of simple folk who were willing to sacrifice all their savings, the fruit of their labors in tiny laundries or shops. To Sun
Yat-sen this money seemed an even more desirable contribution
than the more liberal donations of the wealthy.

Once again, at Canton, the revolutionary banner was un-
furled. But not for long. In 1904 Sun Yat-sen returned to China,
but was soon discovered and had to flee—in women's clothes.
Then he went to Europe. As a "traveling prophet" he knocked
indefatigably on new doors. Proudly and naïvely he reported
afterward that on this world-wide trip he had succeeded in gaining ten students in Paris, twenty in Berlin, and all of thirty
in Brussels.

In Japan again, he united his followers in a new organization called Tung Ming Hui, the "Revolutionary League." Its
program was to be the struggle for "a state belonging to all the
people, a government controlled by all the people, and rights and
benefits for the enjoyment of all the people."

This program contains most of what he later molded into his
Constitution for China. Lincoln's ideas occupy a prominent position, but political democracy in the opinion of Sun Yat-sen is not
sufficient. Social democracy is indispensable. The goods of this
earth must be more equitably distributed. Above all, the land
belongs to those who cultivate it.

There must be no want, no poverty. Only a united brotherly
people can achieve this. Social revolution, therefore, must be preceded by national revolution. Since there were so many obstacles
to this process in China—the clan system, corruption, ignorance
—the revolution would have to be followed by a brief military
regime, which then would step aside permanently in order to en-
dow an enlightened people with a true democracy.

Sun Yat-sen hoped that the success of his revolutionary movement might come to pass within his lifetime. Had he not gathered
ten thousand Sunyatsenists? Soon, however, the Manchu government exerted pressure on Japan, and he was banned from that
country. He went to Hanoi, in French Indo-China. Five times

he dispatched armed revolutionists across the border to the homeland and five times they were defeated.

Sun Yat-sen's tenacity was astonishing. It can be explained only in the light of his inflexible, placid disposition. None of his failures affected him deeply, for it seems that he did not intend to break down the door to freedom with one fierce blow. Rather, he would wear it down with small, sharp thrusts until it finally would give way of itself.

In all those years of bitter disappointment and endless waiting, years never eased by a woman's soothing smile, not once did he complain of his banishment, of the cruel fate that forced him to live in foreign lands. With an almost inhuman self-effacement he kept silent. But when he spoke of China he became eloquent— China, that was waiting to be liberated.

Why should he complain? It was not he who had to wait, but China. Of what importance was his personal destiny compared to the task before him? Truly great men are truly selfless. Exile, therefore, did not drag this great patriot into the depths of effort-shackling gloom as it did so many of his fellow sufferers. Instead, it lent him wings, which carried him back in spirit across oceans and mountain barriers to the peaceful valleys of his childhood. He was in exile, but it was only his body that wearily sought rest in a foreign bed. His spirit was free, indefatigable. It roamed unhindered in a tenderly, patiently, and passionately beloved homeland.

What was this homeland? It was the four hundred and fifty million human beings, suffering as he was, but not privileged to speak. He would speak for them, he must speak for them; he could not look on while they lived in medieval bondage. What mattered his own fate in comparison to that of those millions? He was silent when others spoke of banishment and exile. The suffering of his brethren was greater than his own.

Once more the movement was in need of funds. Sun started a newspaper, the *People's News* (*Min Pao*). His comment was significant: "A single newspaper is worth 100,000 soldiers." Another journey across America, via Seattle, Spokane, Kansas City, and St. Louis, yielded about half a million dollars for the cause. But when Sun Yat-sen sailed for the Far East, he found all Asiatic ports closed to him. He was now "Public Enemy No. 1 of the Orient."

A fresh revolt, again in Canton, ended in failure, whereupon he decided to go back to San Francisco. Here he lived in shabby hotels, dined in obscure restaurants. He solicited funds, he lectured, debated. One evening a member of his audience came up and told him: "I would like to join you. I believe in your success." Sun Yat-sen looked at the speaker with astonishment. The man was introduced to him.

He was Homer Lea, an American who was supposed to be an expert in military strategy and had just written a book called *Valor of Ignorance.* Sun Yat-sen resolved to make the strange, hunchbacked fellow his military adviser someday.

Sun was on his way to Denver in the spring of 1911 when he received a cable from a friend in the fatherland: "Send funds immediately. The Revolution has begun." But he had no funds and he spent a sleepless night in his hotel room, for the cable was already twenty-four days old. Next morning he read in a newspaper: "The revolutionary troops have captured Wuchang." He was greatly relieved. So they were succeeding without direct aid from him! Still he did not rush back home, explaining later:

"I could have directed the revolutionary war myself. Nothing would have made me happier. But on second thought I decided that my place in the revolution was not on the battlefield but among the diplomats. I would not return until I had solved the most important diplomatic questions."

Soon he found confirmation of what until now he had but suspected. Of the six top world powers, only America and France were favorably inclined toward the revolution. The autocratic governments of Germany and Russia were open enemies. "The people of England sympathized with us," he wrote later, "but the attitude of the government was uncertain."

In St. Louis the shabbily clothed, weary traveler learned from the well-informed newspapers that the revolutionaries contemplated proclaiming him president of the Chinese Republic, should the Manchus abdicate. He went to New York, incognito. On his arrival he learned that Canton had already fallen. He took the next steamer to Europe and conferred in London with a group of financiers. He had to prevent the Manchus from being granted any further loans.

Again he was sitting at the home of his friend, Dr. Cantlie, when a cable arrived:

"The Revolutionary Assembly has chosen you President."

His expression was grave, he realized the difficulty of the task that lay before him. His thoughts were on the future while he bounced his friend's child on his knee as though nothing in the whole wide world had changed. Later he conferred with Homer Lea, who had joined him in England. They arrived in Shanghai, December 24, 1911, and the first request made by Sun's old friends was for money. He was forced to shake his head. "I have brought no money with me—I have brought nothing but the revolutionary spirit."

Never before had a revolution—almost bloodless, insufficiently prepared, carried out by a small group of men whose leader was absent—swept before it such a vast empire with such unexpected rapidity. Scarcely a month after the first outbreak in Szechuan fourteen of the eighteen Chinese provinces fell in with the revolution. In Nanking 100,000 government troops gave up the city without a battle.

The Manchu emperor's general, Yuan Shih-kai, was ordered to take up negotiations with the Sunyatsenists. The general, however, sensed the irresistible force of Sun Yat-sen, and advised the emperor to abdicate. Yuan apparently had big plans for himself, for he believed Sun Yat-sen still to be a disciple of Confucius, still reluctant to use force, still accustomed to patient waiting.

Sun was torn between two alternatives. He could come to terms with Yuan Shih-kai, who held the power in Peking. Thus, choosing the golden mean, he would spare the land further bloodshed. On the other hand, he was certain that the republic would be safe only in his own hands. This, however, would mean civil war.

Sun Yat-sen decided, as in his youth, in favor of the golden mean. He came to an agreement with the general from Peking. The Manchus abdicated. Sun Yat-sen also resigned after only a short term as president of the Chinese Republic. His successor was—Yuan Shih-kai.

This decision must have been the result of a fierce inner struggle. There is something superhuman, almost saintly about this sacrifice. Sun let another take the helm, very much as had Garibaldi after he had unified Italy and conquered Naples. Could one possibly imagine a Mussolini or a Hitler withdrawing into private life the moment he reached his goal?

Sun Yat-sen never suspected that a person as trusting as he was always in danger of being used by others, who were adroit, to gain their own ends. Exile had not made him hard. As is the case with most great men, he could never be embittered by suffering.

Before he decided to resign, however, he had established a provisional constitution ensuring abolition of racial and religious discrimination, the founding of a parliament, and freedom of speech and press. Simultaneously the pigtail was outlawed, along with footbinding, the kowtow, and the Chinese calendar.

Sun Yat-sen was neither vain nor autocratic. As Director of Railways he faded into a colorless background. Yet for more than a decade he was dragged into civil war, when it became apparent that he had been cherishing an illusion. For all too soon Yuan Shih-kai's real plan manifested itself.

Yuan Shih-kai was actually a reactionary; after he had obtained a foreign loan he became increasingly autocratic. Sun Yat-sen was aroused. He conferred with his Chinese associates— Homer Lea had died in the meantime. One of his confidants was Chiang Kai-shek, then regimental commander, later marshal of China. Another friend was simple, honest Lin Sen, just returned from California. Later he became China's president. They were agreed: once more the nation was in peril.

Sun Yat-sen wrote to Yuan Shih-kai:

"You have been a traitor to your country. As I rose against the Manchus so shall I rise against you."

In July, 1913, he proclaimed the "Second Revolution." From

the mast of the cruiser which he boarded in Shanghai there now waved a new banner: the white sun in a blue field. In the decisive battle before Nanking, however, Sun's troops were defeated. While his wife and children were driven from their beds he fled again, accompanied by Chiang Kai-shek, and once more landed safe in Japan.

Another exile lay before him. It seemed as if he were destined to gather strength in banishment, to gain courage through a moment's weakness, or when for an instant he had lost sight of reality. He was unbowed in spirit, declaring:

"It makes no difference if China is divided into ten parts— each would still be as big as Japan."

For many years Lu Sze, a simple, gentle creature, had waited for her husband while he traveled abroad. Now for the first time it was evident that she took her duties as a mother more seriously than her obligations as a wife. She refused to accompany Sun into exile. And true to the ancient custom of the land she suggested that he take a "concubine" instead. She would guard his house and children in his absence. Sun Yat-sen did not understand. He was a Christian.

Abandoned by many of his friends, by wife and children, the forty-eight-year-old man languished in Yokohama. Then, from an entirely unexpected source, came relief.

The daughters of Soong, the friend of his youth, placed their services at the disposal of Sun Yat-sen. Ay-ling, twenty-six years of age, was serious, energetic and ambitious, a financial wizard. She became Sun's secretary. But he was far more attracted to Ching-ling, who was pretty, more dainty and warmhearted. He fell in love with her. The girl was two years younger than Ay-ling, and six years older than May-ling, who was later to become Madame Chiang Kai-shek. She looked up to the great man with deep respect. Sun Yat-sen succeeded in arranging a divorce from his wife, and soon after married Ching-ling. The ceremony was performed at a Yokohama church.

Thus three men who had been his friends in the revolution simultaneously became his brothers-in-law. The brothers Soong are all gifted financiers. When Ay-ling married the millionaire

Dr. Kung, Sun found himself in a family circle of financial magnates. The Soong and Kung families were the richest in the land.

Sun, however, remained the simple man of the people, not in the least influenced by his new surroundings. It was characteristic of him that, on the contrary, in those very days he terminated the political revolution to devote himself entirely to the social revolution. His attention was turned to purely economic problems. In Russia, Lenin had come into power and fought for many of the concepts which Sun Yat-sen had long ago adopted. From now on, surrounded though he was by millionaires and friends who had been educated in America, he looked on Soviet Russia with increasing interest.

Neither at this time nor in the future did he amass a fortune. At his death a house and some books were his sole assets.

The course of events in China continued to be a source of anxiety. Yuan Shih-kai had himself proclaimed emperor and shortly afterward died under mysterious circumstances. Then the tuchuns (province governors) fought among themselves. Each of them wished to succeed to the presidency. Three presidents came and went and the confusion grew.

Once, briefly, Sun Yat-sen sojourned in Canton. He named himself "generalissimo," thinking perhaps that the people would be naïve enough to pay more attention to him. A photograph taken during this time shows him in a resplendent uniform, with epaulets and a helmet decked with flowing plumes. It is evident that Sun Yat-sen, like Lincoln and Masaryk, felt more at home in civilian clothes.

Since the military trappings did not bring the desired results Sun had to return to Shanghai and exile. This time the presence of his son, Sun Fo, was a great comfort to him. Sun Fo had just completed his studies in California and wished to serve as adviser to his father.

Sun's mode of living in Shanghai is revealed to us through the report of one of his close friends. His house in the French Concession was small, furnished in the Western manner, with a touch of Chinese influence. A gentle breeze from the garden cooled the wide verandas on even the hottest summer days. In this house one usually found the perennial exile dressed in a white, uniformlike Chinese coat. In the winter he wore a gray woolen robe, donning his European clothes only on rare occasion.

These years were the most productive for Sun Yat-sen the author. He worked on a "Program of National Reconstruction," and on the "Five Power Constitution" for the new state, which may be described as a kind of state socialism or "democratic collectivism." China, thought Sun, would have to go its own way. To the American system of executive, legislative, and judicial branches of government, he added those of "inspection," or "control," and "examination." The first was a check on the executive department, the second constituted the civil service system.

Had Sun Yat-sen been a scholar by nature this work at his desk would have satisfied him. But his heart belonged to the revolution. At last there was news from China that cheered him. For the first time the students of the nation were endeavoring to develop the purely political movement into a social movement for the masses. From now on the Kuomintang (People's party) became a party of the people. Propaganda and education for democracy were given greater prominence; above all, the leaders began to realize that it was foolish to depend on foreign aid. China would have to free itself. But was the new China mature enough to rid the country of its quarreling governors and generals?

Sun Yat-sen took no active part in the movement these days. He remained in exile. His methods of revolution have been compared to that of a Japanese wrestler, who makes use of his opponent's strength to defeat him. And soon even better news came. In Peking, the lean, sly, conniving General Chang Tso-lin wanted to have himself proclaimed emperor. Chen Chiung-ming, the governor of Canton, begged Sun Yat-sen to return in order to prevent this.

For the second time then, in 1921, Sun Yat-sen was elected president of the new republic. From now on he was no longer inclined to make compromises. He had profited by his previous failures. He decided to send an army to march on Peking. But Governor Chen refused to sacrifice his troops in a civil war. Sun was forced to retire into banishment for the nth time. Perhaps he himself had lost count.

His flight this time was more picturesque than usual. In it we find an excellent example of the power that emanated from his simple, buoyant spirit. He boarded one of his cruisers. After a time the officers, bribed by Chen, entered his cabin to inform him that they intended to give him up. Sun regarded them calmly and asked only for permission to make a farewell speech. This was granted him. Then he addressed them and continued to talk for three hours. He did not plead with them to free him. He accused them. He called them traitors. He told them that China must be united and that they were hindering this union. He reminded them of their love for China. Were they not patriots? Was he not one of them?

The officers burst into tears, and transferred him to a British ship.

This incident reveals the secret of his success. He was a man in whom kindness, wisdom, and will power united with the absolute conviction that he was "chosen," predestined for his task. But he was incapable of judging his fellow men; that was his only great weakness. He forgave easily. That is why he never became a dictator, although the temptation was often at hand.

Back in Shanghai he saw three more presidents come and go. Then he received new aid: from Russia. Adolph Joffe, the shrewd Soviet diplomat, came to tell him that Russia was ready to provide him, as it had provided Mustafa Kemal, with military advisers and propagandists, and lend its powerful prestige to his cause. Sun accepted.

Was it the certainty that he could hope for no assistance from the Western powers? Was it a growing conviction that the imperialistic world order was on the decline? Whatever motives prompted him, it is certain only that he agreed not to impede the dissemination of communistic ideas in China. On the other hand, he declared he was convinced that "the communistic order, or even the Soviet system, cannot actually be introduced into China because there do not exist the conditions for the successful establishment of either communism or Sovietism." Yet he also remarked: "I am a coolie and the son of a coolie. I was born with the poor and I still am poor. My sympathies have always been with the struggling masses."

In the meantime Chiang Kai-shek had organized a new army in Canton and so, in 1923, Sun Yat-sen returned home—for the last time. Soon thereafter thirty Russian officers arrived. Chiang Kai-shek himself journeyed to Moscow to study revolutionary tactics. He advised Sun that he found the Russians highly desirable allies.

At this point Sun Yat-sen gave vent to one of his rare smiles as he remembered an incident of years ago.

"Once I met several Russians in London," he recalled. "I was then in exile after my first defeat. The Russians asked me, 'How long will it take the Chinese Revolution to succeed?' I said, 'Perhaps it will succeed in thirty years.' The Russians were surprised. I asked the Russians, 'How long will it take your revolution to succeed?' They answered, 'If we can succeed in one hundred years we shall be satisfied.' "

Sun Yat-sen was now absolute master of southern China. He addressed a manifesto to the peasants and laborers of the country. It was conceived in the revolutionary spirit, but with an undercurrent of the Confucian utopia, "where all peoples, everywhere, live only for the common good."

In a series of lectures to his friends he then finally summarized his beliefs. It was evident that he was familiar with the precepts of Mazzini, Montesquieu, Bismarck, and Lenin, no less than with those of Jefferson, Marx, and Wilson. In these talks he gave his people a new, scientific religion, a religion of common sense; in other words, a typical Chinese religion.

Later he went to Peking, to negotiate with General Wu Pei-fu, ruler of the North. Suddenly he became ill, an operation was necessary. It was too late—he had cancer of the liver.

When he felt that his end was near he dictated to Ching-ling, his wife, a last will and testament. This message was to become tantamount to a religious creed in China. Today, every Monday morning it is read aloud ceremonially in all schools, factories, and government offices and at all political and military gatherings:

I have devoted forty years to the work of the Revolution, the aim of which is to secure the freedom and independence of China. After forty years of experience I am profoundly convinced that in order to reach this aim we must wake up the masses of the country and unite with those nations of the world who treat us on the basis of equality, and continue the struggle together.

At present the revolution is not completed! It is my sincere hope that all my comrades will continue to fight for the ultimate realization of our goal, in accordance with the Three Principles of the People and the Declaration of the First National Congress of the Kuomintang. Recently I have proposed the convening of a national people's conference and the abolition of unequal treaties. You should work toward the realization of these aims within the shortest possible time. That is my final message.

Sun Yat-sen died on March 12, 1925, like Moses leading the Exodus: his eyes on the Promised Land that he was never to enter. Today China worships him as a kind of saint, this man who lived in China for barely twenty-five years, and far longer in exile. But the seed he sowed in his homeland has borne fruit not only there but also in the countries from which he derived strength over and over again, and where for many years he had remained practically unknown.

Today they call him not the Napoleon, but the George Washington of China. He was, we may add, China's Lincoln and Jefferson as well.

NIKOLAY LENIN

by

LYDIA NADEJENA

LYDIA NADEJENA

was born in Moscow. She was a member of the group of young Symbolist poets and her work was included under the pen name of "Solitaire" in the *Anthology of Universal Poetry*. She was graduated from Kiev University for women and she worked in art and cultural anthropology in Russia, Italy, and Turkey. Through Maxim Gorki's wife, E. P. Peshkova, she came to know Lenin during his second Swiss exile. While abroad during the revolution, she lost track of her family and chose America as her home. She revisited Russia and worked there as assistant to Professor Bogoraz of Leningrad University and as consultant in art for the Moscow Restoration Expeditions. In the United States she has been an editor, an art critic, and a research associate at the Fogg Museum at Harvard and at Princeton in the Art and Archeology Department. She has taught and lectured in outstanding American colleges and other educational institutions. She has contributed to leading American magazines and to the symposium *Woman's Coming of Age*.

LENIN
by Lydia Nadejena

"FREEDOM warms me," said Lenin to the women who worried about his getting chilled in the sled on his way from Siberian exile. Wearing a lightweight coat, with his hands in his mother-in-law's muff, he sang gaily on that trip, and saw that his three women companions—wife, mother-in-law, and another exiled fellow traveler—were tucked in and comfortable.

The man who has come to be known to the world as Lenin, was by birth Vladimir Ilyich Ulianov. He was born in Simbirsk on the Volga, in 1870.

His father, Ilya Nicolaevich Ulianov, taught mathematics and physics in Russian classical schools. He finally became director of public education in the state of Simbirsk, with the rank of civil general, thus making his children hereditary nobles. In the course of seventeen years of quiet, persistent work, he opened four hundred and thirty-four public schools in the state of Simbirsk alone, and instituted teacher training courses which were known throughout the Volga region as the Ulianovskie Kursi. In these courses he created educators out of yesterday's serfs.

Of old Russian stock, Vladimir's mother, too, was a native of the Volga region. She was the daughter of a very liberal physician in Kazan, and was disciplined by a Spartan education, by sports and studies, and by the simplicity of country life. She was well-educated in languages and music.

Vladimir adored his mother, her quiet courage, kindness, and yet firmness. She disliked town talk, was hospitable and friendly. Like his father, she preferred a small but congenial circle of friends who shared her ideas and interests. Both parents taught their children—Alexander, Anna, Vladimir, Olga, Dmitri, and Maria—pride in work, responsibility, and consideration for others. Each was expected to set an example in working habits, devotion, and independent thinking.

Vladimir's father died in 1886, when Vladimir was sixteen years old. A year later his older brother, Alexander, was charged with organizing the March 1st plot to assassinate the czar. Alexander admitted it. He assumed responsibility for many of the charges against others. He refused to have a lawyer defend him and said he would himself explain why peaceful people performed acts of terrorism. His mother went to Petersburg to be near him.

Alexander was executed by hanging in the Fortress of Sts. Peter and Paul on May 5, 1887.

In the light of the tragedy of his beloved brother's death for Russia's freedom, Lenin grew up quickly. Ready for direct and constructive action at the age of seventeen, he had already discovered the truth that he was to preach all his life:

"One has to find his relation to the universe. Unless one finds it, he is overpowered and crushed."

At the end of that same May, Lenin and Olga, a year his junior, graduated from school with the highest honors, and received gold medals. But in spite of his academic record, Lenin was refused admission by the Petersburg University on the ground that he was the brother of an executed revolutionary. Thereupon he applied at the nearest city, Kazan.

With Lenin's entry into the University of Kazan, the Ulianov family said good-bye to their hitherto unperturbed life in Simbirsk, to the quiet city with its big estates, parks, and classical buildings.

Lenin's student life was cut very short. He was expelled three months after entering the University of Kazan, together with forty other youths, accused of "student turmoil." An inspector had been slapped. A professor resigned and forty students were sentenced to banishment after a short arrest.

Gorki, who was living in Kazan at the time, wrote in his journal: "The students are rebelling. I don't know why." Even the monarchist papers in the capital made light of the episode and regretted that so much was made of "children's pranks."

The students were the only group in Russia who in the "dead silence" of the "slushy eighties and nineties" kept alive the spirit of freedom. When Lenin was on the way to prison the officer accompanying him said: "Young man, why do you rebel? Don't you see that you are facing a wall?"

"Yes, but a rotten wall," Lenin answered. "Push it and it will fall."

Lenin's arrest occurred on December 4, 1887. After a few days in prison he was sentenced to one year of exile.

Thus, at the age of eighteen began his years of exile. He was banished to the village of Kokushino, forty miles from Kazan, where his older sister Anna was living under the surveillance of the police.

They both served their respective exiles on their mother's grandfather's estate, in Kokushino. They lived in a cold cottage, buried in snow, in complete solitude except for the weekly call of the policeman and the occasional visit by a cousin. The mail, letters, Russian and foreign magazines, reading, talks and dreams of service to Russia filled their days.

After this year of exile was over, Lenin expected to re-enter the university. Both Petersburg and Kazan refused to accept him. The Kazan record said: ". . . brother of the Ulianov executed for a political crime. With his outstanding abilities and being well-informed, Ulianov cannot as yet be considered a reliable person, either morally or politically."

Though Lenin was interested in revolutionary questions, he did not join any active movement at this time. He was determined to go through a four-year university course by self-tutoring. In less than two years he was ready for the examinations. His self-tutoring had taught him to check his own progress, to impose upon himself definite tasks, a program of work.

He had begun to study Marx. He found Marx among his brother's books.

In Kazan his oldest sister often came for a visit to his room, which faced a garden and was built to serve as a summer kitchen.

The slight red-haired youth would sit on the paper-covered stove and speak animatedly of the "new horizons" which Marx and other reading were opening to him. He gesticulated, explained. He was co-ordinating dreams and logic, eager to share his thoughts. He realized that it was not chaos and accident, but the powers of deadly struggles between the existing order and the aspiring order that brought about exploitation, terroristic acts, and the execution of revolutionaries.

As he wrote later: "It is unfortunate for people who wish to be revolutionaries to think only of the chaos of the revolution and forget that the most natural state in history is the normal state, that the chaos of the revolution must be followed by the new and the normal revolutionary state."

Lenin believed in order and in the creative forces of revolution, not in chaos, which he detested in any guise. And out of the chaos of an uncontrollable upheaval, out of want and wars, has come a state, which after twenty-six years of existence still raises questions abroad, but which for the Russians and the new generation who have known no other, has become the "normal state."

In Kazan, Lenin made friends with the Narodovoltzi, the members of the Narodnaya Volya (the People's Will) party. Its right wing was opposed to capitalism and the industrial development of Russia, the possibility of which it vastly underestimated, as Lenin was to point out later. It also based its hopes on the peasants and the messianic role of Russia's intellectuals, on the heroic spirit of the group that united many classes. At the time it was the only party in Russia with a political and economic program. Stemming from the Narodniki, or Populists, who initiated the movement of "going to the people," it had a heroic tradition. Some of the greatest and noblest men of Russia belonged to it. His brother Alexander had belonged to the scrupulously selected terrorist group within the party.

The revolutionary in Lenin matured in this atmosphere. It taught him to be a realist, taught him methods of keeping direct contacts with the nation. Both groups of the Narodovoltzi liked Lenin's modesty, his earnestness and poise, his humor, his quick mind and warm laughter. They appreciated his simplicity, not complicated by nervousness. They admired his firmness and dili-

gence in the face of tragedy and of his own early trials. He was
very pleasant personally. His smile was warm, open and friendly,
and he was loyal by nature.

Their revolutionary traditions became his, though he eventually chose another approach to the problem of Russia's liberation.

After the winter in Kazan, Lenin's mother bought a small
estate in Alakaevo, near Samara and gave up the house in Kazan.

In his years in the country, at Samara, Lenin gained an intimate knowledge of the village and the poverty-stricken peasants
of Russia. "There is hardly another land in the world," Lenin
wrote in 1905, "where the peasants go through so much suffering,
so much oppression and abuse, as they do in Russia."

The years of preparation in Kazan, in Samara, and later in
exile in Siberia were the most important years in making of
Lenin the personality that emerged from exile, to become the historic man of the twentieth century. As foe and friend alike agree,
Lenin was unassuming and puzzling in his simplicity. Wanting
nothing for himself he nourished grandiose dreams for Russia's
future. Relentless in his course and stopping at nothing in his concentration on all-out action at the moment, he aroused hatred and
animosity against himself and his proclamations.

In 1891 Lenin went to Petersburg for his university examinations. On his arrival his sister Olga, a student there, became violently ill with typhus and died in a poorly equipped hospital. Olga
has been his best friend. Lenin loved his sister deeply. But he
had to go from her deathbed to his examinations. He passed
them, covering a four-year university course, on one of his saddest days, impressing the professor with his unusual knowledge
and precision.

From 1891 to 1893 Lenin lived with his deeply grieved
mother in Samara. He worked as an attorney's assistant. He did
not want a professional career as a lawyer, but when he began
the life of a revolutionary his legal knowledge helped him to
advise the workers and peasants.

In 1893 he went to Petersburg and was at once recognized
as an erudite Marxian of great organizational ability. He made
friends with the literary Social Democrat group. But he wanted to

know the workers. He began to hold Sunday classes among the
most skilled laborers of Russia.

In Petersburg, at the home of friends, he met Nadejda Krup-
skaya at a Carnival Week party. She, too, worked among the
Petersburg industrial workers. She conducted geography classes.
They became inseparable friends and coworkers.

In the summer of 1895 Lenin went abroad for the first time.
He visited Berlin and Geneva. The Russian Marxists, the leaders
of the "Liberation of Labor" group, who lived in Switzerland,
invested him with authority as a party organizer in Petersburg
and as editor of the proposed illegal periodical, *The Worker's
Newspaper.*

Years later, Aksel'rod, the theoretician then living abroad and
formulating theories on the conduct of revolution, described his
first impression of the twenty-five-year-old Lenin: "I felt from
the very start that I was dealing with a man who would be the
leader of the Russian Revolution. He was an erudite Marxian.
There were many such but he knew what he wanted to do and
how it ought to be done. He smelled of Russian earth."

On Lenin's return to Petersburg he began to lay foundations
for broader activities. But the Russian police were not dormant.
At the end of 1895 Lenin was arrested and imprisoned.

Lenin lectured to his fellow prisoners from the window of
his cell, wrote pamphlets which were smuggled out and distributed among workers. They were legal explanations for workers
who found themselves with little of their small wages left after
deductions by the complicated system of fines for illness, tardi-
ness, etc. In prison Lenin also drafted his first plan for the party
organization of a revolutionary social democracy.

Thus Lenin took "the case" of the workers vs. oppression
early in life and made it his only concern to the end of his days.
Here he had started work on his book, *The Development of Capitalism in Russia.* His sister, Anna, and friends were bringing him
books.

Library slips show that, while in prison, Lenin ordered and
examined 651 books and a multitude of pamphlets and papers. At
the time of his release—before he was exiled to Siberia—Lenin

told Nadejda Krupskaya: "What a pity to be released so soon. It won't be so easy to get books in Siberia."

He was sent to Shoushenskoe in Minusinsk State and settled there, reading, writing, hunting, waiting for mail that took about thirty-five days to come, always waiting for the return to freedom.

Lenin's prisoner allowance for maintenance was eight rubles a month, four dollars. He paid four rubles rent for half a cottage. His mother sent him money. Later he earned money by writing book reviews and translations from English and German.

His younger brother, and disciple, Dmitri, came once to visit him, on the plea that he was "in need of dentistry." In 1898 Dmitri himself landed in prison.

A year after Lenin's arrival at Shoushenskoe, Nadejda Krupskaya had come to Minusinsk to serve her own exile. They were married. Her mother came with her to keep house for them and for three years Siberia was their home.

After half his exile was over, Lenin wrote home asking for a chess set: "I was wrong in thinking that East Siberia is such a wild country that chess would not be needed." He received a set that his father had carved. For a while after it arrived he would do nothing but play chess, and he was very happy. Later he confined his chess games to certain hours. "One must remember the essentials," he used to say. Always he was exacting, a self-disciplinarian.

More than anything else he missed the contact with friends. In very acute moments of loneliness a way would be found for him to come together with some other exiles in the vicinity. Such meetings would be planned specially when burning questions of principles arose.

Lenin began party organization and collective action while in Siberia. The celebrated "Protest of the Seventeen" against the group of "economists" was signed at the deathbed of a comrade. They called it "Credo," and it was an expression of their strong feeling against labor organization on an economic basis only, without simultaneous political education. He said: "Are heroes perishing in prisons of Siberia for the bowl of lentil soup?"

In Shoushenskoe, Lenin finished writing his book on *The Development of Capitalism in Russia,* begun in the Petersburg prison. Here he planned his coming work in freedom.

In November, 1898, Lenin wrote to his youngest sister, Maria, who was now studying in Belgium. The letter reflected Lenin's own feeling about his Siberian exile:

> We have received your letter, Manyusha, and were very glad to have it. We immediately took out our maps and began to hunt for Brussels. We found it and began thinking how close it was to London, that Paris was near and also Germany. One could call it the center of Europe. Yes, I envy you. At the beginning of my exile I decided never to touch a map. It would mean too much bitterness as I looked at those various black spots. But it is not so bad now. I have grown patient and can examine maps more calmly. Sometimes we even dream in which of the "spots" it would be interesting to land later on. During the first half of my exile I have been constantly looking back, now I look forward. Ah well, qui vivra—verra!

In Siberia, Lenin studied philosophy and foreign languages. But life in Siberia was not all serious. Siberia taught him patience. He was gay and sang. He included hunting in his outdoor activities, for its own pleasure, and as a means of studying the countryside and the Siberian people. Later he announced his hours for consultation as a lawyer. Lenin gave his time gratis and the work kept him busy.

He became the popular attorney of the near-by Siberians. Some took hours of his time relating trivial grievances. One wanted to know: "How can I punish my brother-in-law for not inviting me to a party where there was lots to drink?" He wanted the man executed.

Lenin asked: "Would he offer you a drink now?"

"Yes, now!"

So Lenin persuaded the man to forget the oversight and have a drink with his kin at the next party.

Lenin did not feel that his time in Siberia was wasted. He gained direct human contact with simple people and an insight into their mentality in various situations. With his truly Tolstoyan trend for generalizations, the individual became to him the typical, the incarnation of his class, of his cultural level. A soldier was the army, a peasant the abused and suffering peasantry, a boy or girl the coming generation, a student the potential revolutionary, a worker the revolutionary class.

With full knowledge of all the elemental forces in Russian life, knowing it as a scientist and by human contact, Lenin emerged from the Siberian exile with a clear idea of how the Russian revolutionary party was to be built so as to belong to the Russian soil.

With the Siberian exile ended the second period of Lenin's preparation for leadership from exile abroad and afterward from the Kremlin.

As within his own personality he merged the different elements of his make-up, so he did in his revolutionary life. "Not ideas in one pocket and personal life in another," he said.

Though his wife had left Shoushenskoe at the same time as Lenin, she had another year of exile to serve and was sent to Ufa on the Russo-Siberian border. She became seriously ill, had poor medical facilities and needed care. But Lenin, in spite of an urgent petition, was not permitted to join her. He entrusted her to the care of friends and placed himself at the disposition of the party.

By law he was barred from right of residence in university and industrial centers. He decided to go into voluntary exile abroad and create a party center out of reach of the Russian police.

He called a conference at Pskov. The party came to the conclusion that Lenin should leave Russia before his wife's exile expired. After Lenin had planned the details of a party paper to be published abroad and distributed in Russia, he began the new century by going into voluntary exile in Western Europe.

Lenin did not look noticeably Russian even at this time. If one knew that he came from the Volga region, one would attribute his ease and lightness of movement to that sea of land and rivers. But if one did not know, he could have passed for a Welshman, redheaded, agile, neat and simple, without deliberation; or for a Lombard, or for any cultured European intellectual. He had elusive, highly mobile features. His blue eyes were dreamy, intent, or humorous.

To the Russian intellectual revolutionaries in Western Europe, Lenin came as a new type of leader. Away from Russian lives, the old exiles had no tie with the land they wished to liberate.

Lenin was organically a piece of Russian earth and life. Among the Russian Social Democrats he was the first and only one who always kept contact with the representatives of the Russian workers. He went to Sweden and Finland every summer not only for a stay with his mother, whom he adored, but also because it brought him closer to the Russian border, and made it easier for the Petersburg workers to visit him.

It was Lenin who established a custom of periodic trips abroad for revolutionary workers. Here, away from the danger of being arrested, they could meet, study, take rest and medical cures. One such visitor said: "Lenin made Europe to us an open and interesting book."

Lenin merged scientific social theories with Russia's own form of revolutionary development, and endowed it with national characteristics. His first and last concern was Russia and the destiny of her people, whose self-appointed attorney he had made himself.

The world outside Russia interested Lenin objectively, historically. Throughout the seventeen years of his life in Western Europe, Lenin remained the congenial, keen, unobtrusive, Russian resident-émigré, who loved its libraries, studied its life, but who never tried to affect in any way the life and destinies of the lands of hospitality.

But it was different in Russian political groups. Here he was the electrifying force, the fierce polemist, the unpredictable tactician, attracting, repelling, stimulating, and antagonizing. He believed in polemics for the sake of clarity. Yet he managed not to forget the strong and pleasant qualities of opponents.

He took part in international conferences as a Russian delegate. His limited participation in world events and concentration on Russia is a mark of his dominant sense of direction. His preoccupation with Russia's own destiny, which was a living reality to him throughout his life in exile, did not make for an understanding between Lenin and his Western associates and the German-influenced Russian theoreticians abroad. They considered his talk about Russia's future as "wishful thinking" and not the logical conclusions of a radical theoretician. He judged Europe in the broad terms of a detached student of the West. Although Lenin opposed vehemently the application of pure theory to problems of immediate reality, he himself based his expectations of the world revolution primarily on the Marxist theory of economic determination, and not on the full complex of Western life and traditions. As a result he miscalculated. The revolution never came to pass. Each group lacked the key to the other's mentality and lacked, too, that elemental sense of the inherent forces in national life, which furnishes an understanding of events beyond the evidence of sheer facts. The consequences were greater isolation and the parting of the ways.

When Lenin saw his mistake, he limited himself to Russia's domestic problems, which he knew best. Never separating Russian civilization from that of the European continent at large, he recognized her peculiar historic conditions, and grieved over her imposed loneliness. Because of it he saw Russia's road to progress as slow and hard. But he cherished supreme faith in the creative power of the nation, and set for himself the task of finding a way that would release that creative power "for the good of many and not the few." The will to revolution, he believed, was the only solution for Russian political and economic problems. The Russian state and this alone occupied his life in exile.

On going into voluntary exile, Lenin chose to live in Munich because there were fewer Russians there to endanger the work of his group by attracting attention, and Russian spies. He lived under an assumed name because the spy system of the czar was active abroad.

Lenin determined to establish a paper for wide distribution in Russia but out of reach of the Russian police. *Iskra* (Sparks) was first published in Munich, later in London, and finally in Geneva. To the exiles *Iskra* was part of Russia. The thought that it would reach even a few workers in Russia was Lenin's reward.

His task was difficult. He aimed to assimilate the system of Marxian thought with Russian universality through his profound knowledge of Russian life and his instinct for it. He always thought of the worker not merely as precious material in the revolutionary movement but as potential creative power in life.

So acute was Lenin's sense of Russia that a letter about conditions there would keep him pacing the floor for hours. In Munich a new arrival from Russia was received like a member of the family. The exiles were like the inhabitants of a surrealist land, in which dreams of far-off Russia were their most vital reality.

When Krupskaya went into exile from Russia, also voluntary on a legal passport, she had some difficulty in finding her husband because of his assumed name, secret address, and the confusions of the code instructions she had to follow. She first went to Prague. She used to write to Lenin addressing her letters to a Mr. Matchek in Prague, and was sure she would find him living under this name. She found Mr. Matchek to be a Czech laborer. He told her he did not know Lenin nor his address, but he gave her the address of a Munich man where all the Russian letters went.

In Munich, Krupskaya looked for her husband under the German name. She found the man bearing the name. He was a fat bartender who had never heard of Lenin. Finally Krupskaya was led through a dismal courtyard into a vacant apartment. Here she found Lenin working in a single furnished room. His friend Martov and his sister Anna also were there when Krupskaya arrived.

The little Russian group merrily joined the May Day parade. They rejoiced in seeing children in it, which indicated its peaceful and lawful character. They were somewhat embarrassed by the quantity of beer bottles and pocketfuls of radishes. There were no posters, no songs. They did not feel a part of it, as they had hoped, at the dull picnic. No one seemed to be interested in anything but food. The orator made a matter-of-fact speech and departed. There was none of the folk festival spirit of Russia. So they walked home tired and disappointed.

Lenin liked Munich. He enjoyed walking with his wife, studying German, following literature. "If we could only inherit a higher level of bourgeois culture," he said at this time, "everything would be easier."

But in preparation for the Second Party Conference planned to take place in London, Lenin decided to leave Munich, giving up the little apartment which Krupskaya had furnished so carefully and selling the furnishings for a pittance.

In London, Lenin was thrilled with the urban vitality, with London's movement, energy, and sense of organization. "Capitalism has something to be proud of," he used to say. Often he went to Hyde Park to listen to all kinds of orators. He was eager to feel the surrounding life, to understand the English. He discovered, much to his astonishment, a Socialist Church. He went to the service. After the service the priest prayed: "Lord deliver us from the inferno of capitalism and deliver us to the haven of socialism." The British Museum Library was his constant delight.

He attended trade-union meetings and realized how differently the Russian and Western workers' movements had developed. He was saddened that in England most of the discussions centered on the standard of living in wages and hours and not on broader cultural issues and interests. He was also saddened to hear one of his English conversation teachers say that he had always been a confirmed Socialist but would not confess it for fear of losing his job.

But he liked the English laborer, his interest in civil affairs. He called it "class sense."

The year 1903 was fateful for Lenin and the party. At the Second Party Conference an amendment was made to swell the party ranks by a passive, sympathizing membership. Lenin insisted that a revolutionary organization of workers remain a closed, well-guarded party, with a membership based entirely on *active* participation. He hammered on the idea that only a membership willing to throw in its lot with the party is a dependable revolutionary membership.

The proposal to swell the party membership with dues-paying *passive* sympathizers spelled horror to Lenin. This was a matter of life and death for him, since under existing political conditions in Russia such a step would expose the party to destruction.

He won the majority. The word "Bolshevik," which means majority, came into being as a political term and was, from that time, applied to the group which followed Lenin. The other group was known as "Menshevik" or minority.

There was plenty of friction in the uprooted life of exiles abroad. The older émigrés had little contact with the masses at home, and were more of a theoretical and Western type.

Lenin's force affected them like electric shocks, and the repelling effect was more pronounced when he was most insistent on the undercurrent in Russian life.

His conclusions seemed too farfetched and purely visionary to them. They struggled against him.

But Lenin always had a few strong adherents, and though he was sometimes ill in bed when squabbles grew too painful, he could be gay.

Living at Geneva at the time of the Escalade Festival, Lenin made the rounds from the Café Landolt, where Bolsheviks met and dreamed over glasses of beer, to homes of depressed friends. He made them come out and rejoice with the Swiss crowds. He was the first to join in the singing and before long was in a circle of merrymaking and dancing Geneva folk. This spirit of companionship, of festivity, was prolonged into the night with songs and laughter, Lenin leaning across the table, urging friends to laugh and perform. But such festive moods in which the exiles felt themselves a part of their surroundings were rare.

Lenin, too, often felt lonely in those Geneva days. He was threatened with a united enmity. He would sigh and say: "There is a time when one has to stand alone. . . . They follow personages, not principles." He turned to his never-failing family—his mother, sisters, and brother. At darker moments he would walk the water front of Geneva silently with his wife. Or alone on winding hilly streets.

His first period of exile was brought to an end by the revolution in 1905. But before the exiles started for Russia there were more conferences in Germany, more conflicts, and more studies. Lenin revised his agrarian program. He now took the stand that the workers must help the agrarian movement, and that the revolution could not be won without the peasants. In support of his stand he quoted Marx on the value of peasant participation in case of a German revolution.

But neither his knowledge of Russia nor his erudite knowledge of Marx and Engels convinced the German socialistic hierarchy. Kautsky, the leader, advised Russian labor to stay outside the peasants' movement. The controversy with the German Socialists caused Lenin, who left nothing to chance, to make a thorough study of the American agricultural questions and the Negro suffrage provisions. Meanwhile he studied military strategy.

In October, 1905, Lenin returned to Russia. He lived in hiding, but attended meetings. Once he could not refrain from speaking, pale and tense, from the gallery. The workers recognized his voice, his face. Red shirts were made into banners. Lenin had to leave quickly. Then the man hunt started. Krupskaya sat nights at the window expecting the worst. But Lenin went on writing and editing many workingmen's papers, which were now legally permitted.

In December, 1905, as he was coming to the newspaper building of the *New Life,* which he and Gorki edited, a newsboy ran up to him presumably to sell papers, but whispered: *"New Life* is being raided now." Lenin said to his wife: "The people are for us." It was this never-failing eagerness to feel the reaction of the Russian people and his regard for it that won him both the name of demagogue and the trust of the masses during his life—and after his death.

The January 9th Massacre of workers on strike, of paraders and rebelling peasants, fortified his camp. Lenin considered the 1905 armed uprising in Moscow a lesson in revolution. Not all his actions proved successful. He anticipated a real peasant revolution in 1905. It did not materialize. The revolution was ruthlessly crushed. Prisons were packed. Siberia became a new colonization camp with thousands of peasants at hard labor. The work of the People's Will party was paralyzed.

Lenin's answer to his opponents was "We learn by mistakes." And again he found himself in exile.

Until 1907 he stayed in Finland, in close touch with Petersburg workers, "in heaps of work, with people coming and going."

There were conferences in Stockholm, illegal trips to Petersburg. He slept each night in a different place. But summing up the experience, he was organizing the party "on new unprecedented grounds."

Stalin, who had been active in the Caucasus, came to Petersburg where he was to meet Krupskaya. He brought a present to the Engineering Institute students' dining room, something huge and round, covered with a white cloth. Tall and lanky, in national costume, he carried it carefully, ceremoniously. He attracted attention. Everyone stared. A bomb? It was a watermelon from the Caucasus. Lenin's wife was to take it to her husband.

Then Lenin and Stalin met at a conference at Tennfors in Finland. Stalin was surprised to see that Lenin did not resemble the giant he had expected.

At this time Lenin visualized the Second Revolution. He predicted it would be different, would go beyond political issues, and that the intellectuals and liberals would be the fiercest opponents of the coming social revolution. In 1907 he went with a heavy heart back to Geneva. "I feel as if I come to enter my coffin here."

The saddest and loneliest years of Lenin's exile were 1907 to 1912. Revolutionary writers and youth turned away from revolution and political issues. They were disillusioned and turned to eroticism, philosophy, mysticism, or serious university studies— but away from politics, from social problems.

Lenin was on the verge of a break with the mystically inclined intellectuals. He went to Paris, where he worked on his book, *Materialism and Empiro-Criticism.* He worked for more than a year at the Bibliothèque Nationale before he published the book. The library slips on record show that he examined over five hundred books and many more periodicals.

He explored Paris at this time. Near the Hôtel de Ville, the citadel of the French Revolution, he found a ghetto and discovered many Russian Jewish émigrés living there, away from Russia and the Russian colony but victims of Russian reactionary forces, victims of the 1906 pogrom.

Lenin felt sorry for them. For three months he gave weekly lectures for them, sometimes with only a few in the hall.

He longed for direct contact with the homeland, with friends living in Russia. He started a sort of academy, not in the gardens of Plato's time but in a poor working suburb near Paris. Six of his friends moved there and lived in separate parts of the community.

The Mensheviks refused to participate. But Zinoviev, Lunacharsky, and Semasko lectured on the history of the Russian Revolution, on labor laws, on the history of art, and on newspaper techniques.

Lenin's meetings were the earliest, from eight to ten o'clock. He lectured in the form of questions and answers, trained his students in research, spoke on revolutionary theory and practice, on the agrarian question, and on political economy.

In the evening the group took bicycle trips to Paris, to visit friends and their cafés where Lenin played chess. But he lived outside the Russian colony with its thousands of Russian students, who now considered the revolutionaries narrow-minded, provincial, and too puritanical.

By 1912 Lenin's contact with the Russian working groups was again well-established. He felt it was time to have another congress, now after three years of blackest reprisals in Russia and disintegration abroad. He hoped that a common ground could be found for all for the sake of what was primary in his mind. Gorki was the only one willing to come from Italy to Prague but he was afraid that his presence would bring a horde of journalists and defeat the plans for secrecy. Few real organizers had survived the reaction in Russia, but most of them were present at that conference.

The 1912 conference in Prague became a conference of the Bolshevik party members alone. A resolution expelled the advocates of the "liquidation" of the Duma platform, the leftists in the Social Democrat party.

The conference, which was not attended by the old guard, became the foundation of an independent Bolshevik party. Lenin's polemics against the Mensheviks were accepted more easily than at other conferences. Now he was sure that "there will be a new form of government the very first day after the next revolution."

He was happy. He was at ease with simple people. He had a

Petersburg worker move into his room. One day he was so stirred by the closeness of Russian people near him that he craved movement, swift, bracing, breath-catching. So he skated for hours during the night—and was sick the next morning with a bad cold and high fever.

Once, when the Russians were assembled on a square, a group of Carpatho-Russians started to sing a Russian song. The delegates were thrilled; and, true to the temperament which makes a few Russians a choir, they were ready to join the song. But here Lenin's talent for summing up the situation quickly made him suspect that the song might be a provocation arranged by the secret police. He prevented the delegates from joining the song and got them out of the way. (Not until 1917 did Lenin find out that among the delegates had been a czarist spy, Malinovski, playing a double role.)

At the end of the conference, the Czech Socialists gave them a banquet. Lenin had a complicated task to explain to them the differences between the labor movement as a Russian revolutionary development from that of legalized trade-unionism in Western Europe.

The break with the exile theoreticians and the presence of Russian workers made Lenin wish to be nearer to Russia. This led him to move to Cracow and afterward to Poronin, Galicia. He liked Galicia. He found it very homelike. The Austrian-Polish authorities, disliking the Russian police, were more lenient to the Russian political exiles. Lenin also liked the natural friendliness of the peasants, the simplicity of their lives, the good food, all resembling the Russian. He took issue, however, with the Polish intelligentsia and Socialists on their hypernationalism. He was free from any nationalistic discrimination and nourished the highest sympathy with the deprived minorities, including the Poles. He was against chauvinism at home, and coming face to face with it abroad he began to study, to work, and to write on national problems.

To his mind all these problems could be solved very simply. The Revolution would solve them. Nothing seemed complicated to Lenin. He was a sober dreamer, and he always lived in the future.

And then the First World War broke out. Lenin was arrested as an alien. In the Austrian prison he found his legal education very useful. Again there were many peasants of different nationalities whom the Austrian Empire had scrabbled into its power. Lenin helped them with their legal difficulties and soon he became their counselor in his cell. The peasants liked him and called him "the Strong Mujik."

The German Social Democrats supported the Kaiser on the grounds that Germany, by the defeat of Russia, would defeat czarism. Lenin kept on repeating: "We do not want such assistance." He called the attitude of the German Social Democrats a betrayal, and he called Kautsky and his party "traitors who will be forever despised." In turn he was accused of all sins. The Russians supported the Russian war on the ground of the deep aversion to German militarism and in sympathy for the Serbs. So his Russian opponents condemned his pacifist stand as evidence of a lack of national feeling for Russian people and his country. But Lenin did not consider the Kaiser's defeat of Russia a revolutionary performance.

"The opportunists of the Second International helped the bourgeoisie to deceive the people," he said. To him World War I was waged for the redivision of foreign lands and markets. He sympathized deeply with the Serbians, however, who were fighting a defensive war against the aggressor and enemy of their peaceful national life.

National and world problems absorbed his entire time and interest in these days. At that time he wrote *On the Pride for the Great Russians:*

"We, the Great Russian workers, who are filled with the sentiment of national pride, want at all costs a free and independent, a democratic republican and proud Great Russia, which will base its relation with its neighbors on the human principles of equality, and not on the feudal principles of privileges, which are degrading to a great nation." . . .

In 1915 Lenin was ordered to leave Austria and go to a neutral country. So he went to Zurich. It was a little nearer to Russia than was Geneva.

The Torch of Freedom

The last two years of his exile, 1915 to 1917, seemed the longest. But here as everywhere else he followed his customary mode of life in exile.

The apartment occupied by Lenin and Krupskaya was in a narrow street of the poorer section of Zurich. They had two rooms with a stone-and-tile floor. They ate in a modest little restaurant. During the day, Lenin worked in the library on *Imperialism,* his next book. The library call slips show that he used over six hundred books and three hundred and fifty-three articles for this work. In the evenings Lenin and Krupskaya used to go to the lake for a walk and also to see the latest issues of newspapers, which were always posted in a kiosk at the shore.

He followed the press closely. World affairs and conditions in Russia now seemed to him inseparable. But his manner of reasoning about what was happening in Russia as a result of the war was unconvincing to his Western audience. His address to Swiss workers, shortly before the Russian revolution, in which he predicted Russian events of universal significance, left them cold. Kautsky discarded it as "delirious chatter."

In one way the life of the exile and his work had changed. There were no contacts with Russia; no Russians arrived in Zurich. Across the border in Germany were Russian prisoners of war. Lenin did what he could to help them; he sent them books and letters.

Every Thursday the Russian Socialist group met. One man used to bring his little son. Lenin, always the first at the meeting, would bring toys and play with the child. He loved children. In Zurich he conducted a school like the one in the Paris suburb. There were a few foreign students in Zurich: Italians, Austrians, French.

One eventful day when Lenin was just about to leave for the library and his wife was just finishing the dishes, an émigré ran in.

"There is revolution in Russia!" he shouted.

As soon as he had left, Lenin and Krupskaya went to the lake to read the posted extras. They read them many times. Yes, there was revolution in Russia. Lenin's "case" was coming up in the high court of history. He had given thirty tireless, anxious years to the preparation of his brief. Now he had to hurry. He had to be on the spot. In his mind he was in Russia already. Exile was behind, he believed.

A. M. Kolontai telegraphed from Sweden the second day after the Duma revolution, asking for directions about tactics. Lenin replied at length and concluded: "New elements must be awakened, new initiative aroused, and new organizations in all groups. They must be convinced that peace will be won only by the armed Soviet Deputies if it will win power."

As a pacifist, Lenin was refused a visa to Russia.

He wrote articles for *Pravda*, calling them "Letters from Afar." Only one article was published: "The First Stage of the First Revolution." Lenin was still thinking in terms of the "first." The second article, "On the Proletarian Militia," which was published after his death in 1924, already dealt with government organization as it later came to be in Soviet Russia.

On March 18th, the Petrograd Central Committee sent a dispatch to a Stockholm member: "Ulianov must come immediately."

When Lenin was barred entry to Russia by France, England, and the Russian Provisional Government, he lost sleep. All his life he had waited for this event—and now he could not go.

He made the most fantastic plans about the realization of his life dream. He would take a plane. He would travel as a Swede —but he did not know the Swedish language. He thought of going as a deaf-mute. But his wife laughed and reminded him that if he should dream of the Mensheviks, he would cry out: "Scoundrels! Scoundrels!" He discarded this plan with a heavy sigh.

Then, at a meeting in Berne, one of the exiles, Martov, conceived a plan to get visas through an exchange of German and Austrian prisoners. At the time no one seconded the plan. But later they went on these very visas. Two hours after the notice came they left for Berne.

Lenin said: "We leave by the first train." All his bills paid, library books returned, and a farewell letter to Swiss workers written.

On March 27, 1917, thirty exiles and a four-year-old boy took the train for Russia. They went through Germany in a sealed train, to be opened only at the Russian border. They were branded as German agents, in German pay. Elaborate stories were later written on this event.

For once Lenin wrote no polemics. He did not care what was in the minds of the German authorities. He wanted to reach Russia. Later, by the same route, two hundred exiles followed him —Martov and other Mensheviks among them.

In Stockholm, Lenin was met with banners and parades. He was in a daze. He wanted to see Russia. In Finland his sisters met him. There were Russian soldiers. One treated the little Robert to Russian Easter cake. Lenin was happy. A young officer of the Provisional Government started to talk with him. Lenin said what he thought. Soldiers crowded in to listen.

In Petersburg, Lenin expected to be arrested. Throngs of people met him with banners, with songs and cheers. There were workers, soldiers, old friends and old pupils from Paris. Some cried. He was put atop an armored car. Searchlights illuminated his way from the station. They were projected from the distant Fortress of Sts. Peter and Paul where his brother Alexander had been hanged as a revolutionary thirty years ago almost to a day.

Lenin stayed with his elder sister, Anna. The younger, Maria, was there too. His only remaining brother, Dmitri, soon came from the Crimea for a visit. The Ulianov family was at home again, and united.

But the life of an exile was not finished for Lenin. On June 6th the government ordered him arrested on the strength of a rumor that he was a German agent. On June 18th the government started an offensive at the front, and on the same day the first political demonstration took place. The soldiers behind the soviets and those behind the government clashed. The latter fired the first shots of civil war and killed a few of the Bolshevik soldiers. The strife began.

Lenin, with a price of 100,000 rubles on his head, lived in a worker's house at Sestroretsk. He was finishing his work on *Government and Revolution*. The place was too close to Petersburg. A Finnish worker who needed only a pass got Lenin across the border. A wig on his bald head and a little make-up took "Ivanov" beyond the reach of the man hunt. Lenin was in exile again. . . .

Zinoviev and Lenin lived in a barn from which they could see anyone approaching, and hide if necessary. They slept on hay in the loft. Lenin became very ill there. The peasant was afraid to be responsible for these "vagrant-farm hands" who had implements but no work.

Lenin's wife crossed into Finland the same way, as an old woman laborer. She wore a shawl, once the sure class distinction of a commoner. She found Lenin depressed, pained to be so near the turbulent sea of the Russian Revolution and still having to direct it from exile.

He moved to Helsingfors, then to Viborg, as close to Russia as he dared.

On her visits, his wife told him of the soldiers' conversation in the trains, about the uprising that was in the air. She recalled that "a shadow fell on his face, never to leave it. He talked of many things and thought of something else."

Then, on October 23rd, he wrote a message on two sheets of a small notebook and sent it to Petrograd. It read in part: "Everything indicates that if the insurrection is delayed now it will be fatal."

The uprising took place on November 7th. It culminated "in a new form of government the next day," as Lenin had predicted many years before from his Swiss exile.

And a few days later Lenin was back in Russia, as premier of the new state—Soviet Russia.

Whether seen as social philosopher, fanatic, reformer, or dreamer, Lenin will go down in history as the moving force of an unprecedented epoch, which led to immeasurable sufferings and an hitherto untried way of life. Gorki recalls that Lenin, in a moment of meditation after listening to Beethoven's music at the home of Peshkova (Gorki's wife) said:

". . . I always think with pride, perhaps with naïve and childish pride, What wonders man can perform." And narrowing his eyes slightly, he added with a joyless smile: "But I cannot listen to music often now. . . . I feel like saying sweet nonsense, like patting people on their little heads, because they can live in such swarming hell and still create such beauty. But one cannot pat people on their heads today—they will bite off your hand. Instead one is obliged to beat them on their heads pitilessly, although our ideals are against the use of force. Ah, it is a difficult task."

Lenin longed, as always, for the "normal state."

STEFAN ZWEIG

by

RAOUL AUERNHEIMER

RAOUL AUERNHEIMER

Austrian novelist, playwright, and essayist, was born in 1876. He was arrested by the Nazis in 1938 because he had been chairman of the Austrian Pen Club, and in that position had opposed Nazism in the field of literature. After having been confined for five months in the Dachau concentration camp, he was released through the mediation of American friends and came to the United States. His last book published in Austria was *Vienna, Picture and Destiny*. His first book written on American soil was *Prince Metternich, Statesman and Lover*. Auernheimer was awarded the Palmes de l'Académie Française in 1922, when he was the Austrian delegate to the Paris Tercentenary of Molière.

STEFAN ZWEIG
by Raoul Auernheimer

Stefan Zweig, born November 28, 1881, in Vienna, was the descendant and rich heir of an epoch known as the "Founder's Age" in Austria, the land of his birth.

It was an age of materially successful, industrial pioneers, made secure through the pledges of a liberalism attained only a short time before. Like so many other sons of captains of industry who had become and remained wealthy, Zweig grew up sheltered by a newly acquired and therefore anxiously guarded luxury which could be compared metaphorically to the garden of the young Buddha. Vienna was still the Imperial City, and the emperor watched over the peace; the last war had been completely forgotten when the next broke out almost half a century later. In the meantime the fathers gathered sheaves and the children flowers.

Stefan was one of these happy children. Walking along a meticulously graveled, well-kept garden path, he could gather flowers on every hand. It is characteristic that a collection of poems by the youthful Zweig is entitled *Early Garlands*. Another volume has the no less revealing title, *The Silver Strings*.

Yet the picture of young Zweig showed even then a few individual traits distinguishing him, not to his disadvantage, from more settled contemporaries in "Young Vienna." My junior by a few years, he was introduced to me in a Vienna literary café by another young poet, a professional officer, during a game of billiards. Zweig, too, was in uniform because he was serving his year in the army—a fact which fortunately did not hinder him from pushing, in company with other poets, ivory balls in the clubroom of our literary ivory tower.

I can still recall the slim young man handling the billiard cue in cavalierlike fashion and walking around the green table with elastic steps. It was his marked endeavor to appear, not as the lyricist he was, but as the officer he was not. I can't remember what we talked about; that he was introduced to me as "poet" was, I believe, the only topic connecting our conversation with literature.

A few months later I went to the same café and asking the headwaiter, who was well versed in literature, after Herr Zweig, I learned that he had disappeared, was traveling. In Sicily, said the waiter, or even in Tunisia. According to Austrian ideas of those days, this was a long way off.

Soon young Zweig became only a guest in his homeland. Vienna was not his parents' birthplace, and therefore he might have looked at it with more critical eyes. At first, considering it a metropolis, he had welcomed the family's move to the capital as a felicitous and progressive step. But soon after his military service he evidently discovered that the great city of Vienna, though more beautiful than other cities, was nothing but a larger provincial town. Berlin was a little less so; but that capital, too, could not give to Zweig what he was seeking as, driven by a demonic thirst for the whole world, he stormed up and down the Friedrichstrasse.

He went to Paris, which came still closer to his conceptions, perhaps because it was also a capital of the spirit and the "Ville Lumière" of talent. But even Paris was not without provincial traits that could not remain hidden to his trained observer's glance; yet these had charm and seemed more endurable than stuffy Vienna with its castes and hierarchies and a thousand prejudices.

At any rate, Paris was Zweig's favorite and most constant residence in those sultry years before the First World War. Two books were the fruit of this sojourn: *Verhaeren* and *Romain Rolland*. The centrifugal lyricist—for Zweig a new event since lyric poetry, in Austria, was always centripetally directed—and the author of *Jean Christophe*, stemming as an artist from

Richard Wagner and using the leitmotif in his epic composition, had in common one thing which was totally un-Austrian, un-Viennese: the dithyrambic element.

Stefan Zweig, developing into an expressionistic artist, acquired this element in Paris amidst a circle of kindred young Frenchmen including Jules Romains. Zweig's attitude toward the war also was influenced by his Paris circle: Romain Rolland's "au dessus de la mêlée" position.

The encounter with Rolland, playing almost the part of a conversion in Zweig's inner history, is mysteriously connected with the history of a letter that seems like a chapter from a moral tale. It concerns a missive written by the young Rolland, while laboring under a severe mental strain, to the world-famous Tolstoy, living at the other end of Europe on his estate of Jasnaja Poljana, and totally unknown to the young Frenchman.

And what happened? Leo Tolstoy, engrossed in an immense literary production, found time to answer this quite superfluous epistle of his young Parisian admirer in a handwritten letter having the truly Russian dimensions of thirty-eight pages. This sounds like a fairy tale, especially today when such letters are no more being written, much less answered. It was indeed a miracle—and it had miraculous effects. Thousands of letters pennned by Zweig during his lifetime, dozens which he felt obliged to write during his last days when already irremediably committed to a voluntary death, go back to Tolstoy's great letter, great example.

Two new works resulted from this letter: the one was Zweig's incomparable essay on Tolstoy; the other, his most beautiful story, deservedly placed at the end of his American anthology, *The Eyes of the Undying Brother*. This is, in effect, the story of Tolstoy's last adventure, wrapped in the garment of a Hindu legend but still clearly discernible under the veil. He describes how the aged Tolstoy left his beautiful estate, his family, and his accustomed manner of life shortly before death so that he might die, unknown, in the railway station of a small Russian town. In the same year Zweig wrote and published his legend, flowering so far beyond his own life path that it could never have blossomed without the inner illumination caused by Tolstoy's letter.

This proves the great truth that in the moral as well as in the physical world nothing can be lost, and that every high-minded deed continues in active operation forever.

Among all the biographies of Stefan Zweig his *Erasmus* is the most autobiographical. Generally speaking, Zweig concealed rather than revealed himself in his writings, and did not poetically express his inner experiences as Ibsen had done, whose verse

> To write is to summon one's self
> And play the judge's part

had shown the way to the young generation living at the turn of the century. On the other hand, he escapes the rebuke of the American playwright, N. Behrman, who has coined the pointed phrase of the "loudspeaker in the confessional." Zweig had exposed himself to the danger of loud or half-loud confession only during his lyrical beginnings, when he was still counted as a member of the literary group called "Young Vienna"—merely because he was young and lived in Vienna.

Then came the First World War, an experience that gave an entirely different direction to his whole work. It was then that he wrote *Jeremiah,* his first creation permeated by the idea of humanity. Here, relinquishing a pretentious individualism, he allowed his war-weary self to be consumed by the oratorical fire of the Biblical prophet so that he might express what not only he but millions of his contemporaries were burning to utter. After the war he continued in the same direction, pursuing, with passionate realism, the path which leads from the ego to the fellow man, in a series of broadly conceived biographies. All these life portraits, drawn from the most diverse times and regions, have one thing in common: in them a creative artist, eliminating his own person—though by no means his own personality—penetrates and transposes himself into a foreign ego. And only once do we see Zweig deviate from this direction which he had seemingly chosen and intended to maintain constantly—in the *Erasmus.* This is a portrait, but also a confession.

Of exactly the same age as Erasmus when Erasmus wrote to

a friend, "Why are they trying to thrust me into a party?" Stefan Zweig could have made this sentence the motto of his book which betrayed, in its successive headings, the nature of autobiographical confession and apology. Especially toward the end, the titles of single chapters become uncannily allusive and frighteningly candid.

In one of the main sections, most significantly entitled "The Titanic Adversary," Zweig confronts Erasmus' European outlook with German nationalism. For the great humanist is not so much concerned with the Lutheran religious reform as with the political fanaticism into which it degenerated and which finally drove even Erasmus out of the country. "Settlement and Account," the heading of the third chapter before the last, signifies Erasmus-Zweig's futile attempt at a temporary compromise.

This is followed by the penultimate chapter, called "The End." Zweig knew already then that this end would be, could be, no end. The final section, called "Erasmus' Legacy," adds an inspiring note. Here again Erasmus' legacy coincides with that of his biographer. Both hand down, as an eternal bequest, the idea of humanity which each had shaped and carried onward in his thoughts.

Accompanying the biographer on his simultaneously autobiographical path in this prescient book, one repeatedly encounters glimpses which seem like mirror images of uncanny timeliness. This becomes apparent when Zweig describes Erasmus' facial expression in the great Holbein portrait with these words: "Fine, reflective, shrewdly apprehensive."

It is not certain whether Erasmus looked exactly like this, but it is certain that Zweig did while writing his book on Erasmus in his early fifties. He, too, was an "Epicurean by nature," as he calls the great humanist who liked to sample choice wines. At the same time his industry was remarkable—to call it love of work would be an understatement—as on Zweig's hand, too, "sat the pen like a sixth finger." He, too, safeguarded himself "behind a barricade of books above the fight between God and Lucifer, too prudent to be a hero." The demand to join the rank of fighters he repudiated by quoting from the *Letters to Obscurantists:* "Erasmus est per se!"

But, in order to excuse himself *and* Erasmus, he adds, slightly embarrassed, that this desire to remain independent of both right and left, of the emperor and Luther, constituted the foundation stone in Erasmus' character—"A foundation concealed beneath the completed edifice." And then, harmonizing the character portrait with the hero's destiny, he condenses—here, too, with prescience—Erasmus' tragedy into one sentence: "The tragedy of his life, and one which binds him to us in closer brotherly affection, was that he sustained defeat in the struggle for a juster and more harmonious world."

Characteristic of Zweig's viewpoint at that time is this "more harmonious," visualizing, quite in the spirit of the more or less heedless English appeasers, an understanding as being still possible and desirable. And this fully agrees with the following character description: "Erasmus loved many things we are fond of— books and arts and languages and peoples, without distinction of race and color." All this is the Zweig of 1934—and the final statement that he (Erasmus) negated only one thing, fanaticism, sounds again like self-defense. "It is the duty of each of us to keep a cool head until the disaster is over." So runs a warning sentence in the preface of this book, written in 1934, immediately after Hitler had invaded humanity's front.

Still the author seems inclined to ask himself: Is there not something higher than the quarrel of parties? And is not reason, the supreme judicial court of liberal thinking, this something higher? It is "reason," of which Zweig says expressly in this connection: "Often, while the drunkenness is at its height, she [reason] must needs lie still and mute. But her day dawns and ever and again she comes into her own anew."

Erasmus did not live to see this day, neither did Zweig. He too preferred, like his admired Erasmus, to seek refuge in work: "He retained his independence. He was free." Separated from his friends, Erasmus-Zweig consoled himself with a last friend who had remained faithful to him during his whole life: "One friend alone, his oldest, best and trustworthiest friend, shared study and writing table with him: Dame Work."

And again it is his own fate that this Dame Work, a poetically imagined half sister of Dürer's Melancholia, presages with sorrowful foresight, although our friend could not know and could hardly foresee that he, too, would have to die "outlawed and alone." In spite of the pessimism inborn in this man spoiled by fortune—like the pessimism in all late descendants of a prosperous European bourgeoisie—Zweig, looking down on the events in Germany from a high London rampart, still believed in the mild possibility of Erasmian solutions.

Seven years later, in Petropolis, Brazil, we see him so thoroughly cured of this delusion that he erased his life like an untenable sentence in an earlier manuscript: "The exalted dream of a spiritually united Europe had come to an end." This was written in 1934, in the preface to *Erasmus*.

There are barricade fighters without barricades, and as such the Erasmian appeaser Stefan Zweig finally revealed himself.

Stefan Zweig was a high-ranking poet, a dynamic storyteller, and one of the subtlest essayists of our age. But it was the art form of modern biography, invented and developed in our days, that aroused in him that synthesis of talent and personality recognized and known by us as mastership. From *Fouché* to *Magellan* stretches a gallery of biographical murals—including the unfinished *Balzac*—which forms Zweig's literary contribution to the artistic method, first devised by Lytton Strachey, of poetically re-creating a personality. Alongside of Emil Ludwig and André Maurois, Zweig fostered and enriched this art's Continental wing for twenty years.

What is the nature of this new school, and why do we call it modern? Its protagonists have repeatedly discussed this question —with the exception of Zweig, who seldom theorized about his art. For it is an art; and this fact above all makes it something new. Representation—not to be confused with reporting or scientifically accurate evaluation—is in every case this art's fundamental postulation. But what do we mean when speaking of representation? What else than the faculty of pictorially creating, through a mere appeal to the reader's intellectual capacity and imagination, a character and a fate—one could also say a character *through* a fate—out of the fleeting reflexes of reality by conjuring up, and at the same time revealing, a personality?

Modern biography has been visibly stamped with the mark of the actor. Figuratively speaking, it does not stem from Gibbon but from Garrick; not from Lamartine but from Talma; not from Mommsen but from Kainz, who impressed Zweig as deeply as he impressed all the other young Viennese poets living at the turn of the century.

The biographer is the actor among writers. This applies to Plutarch, to Strachey, and also, in its own way, to Stefan Zweig as he wrote his *Fouché,* his *Marie Antoinette,* his *Mary Stuart* and, above all, his literary masterpieces: animated portraits of Dostoevski, Kleist, Tolstoy, Romain Rolland, Balzac, Hölderlin, Stendhal, Dickens, and once more of Balzac—probably his standard work, which he had conceived in epical breadth and took with him, unfinished, into the grave.

The mimic element in the nature of modern life-portraiture brings us closer to its secret. What is the actor's art but the animation of a character and a destiny—on the stage as well as in biography these go hand in hand—through the material furnished by his own personality? The actor is confronted with the problem of being and representing somebody who is not himself. This cannot be accomplished without a personality, nor without a fitting object; least of all, without betraying neither oneself nor one's part. A most complicated procedure, to be mastered only through the miraculous gift of talent! At any rate, Romeo can be played only by someone who was once in love, Hamlet only by an artist of spiritual endowments.

Thus the biographer's art presupposes, as contribution to the performance, the measure and richness of his own personality: in ideal cases his own greatness, in others at least the actor's ability to "cut a fine figure" before a strange public.

Transformation is the password; and it is an interesting fact that a one-act play by the very young poet Zweig, then still unaware of his biographical mission, was called *The Transformed Comedian.* Both fundamental elements in the future masterful delineator of other men's lives are here anticipated—drama and transformation. For only a character who has undergone a development through suffering is worthy of a biography; and only a writer whose experience has been similar will be able to write one.

Stefan Zweig was an Austrian. He was one by descent and education—though not by self-education, which is possibly the more important part of a superior man's schooling. Nevertheless, he was able to change his innate status through his own efforts only to a certain degree, and least of all beyond a point which, anchored in his inherited nature, lay deep beneath the threshold of his consciousness.

The Austrian, through the course of many generations, had been educated to indifference in political matters. Descendants of an old autocracy whose twelve different nationalities had never been able to unify their divergent interests, the youth of Austria—which consisted, in their opinion, mostly of a landscape and an Imperial House—had learned to speak only when spoken to; and then without touching the foundations of a traditional order or disorder.

The "social problem," merely discussed after supper just for fun as if cracking nuts on a full stomach, did not penetrate the ears and still less the mind of the Austrian Zweig. Also the anti-Semitism, then disseminated in Vienna by the witty Mayor Lueger, escaped him, and he it. For this well-bred Viennese, anti-Semitism, not to be compared with the persecution of today, was polite enough to leave the wealthy and cultured classes in peace. And Zweig belonged to both categories.

So far as the nonpolitical Austrian Zweig and others were concerned, a further fact prevented them from having political interests and assuming responsibility for what was happening and brewing. The autocratic state, even in its milder contemporaneous form, educated the Austrian subject to political abstinence, granting him in exchange a completely untrammeled private life. The license made up for the far-reaching limitations imposed in other fields; egotism usurped the place of the idea of liberty, which withered away more and more. Anyone who did not displease the government with vexatious speeches could live, within the framework of a wide-meshed, wisely amended legal code, wholly as he pleased. The more he enjoyed himself, the better; for an undisciplined life weakened the citizen's power of resistance.

This was the way in which the Middle European generation living at the turn of the century grew up, this the way in which the so-called liberal Vienna educated Stefan Zweig. Without religious faith, which liberalism had discarded as superfluous, but also without the belief in humanity that can to a certain degree take its place because it is a religion of its own in an ethical-social sense, the young well-to-do generation refused on principle to worry about the welfare of the community, let alone eat their hearts out over this question.

What was the common welfare if not the sum of all individual well-being? Therefore, it was easier to solve this mathematical problem by looking out for oneself. The command of the Sermon on the Mount, "Love thy neighbor as thyself," was considered by the bourgeois Vienna of those days, and also by literature, as an exaggerated demand impossible of realization. As thyself! How could one possibly be expected to begin with the maximum?

But then came the First World War, and then came Hitler. The first of these secular events caused Zweig's awakening—just as the first sight of a corpse in his royal garden had awakened the young Buddha; the second made him finally, ten years later, a torchbearer in our sense. Between these two dates, marking awakening and culmination, an inner development is threaded. It makes the life of this great author, as representative of his generation, the richer in affiliations, and his voluntary death so deeply touching.

Stefan Zweig had answered the moral challenge of the First World War by becoming and remaining a pacifist. As his messenger he chose the Biblical prophet Jeremiah, who had the misfortune to foresee the Babylonian captivity in advance of his contemporaries and for this reason was thrust into the cesspool of the palace by his royal master. Emerging from it, he took upon himself his people's fate and joined their pilgrimage into servitude.

But the new Babylonian captivity, so accurately predicted by Zweig's superior judgment, concerned not only his closer compatriots; nor was it only the disfavor of the Austrian government which he called down on himself by writing his dramatic "mene tekel" on the wall. He already knew that the situation was one which concerned all of Europe and that the events in Austria had started the landslide that was destined to bury the whole European civilization within a short time.

Zweig, when becoming a pacifist in 1918, became at the same time a European out of inner conviction, and such he remained during his whole life. "Le grand Européen," Jules Romains called him twenty years later in a booklet dedicated to him and published under this title.

With this postwar pacifism, temporarily uniting a world weary and sick of war, began the international renown of the writer Stefan Zweig. As, ten years earlier, he had left Austria, his closer home, and moved, in a spiritual sense, to Europe; so now he relinquished Europe, in an ideological sense, and settled permanently within the frontiers embracing all five continents. It was a logical, and at the same time a psychological, development. The roots sunk by Romain Rolland, by Tolstoy, into his soul had taken firm hold and were growing.

He published his book on Rolland and the great essay on Tolstoy. Accepting an invitation of the Soviet Union, he delivered the commemorative speech in Moscow at Tolstoy's centennial. Meanwhile, in the early twenties, *Fouché* had appeared, in which he condemned the heartless professional politicians who bore part of the guilt for inflicting the disastrous World War on mankind. In this work, perhaps his most successful—though still clinging to negative premises and totally unheroic—the author shows his new belief in humanity in reflected form, as it were, by treating with contempt the cynical and egotistical go-getter who thinks only of his own advantage.

In the meantime Zweig's new cosmopolitan feeling had engendered a change in his mode of life. He had married and moved to Salzburg with his wife Friederike and her daughters. There he dwelled from then on in a musty, beautifully situated old castle dating from the time of Emperor Francis, living in solitude like Voltaire in Ferney, although still connected with the world.

And though Salzburg lies in Austria—if at its farthest frontier—Austria now lay far behind him. The "short trips across the frontier" into a still Republican "Reich" and the night express to Vienna, sometimes used by him for the purpose of visiting his family and meeting a friend in front of the Vienna Goethe monument made life endurable amid the narrowness of a provincial town, which struts like a world capital during the summer season and does not indulge in a merely wintry anti-Semitism until the Salzburg Summer Festival plays are over.

But then Hitler burst in—not yet into Austria, but into Germany—and the "short trips across the frontier" came to a sudden end. Zweig immediately recognized the greatness of the danger; this in contrast to his class which, soft and flabby, did not heed the past and present happenings or, in order to avoid a decision, stopped short in its thoughts. Although renouncing every interference, Zweig drew his personal, private conclusions.

After selling his estate in Salzburg against the wishes of his family, he went alone to England where his books had already blazed a trail for him. Nazi Germany erased him from its literary calendar, the German publishing house, whose pride and ornament he had been, dropped him.

Ignoring all this, he continued to work in his small London student's flat, and still more in the British Museum, on *Erasmus,* finally publishing the book which, among other things, contains Erasmus' great repudiation of Luther's challenge: "I wish to keep neutral in order to continue to do my share in promoting the renascent sciences; and I believe that a shrewdly manipulated reticence will achieve more than impetuous interference." If one substitutes "literature" for "sciences" in this sentence, one obtains an X-ray photograph of Zweig's spiritual attitude eight years before the heroic turning point prepared for him by fate.

Without the remotest initial intention of becoming a martyr, this descendant of the soft-living bourgeoisie became one anyway. This fact does not diminish, it only delays his merit. He worked too long at his desk, while fate was already waiting for him in the antechamber.

Why did he not write against the brown pest immediately after arriving in a foreign country, as Thomas Mann, Emil Ludwig, Schwarzschild, and many others had done? It is true that

one stroke of his pen might have cost the life of his beloved rela-
tives—among them his mother—who remained in Vienna till
after 1938. But as he did nothing even then, this cannot have been
the only reason.

The explanation is indeed obvious, but has been overlooked up
to now, being replaced by a very unsatisfactory shutting-one's-
eyes to the facts. Zweig's completely clear and accurate judgment
recognized at once that Hitlerism was bound to lead to war. But
war was a thing he had rejected on principle when he became a
pacifist during the First World War.

Should he change his convictions because the times had
changed? He could not. By staying away from the struggle, he
sided with himself. He remained true to himself and to a pacifism
which had become the central point of his world view and corresponded to the deepest things in his nature.

During the First World War he became the pacifist he had
always unconsciously been; twenty years later this pacifist became
an appeaser. Nothing could be more natural, nothing more terrifying. Moreover, his attitude was in accord with that of his new
English surroundings in the decisive years before the Second
World War. The English air invigorated his weakness, as it were.
Chamberlain had been in that air a long time before, clutching
his umbrella, he parachuted down to Munich as peacemaker.

Half a year before the outbreak of war in 1939, I had a talk
with Zweig in New York. This conversation, most characteristic of his attitude toward the one great issue, was conducted
—as between old friends—in a semijocular tone; but we both
knew perfectly well that this banter covered serious questions.

It was in connection with Zweig's first extended lecture tour
through the United States in February, 1939, that the Theatre
Guild had brought out a revival of his *Jeremiah*. Zweig, not quite
satisfied with the performance, asked my impression. I answered
that I could only repeat what I had said in Vienna twenty years
ago when critically appraising the play after its initial performance. The only difference was that now, in my opinion, a final
scene was lacking which would have rounded out the preceding
nine scenes in a timely sense; in other words, a tenth scene. "A
tenth scene?" asked Zweig, amused and curious. "Jeremiah has

followed his people into the Babylonian captivity. What else is there to say?" "Nothing," I answered, "except to show how Jeremiah there was transformed from a convinced pacifist into a convinced 'warmonger,' using all his former arguments in the opposite direction. For in Babylon remained no other salvation even for him than war!" Zweig laughed and changed the subject.

In July, 1940, Stefan Zweig, anticipating a foul peace after the collapse of France and probably also counting on an invasion of England, came to the United States, just after Dunkirk. Once more he evaded the war, warding it off with all the forces coiled up at the core of his nature. The possibility that the United States might have to enter the struggle was in no wise excluded from his realistic travel plans. In that case, he thought, he would go to South America.

Zweig loved South America no less for its beautiful landscapes and pristine vigor than for its predilection for peace. Thus he saw in it the "Land of the Future." Out of this love, this spiritual and political attitude, grew his last book, *Brazil*.

But on the day of its appearance he committed suicide—an act unprecedented in the history of literature. Hand in hand with his faithful mate, who had been his secretary and became his wife, this ever-enthusiastic traveler embarked on his last journey.

Death came to him in Petropolis, near Rio de Janeiro. "Two empty glasses" was the headline above an article in the San Francisco *Chronicle* of January 22, 1941, telling me of this soul-stirring event.

What had happened? Outwardly nothing beyond the fact that our friend had gone to Rio a few months before Pearl Harbor. But inwardly? To raise this question is tantamount to searching out the way in which the appeaser Stefan Zweig finally became a torchbearer in our humanitarian sense.

It must have been his way from the beginning, only he was not conscious of this before taking the final step. At the same time, another realization might have matured within him: that we can choose many things in our lives, but not the place in which we are born. To this place and to the implications of its spiritual climate we are joined by a fate from which we cannot flee even

on a thousand paths. Zweig, an Austrian though not wanting
to be one, had to experience this truth. And this experience was
his last.

If we disentangle the interwoven motives twisted into the
deadly net enmeshing Stefan Zweig and his wife Elizabeth, we
must keep one fact in mind: that Stefan Zweig, passionate thinker
that he was and believer in the spirit out of inner conviction,
never in his life did or could do anything without a mental approach to it. He was not impulsive, nor did he believe in intuition.
Thus we must raise this question: What caused the man of sixty
and the woman of thirty to empty those two fateful cups?

Looking around with his restlessly searching glances that
missed but little, he had realized in the last months that the
entrance of Brazil, and sooner or later of all of South America,
into the conflict had become inevitable. What then? asked his
sovereign reason.

Pondering his plight and not knowing where to turn, he realized that, if the war spread any farther, he would be able to
return neither to England, where his unfinished *Balzac* was awaiting him and the rest of his former fortune was frozen, nor to
the now belligerent United States.

Perhaps he did not even wish to return, because he had sworn
to himself that he would never again live in a country at war.
Was it not for this that he had left Austria, Middle Europe,
France, England, and finally North America? Could he relinquish
his Erasmian principles, now that the war had seized the other
part of the New World? He could not bear the responsibility of
deserting his own cause. A certain loyalty of character and also
a certain stubbornness prevented the aging man from such a
course. Stubbornness is an Austrian characteristic which has been
fraternally divided between the succession states of old Austria,
however little they may have in common in other respects.

However, it was not only Austrian stubbornness and that
easily irritated authoritarian bent which had been left as a legacy
from the Hapsburgs to their former subjects. For this family had
ruled Austria so long and so thoroughly that finally every Aus-

trian became a miniature Hapsburg who could brook no contradiction; not even—and this was especially disastrous—his own.

But the Austrian is not only half a Hapsburg, but also all a Hamlet. Not without reason has this figure, despite his curious mental idiosyncrasies, been positively popular on the Vienna stage for centuries. How often may the young and the elderly Zweig have heard Hamlet soliloquize on the stage of the Vienna Burgtheater, "To be or not to be," as the actor walked up and down behind the footlights. Why endure what Hamlet calls in his monologue "the insolence of office," considerably increased since officials have begun to grant visas? Why bear the "spurns that patient merit of the unworthy takes"? Bear them at a time when spurns have been changed into kicks, if not into arrests and concentration camps?

Besides, there was another factor in Zweig's case—a factor omitted even by Hamlet from his melancholy meditations: old age. Zweig, who had never been ill—a favorite of fortune in this respect also—feared old age like a deadly sickness. Why, impoverished, expose oneself to the unavoidable danger of seeing one's vigor diminish and being always confronted by the end? Why not, wiser than nature and kinder than Hitler, drink a painless death from a cup filled to the brim? Thus the Epicurean, hidden in every Austrian, may have whispered to him to choose the most palatable of all possibilities.

But Zweig was not only a follower of Epicurus, but also a Stoic. This, too, conforms to Austrian tradition. Enjoyment of life and willingness to die have not contradicted each other in the realm of the Hamletic Hapsburgs. Already Thomas Mann and many others have noted the blissfulness with which the Austrian embraced death. Stefan Zweig, in his last meditations, may have detected similar feelings within himself.

It is most enlightening that, in his last book on Brazil, he returned again and again to Austria in spirit. Having at first condemned Austria, then turned his back on it, and finally believed himself to have overcome it, he was, just before the last departure, beset at every turn by memories of his Austrian youth. Everything around him reminded him of his home and seemed— we cannot express it in any other way—homelike. The architec-

tural style of the Brazilian patrician houses; the social organization—it is characteristic that he praised the friendliness of the
"lower classes" while describing the slums; the hand-kissing
children; the smiling contentment of the poor; the exaggerated
politeness of the higher classes and their equally great, pretentious sensitivity; the style of life of the aristocrat—"his love of
art and intellectual liberalism"; the lottery, the unpunctuality, and
above all, the Brazilian folk character; he is "peaceful, negligent,
lazy, and somewhat melancholy," and a charming fellow withal—
almost like a Viennese.

And in the same light the Austrian saw Petropolis, reminding
him, with its winding streets and luxuriant gardens, of Salzburg
or Baden, near Vienna. Had he not walked to school in Vienna
as a boy through the same labyrinthine maze of small streets,
wended his way between flower beds to the exits of richly blossoming parks? What was the Latin saying he had memorized on
the way? Ah, now he had it—*Patet exitus!* Seneca had said it,
but of course without having the exits of richly blossoming parks
in mind. Nevertheless, faithfully accompanied by his second wife
Pompeia Paulina across death's threshold, Seneca had finished
his life at the right moment. Strange that such things should
come back to one all of a sudden at the other end of the world. . . .

Seneca was a great Roman philosopher, a sage, a poet, and
a man blessed by fortune. But he was also—let us make no mistake about this—a hero at the end, though fighting in his own
way. Through his death in the lukewarm bath he eventually
hurt Nero more than himself. He *wanted* to hurt him, wanted to
contribute to Nero's moral condemnation.

Stefan Zweig wanted the same. Before killing himself he had
to kill the Erasmian nature within him and he did; this was his
great development, human as well as biographical.

"Before I depart from life by my own free will I want
to do my duty," he wrote to a friend; and to another: "After
one's sixtieth year unusual powers are needed in order to make
a new beginning. Those that I possess have been exhausted by
long years of homeless wandering. So I think it better to conclude in good time and in erect bearing a life in which intellectual labor meant the purest joy and *personal freedom the high-*

est good on earth." What an unheard-of, new tone on his lyre, a heroic, Fidelio tone. In sounding it, he had fought his way to the final realization that delay was mutiny, and that everyone, in order to defend freedom, must join the rank and file: each with the weapons at his disposal.

Zweig's weapon was the martyr's death which he courageously chose. There are two kinds of torchbearers in history: some carry it onward, the others convert their own person into a torch. Stefan Zweig did the latter. In the afterglow of this image he will live on.